The Making of a Nation in the Balkans

The Making of a Nation in the Balkans

Historiography of the Bulgarian Revival

by

ROUMEN DASKALOV

C E U PRESS

Central European University Press
Budapest   New York

Published in 2004 by

Central European University Press
An imprint of the
Central European University Share Company
Nádor utca 11, H-1051 Budapest, Hungary
Tel: +36-1-327-3138 or 327-3000
Fax: +36-1-327-3183
E-mail: ceupress@ceu.hu
Website: www.ceupress.com

400 West 59th Street, New York NY 10019, USA
Tel: +1-212-547-6932
Fax: +1-212-548-4607
E-mail: mgreenwald@sorosny.org

ISBN 963 9241 83 0 cloth

Library of Congress Cataloging-in-Publication Data

Daskalov, Roumen.
The making of a nation in the Balkans: Bulgaria, from history to historiography / by
Roumen Daskalov.
     p. cm.
Includes bibliographical references and index.
ISBN 9639241830 (hbk.)
     1. Bulgaria–History–1762–1878–Historiography. 2. Nationalism–Bulgaria–History–19th
century. I. Title: Bulgaria, from history to historiography. II. Title.

DR83.D37 2004
949.9'015–dc22
                         2004000869

Printed in Hungary by
Akaprint Nyomda

Table of Contents

Preface

A few paragraphs to explain the motivation behind this work would seem to me appropriate. Generally speaking, the book contains a presentation and critical consideration of the ideas of historians on the major problems, processes, events, and personalities of the era of the Bulgarian (national) Revival. I trace how the Bulgarian Revival was viewed by historical scholarship, and how notions and representations have changed over time. In so far as historical scholarship is meant to reveal, and so help towards an understanding of, historical events, a representation of the movement of ideas and of the debates on various problems inevitably has a bearing on the past itself. The epoch is "contained" in the attempts to conceptualize, represent, and make sense of it. The various notions and narratives are mutually complementary or mutually corrective, and even entirely wrong ideas have some (negative) usefulness in showing what the Revival was not. The "truths" of the Bulgarian Revival can be glimpsed through the conflicting ideas about it, and through their evolution. My own views and opinions, where not stated directly, may be inferred from the manner in which the various authors' views and the polemic surrounding them are introduced and represented, and from certain general reflections, etc.

The Revival is often approached—and understood—by way of comparison with other regions, epochs, ideological trends, or events. The various analogies and more elaborate comparisons employed in making sense of the Bulgarian Revival are based on phenomena (and mental constructs) from two major areas that were, in fact, the source of the actual influences: Western Europe ("Renaissance," "Reformation," "Enlightenment," "Romanticism," the French Revolution, national liberation movements, and capitalism) and Russia (the "agrarian question," "populism" and "utopian socialism," "revolutionary democratism," and the Russian revolution of 1905. These analogies or parallels between developments in Bul-

garia and other historical phenomena may be revealing, but, as we shall
see, they may also be misleading.

In realizing my initial intention, I was also led in other directions. To
begin with, it was fascinating to trace connections between the ideas of
historians, on the one hand, and the social context and political power on
the other. This revealed how historical facts about the Revival were instru-
mentalized for ideological purposes, such as the fostering of national and
state loyalties through the reproduction of identities and their reinforcement by an image of the enemy, or for directly political purposes, such as
the legitimating or contesting of a current political regime under the guise
of disputes over historical legacy. Bulgarian historical scholarship, including that which passes for "serious" or "scientific," offers plenty of material
of this kind, accumulated in successive epochs of ideological mobilization
under the banners of nationalism, right-wing authoritarianism (shading
into Fascism), and Communism. In fact, it is difficult to draw the line between professional historical scholarship, as represented by many scholars,
and the more popular versions of historical writing, where the biases stand
out more graphically. Still, I hope that the present work is not dominated
by ideologo-critical negativity but rather by the hermeneutic effort to understand how the Bulgarian Revival has been conceived of and imagined,
and by the keeping of a certain distance from the various views presented—
whether critical, ironic, or simply that inherent in the presentation of another person's view. In this respect I have been greatly inspired by François
Furet's book on the French Revolution.

Particular attention is paid to the way that the Bulgarian Revival has
been narrated, with respect to selectivity, the principal meanings, protagonists and plots, continuities and breaks. Without presenting a radical de-
construction of the grand narrative of the Bulgarian Revival, or, to be more
precise, of the two grand narratives under the banners of nationalism and
of Marxism, the present work sets in relief some of their mechanisms,
logic, fictions, etc., and thus to some extent relativizes them. The very
demonstration of the "movement of ideas" in historical scholarship,
through theses and their revisions, has a sobering and humbling impact.
This is due not least to the fact that it demonstrates the indelible impact of
standpoints, values, and theoretical frameworks. (According to some postmodern historians, theoretical reasoning itself proceeds by way of likening
in the generation of "true knowledge.")

Finally, and somewhat in the spirit of the "history of concepts" (*Begriffs-
geschichte*), I briefly address such issues as the semiotic reworking of the

historical happening into a "Revival epoch," the participation of phe-
nomenological (life-world) experiences and the role of secondary reconstruction in this process, and the specific temporality of this epoch and its
delimitation from (and contrast with) what preceded and succeeded it, etc.

It should be added that the Bulgarian Revival has been a privileged period within Bulgarian historical scholarship. Enormous interest has been
shown towards it, and understandably so, as an epoch of national formation (in which the national foundation myth is embedded), as the beginnings of modern Bulgarian development, and, as such, as having a crucial
impact on the subsequent history of the country. Various views have been
set forth over the years and a number of comparatively free debates and
discussions were held even during Communist times. One might say that
the specific intensity and sharpness of the debates on the Revival reveal
them as an indirect expression of a (dissident) stand on actuality and re-
flect the absence of free political life under Communism that made the
past into an arena of *Ersatz* politics.

A venture of the kind undertaken here is quite novel for Bulgarian historical scholarship and entirely absent in the sparse foreign writing on the
Bulgarian Revival. The (historiographical) systematization and stocktaking
carried out by scholarship on the Revival epoch so far has dealt mostly with
particular issues with limited goals, and it has been less critical as to fun-
damentals. For that reason I hope that this work will arouse the interest of
many students of modern Bulgarian history, and, beyond that, of those
involved in national (and nationalist) historical scholarship more generally.
In a way, my effort is inscribed within the post-Communist rethinking of
history and historical scholarship, but hardly as straightforward and negative revisionism.

Given the immense number of historical monographs, studies, papers,
and general courses on the Bulgarian Revival, omissions and gaps—even
important ones—are almost inevitable here. But in pursuing the kind of
conceptual review of historical writing (or "conceptual historiography")
that I have in mind, exhaustiveness is less important than establishing conceptual continuities and changes. However, even here there may be lacunae, and some ideas may not be traced to the source.

A comment should be made regarding the considerable imbalance in favor of views that go under the banner of Marxism, or, in fact, of certain
Marxist vulgates (Leninist, Stalinist, Chervenkov-Todor Pavlovist) and of
their subsequent implicit or explicit revisions by nominally Marxist
authors. This results from the fact that the field of the Bulgarian Revival

was most intensively cultivated during the state socialist period, which saw a characteristic increase in the number of "scholarly workers" (historians), many of whom took refuge in the Revival period from the even more ideologized more recent history, and some of whom used the opportunity to smuggle in dissident views of their own. More substantially, as we shall see, some of the fundamental thoughts on the Bulgarian Revival then established have been preserved in some guise until today, after "overcoming" so much.

A note is needed in order to justify my returning to a given problem (or a certain author) in a different context and from a different perspective. The necessity for this comes from the thematic method of presentation, where the same thing recurs in various contexts, for example, the bourgeoisie as social class, in connection with capitalism, as bearer of certain political ideas, as leader of a bourgeois revolution, etc. Thus apparent repetitions are not in fact repetitions.

Finally, a word of thanks to the Humboldt Foundation and the Central European University for their generous support in the carrying out of this research. My thanks go also to Rachel Hideg for the careful copy-editing of the manuscript.

INTRODUCTION

From Metaphor toward Historical Epoch

The Bulgarian Revival[1] is commonly understood as an epoch in Bulgarian history comprising the last century or so of Ottoman rule, which ended in 1878. Its interpretation as a process of the formation of the Bulgarian nation—or, in contemporary parlance, its revival, awakening, coming to its senses, being brought back to life, resurrection, etc.—began while the Revival was still under way (not, admittedly, from its outset, but in its final phase). This self-consciousness can be explained by the reflexive and ideational (or ideological) character of the process by which a group of people becomes aware of itself as separate and different from others, and begins to mobilize itself in the struggle for national recognition.

The term "revival" (*vŭzrazhdane*), which literally means "rebirth," and the related terms, were first employed metaphorically to designate the sudden and profound change experienced by the Bulgarian people, much like a magical return to life (after having been asleep or dead). At the same time, the Revival was thought of as a process with a certain duration, which led the Bulgarians to a state of being "awake," "returned to its senses," "alive again," etc. The conception of it as a historical epoch is potentially present here. In describing what was going on around them, observers of and activists in the unfolding processes in the 1860s and 1870s were actually writing "history of the present," and were imbued with a sense of its historical significance. The meanings of this experience were still open to the surrounding world with its shifting horizons, since the process was not complete. But observers already had a certain "historical" perspective at their disposal. Especially in the 1860s, when the struggle for an independent Bulgarian Church was entering its crucial phase, and with the establishment of a Bulgarian Exarchate in 1870 (which in practice meant the recognition of the Bulgarian nationality), one could look back to the beginnings of the process and trace its turns. The first historians of the Bulgarian Revival to be regarded by later scholars as their "predecessors" were thus involved in its "making."

The initial elaboration of the Bulgarian Revival into a historical epoch is signaled by attempts to define its chronological boundaries and to pay tribute to its first leading personalities. Vasil Aprilov (in 1842), Georgi Rakovski (in 1860), and Marko Balabanov (in 1870) all dated back the beginning of a Bulgarian revival to 1826, with the reforms in the Ottoman Empire initiated by Mahmud II and continued by his son Abdul-Mecid. In their view, the Revival was signaled by the literary activities of Vasil Aprilov, Neofit Rilski, and the Ukrainian scholar Yuri Venelin.[2] In his influential article in the *Periodical Journal* of the Bulgarian Literary Society (1871), Marin Drinov, regarded as the first professional Bulgarian historian, moved back the initial date to the middle of the eighteenth century (with Paisii Hilendarski as the first "awakener"), and this view became widely accepted.[3] The two principal trends of the Bulgarian Revival—the scholarly-educational (connected with Vasil Aprilov, who lived in emigration in Russia) and the revolutionary (initiated by Georgi Rakovski in emigration in Serbia and Romania)—are mentioned in the foreword to the first issue of a newspaper characteristically named *Revival* (in 1876).[4] One can observe how a spontaneous interpretation of the process by its participants was being gradually shaped into an awareness of a historical "epoch" in Bulgarian development. It is worth noting that the national process gave the epoch its name. The term "revival" (*vŭzrazhdane*—"rebirth") imposed itself as a technical term in competition with "awakening" (*probuzhdane*) and Dinov's "resurrection" (*vŭzkresenie*).

The Revival remained part of the biography and memories of several generations, as something experienced personally. The liberation that followed the Russo-Turkish war in 1877–78 does not present a boundary in this respect, since many activists of the epoch lived long afterwards and some wrote memoirs and historical works late in their lives. Soon after the liberation there began an urgent gathering and publication of materials about the preceding epoch from personal archives—letters, notes, proclamations, projects, telegrams, etc., which were usually introduced as "materials from the Revival."[5] The writing of memoirs continued until after World War I.[6] Such efforts were motivated by the idea that the deeds of the past must be rescued for future generations, and for history. They were regarded as "building blocks" (*gradiva*), the very word attesting to the fact that the authors imagined their contribution as something to be used in erecting an entire edifice.

The memoirs are narrated from the standpoint of the author and they are typically local and loosely structured, containing gaps in time and often relating trifling everyday events. Generalizations are rare, and at best they add details to the struggle for a modern educational system or an independent church. But it is exactly because of these peculiarities that the memoirs present a specific picture of the years under Ottoman domination, quite at odds with the grand national narrative constructed by professional historians. They abound in colorful descriptions of places and persons, and of events with local significance. They are low-pitched in tone, and the actors act mainly out of pragmatic motives rather than being driven by great ideals. As to language and style, theirs is a concrete and particularistic language, replete with words from the material sphere (and Turkish words) as opposed to the abstract terms and general assertions of the professional historical narrative. Only here and there do the memoirs refer to the central meaning of the grand narrative, then known as the "people's affairs" or "Bulgarian affairs."

The Bulgarian historians of the Revival generally play down the value of the memoirs as historical evidence by pointing to the gaps and errors that result from memory failure or attempts at self-justification. While this may be true, the often condescending attitude towards the memoirs conceals something more important. The point is that they actually subvert the grand ("high") historical narrative of the nation, which is unitary, coherent, teleological and emotionally tense. In reading the "debasing" testimonies of the times, one becomes aware of the all too active role played by the historian in constructing a historical narrative with a supra-local (national) meaning, and in making generalizations in terms of factors, forces, processes, tendencies, etc. With their localism, particularism, disparateness, pragmatic lowering and personalism, the memoirs generate skepticism toward the encompassing narrative with its generalizations, continuities, and the ascription of attitudes or actions to collective protagonists such as "the people," "the nation," or a certain class.

The "genre" of local histories, most often of a town and its surroundings, should also be mentioned in this context. These were written, in most cases, by local amateur historians who sympathized with all things local and did research using various materials: personal, community, and parish archives, oral testimonies, and sometimes personal recollections. In fact, some do conform to the highest scholarly standards of exactness. The intriguing thing about them is the comparatively rare mention of the term "revival," which occurs mostly when speaking of certain personalities who made contributions toward it; normally they prefer to date events as happening "before" or "after" liberation, "under the Turks," etc. One can infer from this that revival is not meant in a comprehensive epochal sense but in the sense of particular aspects and processes, especially educational and church struggles, situated within a broader profane, that is, nationally non-accentuated, time. This can be contrasted with works of professional historical scholarship, in which the Revival spans all aspects of life and imbues them with its meanings. One can also note, in relation to the previous point, the existence in the local histories of breaks and displacements between the local and the national, with little "communica-tion" between them.[7] No encompassing narrative is developed to bridge them and raise the local to the level of the national.

Some works about the Revival written shortly after the liberation belong to a peculiar hybrid "genre" between memoir, historical scholarship, journalism, and historical fiction. The broadness and significance of the events depicted, the presence of general reflections, and the retreating of the personality of the narrator to the background impart such writings with a scholarly quality even when they are based primarily on personal experience, memories, and imaginative writing. On the other hand, they are strongly rhetorical and strive to impart to the readers the opinions and biases of the author. The most powerful work of this type is Zakhari Stoyanov's *Notes on the Bulgarian uprisings* (published between 1884 and 1892).[8] Similar, though of less artistic value in spite of its perhaps more solid historical qualities, is Stoyan Zaimov's *The Past* (1884–1888).[9] Both authors were among the organizers of the April uprising of 1876, and their works focus on the revolutionary struggles of the receding past with the clear objective of glorifying and immortalizing the revolutionaries. Zakhari Stoyanov, especially, points out in the introduction to his famous *Notes* (and in the introductions to his biographies of Levski and Botev) that he was guided by the purpose of showing that "we Bulgarians," too, have heroes, who would do credit to any nation.[10] These honest, pure, and ideal heroes are contrasted with the times after independence, when disinterested patriotism gave way to job hunting and the all-engrossing pursuit of things material.[11] One can see the elaboration of national heroes at work, as well as the accumulation of a symbolic capital of heroism. The heroes and heroism thus extolled would subsequently be used to various purposes— nationally affirmative and state-building, or subversive and revolutionary.[12]

The establishment of a cult of heroes and of the entire Revival epoch was helped enormously by the great Bulgarian national poet and novelist

Ivan Vazov, and especially by his collection of poems *The Epic of the Forgotten* (1884) and the novel *Under the Yoke* (1894).[13] Vazov became a true "ideologue of the nation," as the title of a recent book about him puts it. As pointed out by the author, he selected a glorious, heroic image of the past and projected it onto the collective consciousness in such a powerful way that it came to be accepted as the "sacred truth" by future generations. In various ways he imparted the impression of authenticity and historical truth to his works of fiction and blurred the boundary between poetry and history. All in all, Vazov succeeded in creating a positive self-portrait of the nation, a reassuring one with which the individual could readily identify.[14] He also made an enormous, though non-avowed (coming from fiction, as it does), impact upon the scholarship of the Revival. Together with Zakhari Stoyanov, he sanctified the epoch and its personalities and inspired a strongly emotional, truly pious attitude that excluded a distanced, many-sided, and critical treatment, that is, a scholarly approach. Both authors promoted a vision of Bulgarian history in black and white, consisting of treason or heroism (or martyrdom), that goes together with strong partisanship for one's own "kin" and hatred towards one's enemies.

In parallel to the memoirs and historical fiction, there began the systematic treatment of the Revival epoch by the nascent historical and literary scholarship.[15] The first professional historians actually spanned the times before and after the liberation. With the passing of time, the Revival receded from actuality and from the memory of the living, and the perspective changed. Attitudes toward the past could now be more neutral and theoretically distanced. Not possessing a personal experience of the epoch, later historical scholarship reconstructed it entirely from documents and earlier testimonies.

Three main points of concentration of scholarly interest in the Revival may be distinguished thematically, corresponding to the major public movements of the epoch. The key words are church, that is, research on the struggle for an independent Bulgarian Church; culture, that is, research on education, literature, the printing press, art, etc.; and revolution, that is, interest in national revolutionaries and their organizations, conspiracies, and revolts. To these, one should add specialized works on the economy.[16] There was also the great interest in the Bulgarian compatriots in Macedonia, most of which was lost in the wars.[17] There follows a brief and simplified outline of the dynamics of the scholarly field.

The first "strictly" scholarly work—Todor Burmov's *The Bulgarian-Greek Church Controversy* (1885)—is dedicated to church struggles to establish a national church separate from the Greek patriarchy in Constantino-ple (Istanbul), which were, for a long time, the driving force of the national efforts.[18] During the interwar period the church movement was researched by Petur Nikov, who considered it to be the most important part of the Revival, being, in effect, a movement for the recognition of the Bulgarian nationality.[19] Ivan Snegarov is another well-known historian from the same period, whose research centered on the evolution of the Bulgarian Church from the Middle Ages to Modernity.[20]

For a long time, under the Communist regime, the church's struggles were eclipsed as the center of interest shifted to the more heroic revolu-tion. The neglect and underestimation of the church movement and of its activists reached such a degree that their vindication in the 1970s by the literary historian and critic Toncho Zhechev, in a widely read and much talked about book, made the impression of revisionism and even of dissi-dence.[21] In a detailed study of the church movement before the Crimean War (1853–1856) the historian Zina Markova legitimized it as a valid mani-festation and a necessary stage of the liberation (and bourgeois-democratic) struggle.[22] The author further developed her breakthrough in a monumen-tal book on the Bulgarian Exarchate between 1870 and 1879, in which she vindicated the legal "evolutionist" national efforts in general.[23] Soon after 1989, Iliya Todev coined the neologism "church nation," in recognition of the formative role of the church struggles in building up the Bulgarian nation.[24]

The revolutionary struggles also became an object of scholarly inquiry at an early date. Alongside the semi-scholarly, semi-journalistic works men-tioned, there appeared heroized biographies of national revolutionaries. Dimitur Strashimirov is the first great historian of the revolutionary strug-gles, with his monumental work on the April uprising of 1876 (published in 1907).[25] Several Communist historian-ideologues (Georgi Bakalov, Mik-hail Dimitrov, Ivan Klincharov, etc.) wrote about the great revolutionaries of the Revival during the interwar period. In a more academic vein, his-torical research on the national revolution was conducted by Aleksandŭr Burmov, whose first work, "The Bulgarian Revolutionary Central Commit-tee," appeared in 1943.[26] Under Communism there followed a profusion of works on revolutionary organizations, activists, and ideas. A numerous group of researchers studied the revolutionary movement and its ideology, which became the privileged (and strongly encouraged) topic of the re-gime.[27]

The cultural history of the Revival was the province of the highly respected Bulgarian "bourgeois" scholarship, represented by literary historians such as Ivan Shishmanov and Boyan Penev, historians such as (the early) Mikhail Arnaudov, (the early) Hristo Gandev, etc. In fact, the Revival was regarded by them as a primarily cultural (spiritual) phenomenon. They published extensively on individual men of letters, on foreign literary and ideological influences and cultural relations, and on the general pattern of literary and cultural evolution and world-view changes at the threshold of modernity. Some authors (Nikola Vankov, Stiliyan Chilingirov) specialized in the history of education.[28]

The initial concentration of the efforts of the "general" (i.e., mostly political and social) historians after World War II mainly on the revolutionary struggles left research on the cultural history of the Revival entirely to literary and art scholars and linguists. Petŭr Dinekov, Emil Georgiev, Toncho Zhechev, Docho Lekov, Nikola Mavrodinov (an art historian) and others studied literary trends and styles, personalities and ideas. During the last Communist decades there occurred a characteristic reorientation of an increasing number of historians toward cultural themes, which continued after 1989. The variety of interests is attested by the following list of names and topics: Nikolai Genchev (cultural relations with France and Russia, the intelligentsia, general patterns of Bulgarian culture[29]), Rumyana Radkova (the intelligentsia, various cultural phenomena, changes in morality[30]), Nadya Danova (cultural trends, pilgrimage to the Holy Lands[31]), Angel Dimitrov (education[32]), Ani Gergova (books and printing, the book trade[33]), Krassimira Daskalova (teachers, readers and reading[34]), Miglena Kuyumdzhieva (the intelligentsia[35]), Nikolai Zhechev (Bulgarian cultural centers in Romania), Virdzhiniya Paskaleva (Bulgarian women during the Revival[36]), Raina Gavrilova (the history of everyday urban life, historical anthropology[37]), Nikolai Aretov (representations of other lands and peoples[38]), Ivan Ilchev (advertising in the Revival press[39]), etc. Literary scholarship changed, too, as a younger generation of literary scholars (Svetlozar Igov, Inna Peleva) explored the texts of the Revival in innovative ways.

One might say that after social-economic history (to be discussed at length later) and the revolutionary struggles were subjected to dogmatic hardening, the cultural (and literary) history of the Revival proved to be an especially productive, dynamic, and innovative field. It generated new topics, legitimated new directions of interest, and served to advance revisionist views under the rubric of culture.

Notes

1 "Revival," as the designation of an epoch, will be written with a capital letter when standing for "Bulgarian Revival," and with a small letter when meant as a process.

2 Vasil Aprilov, "Dopŭlnenie kŭm knigata 'Dennitsa na novobŭlgarskoto obrazovanie'." In Vasil Aprilov, *Sŭchineniya*. Sofia: Bŭlgarski pisatel, 1968, 148–189, esp. 152–153. (Originally in Russian: "Dopolnenie k knige 'Dennitsa novo-bolgarskago obrazovaniya'." In Vasil Aprilov, *Sŭbrani Sŭchineniya*. Sofia, 1940, 165–198.); Georgi Rakovski, "Bŭlgarskii za nezavisimo im sveshtenstvo dnes vŭzbuden vŭpros i nikhna narodna cherkva v Tsarigrad." *Dunavski lebed* 1, no. 2 (22 September 1860); no. 3 (29 September 1860); Georgi Rakovski, "Bŭlgarskii naroden vŭpros pred otomanskata porta." *Dunavski lebed* 1, no. 9 (18 November 1860); Marko Balabanov, "Bŭlgarskii napredŭk." *Chitalishte* 1, no. 11 (1870/71), 323, 327–329; no. 12 (1870/71): 358, 360. Reprinted in Marko Balabanov, *Filosofski i sotsiologicheski sŭchineniya*. Sofia: Nauka i izkustvo, 1986, 108–124.

3 Marin Drinov, "Otets Paisii, negovoto vreme, negovata istoriya i uchenitsite mu." *Periodichesko spisanie na Bŭlgarskoto Knizhovno Drŭzhestvo* 1, no. 4 (1871), 3–26, esp. 25–26. Reprinted in Marin Drinov, *Izbrani sŭchineniya*. Vol. 1. Sofia: Nauka i izkustvo, 1971, 163–185.

4 *Vŭzrazdane*, edited by Svetoslav Milarov, Todor Peev, and Ivan Drasov. 1, Braila: 1876.

5 Dimitŭr Strashimirov, ed. *Arkhiv na Vŭzrazhdaneto*. Vol. 1, Sofia: 1908; T. Panchev, ed. *Iz arkhivata na Naiden Gerov*. Sofia: BAN. Vol. 1, 1911; Vol. 2, 1914; Ivan Georgov, "Materiali po nasheto vŭzrazhdane." *Sbornik narodni umotvoreniya, nauka i knizhnina*, 24 (1908): 1–47; Yurdan Ivanov, "Dokumenti po nasheto vŭzrazhdane." *Sbornik narodni umotvoreniya, nauka i knizhnina*, 21 (1905): 1–111; E. Sprostranov, "Po vŭzrazhdaneto na grad Ohrid." *Sbornik narodni umotvoreniya, nauka i knizhnina*, 13 (1896): 621–681; Marko Balabanov, "Po narodnoto probuzhdane." *Periodichesko spisanie na Bŭlgarskoto Knizhovno Druzhestvo*, 16 (1905): 577–598.

6 Vasil Manchev, *Spomeni. Dopiski. Pisma*. Sofia: Otechestven front, 1982. (The memoirs were written in 1904.); Ioakim Gruev, *Moite spomeni*. Plovdiv, 1906; Dimitŭr Fingov, arkhimandrit Sofronii, Asen Kisiov, "Spomeni." In *Sbornik Kaloferska druzhba*. Vol. 1, Sofia, 1908; Iliya Bluskov, *Spomeni*, edited by Docho Lekov. Sofia: Otechestven front, 1976. (The memoirs were written between 1907 and 1917.); Panteli Kisimov, *Istoricheski raboti. Moite spomeni*. Vols. 1–4, Plovdiv, 1897; Petŭr Peshev, *Istoricheskite sŭbitiya i deyateli ot navecherieto na Osvobozhdenieto ni do dnes*. Sofia: BAN, 1993 (first edition in 1925); Efrem Karanov, *Spomeni*. Sofia: Otechestven front, 1979. (The memoirs were written in 1920.); Arseni Kostentsev, *Spomeni*. Sofia: Otechestven front, 1984 (first edition in 1917); Nikola Lazarkov, *Spomeni. Iz robskoto minalo na Dupnitsa*. Dupnitsa, 1924; Hristo Stambolski, *Avtobiografiya. Dnevnitsi. Spomeni*, edited by Strashimir Dimitrov. Sofia: Bŭlgarski pisatel, 1972 (first edition in 1927–1931); Ivan Andonov, *Iz spomenite mi ot tursko vreme*. Plovdiv, 1927; K. Bozveliev, *Spomeni*. Vol. 1, Kazanlŭk, 1942; Ivan Kasabov, *Moite spomeni ot Vŭzrazhdaneto na Bŭlgariya s revolyutsionni idei*. Sofia, 1905; Mitropolit Simeon Varnensko Preslavski, Stoyan Chomakov, "Spomeni." In *Yubileen sbornik Koprivshtitsa*, edited by Archimandrite Evtimi. Sofia, 1926, 15–24.

7 An example of a rather awkward linkage between local and national is provided by Simeon Tabakov, *Opit za istoriya na grad Sliven*. Vol. 2, Sofia, 1924, 392, 414.

8 Zakhari Stoyanov, *Zapiski po buŭlgarskite vustaniya. Sŭchineniya*. Vol. 1. Sofia: Bŭlgarski pisatel, 1983 (first edition 1884–1892).

9   Stoyan Zaimov, *Minaloto. Ocherki i spomeni iz deyatelnostta na bŭlgarskite taini revol-yutsionni komiteti ot 1869–1877 g.* Sofia: BZNS, 1986 (first edition in 1884–1888).

10 Zakhari Stoyanov, *Zapiski*, 29–33; Stoyanov, *Biografii. Chetite v Bŭlgariya. Sŭchi-neniya*, Vol. 2, Sofia: Bŭlgarski pisatel, 1983, 109–110, 116–118, 289–298. (The biography of Vasil Levski appeared in 1883, that of Lyuben Karavelov in 1885, and that of Hristo Botev in 1888).

11 Zakhari Stoyanov, *Zapiski*, 31.

12 Zakhari Stoyanov anticipated this himself when pointing out that Botev was a combatant against foreign domination, and that had he lived after the liberation he would not have acted against his own nation state. See Zakhari Stoyanov, *Biografii*, 297.

13 Ivan Vazov, *Under the Yoke* (translated by M. Aleksieva and T. Atanasov). Sofia: 1955.

14 Inna Peleva, "Epopeya na zabravenite–istoriya, mit, ideologiya." In Inna Peleva, *Ideologŭt na natsiyata. Dumi za Vazov.* Plovdiv: Plovdivsko universitetsko izdatelstvo, 1994, 5–88, esp. 8–20, 79–80.

15 A historiography of the Revival compiled by Kristina Gecheva contained up to 500 pages already in the 1980s. See Kristina Gecheva, *Bŭlgarskata kultura prez Vŭzrazdaneto. Bibliografiya. Bŭlgarska i chuzhda knizhnina, 1878–1983.* Sofia: BAN, 1986.

16 Ivan Sakazov, *Bulgarische Wirtschaftsgeschichte.* Berlin and Leipzig: Walter de Gruyter, 1929; Petŭr Tishkov, *Istoriya na nasheto zanayatchiistvo do Osvobozhdenieto ni.* Sofia, 1922. There are also a number of economic studies in the publication of the Bulgarian Economic Society, *Spisanie na bŭlgarskoto ikonomichesko druzhestvo.*

17 Yordan Ivanov, *Bŭlgarite v Makedoniya.* Sofia, 1915.

18 Todor Burmov, *Bŭlgaro-grŭtskata tsŭrkovna raspra.* Sofia, 1885.

19 Petŭr Nikov, *Vŭzrazhdane na bŭlgarskiya narod. Tsŭrkovno-natsionalni borbi i postizheniya.* Sofia: Nauka i izkustvo, 1971 (first edition in 1929), 40, 44–45, 366–367, 372. See also Petŭr Nikov, "Vŭzrazhdane chrez tsŭrkva." In *Bŭlgariya 1000 godini (927–1927),* Sofia: Ministerstvo na narodnata prosveta, 1930, 321–381, esp. 323, 381.

20 Ivan Snegarov, *Istoriya na Ohridskata arkhiepiskopiya-patriarshiya, 1394–1767.* Sofia, 1932; Ivan Snegarov, *Solun v bŭlgarskata dukhovna kultura.* Sofia, 1937; Ivan Snegarov, *Skopskata eparkhiya.* Sofia, 1939.

21 Toncho Zhechev, *Bŭlgarskiyat Velikden ili strastite bŭlgarski.* Sofia: Marin Drinov, 1995 (first edition in 1875).

22 Zina Markova, *Bŭlgarskoto tsŭrkovno-natsionalno dvizhenie do Krimskata voina.* Sofia: BAN, 1976, esp. 6, 192–195.

23 Zina Markova, *Bŭlgarskata Ekzarkhiya, 1870–1879.* Sofia: BAN, 1989, 5–30, 315–323.

24 Iliya Todev, *Kŭm drugo minalo ili prenebregvani aspekti na bŭlgarskoto natsionalno vŭzrazhdane.* Sofia: Vigal, 1999, 45–46, 63.

25 Dimitŭr Strashimirov, *Istoriya na Aprilskoto vŭstanie.* Vol. 1–3, Plovdiv, 1907; Dimitŭr Strashimirov, "Komitetskoto desetiletie (epokha na komitetite) 1866–1876." In *Bŭlgaria 1000 godini,* 781–888; Dimitŭr Strashimirov, *V. Levski. Zhivot, dela, izvori.* Vol. 1, Sofia, 1929, etc.

26 Aleksandŭr Burmov, *Izbrani proizvedeniya v tri toma.* Sofia: BAN, 1974–1976.

27 To mention some of the most prominent, belonging to different generations: Mikhail Dimitrov, Dimitŭr Kosev, Ivan Undzhiev, Nikola Kondarev, Hristo Hristov, Nikolai Todorov, Krumka Sharova, Georgi Todorov, Strashimir Dimitrov, Nikolai Genchev. See the historiographical review in Nikolai Genchev, *Bŭlgarsko vŭzrazhdane.* Sofia: Otechestven front, 1988 (first edition in 1978), 32–38. Also Nikolai Genchev, "Dvizhenie na ideite i izsledvaniyata v bŭlgarskata istoriografiya." In *Universitetski izsledvaniya i prepodavaniya na bŭlgarskata istoriya u nas i v chuzhbina.* Vol. 1. Sofia, 1982, 31–55.

28 Nikola Vankov, *Istoriya na uchebnoto delo otkrai vreme do osvobozhdenieto*. Lovech, 1903; Stiliyan Chilingirov, *Bŭlgarskite chitalishta predi osvobozhdenieto*. *Prinos vŭrkhu istoriyata na bŭlgarskoto vŭzrazhdane*. Sofia, 1930.

29 Nikolai Genchev, *Frantsiya v bŭlgarskoto dukhovno vŭzrazhdane*. Sofia: Universitetsko izdatelstvo "Kliment Ohridski," 1979; Nikolai Genchev, *Bŭlgarskata vŭzrozhdenska inteligentsiya*. Sofia: Universitetsko izdatelstvo "Kliment Ohridski," 1991; Nikolai Genchev, *Bŭlgarskata kultura XV–XIX vek*. Sofia: Universitetsko izdatelstvo "Kliment Ohridski," 1988.

30 Rumyana Radkova, *Bŭlgarskata inteligentsiya prez Vŭzrazhdaneto*. Sofia: Nauka i izkustvo, 1986; Rumyana Radkova, *Inteligentsiyata i nravstvenostta prez Vŭzrazhdaneto*. Sofia: Marin Drinov, 1995.

31 Nadya Danova and Svetla Gyurova, eds., *Kniga za bŭlgarskite hadzhii*. Sofia: Bŭlgarski pisatel, 1985.

32 Angel Dimitrov, *Uchilishteto, progresŭt i natsionalnata revolyutsiya. Bŭlgarskoto uchilishte prez vŭzrazhdaneto*. Sofia: BAN, 1987; Angel Dimitrov, *Knizharyat, kogoto narichakha ministur. Biografichen ocherk za Hristo G. Danov*. Plovdiv: Hristo G. Danov, 1988.

33 Ani Gergova, *Knizhninata i bŭlgarite prez Vŭzrazhdaneto. Izvestiya na nauchno-izsledovatelskiya institut po kulturata*. Vol. 2, Sofia, 1984; Ani Gergova, *Knizhninata i bulgarite XIX–nachaloto na XX vek*. Sofia: BAN, 1991.

34 Krassimira Daskalova, *Bŭlgarskiyat uchitel prez Vŭzrazhdaneto*. Sofia: Universitetsko izdatelstvo "Kliment Ohridski," 1997; Krassimira Daskalova, *Gramotnost, knizhnina, chitateli i chetene v Bŭlgariya na prekhoda kŭm modernoto vreme*. Sofia: LIK, 1999.

35 Miglena Kuyumdzhieva, *Intelektualniyat elit prez Vŭzrazhdaneto*. Sofia: Universitetsko izdatelstvo "Kliment Ohridski," 1997.

36 Virdzhiniya Paskaleva, *Bŭlgarkata prez Vŭzrazhdaneto*. Sofia: BKP, 1964.

37 Raina Gavrilova, *Bulgarian Urban Culture in the Eighteenth and Nineteenth Centuries*. Selinsgrove: Susquehanna University Press, London: Associated University Press, 1999; Raina Gavrilova, *Koleloto na zhivota. Kŭm vsekidnevieto na bŭlgarskiya vŭzrozhdenski grad*. Sofia: Kliment Ohridski, 1999.

38 Nikolai Aretov, *Bŭlgarskoto Vŭzrazhdane i Evropa*. Sofia: Kralitsa Mab, 1995.

39 Ivan Ilchev, *Reklamata prez Vŭzrazhdaneto*. Sofia: Marin Drinov, 1995.

CHAPTER ONE

Meanings of the Revival I: National and Cultural

The men of the Bulgarian Revival thought of it in a national sense as the coming of the people to self-consciousness, or, as one might put it today, as the forging of a nation by arousing a sense of belonging. Two other meanings were evolved in historical scholarship, which have sometimes been put forward as basic, and sometimes as complementary to this first one. One is the interpretation of the epoch in spiritual–cultural terms—as a spiritual transformation, a transition from a medieval (religious, traditional, folklorist) world-view toward Modernity, with its secular spirit, positive knowledge, etc. Hence the comparisons of the Bulgarian Revival with the great European cultural epochs, especially the Renaissance and the Enlightenment. One can note the bias of the earlier great authors of the "old school" (Ivan Shishmanov, Boyan Penev, the early Mikhail Arnaudov, Ivan Snegarov, etc.) toward the issues of the cultural (spiritual) and national revival, and foreign cultural influences in particular.[1] The other interpretation, elaborated mostly by Marxist authors, is couched in economic and social (class) terms—as a transition from (Ottoman) feudalism toward capitalism, from a feudal society toward a society under the dominance of the bourgeoisie. I will consider the various interpretations/meanings and elucidate the connections between them.

The National Interpretation

The national interpretation/meaning of the Revival gained widest currency. As already pointed out, it derives from the understanding of the activists of the Revival epoch. The uses of the word "revival" (and of related words such as "awakening," "resurrection," etc.) leave little doubt about this. The term "revival" (*vŭzrazhdane*) was first used in 1842 by the

Bulgarian émigré merchant and pioneer of the Revival Vasil Aprilov, in a pamphlet published in Russian in St. Petersburg, in which he referred to the revival of Bulgarian literature and education but also to the revival of the Bulgarian people.[2] Aprilov may have borrowed the term from the Ukrainian Slavist scholar Yuri Venelin, who wrote (in the 1820s and 1830s) about a "nascence" or "new birth" of Bulgarian literature.[3] Its use was still occasional in the 1840s but became more frequent in subsequent decades, especially in the periodical press. The idea expressed metaphorically in so many variations is that the Bulgarian people were "slumbering," had "lost consciousness," "lost memory," "become numb" or even "died" until, all of a sudden (and thanks to the efforts of "awakeners"), they were "roused," "awakened," and "brought to their senses," "recovered from their amnesia," "regained consciousness," were "resurrected," "came to life," "got up," etc. The term "revival" occurs in phrases such as "spiritual revival," "revival of the people's spirit (or genius)," etc.[4] The word "nation" was not used at the time, but references were rather made to "people" (narod) and from this "nationality" (narodnost) was derived.

The understanding of the Revival as a nationalizing process has been widely shared by professional historical scholarship as well, from the end of the nineteenth century to the present day. One can cite numerous examples, but I will limit myself to some of the more prominent historians. In his early History of the Bulgarians, published in Czech and German in 1876 (and translated into Russian in 1878), the Czech historian Konstantin Jireček describes the Bulgarian Revival as the awakening of national feeling "from deep lethargy"; this was accomplished by a "handful of enlightened patriots" by means of education and books in the native language.[5]

The greatest Bulgarian "bourgeois" literary historian, Boyan Penev, regards the period as an epoch of the spiritual awakening and national (and literary) revival of the Bulgarian people.[6]

For Mikhail Arnaudov, who spanned the "bourgeois" and Communist periods, the Bulgarian Revival meant "the appearance of a new nationality on the periphery of Southeastern Europe." To cite him:

"The national element in the historical process that we call the Bulgarian Revival deserves the greatest attention. Even if this revival was due to a number of internal and external reasons, whether of an educational and political or of an economic and social nature, it is beyond doubt that at the center of this system of preconditions was a collective consciousness with considerable dynamics. This consciousness, leaning upon language, traditional material conditions, a poetic tradition, and all that experienced as destiny, gained, slowly but surely, power over the spirit, until it was formed into a first-rate creative force."[7]

Hristo Gandev, who began his career as a historian before the Communist takeover, defined the early Revival in particular in terms of a spiritual and social transformation, that is, the rationalization of the world-view and the emergence of an urban civic society, which resulted in the shaping of the Bulgarian people into an organized society and a cultural nation.[8]

The literary historian Petǔr Dinekov wrote in one of his early books (1942) that the Revival is primarily defined by the fact that the national consciousness of the Bulgarians, which was manifested only incidentally before, "finds a clear, open, and categorical expression."[9]

The formation of the Bulgarian nation is also present as a meaning of the Revival for most Marxist authors, quite strongly before 1944, very timidly (and as a secondary meaning) during the Stalinist and post-Stalinist 1950s and 60s, and increasingly strongly in the subsequent revision until it was restored to its initial importance. We will trace this evolution later.

When the formation of the nation is posited as the principal meaning of the Bulgarian Revival, it is only natural to look at similar processes in the Balkans and in Europe, especially the national-liberation movements of neighboring peoples (Greeks and Serbs) and national unification movements (in Germany and Italy). Indeed, the first great Bulgarian literary scholar (and a prominent public figure), Ivan Shishmanov, compares the last period of the Bulgarian Revival, with its political struggles, to the Italian *Risorgimento*. Research on the ideology of the Bulgarian national revolutionaries confirmed the strong influence of foreign national movements, especially the Italian (the ideology of Mazzini) and the Greek (*Hetairia Philike*), and the more attenuated influence of the ideas of the French Revolution and of the revolution of 1848. The Bulgarian national Revival was thus shown to participate in European political ideas and trends.[10] As emphasized recently by Raina Gavrilova, the Bulgarian national Revival is inscribed within the triumphant march of nationalism all over Europe throughout the nineteenth century, that is, it was part of a pan-European process.[11] The Bulgarian Revival has been explored against the broader Balkan and South-Slav background by Strashimir Dimitrov and Krǔstyu Manchev[12], and as an integral part of the Slav and South-Slav revival by the literary scholars Boyan Penev and Emil Georgiev.[13] All this embedded the Bulgarian national Revival within the Balkan and (Central) European context by recognizing common features rather than treating it in isolation (as was characteristic of so many national historians).

Concepts of the (Bulgarian) Nation

Attempts at a theoretical treatment of the phenomenon of the nation in Bulgarian scholarship, and the application of general ideas to the Bulgarian case, deserve special attention. It is amazing to find out that, although the formation of the Bulgarian nation features as the primary meaning of the Bulgarian Revival, relatively little has been written on the nation in a scholarly, detached manner. One reason is certainly that, for a number of years, the topic was to be found either in the midst of intense nationalist agitation (which would make a scholarly debate appear rather unpatriotic), or was avoided out of the opposite fear of being labeled "bourgeois nationalist." Two issues have been central in the theoretical debates on the nation. One crucial debate (if one may so call views expressed after various intervals of time) is centered on the "objective" versus "subjective" definition of the nation, that is, whether it can be defined by some set of external features or by self-consciousness. Another issue concerns the "universality" of one or another defining trait of the nation. In what follows I will review in broad outline the evolution of the ideas on the nation in Bulgarian historical scholarship, making diversions to more essayistic (or doctrinaire) writings that give a glimpse of the ideological and political stakes of this "hot" topic.

The men of the Revival defined the nation as having an "individuality" (*samobitnost*), characterized by such features as common descent, a single language and a shared religion, a cultural tradition (of folk songs, proverbs, beliefs, arts, etc.), common material conditions of life and customs, etc. But they also emphasized in their view of "nationality" (*narodnost*) the volitional, subjective aspect, the constitutive moment of "self-consciousness" (or self-awareness) and the feeling of belonging. All the more so because they had personal experience of how difficult it was to "awaken" their compatriots to the idea that they constituted a community in its own right (and to prevent some of them from assimilating into the more prestigious Greek people). There is, in addition, the organicist notion that peoples grow and pass through various phases of life, and the idea of a fate forged in the struggle for self-preservation and through God's providence.[14] Even though in such texts the study of the phenomenon merges with national ideology, they may be very insightful.

Historical scholarship at first recognized the importance of both the "objective" and "subjective" aspects, or scarcely saw any contradiction here at all. The ideational (volitional) character of the nation—that is, the idea that it finally comes down to self-awareness and a feeling of belonging—was stressed by the historians Petŭr Bitsilli and Hristo Gandev (in his earlier writings). During the nationalist 1930s, a number of nationalist and right-wing authors paid tribute to this concept in essays devoted to the Bulgarian nation. In contrast, Marxist authors stuck to objectivist descriptions, at first faithfully reproducing the Stalinist definition. However, revisions occurred in the course of time.

The "subjectivist" (volitional) approach to the nation is strongly emphasized in a theoretical paper by Petŭr Bitsilli, a Russian émigré who settled in Bulgaria after the October Revolution.[15] The author argues that the nation is a historically changing concept, which does not have the same contents in different epochs and different contexts. The shaping of a certain nation is the outcome of a historical process with many contingencies. In a number of examples Bitsilli shows that none of the factors that bind people into a "spiritual community"—such as common language, common territory, economic and political activities, etc.—is absolute and obligatory; the role of every factor may differ, and one feature may define more than one nation. The inference he draws is that no general and exhaustive defining formula for the nation is possible. What is crucial is the feeling of spiritual community, however it has come into being. Bitsilli's experience of emigration certainly contributed to his emphasis on the spiritual relationship between compatriots rather than on territorial–political unity.

One might mention here a number of essays on the nation from the 1930s, written in a markedly nationalist spirit, in which the spiritual unity of compatriots stands in the foreground and is often metaphysically construed as the "native spirit," "people's spirit" or "genius of the nation." But the reason why the "spiritual bond" is given priority is different—it is to provide a reminder of the unity of all Bulgarians and to rally compatriots more effectively to the national ideal of "unification" (especially with Macedonia). The national objective is rarely stated but rather implied, and not all authors are prepared to go all the way.

In one such essay (dated 1935), the psychologist and philosopher Spiridon Kazandzhiev enumerates the contents of the national consciousness in terms of "thoughts" or notions: the notion of the spiritual unity of the people, the notion of the individuality of the people and its self-esteem (implying national independence and sovereignty), and the notion of solidarity between individual compatriots and their moral duty to serve the people and the national ideals, especially in times of war. The spiritual unity of the people derives, according to him, from "objective" features such as blood and tribal kinship, geographical conditions, commonalty of language, history, and religion, etc.[16] As can be seen, the role of the objective traits of the nation, including most "primordial" ones, is to ground and secure the spiritual bond.

Yanko Yanev, a rightist author (philosopher and literary critic) of a fascist bent, wrote (in 1933) of the "genius of the nation" that asserts itself historically with spontaneity and will, calling it "cultural nationalism" (in contrast to "political nationalism," whose expressions he leaves the readers to guess).[17]

The nation is described in a still more elevated and spiritually "distilled" manner by Simeon Topuzanov, an ideologue of mandatory trade unionism in the authoritarian Bulgarian state after the coup d'état on 19 May 1934. A nation is not a given people in the present day, nor even the ethnic principle (because it may sweep along "alien elements" in its élan) but it is "an ideal notion, a historical and spiritual process, and an eternity." The nation is, in fact, the designation of a historical mission, carried through ups and downs along the historical path upon the shoulders of a "string of generations" who are fused by shared feelings, thoughts, and aspirations, and handed down from one generation to the next. It is a "supreme form of collective life," linking past, present, and future. The goal of this spiritually exalted definition (or, rather, metaphorization) of the nation consists, in this case, very explicitly in the rejection of class ideology to be replaced by a "healthy nationalism" and the binding of the working class to the nation. The social problem has to be solved along with the pursuit of the national good—prosperity for all (though, as indicated by the author, the partitioning of the Bulgarian nation reduces the opportunities for advance of all its members).[18]

It is worth noting that, apart from the glorification of the "national spirit" and of its historical mission, the Bulgarian nationalist Right did, selectively, emphasize "objective" criteria of the nation, understood as national markers and demarcation lines between "us" and "them." Here is an example of how "objective" features of the nation may be manipulated to one's convenience. The program of the fascist Union of the Bulgarian National Legions accentuates geography in the justification of territorial claims (the flow of rivers being likened to the "natural" striving of the Bulgarians towards the Aegean sea), while religion is denied a significant role (so that the Muslim *pomaks* may be diverted from their "religious fanaticism" and brought back to the Bulgarian nation, whose language and descent they share).[19] After this excursus into patently ideological writings we return to scholarly works.

Hristo Gandev published in 1940 a work that remains a theoretical high point in Bulgarian historical scholarship on the nation.[20] Only ideas relevant to the Bulgarian debates on the nation will be reproduced here. Gandev denies the possibility of defining the nation in the abstract and through a constant set of features such as common territory, ethnic unity, commonalty of language, literature, religion, art, economic conditions and way of life, etc. A nation may exist where some of these are absent (or shared with others). He ascribes greater importance, as a necessary condition, to a common historical life (more dramatically called historical "destiny"). Nor can the "culture" that characterizes the nation (according to the German notion) be objectively defined, and in any case it exists in the beliefs and is held in the imagination.

Gandev considers two (by now familiar) basic notions of the nation—the civic-legal notion defined through the will, of French origin, and the cultural–historical or ethnographic notion, of German provenance. He explains the emergence of these concepts according to the specific historical and social–political circumstances in the respective countries. According to Gandev, the Bulgarian concept of the nation, which received a certain theoretical elaboration during the Revival (then under the name *narodnost*), falls clearly within the German ideological sphere, partly mediated by Russia. Thus the Bulgarian Revival began by revealing a common historical fate and a distinctive individuality of the way of life that divides the Bulgarians from the Greeks and the Turks. Popular songs were collected, and customs were described as testifying to the "people's spirit." The people was conceived of as a natural community (or collectivity), and to serve it was made into the highest goal. In this view, every people has a peculiar individuality and purpose, and makes contributions to human culture and to mankind. Political independence is regarded as a precondition for the fulfilling of this predestination, hence the task of achieving it. In contrast, the French notion of the nation, which underlines individual will, equality, and an elective-representative system of government as an expression of the "common will" while rejecting monarchism in favor of a national republic, remained underdeveloped.[21]

According to Gandev, it is the similarity of the path towards national formation in Bulgaria and in Germany that explains the reception of the German notion, namely, the passing through of a "cultural nation" phase (by way of a growing awareness of "individuality" in history and of a distinctive way of life), followed by aspirations toward political sovereignty in one's own state. In Bulgaria, as in the West, this was a corollary of urban life, of the spread of mass education, and of the creation of a literary Bulgarian language and a Bulgarian literature resulting from the activities of a Bulgarian intelligentsia of teachers and artisan-traders. The intelligentsia propagated "common Bulgarian spiritual values" and nurtured the new generations in "homogeneous knowledge" (but not earlier than the first half of the nineteenth century).

The earlier Marxist treatment of the nation invariably takes as its point of departure Stalin's formulaic and flatly objectivist definition of the nation through the notorious four features: common language, territory, economic life, and psychological make-up or "national character," as manifested in a common culture. The emergence of nations is accommodated within the teaching on social formations at the transition from a feudal to a bourgeois-capitalist society, thus a nation begins as a "bourgeois nation." In the case of peoples under foreign domination, the emerging national bourgeoisie of the oppressed nation becomes the organizer of all classes of co-nationals in a national movement by presenting its own class interests as the common interests of all classes; its interests consist in conquering the market from the bourgeoisie (or the semi-feudal bureaucracy) of the dominant nation.[22] From this point of view, national self-awareness, the will to belong, common representations, etc. appear as secondary in national formation (being part of the ideological "super-structure"). The process of national formation in general seems secondary (epiphenomenal) to the social–economic transition, in accordance with the Marxist primacy of class over nation.

The Stalinist definition of the nation is used in a short paper (dated 1940) by the would-be ideologue of the Communist regime (and versatile philosopher) Todor Pavlov, though understandably the source of the definition is not mentioned at that time. Rather than an application of the definition to the Bulgarian case, this is an argument for the priority of economic communality over psychic (or spiritual-cultural) unity among the features of the nation. According to the author, although all features are important, if we take the psychic outlook as the fundamental feature we risk "psychologizing" the nation, making a "pure consciousness" out of it, and ending up with a "purely mystical essence."[23] Warnings against the mystification of the nation become understandable in view of the nationalist elaboration mentioned earlier.

Stalin's ideas were first applied to the Bulgarian case by the Russian historian and academician Nikolai Derzhavin (in a work on Paisii in 1941). He described the formation of the Bulgarian nation as the struggle of the

Bulgarian bourgeoisie against the semi-feudal ruling bureaucracy of the Turkish "nation," as well as the struggle against the rival Greek national bourgeoisie for the market; the Bulgarian bourgeoisie conducted the struggle by organizing the lower strata with slogans for nation and fatherland.[24] The Bulgarian historian Yono Mitev followed suit in the literal application of Stalin's ideas. He also linked the formation of the Bulgarian nation to the development of capitalism (in its lower stage of crafts and putting-out industries). Characteristically, the author affirmed that an autonomous Macedonian nation was formed alongside the Bulgarian one—a "concession" to the envisioned federation between Bulgaria and Yugoslavia at that time, and ironic with regard to the further developments.[25]

From the 1960s there stems a doctrinaire and rather naive attempt (by Nedyalko Kurtev) to distinguish between types of patriotism on the basis of the class status of those professing it and their "progressiveness" at a given moment. With elaborate casuistry, the author reveals a spectrum of patriotisms, lower and higher, neutral, positive and negative, peaceful and revolutionary. First comes "people's (*narodnosten*) patriotism," undifferentiated as to class, and characteristic of the stage before the nation (when it was just a "people"). This then develops into "national patriotism," which is conceived of in quantitative terms as finding expression in "a stronger love for the fatherland, the native land and the people, a higher awareness of the commonality of national traits and specifics, a greater readiness for self-sacrifice for the freedom of the fatherland, and the conscious revolutionary activity of the great majority of the working masses." At this higher level of "national" patriotism, Kurtev further differentiates between "national consciousness" as a characteristic of all, "patriotism" as the exclusive characteristic of the oppressed and progressive classes, and the "bourgeois nationalism" of the bourgeoisie. The author admits that the Bulgarian bourgeoisie as a class was also patriotic (and not nationalist) for a time and in some of its efforts, notably toward national education and in the church struggles, as this coincided with the "progressive course of the historical development directed at the destruction of the feudal order and the building up of the bourgeois order." The "progressiveness" of the bourgeoisie lasted until the revolutionary political struggles in the 1860s, which it betrayed, while the consciousness of the peasant and urban laboring classes rose to higher revolutionary forms of struggle. The patriotism of the oppressed classes thus grew and passed from educational and church patriotism to higher revolutionary patriotism, while the patriotism of the bourgeoisie deteriorated. Characteristics of the higher form of patriotism (besides its revolutionary nature) are its democratic quality—being directed against the exploiters from other nations but not against their laboring people—and the fact that it went together with love for Russia, which became an organic component of Bulgarian patriotism.[26] (Kurtev does not speak of "internationalism" in this case.) As clearly seen, the modalities of patriotism, although made to appear "objective," are simply predicated on the attitude of the Communist ideologues toward various historical classes and their "progressiveness" at a certain point in history.

The work of historian Rumyana Radkova on the national self-consciousness of the Bulgarians in the eighteenth century and at the beginning of the nineteenth presents a clear advance in relation to the Stalinist views discussed so far.[27] The very fact that a "subjectivist" category such as national self-consciousness is at the center of the research may have seemed bold at the time. But the effect is tempered by the dogmatism of the theoretical discussion (based on contemporary Soviet authoritative authors) and the mere replication of the notorious "features of the nation" on the objective and the subjective levels, that is, their being entered into the national self-consciousness. The "structure" of the national self-consciousness thus appears to be a mixture of heterogeneous (and some quite curious) components, such as the awareness of belonging to a certain ethnic community; attachment to the "national values" of territory, language, and culture; a feeling of patriotism; solidarity in national-liberation (and anti-feudal) struggles; and an awareness of belonging to a nation-state. According to the author, while national self-consciousness is just one feature of the nation among others, "there is no nation without self-consciousness." However, the author feels obliged to attack "idealistic bourgeois philosophy" for the "fetishization" of national self-consciousness (which is "just" a set of ideas) by detaching it from realities and forgetting that it is their "reflection."

Radkova also offers a more sophisticated version of the Stalinist picture (worked out in reference to subjugated peoples) of the birth and the evolution of national self-consciousness. The latter begins as quite undifferentiated, but the growing class differentiation in society results in different attitudes on the part of the various classes to national issues. The formation of national self-consciousness is initially in tune with the economic interests of the nascent national bourgeoisie in conquering the internal markets. But at a higher stage of development, national self-consciousness (now elaborated into an ideology) is combined with the tasks of social transformation, and a progressive democratic trend comes into being, which is in accord with the interests of the majority of the people.

In fact, the major contribution of the author consists in the empirical search in the literature of the Bulgarian Revival (and in the Catholic "propaganda" of the seventeenth century) for traces of national self-consciousness, especially designations of origin, the use of the ethnic eponym, phrases such as "Bulgarian people," "fatherland," "native land" and similar expressions of patriotism, descriptions of territory, praise for the Bulgarian language, pride in the historical past, and advocacy of the historical right to national independence.

The treatment of the nation (at about the same time) by Nikolai Genchev, a historian with a reputation as a dissident, is free from inconsistencies and arbitrary constructs. The author considers the formation of the nation on the basis of Bulgarian ethnicity (*narodnost*) as its "ethnic substratum," under the impact of such factors as the rise of urban life and of the urban economy, increased market exchange, and the role of the bourgeoisie as a "binding element" through its economic activities but also as a bearer of modern cultural standards and of the national idea itself. The formation of the Bulgarian nation is described as a primarily cultural process, whereas the new culture of the Revival was shaped out of three components—a literary language based on the spoken dialects, tradition (a less important component because of the "medieval conservatism of Eastern Christianity"), and the extremely important foreign influences (from modern Europe, Russia, and other Slav and Balkan cultures). The subjective aspect of the nation ("national self-consciousness") receives less attention, except for a mention that it suffered "deformities" by the assimilation of some Bulgarians among the Greeks or Turks. The author enters the rather slippery terrain of "people's psychology" under the rubric of the "cultural–psychological stereotype of the Bulgarian during the Revival," but he keeps prudently to institutional settings (the family, the commune, the church, national organizations) rather than describing problematic "national traits."[28]

Genchev's otherwise rich exposition is mostly confined to tracing the preconditions and formative forces of the Bulgarian nation, while a theoretical construct of the nation itself (or of "national consciousness") is lacking. This is hardly accidental. The (moderately) nationalist viewpoint that underlies this work makes it difficult to approach the phenomenon of the nation in a more critical or distanced manner. On the other hand, it should be noted that the predominantly cultural (historical, linguistic, ethnographic) concept of the nation, characteristic of the Bulgarian case, makes an objectivist treatment, and an explanation in terms of "cultural processes," quite adequate–historical concept and scholarly "method" being in tune. Nation here equals culture (though one still needs the dimension of the perception of that culture as specific and differentiating).

Strashimir Dimitrov was the first to restore the emphasis on the "subjective" factor in the formation of the Bulgarian nation.[29] The author refers to the theoretical discussion of the nation and of the "national question" in the Russian journal *"Voprosy filosofii"* (in 1966–1968), and, after repeating the usual features of the nation, adds self-consciousness. Then, in discussing the formation of the various traits of the nation in the Bulgarian case, he stresses precisely the "subjective" aspect. To cite him: "The turning of these objective features into a fact of consciousness is precisely the crucial moment in the process of the formation of the national consciousness."[30]

Dimitrov then traces the inception and the spread of the national consciousness by way of "national propaganda," initially by single personalities and within small groups, then in a broader national movement, directed by the bourgeoisie, which drew in the entire population. The author points to the interest in the national past (the "historicism" of the Revival), in the language and the ethnography, that is, the customs and folklore of the people, etc., as instruments in the formation of the national consciousness. National "emancipation" and self-differentiation was effected while fighting the Greek assimilative influences. The consolidation of the Bulgarian "bourgeois nation" as a result of the activities of communes and schools, the printing of books and newspapers, the spread of revolutionary organizations, etc. was basically completed with the establishment of the Bulgarian Exarchate (some years before the liberation).[31]

Already in the 1980s, Hristo Gandev (whose 1940 work was reviewed) came back to the issue of the Bulgarian nation.[32] He started by relating the postulates of the Marxist understanding: the linking of the nation with the transition from feudalism to capitalism, and the factors that contribute to national cohesion, such as economy, language, territory, state tradition, psychology expressed in culture, etc.[33] But this only serves him as a kind of "insurance," and as a starting point of the analysis as he immediately sets out to relativize the significance of every single factor as a defining feature of the nation by drawing counter-examples from various countries, especially in Latin America and Africa; thus neither political sovereignty and state independence, nor bourgeois development and the advance of capitalism, and still less the language, may, as Gandev carefully puts it, "ensure sufficient preconditions for the building up of a unitary and internally consolidated nation" in a number of cases.[34]

The author proceeds to highlight the specifics of the Bulgarian case of national formation by considering the candidate features one by one. He asserts the great involvement of "ethno-geographical unity" (common material conditions and cultural patterns, the principle of a "people"), the effect of which was enhanced by the under-differentiation of the culture of the bourgeoisie from the material life conditions and culture of the common people; then the importance of the Bulgarian literary language and of the literature created in it; the significance of Orthodoxy; and, finally, the importance of the "national idea" itself (i.e., the idea of an independent state on the basis of the Bulgarian people), etc. The author points to the time of the formation of each factor, which often (in the Bulgarian case as elsewhere) long predates the transition toward bourgeois-capitalist relations—thus undermining this postulate as well.[35]

After Communism, Ivan Stoyanov reversed quite mechanically the approaches to the understanding of the nation and of the processes of national formation by stressing the subjective moment: "the thought of belonging to a given nation."[36] An essay-style work of the present author may also be pointed out, in which the Bulgarian case is accommodated within the ethno-cultural idea of the nation, and the "compensatory" character of Bulgarian nationalism is pointed out.[37]

The Bulgarian nation has recently been treated by Iliya Todev in a rather nationalistic spirit. The exclusive emphasis on language as a main (and even universal) factor of national formation by this author should not only demonstrate that the population of Macedonia was part of the Bulgarian nation during the Revival; it should also be conceived of as a refutation of the existence of the Macedonian nation in the present. The problem here is that a historical argument is being projected upon present-day realities that look quite different.[38] Todev defines the Bulgarian national idea (as expressed by Paisii) as defensive—an example of "defensive nationalism"—in so far as it was turned against the offensive of the more advanced Greeks and Serbs.[39]

Maria Todorova, a Bulgarian historian who became a leading figure in the field of Balkan studies in the United States, agrees about the very great significance accorded to language as an identification mark of the Bulgarian nation (far preceding religion). This is attested by the fact that the jurisdiction of the Bulgarian Exarchate over the Bulgarian *millet* in the Ottoman Empire was based precisely on the language criterion; the understanding of the Muslim *pomaks* as Bulgarians, and the negation during Communism of the existence of a Macedonian nation, rested again on identity or similarity of language.[40] However, Todorova never affirms that the role of language in identifying a nation is universal, nor does she treat as normative (and sacrosanct for the scholar) this historically evolved "linguistic identity" of the Bulgarian nation, generated clearly by the need for identification through inclusion/exclusion.

Nationalism and Romanticism

The Slav revivals, including the Bulgarian Revival, took place under the strong ideological impact of romanticism, especially of German romanticism with its interest in history, popular culture, and language. The literary scholar Boyan Penev was the first Bulgarian to emphasize the crucial connection between the Slav revivals and romanticism, expressed through the interest of the Slavic "awakeners" toward their own historical past (romantic historicism, patriotic historicism), toward their people, language, way of life and folklore, but also toward Slavdom as a whole (the Slav idea, South Slav Illyrism). Boyan Penev singles out the influence of German and English romanticism, and of German idealistic philosophy (Herder and Fichte), which all received a specific patriotic and political coloration with the Slavs under foreign domination, while Pan-Germanism was important in the reaction it provoked.[41]

Another literary scholar of the "bourgeois" (i.e., pre-Communist) epoch, Bozhan Angelov, subsumed the entire Bulgarian ideology and literature of the three decades preceding liberation under the concept of romanticism (though he offered no theoretical treatment of romanticism).[42] One might also mention a short text by A. Filipov, dated 1933, in which the Bulgarian Revival as a whole is closely linked with romanticism, and especially with its concept of "the people" and the national idea as one of its components. The work of Paisii Hilendarski (of 1762), the progenitor of the Bulgarian Revival, is interpreted by this author along the lines of romanticism as political romanticism or romantic historicism that makes use of history while omitting the philosophical and artistic problems of romanticism.[43]

The connections between romanticism and the "Slav revival" were further worked out by the literary scholar Emil Georgiev during the 1960s and 1970s. He enumerates the following typical features of the Slav revivals— the turning toward the people (which is at the root of everything else), historicism, philologism, folklorism, and the Slav idea. According to the author, the Slav revival, and the Bulgarian Revival in particular, went through two phases—a phase of "Enlightenment" (or "Renaissance-Enlightenment," the period of the "Awakeners"), and a phase of romanticism. The romanticism that followed upon the Enlightenment-Awakeners' phase is understood by Emil Georgiev as not just a literary trend but, more broadly, as an ideological and social–cultural current that began in the 1820s and lasted until the liberation. Its content was formed by the struggles of the already awakened nation for (modern, secular) education and independence. Romanticism, in literature in particular, is characterized by patriotism, the prevalence of civic topics, and an ethos of heroic struggle. Slavic romanticism, under the conditions of foreign domination, is described as "progressive and revolutionary"—turned toward the people, patriotic, and inspired by the national-liberation struggles.[44]

It should be noted that romanticism as a literary trend received a comparatively low valuation under the Communist regime, in accordance with a hierarchy of styles in which it came only below socialist realism, critical realism, and realism. Hence the necessity to vindicate it by emphasizing its "progressive" role and its ethos of combat under the specific conditions of foreign rule.

Petŭr Dinekov is another important literary scholar who dealt with Bulgarian romanticism. He differentiated between romanticism as an "ideological current" (the historical romanticism of Paisii, Yuri Venelin, Vasil Drumev, etc.), romanticism as a "literary school" (and artistic method), and "revolutionary romance" (that he ascribed to some brands of Bulgarian realism).[45]

Romanticism viewed as a purely literary trend forms the subject matter of a book published in 1968 by the literary scholar Krŭstyu Genov. He extended it over the whole of the Bulgarian literature of the Revival, dividing it into two periods: 1) the "romanticism of the national awakeners" from 1762 (when Paisii finished his "Slavonic-Bulgarian History") to the Crimean War of 1853–1856; and 2) romanticism with an ethos of national liberation and social revolution, of the period from the Crimean War to liberation in 1877/8 (culminating in the poets Botev and Vazov).[46] However, this concept of "romanticism without boundaries" came under strong attack by critics.[47]

The literary scholar and historian Svetlozar Igov recently proposed a division of the Bulgarian literary process into an Enlightenment period (from Paisii to the mid-1840s), and a period of national romanticism, "sharing a number of the stylistic traits of European, Slav, and Balkan literary romanticism" (from the mid-1840s to the 1870s). The author draws a distinction (like Dinekov before him) between national romanticism as "underlying the ideology of the national revival as a total-historical process," and romanticism as a "literary ideology, literary trend, and literary style," which dominated only the second period of the Bulgarian Revival.[48] But he then deals only with literary romanticism.

Romanticism in historical writing in particular receives special treatment as an instrument of the shaping of the national consciousness. The influential Communist historian Aleksandŭr Burmov divided the evolution of Bulgarian historical scholarship into two periods—"national romanticism" (of Georgi Rakovski and Gavril Krŭstevich), and "critical history writing" (with Vasil Aprilov and Spiridon Palauzov as its forerunners). Historical scholarship under the banner of national romanticism is described as uncritical, and as containing patriotic exaggerations aimed at reinforcing the national consciousness.[49] Interestingly, the beginnings of critical (or "scientific") historical scholarship are placed at the end of the Revival period (with Marin Drinov).

The historian Dimitŭr Tsanev takes as the focus of his interest the "romanticism" of Bulgarian historical scholarship. According to him, romanticism accompanied the national-liberation movement in the form of romanticism in history writing, more precisely as "national romanticism," where the national idea received a political edge. While Paisii's followers in history writing, and the works of Rakovski and Krŭstevich from the first half of the nineteenth century, are considered by the author as examples of Bulgarian historical romanticism, Paisii himself is viewed as more of an Enlightener.[50]

The link between the South Slav and Balkan national-liberation movements and romanticism was recently studied in greater detail by the historian Nadya Danova. Starting with a more general description of romanticism and its manifestations and specifics in various European countries (England, France, Germany, Italy), the author focuses on romanticism in the writing of history in particular, which shaped the Balkan nationalisms. It was within the matrix of historical romanticism that a set of ideas evolved, such as the understanding of history as a history of "peoples" (rather than of mankind or Christianity), the idea of the "primordiality" of the nation and its "organic unfolding" in time, of the peculiar character and "originality" of a certain people that finds expression in its "genius" (or "spirit"), the exceptionality and special mission of the nation, the notion of national belonging as a feeling with deep, irrational roots, etc.[51]

To sum up, the Bulgarian national Revival has rarely been generalized into an epoch of national romanticism, in contrast to the frequent analogies with the Renaissance and the Enlightenment. Romanticism is mentioned as a rule in a more narrow sense, as romanticism in history writing or as a literary style and an artistic ideology. Only a few scholars (Boyan Penev, Emil Georgiev, Nadya Danova) operate with a broader understanding of romanticism as an intellectual (or ideological) "climate" and a shared set of ideas that marked the national ideology of the Bulgarian Revival but also of the Balkan and Slav revivals in general. Emil Georgiev in particular comes closest to describing the Bulgarian Revival (within the context of "Slav revivals") in terms of romanticism when speaking of its first (Awakeners') phase as one that "posed the tasks of the Revival," followed by a second, romantic period of "stormy national upsurge" that "began to put them into effect."[52] While Svetlozar Igov views "national romanticism" as expressive of the Bulgarian Revival in general (its "pathos"), he is primarily interested in literary romanticism. Among the historians, Dimitŭr Tsanev spoke of a Bulgarian national romanticism in the nineteenth century but narrows it down to historical works, literature, and the arts.[53]

One may pose the question as to why the link between the Bulgarian Revival and romanticism does not stand out more graphically in Bulgarian historical scholarship, and especially in "purely" historical works (in contrast to literary scholarship). Why is the Revival (or part of it) not defined—at least not typically—as an epoch of "national romanticism"? One may speculate that the blindness regarding the romantic ideological contents of the Bulgarian Revival is due to a conceptual blockade of authors, who stand very much on national-romantic ground themselves. When filtering the world through such lenses, the lenses themselves remain invisible. It is as if a dose of national romanticism remains unsurpassed in the Bulgarian historical scholarship more than a century after its announced entry into a "scientific–critical" stage.

The National and the Spiritual (Cultural) Meanings

In another major interpretation, the Bulgarian Revival is viewed as a profound spiritual transformation, a transition to the world-view and culture of Modernity—secularism, belief in reason, science, individualism, pragmatism, etc. This meaning will be dealt with in the following sections on the parallels with the great European cultural epochs. But its close association with the national meaning (which is of a "spiritual" nature, too) should be pointed out first. In fact, it was developed as complementary to it, and the two meanings have often been conflated into a "national-spiritual" interpretation of the Revival. To cite an early example, Dimitŭr Mishev described the Revival (in 1925) as a "Bulgarian awakening," that is, in the national sense, but in the same breath he compared it to the Renaissance in Italy. He meant the Renaissance in the broadest terms—as a spiritual upheaval, "a regeneration of spirituality," "the liberation of literature, the arts, science, the mind, and the individual from the medieval scholastic, ascetic, and mystical spirit." He admitted that in contrast to the "cultural peoples," the Bulgarians did not have literature, arts, and sciences waiting to be regenerated and renewed. However, the Bulgarian people had "dormant creative capacities," "a latent creative spirit," which had to be awakened and regenerated, hence the Revival consisted in the awakening and the renewal of the "Bulgarian soul."[54]

The very expression "spiritual awakening," often used in the literature of the Revival and on the Revival, is characteristically ambiguous—it links intellectual advance with national self-awareness, Enlightenment with nationalism. Such a conflation of two moments is not accidental. It is rooted in the specific conditions in which elementary education (*prosveta*), conducted in the native language and making use of patriotic contents, simultaneously arouses national self-awareness. A passage by an earlier historian makes the connection explicit:

"The Bulgarian was called to awake, to come to his senses. The awakening brought about a desire for education. The Enlightenment of a certain people is manifested in literacy, books for the people, and schools for the people. [....] The schools reinforce the natural aspiration of every people for freedom. The teachers and the pupils in the newly-opened schools studied and already knew that our people had been strong, enlightened, and respected in the past, but that now it is a slave."[55]

The close association between the two meanings of the national Revival is also due to the belated Bulgarian development that "collapses" into one the epochs of earlier Western development (or makes up for them). The overlap between spiritual (world-view) renewal and the age of nationalism in the Balkans is made explicit by the literary historian Petŭr Dinekov (in a passage from 1942):

"The middle of the eighteenth century is, in our history, the beginning not only of a national, but also of an ideological, world-view revival in the broadest sense—the end of the Middle Ages and the beginning of a modern

European culture. In Western Europe this transition occurred some centuries earlier, but the ideas of the new European culture came late to us and to the Balkan peninsular in general because of the peculiar political and economic conditions. [...] Thus the ideological revival of our people coincides with its national revival."[56]

Alternatively, Hristo Gandev posits an earlier part of the Bulgarian Revival (beginning with the eighteenth century) as a gradual spiritual–cultural process of overcoming the medieval religious world-view and its replacement with a pragmatic, secular, civic, and rationalist world-view, and, as a result, the formation of a modern cultural nation.[57]

While the spiritual (intellectual, cultural) and national meanings of the Bulgarian Revival are closely related and, in a sense, complementary, they are still different and autonomous. The spiritual–cultural meaning is broader and more vague. It encompasses the transition to the modern epoch (of which the formation of the nation is only a part). In the West, the transition to Modernity was effected by the great intellectual (cultural) epochs—the Renaissance, the Reformation, the Enlightenment. When conceiving of the Bulgarian Revival as a spiritual–cultural process, it was only natural to look for analogies there, the more so as there existed strong actual influences. In what follows I will consider the comparisons that were drawn between the Bulgarian Revival and the European cultural epochs. By the same token, those comparisons present attempts to synchronize Bulgarian historical development with that of the West.

The Analogy with the Renaissance

The first serious attempt to juxtapose the Bulgarian Revival (the word for which in Bulgarian means "rebirth," as does "renaissance") with the Italian Renaissance and its great personalities was made by the Bulgarian literary scholar Ivan Shishmanov (in 1928). He points out the following "parallels" (similarities): a transition from the Middle Ages to Modernity (and from a natural type economy to capitalism); a developed urban class as the promoter of the new ideas; one great personality as leader of the movement; a new "national" spirit and a return of language and literature to their source (for the Bulgarians, the "Slavonic-Bulgarian trend"); the growing role of the individual; and a belief in the value of knowledge, science, and education. The differences mentioned are the absence of the revival of an antiquity in the Bulgarian case, and the lack of profound

changes in religion, science, morality, and aesthetics. After due cautioning
about comparing "two so unequal magnitudes," the author concludes that
"we actually have the right to speak of an epoch of Revival with many of
the symptoms that distinguish the West European Renaissance."[58]

Shishmanov dates the Bulgarian transition to Modernity to the end of
the eighteenth century, with the monks Paisii Hilendarski and his follower
Sofronii Vrachanski as "Renaissance types," followed by transitional and
modern figures.[59] The comparison with the Italian Renaissance (*Rinasci-
mento*) by this author regards, in fact, what he calls the Bulgarian "spiritual revival," which ended with the establishment of the Bulgarian Exarchate in 1870, and which was followed by a "political revival" of struggles
and uprisings (similar to the Italian *Risorgimento*).[60]

In a similar vein, the literary scholar Emil Georgiev conceives of the
Bulgarian Revival in general, and of its first and longer part in particular,
as a sort of Renaissance. According to him, in spite of its specific traits the
Bulgarian Revival was similar "in essence" to the Renaissance of the other
European peoples, although occurring a few centuries later—a kind of
"belated Renaissance." It turned the eyes away from the divinity, although
it discovered the nation rather than the individual and was inspired by
history, popular traditions, language, folklore, and kinship with the Slav
peoples rather than reviving a classical antiquity.[61] Emil Georgiev posits an
initial "Renaissance-Enlightenment" period of the Revival, somehow making up for the Renaissance as well.[62] In addition, he speaks of an earlier
"pre-Renaissance" period of the South Slavs and the Bulgarians in particular, encompassing the authors of *damaskini* (Readers with mostly moralist-
religious readings) in the seventeenth century, the activities of the Bulgarian Catholics under Renaissance influences issuing from Dubrovnik in the
mid-seventeenth century, and the Enlightenment of Serb and Bulgarian
emigrants in the Habsburg Empire.[63]

In a more cautious way, the literary scholar Tsveta Damyanova offers a
"functional comparison" for establishing formal similarities and differences between the Western Renaissance and the Bulgarian Revival, especially as regards the representation of time in the literature (but not devoid
of more general claims).[64] According to the author, the understanding of
time in the West European triad Modernity–Middle Ages–Antiquity has a
Bulgarian equivalent in the triad Modern epoch (i.e., Revival)–(Turkish)
Yoke–Glorious past (i.e., Medieval Bulgaria). But while the attitude of the
West toward the Middle Ages in this triad was negative, it is the yoke that
constitutes the Bulgarian "dark centuries"; and it is not antiquity but the

Middle Ages that receive praise from the Bulgarian authors. For the poets, writers, and political journalists of the Revival epoch, all things valuable, and especially freedom, are situated in the past or in the future, while the present day is depicted in dark colors (unlike the hypertrophy of the present in the Western Renaissance). That the Bulgarian Revival could not accept Greek antiquity as its ideal, but rather rejected it, was largely due to the contemporary struggles against Greek cultural influence and attempts at assimilation.

The historian Nikolai Genchev was also tempted by the parallel with the European Renaissance.[65] He justifies it by employing a very generalized concept of "Renaissance" (with reference to Arnold Toynbee and Nikolai Konrad) as an epoch of deep social and world-view transformations by, presumably, resuscitating the values of the past and evoking the spirit of older civilizations. He argues that both phenomena constitute a transitional phase between the Middle Ages and Modernity (or "bourgeois civilization"), that humanism and individualism played a role in both, as did towns and the urban class (of burghers). The author makes a few strong statements to the effect that the Bulgarian Revival took place "in the shadow" of the European Renaissance, and that it "repeated some common and specific traits of the European Renaissance." But he dilutes them by citing such specifics of the Bulgarian case as different "ideological and cultural loading" and motivation, a different point of departure, a different social and civilizational context (Islam, the Balkan-Ottoman model), and different components of the cultural synthesis, since, in the Bulgarian case, one cannot speak of the renewal of past cultural patterns but of borrowing and adapting ideas and achievements from Western bourgeois civilization. In the end Genchev returns to his earlier idea of the Bulgarian Revival as a mixture of intellectual components (to be considered below).

Although the parallels between the Bulgarian Revival and the West European Renaissance are very formalistic, and even so very tenuous, this has remained a favorite association and reference point for a number of authors up to the present day.[66] The Renaissance is a beloved image of the Bulgarian Revival, a bright dream that Bulgarian scholars are reluctant to renounce. Even when the comparison ends up establishing substantial differences rather than similarities, the two phenomena are implicitly identified by the very fact that they are brought together. But when the common ground of the comparison is merely "spiritual transformation," it remains a purely metaphoric figure, empty of substantial contents. It then makes little sense to compare the Bulgarian Revival precisely with the Ren-

aissance instead of representing it simply as a (world-view) transition to
Modernity.[67] This does not preclude the possibility of speaking about the
borrowing of Renaissance ideas and values, mediated by the contemporaneous Enlightenment.

The analogy with the West European Renaissance has recently been emphatically rejected by the literary scholar Svetlozar Igov. According to the
author, the Bulgarian Revival (and the revival of most of the Slav and Balkan peoples) not only does not correspond to the European Renaissance
chronologically but also fails to do so as a cultural typology and as a historical process, even though both replaced the religious-theological concept
of the Middle Ages with a secular one. The fundamental difference is that
the European Renaissance, in the form of humanism, replaced God with
the individual as the highest value and as center of the universe
("anthropocentrism"), while the Bulgarian Revival replaced God with the
fatherland and the people (an "ethnocentric" vision of the world). The
individual here serves the nation and the fatherland, which might easily be
substituted for other "supra-individual" idols (e.g., party, leader, revolution, etc.). The basic orientation of the Bulgarian Revival is not Renais-
sance-humanist and individualist, but national awakening and national
liberation—hence it is not a "belated" Renaissance.[68]

Curiously, in a recent work by another literary scholar (Kiril Topalov)
the contrast between "anthropocentrism" and "ethnocentrism," instead of
establishing a fundamental Otherness between the European Renaissance
and the Bulgarian Revival, is accommodated in its turn within the old
comparative framework, as just another difference.[69]

The Bulgarian Revival and the Enlightenment

The Bulgarian Revival, widely assumed to start with Paisii's *Slavonic-
Bulgarian History* in 1762, has also been searched for Enlightenment contents. Among the advocates of the thesis of a Bulgarian Enlightenment is
the historian Iliya Konev.[70] The slant of a monumental work of his is the
refutation of the view that the Bulgarians did not have an Enlightenment
because of their "belated" development, or that they had, at best, Renaissance and Enlightenment ideas subsumed under the ensign of a primarily
national revival.[71] The problem is that the author does not state clearly and
unambiguously his thesis (implicit in his critique of other authors),
namely, that a certain period presents a "Bulgarian Enlightenment," and

that the Bulgarian spiritual–cultural development then had an original local character. He speaks instead in roundabout terms[72] and only occasionally hints at a Bulgarian Enlightenment in connection with the *damaskini* (mistakenly, as will be seen), with Paisii, or with the "philological movement."[73] The contribution of this author actually consists in tracing specific influences of the Enlightenment on Bulgarian literature (especially in history and in philology) and on school education, and a connection with national-liberation ideas.[74] Finally, he admits that the Enlightenment had stronger expressions in Greece, Serbia, and Romania than in Bulgaria.[75]

A quite different view on the impact of the Enlightenment on the Bulgarians is held by Donka Petkanova-Toteva. She finds no traces of Enlightenment ideas in the *damaskini* (books with "mixed" semi-religious contents), which are chronologically earlier, have an entirely different origin, and still express a religious world-view. Paisii Hilendarski, the originator or precursor of the Bulgarian Revival in 1762, already goes beyond religiosity and stands closer to the Western Enlightenment, but only in a general sense as he had no knowledge either direct or indirect, of Rousseau, Voltaire and other Enlightenment figures, and he dealt with specifically Bulgarian and Balkan themes. Sofronii Vrachanski, a follower of Paisii in the next generation, is already a "new type of Enlightener" (comparable to the Serb Enlightener Dositej Obradović); he was influenced by Enlightenment ideas mediated by Greeks, Serbs and Romanians, and expressed such ideas in a modified (national, Balkan) form. Donka Toteva notes a number of peculiarities in the manifestation of Enlightenment ideas among the Bulgarians (but also in Serbia and Greece), such as the absence of a sharp conflict with the church and religion (which played a protective role under foreign domination: Enlightenment ideas were sometimes advocated by monks and priests), the close link between Enlightenment ideas, ideas on education, and national feeling (e.g., education as a path to intellectual and moral improvement, but also to freedom), and, finally, the absence of the philosophical, aesthetic, and political questions that concerned the Western Enlighteners. Enlightenment ideas among the Bulgarians found expression mainly in propaganda about the need for education, which led to the great educational upsurge in the nineteenth century and to the setting up of schools of a new, secular type (that also propagated national self-awareness).[76]

A Bulgarian Enlightenment, as a period in Bulgarian literary and cultural development (dated from Paisii in the middle of the eighteenth century until the mid-1840s), features in a recent work by the literary scholar Svetlozar Igov. It is characterized as a period of national awakening and of the laying down of the organizational (institutional) foundations of the subsequent literary and cultural development—schools and education, printing presses, books and periodicals, all of which played a role in the formation of a literary language. The Bulgarian literature of the time still presented a syncretic, publicistic form and had an educational-didactic character in the main; it was subject to strong foreign influences, especially Greek and Serb, and spread universalistic rationalist and humanist ideas.[77]

The arguments pro and contra a Bulgarian Enlightenment often focus on the outlook of Paisii Hilendarski, who was chronologically a contemporary of the Enlightenment. Some authors place him under the label of romanticism and regard him as a romanticist historiographer (Boyan Penev, Krŭstyu Genov[78]), for others he was primarily a man of the Enlightenment (Ivan Shishmanov, Iliya Konev, Emil Georgiev[79]), while others detect the influence of both the Enlightenment and romanticism on him (Emil Georgiev in some pronouncements, Dimitŭr Tsanev, Svetlozar Igov[80]). The main reason for the controversy in the interpretation of Paisii is the absence of direct and strongly expressed Enlightenment influences in his oeuvre, and the mostly nationalist character of his message, in contrast to the universalism and liberalism of the Enlightenment.

A number of authors have spoken more generally (and less problematically) of "Balkan" and "South Slav" enlightenments. As mentioned, the literary scholar Emil Georgiev divides the Slav (or South Slav) revival into two periods: Enlightenment (or "Renaissance-Enlightenment") in the second half of the eighteenth century and the beginning of the nineteenth century, and romanticism from the mid-1820s onwards.[81] The Renaissance-Enlightenment period is defined by the author as a period of "national awakening," in which the national upsurge and struggles of later times were prepared.[82] According to him, there existed a "literary community" of the South Slavs during their revival, whereas the Serbs and Croats, who were in a more favorable situation under Austrian rule and who experienced earlier revivals, gave more to the Bulgarians (while the Serbs of earlier times were indebted to medieval Bulgarian literature). Moreover, some authors (Hristofor Žefarović, Partenii Pavlović, Andria Kačić-Mioşić, Jovan Rajić) were either indistinguishable as to nationality and lived in a common South Slav milieu, or else worked with the idea of South Slav unity. As Emil Georgiev puts it, the ideas of the Enlightenment and its rationalism "came into the possession of the South Slavs in conditions of unrestricted exchanges." The South Slav literary community is cited to explain the literary work of Paisii, who stands, according to the author, at the beginning of a Bulgarian Enlightenment proper and does not look so isolated against this background.[83] (But Emil Georgiev does not pursue the idea of a Bulgarian Enlightenment further, being primarily interested in the South Slav literatures.)

In their work on Balkan history, Strashimir Dimitrov and Krŭstyu Manchev devote some attention to a "Balkan Enlightenment," Greek and South Slav in particular. They point to the "historicism" used as a means of national awakening as a peculiarity of the Enlightenment among the Balkan Slav peoples under Austrian and Ottoman rule. But the authors cite mostly Serb and Croat representatives of the Balkan Enlightenment, which may be interpreted as skepticism regarding a Bulgarian Enlightenment proper (even though Paisii receives a mention in this context).[84]

The problem of a Balkan Enlightenment (and Balkan romanticism) is treated at length by the historian Nadya Danova.[85] She endorses the view of separate (and implicitly equivalent) "national" enlightenments—French, English, German, Russian, etc. But, as regards the Balkans, the author speaks cautiously about specific manifestations of the Enlightenment here, conditioned by the peculiar historical circumstances such as life under foreign domination, the stronger hold of the church over minds (largely due to the role of religion in protecting nationality), and the retarded development of capitalist relations and an underdeveloped bourgeois society. Backwardness has been linked with the discrepancies between the ideas of the new secular Balkan intelligentsia and the mentality of its peasant compatriots, the greater role of the "traditional" church intelligentsia, the phenomena of auto-didacticism and "encyclopedic" knowledge, etc. According to the author, the Enlightenment among the Bulgarians in particular is manifested in the "general spiritual upsurge and the striving toward knowledge and education," the gradual growth of a secular intelligentsia, the efforts of Enlightenment activists to create a common and accessible literary language, a certain critique of the church and its servants, and Enlightenment historicism (Paisii). The Enlightenment ideology reached greatest maturity in the views of Ivan Seliminski and Nikola Pikolo (both of whom lived outside Bulgaria).

Having made the point that historicism was developed not only by romanticism but by the Enlightenment as well, Nadya Danova argues that this, precisely, is the crucial link between the Enlightenment and the processes of national formation in the Balkans and among the Bulgarians in particular. While historicism in France and England was used as a weapon against traditionalist views, in the Balkans it assumed the task of shaping patriots, similar to the role of historicism in the German Enlightenment. The Enlightenment principle of individual freedom and freedom of consciousness was transformed in the Balkans into an appeal to the individual to subordinate his (or her) efforts to the objectives of national liberation.[86] The Balkans took part in the struggle to reorganize education and science toward "positive knowledge," as well as in the propaganda for new bourgeois ethics and values. The issue of the national language became particularly poignant here because of its ethno-formative functions (another analogy with the German Enlightenment). The weak representation of ideological radicalism in the form of materialism, atheism, and republicanism in the views of Balkan Enlightenment figures is explained by the author with reference to the role of the church and the Christian religion as a guard against Islam.

Finally, the treatment of the Balkan Enlightenment by the Greek historian Paschalis Kitromilides deserves special attention because of its more detached manner and broader perspective.[87] The author approaches the issue in terms of regional and local enlightenments resulting from the transfer of new ideas (liberal ideas in the realm of politics and ethics in particular) from the place and context of their genesis to other places and societies, where they become "refracted" through the particular problems of these societies. The "fragments" of the Enlightenment that came to the eighteenth-century Balkans fell upon a structurally and culturally hostile terrain—traditional social structures and mentalities, Orthodoxy, theocratic Ottoman rule, etc.—that accounts for their quite unsuccessful fortunes. The Enlightenment here remained primarily the affair of small groups of Balkan intellectuals (initially clerics and increasingly secular figures), and the result of intellectual exchanges with Western and Central Europe.

According to Kitromilides, the Enlightenment in the Balkans began as a "cultural critique" of the conditions of backwardness and cultural primitivism, and then created visions of political transformation (political reform or radical revolution). From the very outset, these ideas were connected with the beginnings of modern nationalism, which they helped. The Enlightenment found expression in a certain philosophical argument (in favor of rationalist philosophy, mathematics, and natural science); in a concern for a reform of the language, education and literature; and in an awareness of one's own historical past. The Balkan Enlightenment was

especially receptive to German intellectual influences because of its concentration on issues of history and culture; it thus acted in favor of an
"organismic concept" of national community that boded a compromise
with the corporativism of the traditional culture. In fact, the author speaks
only about the Greek, Romanian, and Serb cases, while Paisii's work presents, in his view, "a case of incipient national awakening without the cultural experience of the Enlightenment." The Bulgarian awakening in general is presented by him as an indirect product of the enlightenment of
other Balkan nations and a reaction to the awareness of cultural backwardness that gave rise to a similar cultural critique, a sense of historical
and cultural identity, and a vision of national liberation.

As for the political projects of the Enlightenment, the imagination of the
Enlightened intellectuals in the Balkans was first captured by the "mirage
of Enlightened absolutism," while the new and more radical generations
had the vision (under the impact of the French Revolution) of political
independence in the form of a modern nation state, either in a more radical republican form (as in the Greek case), or as an aristocratic republic (as
in the Romanian case). None of these Enlightenment political ideals was
realized, because the Greek and the Serb national revolutions were in
essence peasant wars and the outcome was actually a defeat of the political
aspirations of the Enlightenment in tune with the new international climate of the Restoration in Europe; the "residual liberalism" among students and the liberal intelligentsia in Romania was defeated in the revolution of 1848. The conclusion of Kitromilides is that the Enlightenment in
Southeast Europe was submerged by the nationalism that it helped initiate,
and by confrontation with the traditional culture.

To sum up, when the Bulgarian Revival (its first stage in particular) is
juxtaposed with the Enlightenment, a number of caveats and qualifications
become necessary: to begin with, the rather mediated (through the Greeks
and Serbs) and diluted influence of Enlightenment ideas; then a certain
delay (especially if Paisii is not counted as an "Enlightener") and the small
number of manifest Enlightenment figures; and, finally, the existence of
strong peculiarities and specifics—Bulgarian and Balkan in general—due to
the very different circumstances under Ottoman domination. The political
liberalism and civil rights associated with the Enlightenment are translated
here into a struggle for national independence; the national idea that may
have received impetus from the historicism of the Enlightenment soon
passed under the auspices of romanticism and was shaped into cultural-
historical and "organic" nationalism (hard to reconcile with the universal-

istic and individualistic claims of the Enlightenment). The Enlightenment in general found a stunted reception in the Balkans, confined mostly to its literary and educational aspects, and to a lesser extent, and quite superficially, its philosophical–scientific aspects, while radical social and political projects in its spirit were almost absent. The Bulgarian case is characterized by a broad local movement for education in the native language and in a secular spirit, though this can hardly be defined as Enlightenment proper.[88] What do qualify, however, are ideas about the importance of knowledge and education, disputes regarding literary language, and probably some influences on "historicism."

The existence of Enlightenment ideas in the Bulgarian milieu during the national revival—the praise of education, the popularization of science, and secular and rationalistic ideas in general—is certain. The question is whether these ideas put their stamp on the times, marking them as a distinctive "epoch." In order to do so, prominent adherents and propagators of these ideas, that is, prominent "Enlighteners," are required, as is the spread and impact of their ideas.[89] Candidates in the Bulgarian case are Paisii and Sofronii, but only the latter is more of an Enlightener. The more accomplished Enlighteners Ivan Seliminski, Nikola Pikolo, and Petŭr Beron lived (somewhat anachronistically) in later times and in a foreign milieu. Enlightenment ideas were present among the Bulgarians, but in quite diluted forms. This leaves the concept of a "Bulgarian Enlightenment" with little substance.

In general, the debate as to whether or not one can speak of a "Bulgarian Enlightenment" is a function of the concept one applies and the claims and expectations that go with it.[90] The stronger concept, put forward by Kitromilides and oriented more substantially toward the Western cases, excludes not only a Bulgarian Enlightenment proper but makes even stronger instances of Enlightenment in the Balkans problematic—a failed political project in any case. The various Bulgarian authors discussed in this chapter can be taken as a demonstration of the fact that while the thesis of a "Bulgarian Enlightenment" in the strong sense is untenable, it is legitimate to look for Enlightenment influences among the Bulgarians, and such have been discovered in a number of spheres. There is also the possibility of treating the Bulgarian case as part of the more comprehensive processes of a regional "Balkan Enlightenment" or a South Slav Enlightenment with brighter representatives elsewhere. Another possibility (suggested by Svetlozar Igov) has been to consider the Bulgarian Enlightenment as a primarily "cultural-organizational" phase, in which the institutional prerequisites for the development of secular literature and culture were being laid down.[91] Clearly this circumvents the necessity for manifest individual achievements.

Analogies with the Reformation

There also exist attempts to interpret a certain part of the Bulgarian Revival, its earlier part in particular, in terms of Reformation. As far as I can see, the first such attempt was made by Hristo Gandev (in 1939).[92] The author points to a host of new phenomena in religiosity—the emergence of a "new Christianity" in the eighteenth century and the first half of the nineteenth century, which rediscovered the Gospel in a rationalist and practical, concrete sense; a striving toward a new morality "deriving from the depth of real faith"; moralistic and instructive appeals in the spirit of "social love" (in contrast to the "individualism" of magic customs); and the romantic aspiration of the burghers toward a "lay spiritual community." The new religiosity was directed against popular paganism but also against the religious formalism of the clerics and the ignorant insistence on simple faith. Promoters of these phenomena were religious moralists, preachers, and educators, authors of books against magic (pagan) popular beliefs and of manuals on virtuous behavior, etc. Spiritual transformations in the spirit of the Reformation were observed among artisans and traders and their teachers and priests (but not among the peasants, tied to the cycles of nature and immersed in magic notions). Gandev makes an explicit analogy between this "reform movement" and the early West European movements, with the reservation that, unlike them, it did not change the dogmatics.[93]

A similar treatment of the earlier part of the Revival (and a previous period) as a kind of Reformation was recently offered by Svetla Strashimirova, in a book focusing on the transition of the Bulgarians to Modernity. According to the author, although the Orthodox Balkan Christian did not experience the dramatic problem of faith faced by the Western Christian in seeking personal religious autonomy from the Catholic monopoly, for the Orthodox as well the value and world-view transformation at the end of the Middle Ages and the threshold of Modernity initially assumed a religious form. This is attested by the *damaskini* (books with religious-moralist contents) of the seventeenth century, the edifying sermons in the early Revival, and the Christian preachers-moralists of the beginning of the nineteenth century. The transformation found expression in a strong striving toward the "moral contents" of Christianity, a turning toward the sources of the faith (the Holy Scriptures), a renewal of the faith by freeing it from formalism, the preaching of virtues and moral values, the addressing of the practical life of man, etc. All this served as the spiritual background of the nascent bourgeoisie and as a "spiritual catalyst for the civic revival of the medieval personality—among the Bulgarians as in the West," preparing the ground for the shaping of modern individuals, citizens, and nationals.[94]

Finally, a more formal parallel has been drawn between the Reformation and the Bulgarian struggles for church autonomy from the Greek Patriarchy (around the middle of the nineteenth century). According to the historian Iliya Todev, the Bulgarians actually wanted not to reform but to nationalize the church. In contrast to Western Europe, where the secularization (of the Enlightenment) was dominated by anti-clericalism, the secularization of public life among the Bulgarians did not abandon the framework of the church. The Bulgarian Revival was thus a "correlate of the Reformation and Enlightenment at the same time" and it can (paradoxically) be called "an Enlightenment in the form of Reformation." All the more so as the church and its clergy contributed greatly to the "enlightening" of the Bulgarians in a modern, secular spirit, not least by spreading rational knowledge. The struggle for an independent national church led, in practice, to the secularization of the public domain, in spite of the absence of radical anti-clericalism and atheism.[95] As can be seen from this example, when the parallels are primarily external and formal, and primarily establish differences (the different role of the church, a different meaning of "reform," etc.), their usefulness diminishes.

To summarize, the comparison of the Bulgarian Revival with the cultural epochs that effected the transition toward Modernity in the West has resulted in the asserting of numerous similarities and differences. The comparison assumes different methodological forms according to the degree of similarity claimed by the authors: the pointing out of formal "analogies" or "parallels"; the establishing of "functional equivalents" (under different conditions); the detection of Western ideological influences on the Bulgarian Revival; the conception of the Bulgarian Revival (or part of it) as the "reflection" or "repetition" of a Western cultural epoch, eventually with peculiarities; and, finally, the positing of an equivalence between "national" cultural epochs (and the rejection of a unitary model). The similarities, contrasts, analogies, parallels, correspondences, etc. that are established are located in the continuum between total difference and complete identity. The undertaking of comparison in general rests on the

assumption of a fundamental comparability between Bulgarian development and that of Western Europe, that is, the rejection of the radical difference (total "originality") of the Bulgarian case and the assumption that
it participated, to an extent, in a "common European" pattern of cultural
development.

The Bulgarian Revival and European Development

In addition to comparison with separate cultural epochs, the Bulgarian
Revival has been juxtaposed with the cultural evolution of Western Europe
as a whole. The most ambitious and highly speculative attempt of this sort
was undertaken by Georgi Gachev, a Bulgarian living in the Soviet Union.[96]
It is premised upon a number of historico-philosophical tenets. First, humanity in its evolution passed from a syncretic, folklore-epic form of collective consciousness (characteristic of a patriarchal stage), through a religious mentality (characteristic of the feudal social structure, and as reformed Christianity presenting the first ideology of capitalism), toward a
secular ideology and a bourgeois life-style (characteristic of "civic society"
and of the capitalist social structure). Second, backward or arrested societies and cultures reproduce in their development (in a specific way) the
stages passed through by advanced societies and cultures, in a way reminiscent of the "law" of biological evolution, in which the ontogenesis repli-
cates the phylogenesis, that is, the development of the individual repeats
the evolution of the species. Third, one can approach the collective consciousness of the society and its culture through the study of literature; the
relation is even closer, so that one may actually speak of an ideological (and
literary) form of the social-economic processes or of parallel processes of
social and literary development.

These Hegelian and evolutionist premises hardly deserve a critique.
What is interesting, however, is the idea that societies that have been held
back eventually undergo a peculiar type of "accelerated and condensed"
cultural development. Applied to the Bulgarian case, this looks as follows.
The evolution of the Bulgarian culture was arrested by the Ottoman conquest and preserved in a patriarchal state with its folklore and religious
world-view. The development was resumed during the Revival in the second
half of the eighteenth century and from then onwards it started reproducing the stages of West European development in its efforts to catch up with
the more advanced culture. However, this reproduction has a number of

peculiarities in comparison with "normal" Western development. It is "accelerated" and "condensed," that is, society covers in less time what has taken longer with others. Furthermore, cultural phenomena and traits that were consecutive in the West are "contemporaneous" and overlapping here, and there is a time lag from what is current in the West.[97] In addition, the ideological (and literary) forms of the belated development cannot reach maturity and classical purity but remain underdeveloped and "abridged," and there exist "hybrid" forms. Finally, in a "belated accelerated" development, processes in the realm of the mind and ideology overtake the processes in the social-economic and political spheres; it thus becomes possible for literature to move to the center of public life and even to become an "arena of revolutionary transformations."

The recapitulation of Western cultural epochs by the Bulgarians is described by Gachev in the following manner: the Renaissance stage barely projected itself onto Bulgarian development but the latter still realized, "in a very concise manner," what was "internally needed" from the Renaissance processes. There was an almost direct transition to the Enlightenment, the asceticism of which coexisted here with a Renaissance feeling for the fullness of life. The transitional stages mentioned so far "ran into" the romanticism and realism characteristic of nineteenth-century Europe. One effect of the accelerated development was the overlaying of stages of the "literary-*cum*-social" development, even within the work of a single author (e.g. Petko Slaveikov). It also made possible an "anachronism" like the "Petŭr Beron phenomenon," who wrote his "panepistemia" (science with claims to integrate all branches of knowledge) in a time of advancing scientific specialization.[98]

Criticism of Gachev's ideas notwithstanding, the notion of "delayed accelerated" development and its implications were taken up by a number of authors. Thus the prominent literary scholar Petŭr Dinekov spoke (with reference to Gachev) about the overlapping and mixing of literary trends in Bulgaria—the coexistence of elements of Enlightenment ideology with sentimentalism, romanticism, and realism—in the effort to catch up with Europe.[99] The concept was taken up by the literary scholar Emil Georgiev to describe the interlacing of styles in the development of South Slav literatures.[100] The author also attempted to rhyme the Bulgarian Revival with West European epochs, chronologically and (implicitly and to a degree) in substance, too. The Bulgarian Revival (which he dates from Paisii in 1762) occurred a few centuries later than the West European Renaissance but it was preceded by a primarily spiritual pre-Renaissance in the seventeenth and eighteenth centuries (the *damaskini*, the literary activities of the Bulgarian Catholics, the Church Slavonic cultural tradition). The revival/renaissance of the Bulgarians took place in the eighteenth century, which is the Age of Enlightenment in the West; it borrowed ideological elements from the European Renaissance, the Enlightenment, and romanticism respectively. It also presents an epoch of the formation of the Slav nations—a Slav revival—in close connection with romanticism. The belated development thus results in the merging of elements that are characteristic of different epochs (i.e., different in the West).[101]

In the same vein, the historian Nikolai Genchev conceives of the Bulgarian Revival, its spiritual–ideological aspect in particular, as an interlacing of ideas from different Western epochs. According to him, it forms part of the "common European transition from the Middle Ages to the bourgeois world" and presents a belated instance of it. The Bulgarian Revival spans, in fact, the various stages of the transition, especially the Renaissance, the Enlightenment, and the bourgeois revolutions, whose ideas are "organically merged" and "closely intertwined." Renaissance motifs made an appearance in the early cultural revival of the eighteenth century simultaneously with Enlightenment ideas, and they all merged during the nineteenth century in the organic whole of the national cultural movement.[102] Elsewhere, Genchev points out that the Bulgarian Revival borrowed and reworked not only Renaissance (humanist) ideas and achievements, but also classicist, Enlightenment, liberal, and romantic ones, and that it did not follow the "classic" sequence of stages of the European transition. To cite him:

"The Bulgarian Revival is a compensatory epoch, which is not only Renaissance, not only classicism, not only Enlightenment, and not only a revolutionary change in social relations, but all that taken together, and realized under specific historical conditions in the course of the national-liberation epoch."[103]

In the last formulation of his ideas (in 1995) the skeptical notes sound stronger. The Bulgarian Revival cannot be defined as Renaissance in a proper sense; classicism is also lacking; it is a "pale Enlightenment"; and though it is a little of them all "under specific historical conditions," the compensation for the Bulgarian historical past and for falling behind was only partial and superficial. The "accelerated development" of the revival processes (a reference to Gachev) was such only in comparison with the slow tempo of the preceding evolution, but in comparison with the European tempo it was actually slower, and presented rather an effort "to stop the degradation processes."[104] The Bulgarian Revival is regarded here primarily as a process of national formation and a bourgeois social transformation that had to join Bulgarian society to European bourgeois civilization. But here again, according to Genchev, the results were partial and inconclusive: an underdeveloped bourgeois society emerged on the basis of a "dragging oriental capitalism"; the Bulgarian national question ended up in partial liberation that predetermined new and also unsuccessful attempts in the next period; and the spiritual union with European civilization through a national reworking of foreign values also remained perfunctory.

To sum up, the Bulgarian Revival in the spiritual–cultural interpretation is a transition to Modernity, conceived as common for Europe but delayed in the Balkans. Because of this, the Revival fulfills the functions of a number of phenomena that inaugurated the advent of Modernity in the West.[105] It has to substitute for a missing Modernity (or early Modernity) in Bulgarian history. Accordingly, it is filled with various contents—with most of what had happened in Western Europe in the previous epochs and while it lasted. The usual formula is that it followed the "common regularities" of the historical process, that is, of the European evolution, with some "specific peculiarities" (such as delay, partial character, specific contents, hybridization, etc.).[106] Thus, apart from an epoch of national formation contemporaneous with the "Age of Nations" in the West, the Bulgarian Revival is (something of) a Renaissance, Enlightenment, and romanticism, and, in any case, it "recapitulates" these cultural epochs and makes up for them, acquiring a clearly compensatory character. One might add that "compensation" is a feature not only of the Revival, but also of historians who insist too much on the similarities with Western development.

Applying an idea of literary scholar Aleksandŭr Kiossev, one may interpret the insistent comparison with Western cultural epochs as a feature of "self-colonizing cultures" (or "cultures of absences"), which build up the Other, especially the admired West, into something Universal that stands for Humanity as such, and then measure themselves in relation to it. This also includes the "universalization" of time by the European "center" and the assumption of a unitary temporal axis of progress, with the various peoples imagined as racing along it (and some falling behind). The self-inflicted trauma of self-colonizing cultures is that they always feel inferior, peripheral, secondary, not sufficiently civilized, and immature in respect to the Universal (model), that must remain always "the Other."[107]

One can cite in this context a recent vehement reaction on the part of the literary scholar Inna Peleva against the imposition of Central and West

European temporalizations and frameworks in making sense of Bulgarian literary development (and, by implication, history). The author rejects the positing of a unitary World Historical Time (of Western provenance), with its meanings and important turning points; the assumption of a "true" and "good" historical model with "presences" (that relegates all the rest to absences and deficits); the acceptance of a disciplining principle of self-representation taken from the outside and of a norm of rationality, which forbids the beginning of the historical narrative "from another place." The interesting thing is that, while reacting against the striving of the self-colonizing cultures and their historiographies to prove, at any cost, "coincidences, contemporaneity, commonalities between local and universal" and their wish to be present "within the correct time network, made obligatory by the winning civilizational model" at the cost of "normalizing" a peculiar native, she also criticizes the presenting of the native as radically heterogeneous and untranslatable into the paragon of others (especially if this is done with the goal of depreciating the native).[108] In fact, she does not close the door on comparability but only on the kind of "bad" comparability that posits an obligatory paradigm that is traumatic for those different.

Whatever their stand on the issue, the authors cited touch a very real problem, namely, that beyond the empirical contents, a comparison with the advanced West engages strong value attitudes. Both the wish to discover identity at any price and the insistence on total difference ("originality") in comparing less successful histories with Western development may be symptoms of trauma. A self-colonizing inferiority complex in comparison with the Other Europe can perhaps be detected in some historical writings on the Bulgarian Revival. But comparing does not necessarily lead to compiling a list of absences, and it is possible to extract from it the sting of self-underestimation, if not in technological and economic matters at least in a human and moral sense. Methodologically, this is achieved by renouncing unitary models and doing justice to the two compared entities, to similarities as well as differences. Equally important is that one frees oneself psychologically from the trap of self-colonization. Admittedly, this is easier said than done, and extra-scholarly circumstances play a role, too.

Modernity and Modernization

The spiritual–cultural interpretation of the Revival is sometimes translated in terms of modernization—as a transformation from a traditional (peasant, "ethnographic," "folklorist") society into a modern (urban, bourgeois) one, with a corresponding transformation of the economy.[109] It is well known that theories of modernization proliferated after World War II in the United States and were characterized initially by an optimistic view of the prospects for the development of the "developing" countries. "Modernization," conceived of either as primarily economic change or in the broadest sense as a change in every sphere, is the process pioneered by a group of West European countries in the last quarter of the eighteenth century with the industrial revolution in England and the French political revolution—the "dual revolution" as Eric Hobsbawm called it. The countries that managed to effect the leap in their development outdistanced all others, which suddenly found themselves in a situation of "backwardness" and threatened by "peripherization" under the pressure of an expanding mechanized production looking for markets. They made efforts to catch up with the more developed countries, but only some were successful.[110] Skeptical authors (such as Andrew Janos) think that there were, in fact, two different processes at work: the ascendancy of a new material civilization in the West, and the efforts of the rest of the world to adapt to it, with dubious means and failing to achieve real progress (actually falling still further behind). From here, we move to the terrain of the very critical and skeptical theories of underdevelopment and "world theories."[111]

The conceptualization of the Bulgarian Revival in terms of modernization (or underdevelopment) in historical scholarship has as a precedent the notion of "Europeanization" among leading figures of the Revival itself, applied to designate the importation of European material goods (clothing, domestic utensils, furniture, etc.) and life-styles. The contemporary so-called critique of the vogues attests to growing apprehensions about the economic effect of European imports on Bulgarian handicrafts, as well as the moral effects of deviating from the native traditions and harming a nascent national self-awareness. One can note the contradiction between experiencing the European expansion as a threat and the aspirations of a modernizing (and Europeanized) Bulgarian intelligentsia then and later.[112]

Modernization has attracted the interest of the historical scholarship of the Revival. Nikolai Genchev, among others, describes vividly the challenges presented to the Balkans by a cosmopolitan and dynamic Western capitalist civilization in the process of expanding its economy and spreading its ideology to the whole world. The Bulgarians came under its impact at an early phase, under complicated geopolitical conditions at a geographical "crossroads" (where the conflicting interests of the European great powers perpetuated the "Eastern question"), and surrounded by the more evolved nationalism of neighboring Balkan peoples.[113] The outcome of the Bulgarian Revival, according to the author, was a modernization of Bulgarian society and culture and an exit from the orbit of "the Orient" and from the Islamic (Ottoman) civilization in particular and the joining of the European bourgeois civilization (admittedly, the Ottoman Empire was also caught up in a process of "Europeanization"); however, modernization remained partial and inconclusive.

A number of authors consider the particular instances of "Europeanization" in the material sphere and urban life-styles during the Revival (e.g., the so-called "*alafranga*" vogue, i.e., in the French manner).[114] The changes in mentalities and attitudes, as well as the new sociability and life-styles that came with the advance of urbanization, are described by the historian Rumyana Radkova.[115] The new phenomena in everyday urban life, arranged according to the calendar of the year and the life-cycle of the individual, form the subject matter of a very well documented recent book by Raina Gavrilova.[116] It can be noted that the relatively narrow focus of historians on "Europeanization" in clothing, material conditions of life, and habits—a "symbolic modernization" so to say—corresponds to the fact that modernization here, as elsewhere, made its first inroads in the sphere of consumption and behavior.

The economic aspect of modernization is treated separately under the label of Marxism in terms of a transition to capitalism. As will be seen, it is presented mostly in a progressist and optimistic perspective rather than from the perspective of underdevelopment. (Only in a few instances is the theory of colonialism evoked.) This is a contradiction with many pessimistic voices regarding Bulgarian modernization heard in the period after independence and the establishment of the Bulgarian state. The Revival remains, in this respect, an ascending bright epoch immune to criticism, for reasons to be discussed later on.

Notes

1 See the critical review of the historiography on the Revival in Genchev, *Bŭlgarsko vŭzrazhdane*, 24–26.

2 Aprilov, *Dopŭlnenie*, 152–153, 179, 188–189.

3 Yuri Venelin, *Drevnie i nyneshniia bolgare*. Moscow: Universitetska tipografiya, 1856 (first edition in 1829), 15; Venelin, *O zarodyshe novvo bolgarskoi literatury*. Moscow: Tipografiya N. Stepanova, 1838, 50. This work was translated into Bulgarian by Mikhail Kefalov under the title "Zaradi Vozrozhdenie novoi bolgarskoi slovesnosti ili nauki" (Bucharest, 1842; Ruse, 1896), in which *"vŭzrazhdane,"* i.e., revival or renaissance, was substituted for Venelin's *"zarazhdane,"* i.e., emergence.

4 Ivan Seliminski, *Izbrani sŭchineniya*. Sofia: Nauka i izkustvo, 1979, 146, 148, 150, 274, 368 (the works date from 1842, 1844 and 1856); Georgi Rakovski, "Bŭlgarskii za nezavisimo"; Rakovski, "Posledni izvestiya vŭrkhu nash vŭpros." *Dunavski lebed* 1, no. 19 (January 31, 1861); Rakovski, "Istinskoto rodoliubie." *Dunavska zora* 2, no. 49 (December 8, 1869); Rakovski, "Velikata ideya na bŭlgarite." *Dunavska zora* 2, no. 51 (December 24, 1869); Marko Balabanov, "Bŭlgarskii narpeduk," 323, 327–329, 358, 360; Balabanov, "Narodno bitie." *Vek*, no. 26 (6 July 1874). Reprinted in Balabanov, *Filosofski*, 141–145; Balabanov, "Sŭvremenniyat dukh na bŭlgarskiya narod." *XIX vek*, no. 11 (13 March 1876). Reprinted in Balabanov, *Filosofski*, 214–224; Balabanov, "Politikata na narodite v tursko." In Balabanov, *Filosofski*, 219–224; "Kŭm chitatelite." *Periodichesko spisanie na Bŭlgarskoto knizhovno druzhetvo* 1, no. 1 (1870): 1–7; Drinov, "Otets Paisii," 4, 25, 26; Drumev, Vasil. "Zhivotoopisanie." *Periodichesko spisanie na Bŭlgarskoto knizhovno druzhestvo* 1, no. 3 (1971): 18–20, 30–31, 36, 39. Reprinted in Drumev, *Sŭchineniya*. Vol. 2, Sofia: Bŭlgarski pisatel, 1968, 201–293; Drumev, "Zhivotoopisanie. Stoiko Vladislavov–Sofronii." *Periodichesko spisanie na Bŭlgarskoto knizhovno druzhestvo* 1, nos. 5–6 (1872): 3–4; Drumev, "Materiali za istoriyata na dukhovnoto vŭzrazhdane na bŭlgarskiya narod." *Periodichesko spisanie na Bŭlgarskoto knizhovno druzhestvo* nos. 11–12 (1876): 3–7; "Predgovor na 'Mati Bolgariya'" *Periodichesko spisanie na Bŭlgarskoto knizhovno druzhestvo* nos. 9–10 (1874): 1–13. As pointed out by Ernest Gellner, the "primordiality" of the nation is a typical representation (and illusion) of the nationalist activists; the nation is like a "Sleeping Beauty" that only needs "awakening." See Ernest Gellner, *Nations and Nationalism*. Oxford: Blackwell, 1983, 47–48.

5 Konstantin Jireček, *Istoriya na bŭlgarite*. Sofia: Nauka i izkustvo, 1978, 553 (first Bulgarian edition in 1886). On the activities of Jireček in Bulgaria, see Vasil Zlatarski, "Deinostta na d-r Konstantin Irechek v Bŭlgariya." *Periodichesko spisanie*, 66, nos. 1–2 (1905).

6 Boyan Penev, *Istoriya na novata bŭlgarska literatura*, edited by Boris Iotsov. Vol. 1, Sofia, 1930, 68, 78, 81, 171–174, 178.

7 Mikhail Arnaudov, *Bŭlgarsko vŭzrazhdane*. Sofia: Bŭlgarska misŭl, 1941, 7–10, 183, cit. on 7. For a similar description, see Ivan Ormandzhiev, *Nova i nai-nova istoriya na bŭlgarskiya narod*. Sofia: Zaveti, 1945, 184.

8 Hristo Gandev, *Faktori na bŭlgarskoto vŭzrazhdane, 1600–1830*. Sofia: Bŭlgarska kniga, 1943, 179–182, 184.

9 Petur Dinekov, *Pŭrvi vŭzrozhdentsi*. Sofia: Hemus, 1942, 6.

10 Veselin Traikov, *Ideologicheski techeniya i programi v natsionalno-osvoboditelnite dvizheniya na Balkanite do 1878 godina*. Sofia: Nauka i izkustvo, 1978, 14, 412–413.

11 Raina Gavrilova, *Vekŭt na bŭlgarskoto dukhovno vŭzrazhdane*. Sofia: Slov-D, 1992, 8.

12 Strashimir Dimitrov and Krŭstyu Manchev, *Istoriya na balkanskite narodi, XV–XIX vek*. Sofia: Nauka i izkustvo, 1971, 127–131, 141–152.

13 Emil Georgiev, *Bŭlgarskata literatura v obshtoslavyanskoto i obshtoevropeisko literaturno razvitie*. Sofia: Nauka i izkustvo, 1973; Emil Georgiev, *Obshto i sravnitelno slavyansko literaturoznanie*. Sofia: Nauka i izkustvo, 1965.

14 Marko Balabanov, "Nachaloto na narodnostta." *Vek*, no. 45 (15 November 1875). Reprinted in Balabanov, *Filosofski*, 135–140; Marko Balabanov, "Narodno bitie." The author underlines that the nation exists on the basis of a number of commonalities, but mainly through being "conscious" of its "individual personality" and thrugh having a sense of its own existence and being.

15 Petŭr Bitsilli, "Shto e natsiia?" *Rodina* 2, no. 1 (1939): 150–164. One can find here thoughts in tune with the contemporary classic view of nations as "imagined communities," Benedict Anderson, *Imagined Communities*, Thetford, Norfolk, 1983.

16 Spiridon Kazandzhiev, "Natsionalno sŭznanie." *Otets Paisii* 8, no. 2 (1935).

17 Yanko Yanev, "Dukhŭt na natsiyata." *Otets Paisii* 6, no. 1 (1933): 8–10.

18 Simeon Topuzanov, *Ideologiya, stroezh i zadachi na Bŭlgarskiya rabotnicheski sŭyuz*. Sofia, 1937, 38–41 (cit. on 38 and 39).

19 *Nashata borba. Kratŭk razbor na programata na Sŭyuza na Bŭlgarskite Natsionalni Legioni*. Varna, 1938, 5–16.

20 Hristo Gandev, "Natsionalnata ideya v bŭlgarskata istoriopis." In Hristo Gandev, *Problemi na bŭlgarskoto vŭzrazhdane*. Sofia: Nauka i izkustvo, 1976, 720–743 (first published in 1940).

21 Gandev's own preference lies with the German notion of the nation, with the significance it accords to the historically evolved community on the basis of living together, common territory, language, religion, etc., and with the concept of the nation as a "spiritual unity." He is more critical of the French individualist and civic idea of the nation, and of the Wilsonian principle of national self-determination by way of a plebiscite.

22 Joseph Stalin, *Marksizm i natsional'no-kolonial'nyi vopros*. Partizdat, 1936, 10–12, 16–25. (English translation: "Marxism and the National Question." In Joseph Stalin, *Marxism and the National Question. A Collection of Articles and Speeches*. San Francisco: Proletarian Publishers, 1975, 15–99, esp. 18–22, 28–38).

23 Todor Pavlov, "Natsiya i kultura." In Todor Pavlov, *Natsiya i kultura*. Sofia: Izdatelstvo Gologanov, 1940, 106–133, esp. 114–116.

24 Nikolai Derzhavin, *Istoriia Bolgarii*. Vol. 4, Moscow–Leningrad: Izdatel'stvo Akademii Nauk SSSR, 1948, 68–69, 89–90; Nikolai Derzhavin, "Paisii Hilendarskii i ego 'Istoriia Slavenobolgarskaia'. 1762." In Nikolai Derzhavin, *Sbornik stat'ei i issledovanii v oblasti slavianskoi filologii*. Moscow: Izdatel'stvo Akademii Nauk SSSR, 1941, 63–124, esp. 63–64, 103.

25 Yono Mitev, "Obrazuvaneto na bŭlgarskata natsiya." *Istoricheski pregled* 4, no. 3 (1947/8): 291–316.

26 Nedyalko Kurtev, "Formirane na bŭlgarskata burzhoazna natsiya" *Godishnik na Sofiiskiya universitet. Ideologichni katedri*. Vol. 57, Sofia, 1964, 87–193, esp. 103, 172–189.

27 Rumyana Radkova, "Natsionalno samosŭznanie na bŭlgarite prez XVIII i nachaloto na XIX vek." In *Bŭlgarskata natsiya prez Vŭzrahzdaneto*, edited by Hristo Hristov. Vol. 1, Sofia: BAN, 1980, 178–238, esp. 178–182.

28 Genchev, *Bŭlgarsko vŭzrazhdane*, 303–323.

29 Strashimir Dimitrov, *Formirane na bŭlgarskata natsiya*. Sofia: OF, 1980.

30 Strashimir Dimitrov, *Formirane*, 24.

31 Strashimir Dimitrov, *Formirane*, 72–73.
32 Hristo Gandev, *Ot narodnost kŭm natsiya*. Sofia: Nauka i izkustvo, 1988. An earlier version is Hristo Gandev, "Burzhoaznata natsiya i osobenostite v neinoto razvitie." In *Bŭlgarskata natsiya*, Vol. 1, 23–43.
33 Hristo Gandev, *Ot narodnost*, 11.
34 Hristo Gandev, *Ot narodnost*, 12–20 (cit. on 20).
35 Hristo Gandev, *Ot narodnost*, 20–35.
36 Ivan Stoyanov, *Istoriya na Bŭlgarskoto vŭzrazhdane*. Tŭrnovo: Sv. Evtimii Patriarkh Tŭrnovski, 1999, 209–210.
37 Roumen Daskalov, "Natsiya, natsionalna ideya i nie." In Roumen Daskalov, *Mezhdu Iztoka i Zapada. Bŭlgarski kulturni dilemi*. Sofia: LIK, 1998, 187–225.
38 Iliya Todev, "Kŭm problema za genezisa i rolyata na natsionalnata ideya v bŭlgarskoto vŭzrazhdane." In Iliya Todev, *Kŭm drugo minalo ili prenebregvani aspekti na bŭlgarskoto natsionalno vŭzrazhdane*. Sofia: Vigal, 1999, 13–22, esp. 15; Iliya Todev, *Novi ochertsi po bŭlgarska istoriya. Vŭzrazhdane*. Sofia: Vek 22, 1995, 10–65, esp. 16, 21–34, 51, 57–58.
39 Iliya Todev, "Paisii-avtor na bŭlgarskata natsionalna ideya." In Todev, *Kŭm drugo*, 28, 30–31; Todev, *Novi ochertsi*, 14.
40 Maria Todorova, "The Course and Discourses of Bulgarian Nationalism." In *Eastern European Nationalism in the Twentieth Century*, edited by Peter Sugar. The American University Press, 1995, 55–102, esp. 81–82.
41 Boyan Penev, *Istoriya na novata bŭlgarska literatura*. Vol. 3, Sofia, 1933, 163–170. On Paisii's historical and patriotic romanticism, see Penev, *Paisii Hilendarski*. Sofia, 1918, 44–45 (first published in 1910). The same topic is to be found in Penev, *Istoriya na novata bŭlgarska literatura*. Vol. 2, Sofia, 1933, 254–255.
42 Bozhan Angelov, *Bŭlgarska literatura. Chast 2. Istoricheski ocherk na novata bŭlgarska literatura ot Paisiya do dnes*. Sofia, 1923.
43 A. Filipov, "Uchitel na natsionalno sŭznanie." *Otets Paisii* 6, nos. 8–9 (1933): 14–15.
44 Emil Georgiev, *Obshto i sravnitelno*, 55–61; Georgiev, "Paisii Hilendarski–mezhdu Renesansa i Prosveshtenieto." In *Paisii Hilendarski i negovata epokha, 1762–1962*, edited by Dimitŭr Kosev, Al. Burmov, H. Hristov. Sofia: BAN, 1962, 253–283, esp. 277–283; Georgiev, "Tipologichen relef na romantizma v bŭlgarskata literatura." In Georgiev, *Bŭlgarskata literatura*, 236–237, 242, 260.
45 Petŭr Dinekov, "Problemŭt za romantizma v bŭlgarskata literatura do Osvobozhdenieto." In Dinekov, *Vŭzrozhdenski pisateli*. Sofia: Nauka i izkustvo, 1964, 49–79.
46 Krŭstyu Genov, *Romantizmŭt v bŭlgarskata literatura*. Sofia: BAN, 1968, 101–102, 534–537.
47 Nichev, Boyan. *Uvod v yuzno-slavianskiya realizŭm*. Sofia: BAN, 1971, 105–109; Georgiev, "Tipologichen relef," 234–235.
48 Svetlozar Igov, *Kratka istoriya na bŭlgarskata literatura*. Sofia: Prosveta, 1996, 25–27, 184, 221–223 (cit. on 26, 223.)
49 Aleksandŭr Burmov, "Marin Drinov kato istorik na Bŭlgariya." In *Izsledvaniya v chest na Marin Drinov*. Sofia: BAN, 1960, 105–118, esp. 108–109.
50 Dimitŭr Tsanev, "Proyavi na natsionalno chuvstvo i sŭznanie v bŭlgarskata vŭzrozhdenska istoricheska knizhnina prez pŭrvata polovina na XIX vek." In *Bŭlgarskata natsiia*. Vol. 1, 239–263; Tsanev, *Bŭlgarskata istoricheska knizhnina prez Vŭzrazhdaneto. XVIII–pŭrvata polovina na XIX vek*. Sofia: Nauka i izkustvo, 1989, 12–13, 24–25, 52–55, 184–185.
51 Nadya Danova, *Konstantin Georgi Fotinov v kulturnoto i ideino-politichesko razvitie na Balkanite prez XIX vek*. Sofia: BAN, 1994, 56–72.

52 Emil Georgiev, *Obshto i sravnitelno*, 55–57, 60, 83, 91; Georgiev, *Tipologichen relef*, 242.
53 Dimitŭr Tsanev, "Proyavi," 244; Tsanev, *Bŭlgarskata istoricheska*, 25.
54 Dimitŭr Mishev, "Nachalo na bŭlgarskata probuda." *Tsŭrkoven arkhiv*. Vols. 1–2, Sofia, 1925, 10–11; Mishev, *Bŭlgariya v minaloto*. Sofia, 1916, 284–285.
55 Nikola Stanev, *Borba na bŭlgarite za dukhovna svoboda*. Sofia, 1920, 3–4. In a similar sense, on the mutual reinforcement between the awakening of a national spirit and spiritual revival, see Petŭr Peshev, *Istoricheskite sŭbitiya*, 39.
56 Petŭr Dinekov, *Pŭrvi vŭzrozhdentsi*, 7–8.
57 Hristo Gandev, *Faktori*, 179–185; Gandev, *Ranno vŭzrahdane, 1700-1860*. Sofia, 1939.
58 Ivan Shishmanov, "Zapadnoevropeiskoto i bŭlgarskoto vŭzrazhdane." In Shishmanov, *Izbrani sŭchineniya*. Vol. 1 (Bŭlgarsko vŭzrazhdane). Sofia: BAN, 1965, 74–80 (first appeared in 1928); Ivan Shishmanov, "Uvod v istoriyata na bŭlgarskoto vŭzrazhdane." In Shishmanov, *Izbrani sŭchineniya*. Vol. 1, 31–73, esp. 31, 34. (First published in 1930.)
59 Ivan Shishmanov, "Zapadnoevropeiskoto," 78; Shishmanov, "Uvod v istoriyata," 35–36.
60 Ivan Shishmanov, "Uvod v istoriyata," 33–34.
61 Emil Georgiev, "Bŭlgarskoto i obshtoevropeisko vŭzrazhdane." In Georgiev, *Bŭlgarskata literatura*, 149–176, 151, 155, 159, 168–169, 176–177; Georgiev, "Paisii Hilendarski," 254.
62 Emil Georgiev, "Bŭlgarskoto literaturno i obshtoistorichesko razvitie i Prosveshtenieto." In Georgiev, *Bŭlgarskata literatura*, 203–204. According to the author, because of the delay in development, the Renaissance manifestations of the Bulgarian Revival had to merge with the Enlightenment ones or quickly cede place to them. See also Georgiev, "Paisii Hilendarski," 277–278.
63 Emil Georgiev, "Bŭlgarsko predvŭzrazhdane." In Georgiev, *Bŭlgarskata literatura*, 116–148; Georgiev, "Ranniyat Renesans i Predrenesansŭt v yuzhnoslavyanskata literaturna obshnost." In Georgiev, *Obshto i sravnitelno*, 78–82; Georgiev, "Paisii Hilendarski," 258–266.
64 Tsveta Damyanova, "Nyakoi aspekti na renesansoviya mirogled—skhodstva i razlichiya s Bŭlgarskoto vŭzrazhdane." *Literaturna misŭl* 22, no. 5 (1978): 106–119.
65 Nikolai Genchev, *Bŭlgarskata kultura*, 173–181, 266–274.
66 E. g., Krumka Sharova, "Problemi na Bŭlgarskoto vŭzrazhdane." In *Problemi na Bŭlgarskoto vŭzrazhdane*, edited by Krumka Sharova. Sofia: BAN, 1981, 5–44, esp. 6–9. See also the introduction to the volume on the Revival in the multi-volume academic *Historiya na Bŭlgariya v 14 toma*. Vol. 5 (Bŭlgarsko vŭzrazhdane XVIII-sredata na XIX vek.) Sofia: BAN, 1985, 13. It is affirmed here that the notion *"vŭzrazhdane"* (implied is Western Renaissance) has been filled up with different contents in the course of the centuries and that Marxist historiography takes it to mean the sum of the economic, social, political, and cultural processes in the epoch of transition from feudalism to capitalism. In a recent book another author affirms that the Bulgarian Revival was three centuries late compared to the European Renaissance. Ivan Stoyanov, *Istoriya na Bŭlgarskoto*, 39–40.
67 Svetla Strashimirova, *Bŭlgarinŭt pred praga na novoto vreme. Orientiri na vŭzrzhdenskiya svetogled*. Sofia: Universitetsko izdatelstvo "Kliment Ohridski," 1992, 8–11. The author argues that, for all the specifics and the difference in proportions, the Bulgarian Revival and the European cultural process in its entirety from the Renaissance to the Enlightenment have a common "internal logic" and "direction of change," namely, an orientation toward Modernity, change in the widest social sense of world-

view reorientation, differentiation of the forms of consciousness (into political, moral, aesthetic, juridical), change to a bourgeois way of life, and the transformation of man into an individual and a citizen, and of the traditional community into a civic society.

68 Svetlozar Igov, *Kratka istoriya*, 175–177.

69 Kiril Topalov, *Vŭzrozhdentsi*. Sofia: Universitetsko izdatelstvo "Kliment Ohridski," 1999, 5–6. But in an earlier edition of his book (1988, 5–6), Topalov sees the European Enlightenment as the nearest parallel to the Bulgarian Revival. The later revision is also present in Kiril Topalov and Nikolai Chernokozhev, *Bŭlgarskata literatura prez Vŭzrazhdaneto*. Sofia: Prosveta, 1998.

70 Iliya Konev, *Bŭlgarskoto vŭzrazhdane i prosveshtenieto*. Vol. 1, Sofia: BAN, 1983; Vol. 2, Sofia: Universitetsko izdatelstvo "Kliment Ohridski," 1991.

71 Iliya Konev, *Bŭlgarskoto vŭzrazhdane*, Vol. 1, 9–16.

72 Iliya Konev, *Bŭlgarskoto vŭzrazhdane*, Vol. 1, 17, 23, 30.

73 Iliya Konev, *Bŭlgarskoto vŭzrazhdane*, Vol. 1, 19–20, 32–35, 209; Vol. 2, 6. The main slant of the author in the second volume is to oppose, in a patriotic spirit, certain statements by the historians Nikolai Genchev and Toncho Zhechev to the effect that, with the Ottoman conquest, the Bulgarians left the orbit of European culture and that when eventually they looked to Europe again (during the national Revival), they mostly adapted and imitated. Konev argues that the Bulgarians did not stray that far from European civilization and that they preserved ties with Russia and Slavdom (something his opponents would hardly deny). See Konev, *Bŭlgarskoto vŭzrazhdane*. Vol. 2, 21–37.

74 The close connection between the "Enlightenment under Bulgarian conditions" (and of the "Balkan enlightenments" in general) on the one hand, and the national liberation struggles and the primacy of the ideas of national education (which subordinated the bourgeois-democratic ideas) on the other, have also been pointed out by Radkova, *Bŭlgarskata inteligentsiya*, 286–287. Robin Okey, among the foreign historians, stresses the primarily literary character of the Enlightenment in the Balkans in contrast to the philosophical, social, and scientific-engineering aspects elsewhere. See Okey, *Eastern Europe, 1740–1985. Feudalism to Communism*. Minneapolis: University of Minnesota Press, 1985, 40–46.

75 Iliya Konev, *Bŭlgarskoto vŭzrazhdane*. Vol. 1, 59–65, 144–213.

76 Donka Petkanova-Toteva, "Pazvitie na prosvetnite idei v Bŭlgariya prez XVIII vek." In Petkanova-Toteva, *Hilyadoletna literatura*. Sofia: Nauka i izkustvo, 1974, 211–238.

77 Svetlozar Igov, *Kratka istoriya*, 25–27, 184–221.

78 Boyan Penev, *Paisii Hilendarski*, 44–45; Penev, *Istoriya na novata*. Vol. 2, 254–257.

79 Goran Todorov, "Istoricheskite vŭzgledi na Paisii." *Izvestiya na instituta po istoriya*. Vol. 20 (1968): 155–157; Iliya Konev, *Bŭlgarskoto vŭzrazhdane*. Vol. 1, 35, 209; Ivan Shishmanov, "Paisii i Rousseau. Aperçu." *Dennitsa* 1, nos. 7–8 (1890): 353–354; Emil Georgiev, "Tipologichen relef," 236–237; Georgiev, "Paisii Hilendarski," 277–283. The authors are very well aware of the primarily individualist, social, and universalist ideas of the Enlighteners in contrast to the primarily national ideas of Paisii.

80 Emil Georgiev, *Obshto i sravnitelno*, 83–90; Dimitŭr Tsanev, "Proyavi na natsionalno," 244, 246–249; Svetlozar Igov, *Kratka istoriya*, 184–191. According to the author, Paisii's oeuvre presents a "syncretic literary whole," a syncretism of Enlightenment and national romantic ideas.

81 Emil Georgiev, "Bŭlgarskoto literaturno," 203–204. See also Georgiev, "Paisii Hilendarski," 277–278.

82 Emil Georgiev, "Tipologichen relef," 242.

83 Emil Georgiev, *Obshto i sravnitelno*, 55, 59, 76–82; Georgiev, "Renesansovo-pros-

veshtenskiyat period v yuzhnoslavyanskata literaturna obshtnost" In Georgiev, *Obshto i sravnitelno*, 83–90, esp. 88; Georgiev, "Bŭlgarskoto literaturno," 203–215; Georgiev, "Tipologichen relef," 236–237; Georgiev, "Paisii Hilendarski," 277–283.

84 Strashimir Dimitrov and Krŭstyu Manchev, *Istoriya na balkanskite*, 141–152.

85 Nadya Danova, *Konstantin Georgiev Fotinov*, 36–55.

86 See also Gale Stokes, "Introduction: In Defense of Balkan Nationalism." In Gale Stokes, ed., *Nationalism in the Balkans. An Annotated Bibliography*, vii–xvii. According to the author, the principle of social justice was transformed in the Balkans into freedom from foreign political and religious domination. See also Okey, *Eastern Europe*, 97. As pointed out by Okey when treating the revolution of 1948, the Slavs in the Habsburg Empire and the Romanians rightly sensed that their liberation as individuals would only come as a result of the assertion of their solidarity as a group, i.e., through nationalism. Thus their nationalism had liberal goals, while the liberalism of their opponents was filtered through nationalist lenses.

87 Paschalis Kitromilides, "The Enlightenment East and West: A Comparative Perspective on the Ideological Origins of the Balkan Political Traditions." In Kitromilides, *Enlightenment, Nationalism, Orthodoxy. Studies in the Culture and Political Thought of South-eastern Europe*. Variorum, 1994, 51–70.

88 Bulgarian authors do not call the broad educational movement "Enlightenment," though the adjective "educational" (*prosveten*) is sometimes contaminated with "Enlightenment" (*prosveshtenski*), being etymologically quite close. Among foreign authors, Peter Sugar emphasized strongly that the peculiar (and later) local Bulgarian movement for education (which he calls "peasant self-education") is quite different from the Western "Enlightenment." He rejects the ascription not only of Paisii but also of Sofronii to the Enlightenment, while the group of national intellectuals and revolutionaries who came after were already under the influence of romanticist and nationalist ideas. See Peter Sugar, "The Enlightenment in the Balkans. Some Basic Considerations." *East European Quarterly* 9, no. 4 (1985): 499–507, esp. 505–507. In my opinion this does not preclude that the above-mentioned movement for education was stimulated by Enlightenment ideas.

89 In a similar vein Peter Sugar argues that "one sparrow does not bring the spring," posing questions such as: Which of the aspects of the Enlightenment can be detected in the Balkans? How many sparrows (i.e., prominent Enlighteners) are needed? How long a delay is acceptable in asserting a valid connection between the influence and the influenced phenomenon? What is a local adaptation of a foreign influence and what is a local phenomenon *sui generis*? His answer is that we do not possess a precise measurement and that we have to rely on the sense of the well-trained historian, who reaches a solution and pronounces his verdict having studied everything relevant. See Sugar, "The Enlightenment in the Balkans," 500, 503.

90 Bulgarian authors characteristically write "Bulgarian Enlightenment" with small letters (in contrast to Bulgarian Revival), which attests to an attenuated meaning.

91 Svetlozar Igov, *Kratka istoriya*, 27, 184, 195.

92 Hristo Gandev, *Ranno vŭzrazhdane*, 93–131 (the chapter "The Reform movement").

93 Hristo Gandev, *Ranno vŭzrazhdane*, 106.

94 Svetla Strashimirova, *Bŭlgarinut pred praga*, 96–105.

95 Iliya Todev, *Novi ochertsi*, 17–19; Todev, *Kŭm drugo minalo*, 15–16.

96 Georgi Gachev, *Uskorenoto razvitie na kulturata*. Sofia: Nauka i izkustvo, 1979. For theoretical elaborations and summaries see–29, 35, 40–44, 49–55, 58, 68–78, 87–89, 121–122, 125, 129–130, 133–137, 146, 168–179, 220, 342–343, 353–372, 504, 507–508, 512–514.

97 The notion of the "contemporaneity of the non-contemporaneous" has been elaborated by Marc Bloch and Reinhart Koselleck. See Reinhart Koselleck, "Moderne Sozialgeschichte und historische Zeiten." In *Theorie der modernen Geschichtsschreibung*, edited by Pietro Rossi, Frankfurt/Main, 1987, 173–190.

98 Gachev, *Uskorenoto razvitie*, 135, 220–221, 342–343.

99 Dinekov, "Problemŭt za romantizma," 49–79, esp. 53–54.

100 Georgiev, *Obshto i sravnitelno*, 55, 77.

101 Georgiev, "Paisii Hilendarski," 253–254, 258–260, 277–283.

102 Genchev, *Bŭlgarsko vŭzrazhdane*, 11–14. The author speaks rather freely of "Bulgarian Enlightenment" and "Bulgarian Enlighteners" and puts a number of figures under this heading. See also Genchev, *Bŭlgarskata kultura*, 175–176, 266, 268.

103 Genchev, *Bŭgarskata kultura*, 176.

104 Nikolai Genchev, "Za osnovnoto sudŭrzhanie na bŭlgarskiya vŭzrozhdenski protses." In *Kultura, tsŭrkva i revolyitsiya prez Vŭzrazhdaneto*, edited by Krumka Sharova, Sofia, 1995, 40–46. In fact, this is anticipated in an earlier work, Genchev, "Pak po nyakoi vŭprosi ot istoriyata na bŭlgarskoto vŭzrazhdane," *Istoriya i obshtestvoznanie*. 1985, no. 4, 13–22.

105 On disputes on the chronology and the contents of Modernity (the Modern epoch) in Europe, see Reinhart Koselleck, "Das Achtzehnte Jahrhundert als Beginn der Neuzeit." In *Epochenschwelle und Epochenbewusstsein*, edited by Reinart Herzog and Reinhart Koselleck. Munich: Wilhelm Fink Verlag, 1987, 269–282; Koselleck, "'Neuzeit': Remarks on the Semantics of the Modern Concepts of Movement." In Koselleck, *Future's Past. On the Semantics of Historical Time*. The MIT Press, Cambridge, Mass. and London, 1985, 231–266. Erich Hassinger, *Das Werden des neuzeitlichen Europa. 1300–1600*. Braunschweig, 1959; Stephan Skalweit, *Der Beginn der Neuzeit. Epochengrenze und Epochenbegriff*. Darmstadt, 1982. The traditional dating of the beginning of Modernity is around 1500 (the Renaissance being considered as a "bridge" to it), but there are arguments for ca. 1800. The economic spring of the West took place with the spread of the results of the agrarian revolution and of the industrial revolution (ca. 1780–1820).

106 For an example of such a compensating overloading of the Bulgarian Revival, see *Istoriya na Bŭlgariya v 14 toma*. Vol. 5, 13. It is defined here as the sum total of the economic, social, political, and cultural processes characteristic of the transition from feudalism to capitalism, and from a feudal to a bourgeois society, following "the general regularities" of the transition with some specifics conditioned by foreign domination. It then becomes clear that these specifics made the maturing and the carrying out of the "Bulgarian national revolution" into the main content of the Revival.

107 Aleksandŭr Kiossev, "Spisŭtsi na otsŭstvashtoto." In *Bŭlgarskiyat kanon? Krizata na litaraturnoto nasledstvo*, edited by Kiossev. Sofia: Aleksandŭr Panov, 1998, 5–49, esp. 11–20.

108 Inna Peleva, "Natsionalno vreme, kontinentalno vreme–figuri na neprevodimostta." *Literaturen vestnik*, no. 31 (11 October 2000); no. 32 (18 October 2000).

109 Gavrilova, "Vekŭt na bulgarskoto," 5–8.

110 Daniel Lerner, James Coleman and Ronald Dore. "Modernization." In *International Encyclopedia of the Social Sciences*. Vols. 9–10. New York–London: The Macmillan Company and the Free Press, 1972, 386–408; Cyril Black, *The Dynamics of Modernization. A Study in Comparative History*. New York, Evanston and London: Harper & Row, 1966, esp. 5–34; Reinhard Bendix, "Tradition and Modernity Reconsidered." In *Comparative Studies in Society and History* 9, no. 3 (1967):318–344; David Harrison, *The Sociology of Modernization and Development*. London: Unwin Hyman, 1988.

111 Andrew Janos, *The Politics of Backwardness in Hungary, 1825–1945.* Princeton, N. J.: Princeton University Press, 1982, 313–316; Janos, "Modernization and Decay in Historical Perspective. The Case of Romania." In *Social Change in Romania, 1860–1940,* edited by Kenneth Jovith. University of California, Berkeley, 1978, 72–116, esp. 72–75; Janos, "The Politics of Backwardness in Continental Europe, 1780–1945." *World Politics* 41, no. 3 (1989): 323–359; Dieter Senghass (ed.), *Peripherer Kapitalismus. Analysen über Abhängigkeit und Unterentwicklung.* Frankfurt/Main, 1974.

112 On this, see Roumen Daskalov, *Images of Europe: A Glance from the Periphery.* Working Paper, European University Institute, SPS, 94/8, 1994, esp. 11–15.

113 Genchev, *Bŭlgarsko vŭzrazhdane,* 12–13; Genchev, *Bŭlgarskata kultura,* 181. The author demonstrates a keen feeling for the geopolitical factor, without lapsing, however, into geopolitical determinism.

114 Genchev, *Bŭlgarsko vŭzrazhdane,* 128–130, 310–311; Genchev, *Bŭlgarskata kultura,* 271–274.

115 Radkova, *Bŭlgarskata inteligentsiya;* Radkova, *Inteligentsiyata i nravstvenotta.*

116 Gavrilova, *Koleloto na zhivota;* Gavrilova, *Vekŭt na bŭlgarskoto.*

CHAPTER TWO

Meanings of the Revival II: Economic and Social

The economic (*cum* social) dimension is present in explanations of the Bulgarian Revival by "bourgeois" authors of the "old school." There, it is accorded the role of a "precondition" or "factor" for spiritual–national revival but not regarded as the phenomenon itself.[1]

An influential early work by the socialist Krŭstyu Rakovski (published in 1910) deserves special mention. The author, nephew of the great national revolutionary Georgi Rakovski, points to the economic upsurge during the first half of the nineteenth century and the formation of a strong and self-reliant "urban class" of artisans, small shopkeepers and traders, as a major condition and factor of the Bulgarian Revival. He pays special attention to the role of the *beglikchii* (collectors of the tax on sheep—*beglik*—and traders in sheep) as "first representatives of young Bulgarian capitalism." It was the urban (bourgeois) class, with its newly acquired self-confidence, that became a supporter and promoter of the national idea, and thus of the revival. Krŭstyu Rakovski reveals a causal link between the introduction of a regular army in Turkey and an upsurge in a number of Bulgarian urban crafts and domestic industries engaged in supplying it (especially with woollen cloth [*aba*] and decorative braid [*gaitan*], as well as the importance of the opening up of trade along the Danube and on the Black Sea following the peace treaty of Edirne (1829).[2]

A few "bourgeois" economic historians spoke of the emergence of capitalism during the Revival, especially in wool manufacturing. Dimitŭr Mishaikov applied Werner Sombart's definition of capitalist cottage (domestic) industries as different from urban crafts to describe Bulgarian wool production. It was based on the dominant role of a capitalist entrepreneur linked with the market, and laborers working at home for low payment, ensuring the low cost of the product.[3] In his *"Bulgarian economic history,"* published in German in 1928, Ivan Sakŭzov speaks of the development in the 1860s of "factory-like production with clearly manifest capitalist elements" in the manufacturing of woolen textiles along with domestic manufacturing, that is, as entrepreneur-capitalists, merchants or factory owners provided hundreds and thousands of workers with factory wool to work for them at home.[4] This is known as the putting-out system.

However, the "bourgeois" economists were not inclined to exaggerate the development of capitalism during the Revival, still less to make it into a defining feature of the epoch. Characteristic in this respect is the opinion of the authoritative economist and economic historian Stoyan Bochev (admittedly with a more advanced concept of capitalism in mind):

"Thus there began and developed an accumulation of capital in the hands of Bulgarians, on Bulgarian soil, starting from stock raising, trade, and crafts. But the existence of capital by itself does not mean capitalism. There is no capitalism whatsoever, especially when the labor of the owner— and what labor at that!—accompanies the capital and we are still within a very primitive economy, though in the phase of money exchange. This accumulation of capital, painful and slow, gives only the beginnings of economic life, and one can hardly speak of a 'big bourgeoisie' then, as some have remarked."[5]

The Transition from Feudalism to Capitalism

The economic development (and the accompanying social transformation) were elaborated by Marxist authors into the central meaning and basic content of the Bulgarian Revival. The latter is fitted into the Marxist scheme of successive stages of development with corresponding dominant classes. The Revival then appears as a period of transition from feudalism to capitalism, the social (class) corollary of which is the transition toward a bourgeois society. This is imagined as a revolutionary transition—an antifeudal, bourgeois-democratic revolution. But the extreme version of this interpretation prevailed later.

The founder of "scientific socialism" in Bulgaria, Dimitŭr Blagoev, who grew up before the liberation, was nearer to the realities of the Revival period. He was still under the impact of the great national upsurge when characterizing (in 1906) the Revival as a national movement led by the new class that rose on the wave of the economic development after the 1820s (i.e., after the anarchic "Time of Troubles" in the Ottoman Balkans came to an end). The preconditions were created by the rise in upland Bulgarian towns of industries (meant in the older and more general sense of urban crafts) and lively market exchange. In the meantime, the feudal *sipahi* fiefs in the villages were being undermined and replaced with *chifliks* (big commercial estates), and the "serfdom" of the peasant masses was declining. The peasant uprisings from the first half of the nineteenth century were unsuccessful, but the "peaceful urban revolution," that is, the setting up of schools, the printing of books, and the uplifting of the national spirit through these means, was heading toward success. The church struggles were fought for the recognition of the Bulgarian nation and they were led by the commercial-industrial (bourgeois) class, which rallied the entire nation.[6] As can be seen, Blagoev presented the Revival in primarily national terms, although he also stressed the social aspect—the national movement as a kind of social revolution effected by the rising bourgeois class. On the other hand, as later research would show, he was mistaken about the "serfdom" of the peasants and exaggerated the significance of the *chifliks*.

The Marxist theses about the Revival were first formulated in the 1930s, mostly by the Communist Party intellectual Georgi Bakalov and the economic historian Zhak Natan in polemics with right-wing nationalist authors. Their hardening occurred under Communist rule in its early Stalinist phase. Political leaders in the highest positions, such as Vŭlko Chervenkov, head of the Communist Party and of the state; and Vasil Kolarov, president of the National Assembly and deputy premier, etc. were then giving instructions as to how to interpret the past. A rewriting of Bulgarian history was undertaken under the direction of Todor Pavlov, a Moscow-trained philosopher and president of the Bulgarian Academy of Sciences (1947–1961), acting as the leading party ideologue, which resulted in an "academic" two-volume history of Bulgaria (1954). At the same time, a purge of the "historical front" of "bourgeois" historians, and the "realignment" of the remaining ones toward crude Marxist postulates and methodologies was taking place.[7]

The works of the economic historian Zhak Natan, who wrote both before and under Communist rule, give an idea of how the economic factor grew in importance. In one of his earlier works (published in 1938) he treated the Bulgarian Revival in a primarily national sense—as a restoration of the Bulgarian historical process that was interrupted by Ottoman domination; the formation of the traits of the nation; as well as emancipation from Greek cultural influence. The economic process of "transition from the old feudal patriarchal relations to the new commodity relations" is presented as one factor in the shaping of the Bulgarian nation—the main one to be sure—while capitalism is not particularly emphasized.[8]

The economic meaning comes forward strongly in another book by the same author (revised edition, 1949), although the struggle for national independence receives some recognition, too, as a "form" of an otherwise socioeconomic "content." To cite a characteristic passage:

"One should understand as Bulgarian renaissance the process of social-economic transformation that took place in the country around the end of the nineteenth century and had as its content the struggle for the liberation of the country from the fetters of Turkish feudalism, and as its form the struggle for the national, cultural, etc. liberation of the Bulgarian people suffering under the yoke of the Turkish sultans, *pashas*, and *beys*, as well as under the spiritual yoke of the Greek priests."[9]

Passages such as this one coexist with statements (in the same book) about the primarily national sense of the Revival, attesting to the difficulties of the reorientation.[10] It came easier to people just emerging in the historical field, equipped with Marxist (i.e., mostly Stalinist) doctrine. Instrumental in imposing the social (class) over the national meaning at the end of the 1940s and the beginning of the 1950s was Dimitŭr Kosev, who was later to become the "doyen" of Bulgarian historians (head of the academic Institute of History between 1950 and 1963; rector of Sofia University from 1962 to 1968, etc.). In a programmatic paper he attacked "idealist historians" for not taking into account "the basic socioeconomic process that makes up the essence of the Revival, and of which all other manifestations—such as the idea of an independent church, the national idea, etc.—are but a result and an external form."[11] He then proceeds to derive the nation directly from the economy by affirming that the development of the commodity-money economy and the disintegration of feudal relations "led inevitably to the formation of the Bulgarian nation."

The economic interpretation of the Revival is coupled with a social one signaled by class struggles and a social (bourgeois) revolution. Georgi Bakalov was the first to develop polemically, in the 1930s, the thesis that the national struggles were but a veil for the social conflict between different classes and ideologies. To cite him:

"The activists of the Revival do not present a monumental wall against foreign domination, unified and inspired by the same ideal of national independence as they are presented by the bourgeoisie now. On the contrary, they embody the clash between different class ideologies, whose difference is blurred by the national veil. Concealed behind their struggle

against either the patriarchy or the rule of the Sultan are real class interests under a national mantel."[12]

In the same vein, but already during the Communist regime, Dimitŭr
Kosev accused the "bourgeois scholars" of seeing only the national idea in
the Revival, which, according to them, united the rich and the poor, the
learned and the uneducated in the struggle for national independence.
Even if acknowledging class contradictions, they did not use them to explain the national-liberation movement:

"Blinded by their bourgeois-idealistic views, the bourgeois historians did
not see that the 'national idea' itself is nothing but a result and a manifestation of the class struggle of the Bulgarian bourgeoisie against the Greek
bourgeoisie for the internal market, and of the class struggle of the petite
bourgeoisie and the peasant masses against the Turkish exploiters—*pashas*,
beys, and their plunderous rule."[13]

The national character of the revolutionary movement is explained by
the author by the fact that the dominant class belonged to another nationality; it is, so to say, of secondary importance. (Kosev follows in the steps of
Bakalov with this argument.) Proof of the primarily class character is
found in the fact that Levski, Botev, and the other revolutionaries fought
against the "exploitative class" of Turkish *pashas*, *beys*, and Bulgarian
chorbadzhii, but not against the Turkish "people."

The social (and class) differentiation of the societies being a fundamental social fact (like the divisions according to sex, race, ethnicity, etc.), one
cannot object in advance to seeing the Revival in primarily class terms. The
fact of foreign domination itself can be treated, as Marxist authors treat it,
as the occupation of a dominant "class" position by (part of) the Turks.
Hence the purely theoretical affirmation of the priority of "class" in the
above statement is not wrong, simply a priori and empty (as would be the
opposite affirmation of the priority of a common national interest). Both
have a sense only as hypotheses to be tested. The main issue is how relevant
the class factor will prove in explaining the social and political processes of
the Bulgarian Revival—for example, the importance of class descent and
class status in accounting for the views and actions of the national activists
(and how "class" interacted with other factors and motivations), the role of
class struggles in public life, etc. The class analysis can be applied in a
crude manner, caricatured, or treated in a more sophisticated way. This
would form the core of many controversies and revisions.

Once interpreted in an economic–social sense, the Revival had to be accommodated into the materialist historical scheme, with its claims of

global validity. According to this scheme (worked out on the instructions of Stalin and Zhdanov for the Russian textbook of modern history in particular), modern history begins with a revolutionary transition from feudalism to capitalism in the advanced states, dating from the French bourgeois revolution of 1789–1794. The modern development of dependent and colonial states is marked by the unfolding of bourgeois–democratic revolutions, which are simultaneously national-liberation movements.[14] The Bulgarian Revival presented historians with the question of its relation to "modern history," marked by the capitalist transition. To settle this question, a "discussion" on the periodization of Bulgarian history was organized by the Bulgarian Academy of Sciences in 1950/51.[15]

Several major standpoints were elaborated. Zhak Natan placed the beginnings of capitalism in the Bulgarian lands at the end of the eighteenth century and the beginning of the nineteenth century, characterizing it as primarily commercial capitalism with some manufacturing by outworkers. According to him, the advance of capitalism is not equivalent to the victory of the capitalist formation, especially as the land was owned by Turkish feudal lords, there existed feudal obligations, and the political superstructure—the state—was also feudal. Natan dates modern Bulgarian history from the liberation, which destroyed Ottoman feudalism and thus performed the role of a bourgeois–democratic revolution. But even the liberation opened up no more than the possibility for free capitalist development. There followed a period of "primitive accumulation of capital," while capitalist development accelerated only at the beginning of the twentieth century up until the Balkan wars (after the wars came the beginning of its "monopolistic stage").[16] In the discussion, Zhak Natan actually reiterated his previously expressed opinion that until the liberation only the "contours" of capitalism were outlined, so that the Bulgarian Revival is actually part of feudalism and presents the "ending of the Middle Ages, which stayed late in our lands"—or, to be more precise, it is a period of the decay of feudalism. Still, Natan suggested that the lecture course in modern Bulgarian history should nevertheless begin with a short review of the Revival "as a link between the epoch of the decay of feudalism and the epoch of the victory of capitalism," as well as a period of "bourgeois-democratic revolution" and the "preparation of the conditions for the victory of capitalism."[17]

According to the view elaborated by Dimitŭr Kosev, modern Bulgarian history should comprise the entire process of the development of the bourgeois–capitalist formation, from the inception of capitalist relations in the second half of the eighteenth century until the establishment of socialism in 1944. Otherwise, it would turn out that Bulgarian society, until its liberation in 1877/8, was feudal, which he obviously thinks to be wrong. Kosev then indicates two sub-periods within modern Bulgarian history: the Revival, described as the period of the decay of Ottoman feudalism and the initial development of capitalist relations (plus the preparation for, and carrying out of, the bourgeois–democratic revolution that destroyed the Turkish feudal system in 1877/8), followed by a period of the further growth and then decay of capitalism from the liberation to 1944. According to the author, capitalism in the form of factory industry affirmed itself as a dominant system in Bulgaria at the beginning of the twentieth century and was making progress until World War I; after which it entered a period of crisis (as part of the "global crisis" of capitalism after the October Revolution).[18] Kosev reacts against the view that capitalism was already victorious during the Revival (ascribed to him by his opponents). He subscribes to the view that there were only the beginnings of capitalist relations prior to the Bulgarian liberation, and that they were developing within the framework of the still dominant, though deeply eroded, Turkish feudal system.[19] This view was endorsed by Ivan Snegarov, who also dated the beginning of modern Bulgarian history toward the end of the eighteenth century, again not with the victory of capitalism but with its appearance, and who argued by bringing the contrary view—of belated feudalism—ad absurdum (in which case it would turn out that the Middle Ages in Macedonia had lasted until 1913, and that as a native of Macedonia he himself had lived under feudal conditions).[20]

There is, finally, the opinion of Hristo Gandev, to the effect that the bourgeois-capitalist order was victorious even before the liberation, but primarily in the form of the expansion of European capitalism and its semi-colonial exploitation of the Ottoman Empire, especially since the 1830s and 1840s. Bulgarian capitalism and the Bulgarian bourgeoisie are ascribed a mediating "comprador" role, as in colonial dependent states. Modern times for the Bulgarians thus began during the Revival. The liberation in 1877/8 completed an already unfolding bourgeois–democratic revolution by achieving political independence and the total destruction of the feudal order, and by opening the way to capitalist development.[21] Characteristic of Gandev's position is not only the idea of dependent capitalist development but also, and flowing from it, the idea that only the last part of the Revival can be counted as "modern times."

What makes this discussion quite interesting is the a priori nature of the assumptions, which engenders a number of problems. The scheme requires that modernity and "modern history" respectively begin with the triumph of the bourgeoisie and of capitalism (dated in Europe from the French Revolution), though some latitude of "underdevelopment" is allowed for dependent and colonial peoples that also have to throw off the yoke of foreign rule (by way of a bourgeois–democratic revolution). The basic problem is how to define the Revival as belonging to modernity (which is the intuitive feeling of all participants), and how to include it in modern history, given these assumptions and the required development of capitalism in particular (instead of just world-view changes, or the formation of the nation). To speak of a "victory" of the capitalist formation during the Revival would not only be patently wrong but would make unnecessary the liberation from Turkish rule, which, in this case, would be sufficiently "progressive." On the other hand, the participants in the discussion clearly think of the Revival as the beginning of Bulgarian modern times, as they all recognize the considerable changes it brought about. Hence their suggestions may be understood as a search for a way out of the dogmatic dilemma: the Revival as part of modern history (which, in the scheme, requires developed capitalism and a developed bourgeoisie) but without presuming the triumph of capitalist relations. Moreover, the dilemma is aggravated by the need to present conditions under Turkish rule as extremely backward and "feudal" (so that a liberation would be justified in economic terms as well).

Dimitŭr Kosev's suggestion pushes back the inception of the "bourgeois–capitalist formation" as a whole to the Revival (which thus becomes part of "modern history"), but this risks being understood as an early "victory of capitalism" because of the lack of a clear-cut line between the appearance and dominance of capitalist relations. A direct statement to the effect that capitalism had triumphed before the liberation (as proposed by Gandev) would not do, not only because it is in contradiction with the facts but also because it makes liberation (from feudalism) hardly necessary, while the reservation that this was an external, colonial capitalism creates a problem for the internal Bulgarian "bourgeois revolution." The best way out proves to be the assumption of a long period of transition—which saw the decay of feudalism and the gestation of capitalism simultaneously, neither pure feudalism nor a triumph of capitalism, but the preparation of conditions for it. Accordingly, the Revival becomes a somewhat ambiguous "introductory" chapter to the modern history of Bulgaria. This is Zhak Natan's standpoint, which asserted itself in subsequent Marxist historiography (corrected by playing down feudalism before the liberation). Hence the formula that the liberation played the role of a bourgeois revolution and cleared the way for capitalist relations, which were already making progress during the Revival (together with the bourgeois revolution). Thus it was only the tacit change of the initial assumption (capitalism in full sway) that allowed the assertion of the Revival as the advent of Bulgarian Modernity.

Regarding capitalism, the more doctrinal Marxist historians had necessarily to be very ambiguous and to play a "double game." As we have pointed out, capitalism could not be said to have triumphed before the liberation, otherwise no bourgeois revolution and no liberation would have been needed. However, it did need to be well advanced, because it is on capitalism that the entire Marxist interpretation is premised—otherwise the transition to a capitalist formation becomes problematic however far it is stretched, and the bourgeois revolution hangs in the air. Moreover, the Marxist relationship between basis and superstructure makes economic development absolutely necessary as an explanation of world-view and ideological changes, the formation of national consciousness included (at least in a dogmatic reading). Several strategies for the "justification of capitalism"—that is, showing that it was considerable, though not strong enough to triumph—have been employed in dealing with this problem.

A first approach is exploiting all the potential from the condition of "transition." The Revival is regarded as a period of the "decay of feudalism" and a prelude to capitalism, a "preparation of the preconditions" for the victory of capitalism; the new forces of capitalism evolved long before its "full victory" while still in the womb of the feudal society.[22] Sometimes even future capitalism or capitalism "in projection" is evoked to make up for a deficit in capitalism at an earlier stage of affairs.[23]

A second strategy is to exaggerate the significance of the putting-out system and the factory industry, or to speak of capitalism in a very general and indiscriminate manner that includes usury, tax farming, and other premodern forms.[24] Sometimes the very economic upsurge and "commodity-money" (i.e., market) relations or the "accumulation of capital" are identified as capitalism. The widening of the idea of capitalism can be seen in the following contradictory statement (from Zhak Natan):

"That is why it is usually said that Bulgaria in this period was suffering not only from the push of the new, which was being born slowly but surely, but was also suffering from the insufficient development of the new, from its slow pace. For that reason, even commercial capitalism was not able to impose itself in Bulgaria during this period as a complete system. But this does not provide the least ground for affirming that there was no development of capitalism and no capitalism during that period in Bulgaria. Without this impetuous development of capital in its pre-capitalist form, in the form of commercial–usurious capital, all the impressive events that took place in the country during this period of economic development in Bulgaria would remain unexplained."[25]

The last sentence, in particular, performs a trick by inverting logic: instead of explaining political events by the ascent of capitalism (as required by the doctrine), it derives capitalism from them. Since there was a "revolution," there must have been capitalism.[26]

Finally, there is the common idea that capitalism made its way slowly and painfully because the "feudal ways" of the Ottoman Empire obstructed it (as did legal insecurity and administrative arbitrariness). In this case, the "feudal obstacles" are evoked to explain why capitalism did not manifest itself more strongly.[27] Without denying the huge impediments to the development of modern capitalism in the Ottoman Empire, especially physical and legal insecurity, corruption, etc., the picture of modern capitalism heroically trying to assert itself while being handicapped by backward conditions is hardly accurate. Hristo Gandev's reconstruction of the strong involvement of Bulgarian capital with Greek, Turkish, and Western partners, and its strong reliance on precisely the conditions that existed in the Ottoman Empire (even being "parasitic" on them), seems much more realistic.[28] The dominant pre-modern forms of capitalism especially, such as usury and tax farming, are difficult to imagine under other conditions; the role of state deliveries to the Ottoman army and court has also been stressed. Let us now consider in more detail the way capitalism and feudalism, that is, the point of arrival and the point of departure in the transition, are presented in historical scholarship.

Capitalism during the Revival

One of the first Marxist authors eventually to clear up some misconceptions about capitalism was Zhak Natan. As he pointed out, not every accumulation of money leads to capitalism (but only when it functions as capital); commodity production for the market is not in itself equivalent to capitalism (but only a condition for it); although commercial and usurious capital play a role in the ruining of small producers, this does not necessarily lead to capitalism; and, finally, industrial capitalism in Bulgaria developed in the form of manufacturing using the putting-out system, which gave the domestic industry it employed a capitalist outlook.[29]

A description of Bulgarian capitalism using the concept of "Orientalism," and an explanation of "underdevelopment" in terms of an "Asiatic mode of production," is provided by Nikolai Genchev. The emphasis is on the slowness of the capitalist transformation and the lack of dynamics in a backward "Oriental–Asiatic" empire; the hybridization of economic forms and social types that created some intermediate and mixed, rather than "pure," forms (e.g., the *chiflik*, social groups such as the *chorbadzhii*, etc.); and the resulting "immaturity" of the bourgeois class in composition and behavior. In Genchev's view, Bulgarian capitalism bore the deep imprint of the Oriental system, within which it existed.[30]

As already mentioned, Hristo Gandev offers a description of the Bulgarian capitalism of the last part of the Revival in terms of semi-colonialism and dependence. He dates Bulgarian capitalism from the penetration of the big capitalist states into the Ottoman Empire and the semi-colonial exploitation of the empire in the 1830s and 1840s, predated by the existence of crafts for local needs, commodity–money relations, and primitive technology. The author describes the emergent Bulgarian capitalism as based on brokering activities, involving acting as commissioner for somebody else, or buying and selling at one's own risk; the Bulgarian bourgeoisie is accordingly described as a "comprador" bourgeoisie, engaged in import–export trade and dependent on foreign capital and foreign companies. The Bulgarian bourgeoisie was also taking advantage of the "feudal remnants" for its enrichment, for example, tax farming, usury, currency exchange, bidding in public auctions, etc. Things did not change substantially after the liberation: Bulgaria soon became dependent on Western imperialist states while the now dominant bourgeoisie was too weak and continued its mediating role in trade, supplemented by state deliveries and the undertaking of construction works.[31]

Presenting Bulgarian development during the Revival in terms of theories of imperialism and colonialism (or the later "world system" theories and "peripheral capitalism") is an exception among the generally progressist and optimistic Bulgarian Marxist historians. It is also somewhat exaggerated. Attempts to apply the concept of "dependent development" and "world system" theories to the Balkans, that is, the attribution of slow development to Western "semi-colonial" exploitation, have been rejected recently by the Western economic historians John Lampe and Michael

Palairet, on the grounds of the weakness of Western commercial penetration (even after the setting up of post-Ottoman independent states).[32] On the other hand, there is no doubt that the Western powers extracted exorbitant profits from the bankrupt empire through such instruments as the capitulations (i.e., trade and customs agreements, ex-territorial rights and exemptions), and the management of the Ottoman debts. Still, the question of the causes of "underdevelopment" remains far too complex to permit simple solutions as regards the relative weight of internal and external factors of development, and one has to differentiate further between falling behind as the result of an external force holding back progress, or simply becoming aware of other states speeding up ahead.

The issue of Bulgarian capitalism is more fruitfully approached by way of empirical studies. A good example is Hristo Gandev's research on particular cases of Bulgarian putting-out textile enterprises from the 1860s and the 1870s, based mostly in Istanbul and Gabrovo (and some in Kazanlŭk, Karlovo, and Sopot). The author clarifies such questions as the profits and expansion of these enterprises, the use of wage labor, as well as the connection with the development of factories in the same localities after the liberation, that is, the continuity of capitalist development.[33] The study is also noteworthy for its theoretical discussion of the notion of capitalism, in which it is pointed out (with reference to Marx) that the application of wage labor, a certain size of enterprise, an orientation toward profit, etc., are enough for capitalism to exist even before mechanized factory production.

An interesting idea first developed by Stefan Tsonev, and subsequently by Nikolai Todorov (both of them economic historians), is that the emerging Bulgarian capitalism actually concealed itself under the guise of the guilds (esnaf) in order to take advantage of their traditional status and of the protection they enjoyed in the Ottoman Empire. The guilds were profoundly transformed in the process. The estate-like regulations against competition were weakened; commercial capital entered into the marketing of their produce and as buyer of the labor of the craftsmen; big commercial–industrial companies had direct membership in the guilds, etc. Thus instead of functioning to prevent master-craftsmen from becoming capitalists, the guilds actually became a protective roof for capitalists, who formed a sort of "bourgeois elite" within them; moreover, some guilds existed in the framework of bigger capitalist enterprises. The preference among big capitalists to stay within the guild system is explained (by Nikolai Todorov) with reference to the overall insecurity and deficit of legality; for the same reasons, they preferred the lower, decentralized forms of capitalist enterprise (putting-out enterprises, and the employment of the labor of wage workers, journeymen, and master-artisans) and the merging of commercial and production capital instead of setting up centralized factories; again for the same reason (and to reduce risks), investments in production were combined with investments in various other activities (trade, real estate, etc.), and capitalists were ready to take those investments out of production, or even out of the country, at short notice.[34]

It proved especially difficult to identify capitalist forms in agriculture. The only candidate in this sphere is the *chiflik*, that is, the big estates in the late empire, mainly in the hands of rich Turks, which were operated by various arrangements—corvée labor, sharecropping (called *kesim* or *ispolitsa*), that is, the renting of land in return for part of the produce, and wage labor (permanent or seasonal). The grounds for treating the *chiflik* as at least partially capitalist are the commodity character of the production (for the market) and the partial employment of wage labor; conversely, they are characterized as "semi-feudal" by the partial use of corvée and sharecropping, and most generally by the fact that they presumably emerged from the disintegration of the *sipahi* "feudal" fief.[35]

Typical of (vulgar) Marxist historical scholarship is an inclination to present the development in clear-cut stages. In the case of agriculture, there was a transition from the *sipahi* fief system to (semi-feudal, semi-capitalist) *chifliks*, accompanied by a loss of land on the part of the peasants and their liberation from dependency ("serfdom") to the *sipahi* feudal lords. This scheme was briefly indicated by Blagoev and further elaborated by Zhak Natan, Hristo Hristov, and some Russian authors.[36] Thus Hristo Hristov (eventually awarded the highest title of "academician") depicted the development schematically as a transition from a "natural" type economy through "simple commodity" to "capitalist commodity" production, in which the *chifliks* are the intermediary phase. One work by the Russian historian Vasilii Konobeev presents an assortment of all the dogmatic ideas from the earlier period: natural type economy during "classic" Ottoman feudalism; the creation of *chifliks* on a mass scale at the end of the eighteenth and beginning of the nineteenth centuries; a general transition from the "feudal" *sipahi* fief to *chifliks* and a concomitant loss of land for the majority of the (Bulgarian) peasants; peasant struggles for land and freehold peasant property, etc.[37]

Accounts of the processes in agriculture became more adequate and realistic in the course of time. The scheme was subjected to criticism (Hristo

Gandev in 1954, Strashimir Dimitrov and Dimitŭr Kosev in 1954, Nikolai Todorov in 1961, etc.) as regards both the scope and the significance of the *chifliks* and the thesis of the loss of land by the peasants.[38] Research showed that the *chifliks* had a rather limited extent (in certain regions and ca. 10% of the land), that they were rather "mixed" phenomena, and that the trend (asserted by the Ottoman land reform in the 1830s) pointed toward free peasant smallholder property.

A detailed empirical and analytical study by Gandev of the *chiflik* estates in northwestern Bulgaria provides a good example of this type of work. A complex and nuanced picture is created based on the available documents. It begins with a consideration of the ways and methods of establishing *chifliks*, which were various but rarely encroached upon *sipahi* lands (contrary to the thesis of a general transition from *sipahi* fief to *chiflik*). Gandev further discusses the type of ownership of the land—in practice private, essentially like "bourgeois" land property; then the working of the land—characterized as capitalist, with extensive use of wage labor; the marketing of the produce—commodified and market-oriented (traded on the markets of the towns on the Danube). The author differentiates the *chifliks* with which he is dealing from other types of private estate such as the *gospodarlŭk*, which were cultivated in a "feudal" manner, that is, divided into parts and rented to sharecroppers. He also looks for parallels elsewhere (in Serbia, around the town of Russe, and around Sofia), but does not find *chifliks* of the same type and scope there. The implicit inference is that the specific conditions of the weakening of central control in the northwestern Bulgarian lands during the eighteenth century (under the local governor Osman Pazvantooglu), as well as the opportunity for marketing the produce in the Danube ports, encouraged the creation of *chifliks* there (rather than circumstances of a more general scope or some historical "regularity").

Gandev reveals the *chifliks* as an economically dual phenomenon. While the Ottoman treasury remained supreme owner of the land and took from the owner of the *chiflik* a "feudal rent" in money or in kind, there was in practice "bourgeois" private property "from below," a capitalist mode of production, and a capitalist rent. Such a duality is interpreted by the author as an expression of the growth of capitalist relations within the bosom of the "feudal order." It is to be noted that even general and imprecise notions such as Ottoman "feudalism" become less misleading, and even useful, when employed in empirical descriptions and specified in such a way.[39]

The contribution of the historian Strashimir Dimitrov in clarifying agrarian relations and the *chifliks* in particular deserves a mention. He demonstrated their limited scope and extent (284 *chifliks* in the Bulgarian lands on the eve of the liberation) and described some ways of creating *chifliks* (by the seizure of land for debts, the occupation of state and communal lands, or of waste lands, etc.), and their mixed (semi-capitalist, semi-serfdom) character. In discussing the use of labor force and methods of cultivation the author distinguishes "progressive" elements (wage labor) from "intermediate" semi-capitalist elements (sharecropping in the form of renting land additional to one's own–*ispolitsa*) and "regressive" elements (sharecropping combined with corvée–*kesim*, a remnant of "serfdom"). He also differentiates between types of *chiflik* depending on the labor used, and points out that the regressive types were restricted to poor mountainous places (especially in the Kyustendil region), while the more progressive types in the plains were growing in number. This, according to him, proves that feudal-serfdom relations were being pushed out of the *chiflik* economy, which was developing along a capitalist path.[40]

The question then arises as to whether the destruction of such capitalist *chifliks* after the liberation can be considered "progressive," as required by the thesis that presents the liberation as a revolutionary agrarian overturn (which did away with feudal relations). To preserve this thesis, Strashimir Dimitrov feels obliged to note, not quite convincingly, that the most backward *chifliks* and the generally slow and painful (in Lenin's terminology–"Prussian") way of development of capitalism in agriculture were destroyed so as to clear the way for a faster capitalist development.[41] He chooses an appropriate place to stop, because the subsequent strengthening of the smallholder and largely self-subsistent peasant economy actually refutes him.

With post-Communist revisionist ardor, the historian Konstantin Kosev recently made the *chifliks* go all the way to capitalism by defining them as "structures of a farm type," that is, as modern capitalist enterprises.[42] This, of course, makes a bourgeois revolution in agriculture unnecessary, but the implication is not spelled out by the author.

As we have seen, the notion of capitalism is central to the economic history of the Revival as written by Marxist historians (though not for the earlier "bourgeois" economists). Various economic forms are screened for capitalist elements (and for the residue of "feudal" elements). This is so because capitalism is conceived of not just as a certain way of organizing production and exchange, but as a higher social formation, a higher rung in the progress of society.

Some foreign economic historians of the Balkans (John Lampe, and recently Michael Palairet) avoid the term "capitalism" and prefer to describe the Bulgarian economy of the late Revival period in terms of the theory of proto-industrial development (as evolved by Franklin Mendels, Sidney Pollard, and others). From this point of view, the proto-industries present a critical step toward modern factory production, though they do not necessarily lead to it. For proto-industries to develop and to become eventually a point of departure toward real machine and factory industrialization, the following are required: traditionally organized but market-oriented cottage industries; traders–entrepreneurs as organizers of production; regional specialization and work for external–regional or distant–markets; the parallel development of (and symbiosis with) commercialized, market-oriented agriculture in the same region; fast population growth, etc. This was the case with the specialized craft-shop industries that developed in the purely Bulgarian upland towns, oriented toward distant markets. In his empirically well-substantiated work, Palairet in particular traces the beginnings of the mechanized factory production of woollen textiles to the 1870s and rejects the common idea of a decline in Bulgarian proto-industries after the Crimean War (1853–1856).[43] According to this boldly revisionist author, it was actually after the liberation that a "de-industrialization" and dispersal of a large part of the Bulgarian proto-industries occurred (accompanied by "regression" to peasant smallholder agriculture and largely subsistent farming), though not without leaving a residue of factory production.[44]

The theory of proto-industrialization was recently introduced in Bulgarian historical scholarship by Svetla Yaneva, together with an attempt to apply it to some industries during the Revival. The author reviews a number of Bulgarian studies on craft and domestic industries (many of them by older "bourgeois" authors), which keep close to the realities on the ground, and, in fact, contain many of the elements and intuitions of the proto-industrial theory. Interesting in the present context is the implicit criticism by the author of the idea of the inevitability of capitalist development, in tune with the proto-industrial theory as well as the explicit critique of the Marxist interpretation in terms of a (grand and overall) transition from feudalism to capitalism. The conclusion of the author (more optimistic than Palairet) is that though the long-term prospects of these industries varied, they "prepared in a number of important aspects the further industrial development."[45]

All in all, the proto-industrialization theory seems to offer an alternative to the Marxist theory of a global transition from feudalism to capitalism by remaining truer to the "micro-economy" of regions and industries and by taking reversals in the development into consideration. But it should not be regarded as altogether new for Bulgarian economic scholarship, as demonstrated by a number of earlier empirical studies on cottage (domestic) industries and the putting-out system, some of which were published in the authoritative pre-1944 *Journal of the Bulgarian Economic Society*. While capitalism is rarely mentioned here, there are excellent descriptions of the local organization of manufacturing and of its financing and marketing.

Ottoman Feudalism

Ottoman feudalism as the point of departure in the development scheme is also of interest, and all the more so as it has rarely been discussed in Bulgarian historical scholarship on the Revival, except by a few Ottomanist scholars. The Ottoman Empire is commonly described as "feudal" (or "feudal-despotic"), and its evolution as a transition from military feudalism to a feudal-bureaucratic (or "feudal-administrative") order after the abolition of the *sipahi* fiefs (1832–1834).[46] The view of the well-known Turkish Ottomanists Omer Barkan and Halil Inalchik, that the centralized military-fief (*timar*) system of the early period was not feudal in itself but underwent feudalization in times of the weakening of the central authority[47] (and especially during the seventeenth and eighteenth centuries), is disregarded or rejected outright.[48] The oscillation between centralism and feudalism is simply incompatible with a scheme of development that starts with feudalism and allows for one transition only.

The development of Bulgarian Ottomanist scholarship through the efforts of Vera Mutafchieva, Strashimir Dimitrov, Bistra Tsvetkova, Nikolai Todorov, etc., led to a number of corrections in the initial schematization. The defining features of the Ottoman "feudal" empire and its major early feudal institution—the conditional (in return for a service) and revocable *timar* and its *sipahi* (military) holders—became better known. This was helped by the Marxist discussion of the "Asiatic" mode of production and of the Eastern type of feudalism, which also made its mark on Bulgarian historical scholarship.[49] The standard description runs as follows.

The Ottoman Empire of the "classic" fifteenth and sixteenth centuries is defined as feudalism of an Eastern (or Asiatic) type, characterized by a strong central authority uniting the temporal with the religious principle and variously designated as "despotic absolutism" or "military–feudal theocracy." Strong central authority was associated with supreme owner-ship over the principal "means of production"–the land. Two major forms of feudal land ownership stand out–the conditional service fief or *timar* (mostly military, granted to *sipahi* cavalrymen) and the *mülk*, or uncondi-tional land grant. Another division according to owner differentiates be-tween the *sipahi timar* holders, the *vakfs* of religious institutions, and the *has* estates of the sultan and other magnates. The conditional fief did not include the kind of administrative and legal immunities that form the basis of Western feudalism (and that resulted in the far-reaching autonomy of the feudal lords, and in decentralization). What was granted was not actu-ally the land but the right to derive income from it by collecting certain taxes–an arrangement that approximates to a stipend, or even a servant's salary. Though the "serfdom" of the non-Muslim peasants existed legally in the Ottoman Empire during a certain period, it was not energetically im-plemented. Moreover, the peasant was bound to the land (not to a person) and there existed the possibility for the peasant to sell the land and buy the right to move elsewhere.[50]

The central Marxist category used in approaching feudalism, and Otto-man feudalism in particular, is the land rent and its appropriation, in so far as the land was the main means of production and source of wealth under feudalism. However, this implies a certain underestimation of the developed urban life and money economy of the Ottoman Empire, in con-trast to the early Western "natural" type feudal economy, from which the model is derived. The "specificity" of the Eastern empires in this respect is accommodated by citing Marx, that where the supreme ownership of the land belongs to the central authority and there is no private property (in Asia), land rent and taxes coincide.[51] The Eastern type of feudalism, and the Ottoman type in particular, are thus based on a "centralized feudal rent," divided between the central authority and the fief holders. A perma-nent struggle was waged between the central authority and the Ottoman feudal aristocracy, which aspired to convert the conditional military *timar* fief (or feudal stipend) into an outright (unconditional) feudal land estate.[52]

The evolution of the Ottoman Empire was long concealed behind a rather static historiographical picture. What was generally assumed was a long period of decay of the *sipahi* system from the end of the sixteenth century under the impact of commercial capital and usury, ending with its abolition in 1832.[53] The subsequent development of Bulgarian Ottomanist scholarship dynamized the picture by revealing various changes and new practices, although this found its way with difficulty into the writings on the Revival. The existence, even in earlier centuries, of a relatively free exchange of land of all kinds (*timars, vakf*, etc.), and the tendency—sometimes reversed—for it to pass into private ownership, were revealed. The existence of a well-developed urban life and money economy in the initial centuries of Ottoman rule was attested, and, in connection with this, the enormous significance of the institution of the *vakf* as the greatest owner of urban real estate, rented and exploited in various ways. Of particular consequence was the practice of leasing state revenues to private tax farmers (*mukataa, iltizam*) for a longer term, and even for life. This enhanced the power of commercial–usurious capital and its owners, and led to political corruption, the undermining of the central administration, an increased burden on and oppression of the taxable population, opportunities for the accumulation of land into private property, etc. Finally, the possibility of acquiring land through illegal deals with *vakf* property, the seizure of land for debts, the leasing of taxes, etc., led to the formation of a landed aristocracy (*ayans*) in the provinces, which assumed control of the local administration. Its increased autonomy—to the extent of maintaining private armies—resulted in decentralization and the anarchy of the last quarter of the eighteenth century (the "times of the *kŭrdzhalii*").[54]

While the last-mentioned phenomenon can be interpreted as "feudalization" in progress, Vera Mutafchieva was the only one among the Bulgarian authors occasionally to use the term in a contraband manner.[55] Bulgarian historical scholarship as a whole avoided it, preferring to speak of the "decay" of the initial military feudalism, of "decentralization," "troubles," etc. One may speculate as to why, given the need of the Marxist scholarship of the Revival for feudalism. My guess is that an alternation between centralization and feudalization is clearly discordant with the concept of linear progressive development (and there had already been "mature" feudalism in the medieval Bulgarian kingdom). Besides, the idea of an advancing feudalization at such a late date sounds like insulting retardation in comparison with Western Europe (like the "second serfdom" in other parts of Eastern Europe).

Among Bulgarian historians, Vera Mutafchieva went furthest in the revision of the older views on the Ottoman Empire in her detailed studies and analytical discussions, even during the Communist period, followed by the massive problematization of Ottomanist historiography after Communism. She recently criticized the usual periodization of Ottoman history, which presents the military-fief system of the fifteenth and sixteenth centuries as "classic feudalism," followed by a long period of the "decay" or disintegration of the system, in which the new moments are insipidly defined as "changes." As the author indicates, the real "classic" ("high," "mature") Ottoman feudalism was formed during the seventeenth and eighteenth centuries with the spread of unconditional (non-service) land ownership in new forms connected with the leasing out of taxes and the increased power of the landowning and money aristocracy that culminated in decentralization and feudal anarchy in the last quarter of the eighteenth century. Vera Mutafchieva again challenged the notion of strict and consistent centralization and extreme "etatism" of the Ottoman Empire as based primarily on legal regulations but divergent from the realities of a strongly developed "private sector" (trade, tax farming, *vakf* urban real estate, considerable de facto exchange of land). She particularly scorns the presentation of the impoverished *sipahi* (military fief holders) of later times as the major feudal exploiter and indicates that the feudal lords proper were big feudal landowners, tax farmers, higher officials, etc. Finally, she insists on representing Ottoman (and other Eastern) types of feudalism not as "specific forms" or "deviations" in comparison with the Western type, which is taken as a model, but as equivalent forms in their own right.[56]

To summarize, the representation of the Ottoman Empire in Bulgarian historical scholarship has been heavily and disproportionately characterized by military-fief feudalism and its decay, which was supposed to have lasted much longer than its heyday. What is absent are more complex ideal-type models to account for the coexistence and mutual articulation of various arrangements in a number of domains—for example, conditional *sipahi* feudalism (a kind of prebendalism), sultan patrimonialism, theocracy, centralized bureaucracy, provincial administration, religious communities, etc. Some of these, indeed, are mentioned, but hardly as semi-autonomous institutions that interlace in various ways, and always under the label "feudalism," which renders them a "feudal" quality. The definition of the land regime as "feudal" when so many varieties of ownership and use were available can be especially misleading.

The attempts to reform the Ottoman Empire undertaken by Mahmud II after 1926 (when he eliminated the janissaries) and by his successor Abdul Mecid during the so-called *Tanzimat* era (which began with the *Hatt-i Sherif* of 1839) presented Bulgarian historical scholarship on the Revival with special problems. A major problem was the agrarian reform in the 1830s and 1840s, which revoked the *sipahi* fiefs, that is, what was considered as the basic feudal institution, and left the land in the possession of the peasants.[57] To put it bluntly: Was the Ottoman Empire departing from feudalism, and if so, where to? The preconceived answer of the Marxist authors was "no" (or else no bourgeois revolution, closely tied to the liberation, would have been necessary). But one had to show how feudalism persisted.

A naive attempt to argue for the preservation of feudalism until the very end of the Ottoman domination attaches to the character of property. While most authors recognized the full "bourgeois" (i.e., private property) status of the *chifliks*[58] and of the basically free peasant holdings, more dogmatic authors resisted. The a priorism of reasoning is revealed with rare frankness in a passage by Hristo Hristov, who argues his refusal to acknowledge the "bourgeois" (i.e., private property) status of the land in the second half of the nineteenth century (or even its "gradually becoming bourgeois") in the following manner:

"The legal sanctioning of bourgeois land property as an element of the superstructure over the capitalist basis occurs only after the destruction of the old feudal basis and the establishment of capitalism as a dominant formation after the liberation. This should be kept in mind if we do not want to empty of content the bourgeois–democratic revolution maturing in the Bulgarian lands at the end of the eighteenth and in the nineteenth centuries, as a revolution caused by the contradiction between the evolving new forces of production and the old conditions of production, sanctioned by the Turkish feudal public law norms."[59]

In other words, if the liberation has to have its (postulated) meaning as a bourgeois revolution and as the clearing of the way for capitalism, the socioeconomic "order" until that moment should have been feudal, the nature of land ownership included. It follows that the agrarian reform could not have abolished feudalism.

However, all attempts to specify agrarian feudalism failed in the face of evidence to the contrary—basically free *raeti* peasants, firm peasant ownership of the land, the small number of *chifliks*, etc.—the more one approaches the liberation. The normalization of views on the agrarian evolution had already been discussed. To this one should now add the treatment of the agrarian reform. Its meaning was clarified as early as 1954 by Hristo Gandev in a rather indirect way (as "Turkish sources on Bulgarian agrarian history"). As pointed out by the author, the reform basically consisted in ascribing the land to the peasants who worked it. They had to pay directly to the treasury the taxes previously paid to the *sipahi*, who were compensated with yearly money pensions (paid by the state). Thus the goal of the agrarian reform was to create peasant tax payers with land of their own (not to expropriate them). It also legalized the *chifliks* as full private property, but this could lead to competing claims on the land. It was precisely because the reform was not applied initially in northwestern Bulgaria, where local magnates managed to appropriate peasant lands and force the peasants to work for them as wage laborers and sharecroppers, that the peasants rose in revolt in 1850. This prompted the Turkish government to intervene in their favor by taking most of the lands from the *agas* and giving them to the peasants.[60] As a result of the agrarian reform, the free peasant (*raeti*) ownership of land became the norm (legally as well) on the eve of the liberation.

All this became more or less accepted in Bulgarian historiography, or at least the insistence on the expropriation of peasant lands by Turkish *chiflik* owners and peasant "serfdom" was dropped. But if feudalism is not about property relations, and still less about "serfdom" (the tying of the peasants to the land), then what is it about? (The corvée in some *chifliks* as just a feudal "remnant" was not felt as a sufficient explanation.)

To provide an answer, Eastern-type feudalism, with its strong centralization, is once again evoked. The abolition of the *sipahi* fief system then looks not like the abolition of feudalism but as its centralization by means of centralizing the whole feudal rent after "retiring" the former *sipahi* fief holders (who were compensated with state pensions or positions). The state is now portrayed as a peculiar "supreme collective feudal lord" (a "collective *sipahi*," according to one author), who replaced the individual feudal lords and held all peasants (and the urban population) in "feudal subordination," expressed in the collection of "centralized feudal rent" (in fact, state taxes) in the interest of the "feudal class" as a whole, to be distributed among it. This notion (or fiction) made it possible for historians to continue describing the situation of the peasants as "feudal" oppression—as if this adds something specifically onerous to the nature of the exploitation.[61]

While this is a rather artificial construction—a centralized monarchy with state taxation does not have to be "feudal" (as the contemporary Russian and Habsburg Empires were not)—its persistence derives from the Marxist transition scheme, which is also a scheme of "progress," but also from nationalist needs. With its negative value loading and the implication of backwardness, "feudalism" participates emotionally in the description/evaluation of Ottoman domination. Avoiding this rather unfortunate term does not in itself imply the exoneration (or idealization) of Ottoman rule—it may have been bad enough without being feudal[62]—but the end of the career of the concept is not in sight, due to its already automatic connotations. Admittedly, the distortion in representing the decades prior to Bulgarian independence is partly offset by good descriptions of the state of affairs. And the term "feudal" acquires more of a figurative and diffuse meaning.

The Ottoman reforms are taken more seriously in a work by Georgi Pletnyov on the prominent Ottoman reformer Midhat pasha and his modernizing activities as governor of Tuna *vilayet* (i.e., northern Bulgaria) between 1864 and 1868. Midhat was also an energetic promoter of the "Ottomanization," that is, homogenization, of the subject populations under common Ottoman "citizenship" as a way of rescuing the empire, hence the resistance to his policies on the part of the Bulgarian national movement (severely suppressed by him). Without necessarily sympathizing with the Ottomanizing efforts of Midhat, and holding back his national feelings, the author pays tribute to the Turkish statist point of view, in contrast to almost all preceding Bulgarian historical scholarship.[63]

Regarding the *Tanzimat* reforms in general, it is interesting to note that they have been criticized by most Bulgarian historians as half-way, incomplete, undertaken under foreign pressure, etc. While this is certainly true, such criticism on the part of national(ist) historians is hardly sincere, because implementing the reforms successfully would have meant the preservation of the Ottoman Empire and the suppression of the national movement.

The Social (Bourgeois) Revolution
and the Agrarian Thesis

The economic interpretation of the Bulgarian Revival as a transition from feudalism to capitalism is closely connected with the concept of social revolution, a bourgeois one in particular, as a driving force of this transition. In fact, the Marxist meaning of social revolution is superimposed upon the national meaning of liberation through revolt against the Turks ("revolution"), which the revolutionaries of the Revival planned and wrote about. The revolution is thus both national and social. Moreover, the social element is given precedence over the national element through the formula "national in form, social in content." Since, in this dichotomy, the "content" is more important than the "form," the national struggles appear to cloak the class struggle. But they actually coincide, in so far as the social enemy is the national enemy (the Turks are the ruling class).

Georgi Bakalov was the first to put forward such an interpretation in the 1930s: "The class struggle, which had to cope with the foreign yoke, could not but assume a national color, the form of a people's struggle."[64] The revolutionary movement of the peasants in particular assumed the form of a national movement, the landowners being of foreign origin.[65] Zhak Natan followed suit in presenting the revolution as both social and national, with the same underestimation of the national at the expense of the social aspect:

"Feudalism in Bulgaria in this epoch was intertwined with the national yoke of the Bulgarian people. The people was under a double yoke—national and social. That is why the struggle assumed in that period a national form while it was social in its content. The carrying out of the bourgeois–democratic overturn meant, at the same time, a national liberation of the country. This could only be accomplished by way of a mass people's revolution, which had to lead to a radical transformation without compromises, to the elimination of all remnants of feudalism, and to the opening up of the way for a painless and free development of the commodity economy and of capitalism."[66]

The revolution, thus conceptualized, casts its shadow far behind, beyond the political struggles of the last decades prior to the liberation over earlier times, and even over the entire epoch. The Revival is then retrospectively conceived as an epoch that has "tasks" to accomplish, which seem posed from the very beginning, and it becomes the epoch of the bourgeois–democratic revolution. The epoch adopts its revolution as it gradually "matures" for it, and, vice versa, the revolution illuminates the epoch, which becomes "revolutionary" throughout.[67] Thinking of the development according to an a priori scheme acts, in this case, retrospectively, imposing upon the past the meaning of its future. The past peeps into the future and sees through it, because the Marxist author knows exactly where things are going even before the trend has manifested itself, and before the historical agents have grasped it. Here is an example of this kind of thinking: "Bulgaria in Botev's times was on the eve of the bourgeois–democratic revolution. A grand democratic transformation of the country was imminent."[68]

In the same vein, the aspiration to new, capitalist relations in production is ascribed to the peasants by the ideologue–philosopher Todor Pavlov:

"...from an objectively historical point of view, our peasants fought not only for land, in so far as it was still, to a great extent, in the hands of the feudal lords and the semi-feudal lords, but for the kind of development of the rural economy and of the economy as a whole that would eliminate all shackles and obstacles and open up opportunities for a full and unobstructed unfolding of the new production and exchange relations..."[69]

Independent of the truth of the assertion (the peasants were not fighting for land and were, in fact, least active), what is interesting here is how the author attempts to close the gap between the subjective intentions of the historical actors and an "objective–historical" tendency (the replacement of feudalism with capitalism) known to him, but somehow ascribed to the peasants as well.

The concept of "bourgeois revolution" encounters the problem of underdeveloped capitalism, as attested by the desperate effort of Konstantin Kosev to come to grips with it. The author acknowledges the rather low development of capitalist relations in the 1860s and 1870s, somewhat higher in the urban economy than in the agrarian economy. He then asks how we can judge the degree of development of bourgeois relations—and comes up with the following criterion. If the epoch of the bourgeois revolution finally arrives, this clearly indicates a high degree of development of capitalist relations, because it is they that create the objective material preconditions for a bourgeois revolution (or a "revolutionary rising"). Thus the April uprising of 1876, conceived of as the Bulgarian bourgeois revolution, becomes a proof of a sufficiently high level of development of capitalist relations. On the other hand, the fact that the Bulgarian national revolution could not succeed at that time only shows that bourgeois–capitalist relations were still at a lower stage (that of the putting-out system).[70] At work here is a logical inversion and circularity: the bourgeois revolution should be explained by capitalism (itself independently attested), but instead the bourgeois revolution itself becomes the proof of capitalism. (The bourgeois revolution is taken for granted here). The empirical material that may provide independent proof of capitalism is disregarded precisely because it does not provide a strong confirmation.[71]

It should be noted that the absence of advanced capitalism is a problem mainly for adherents to the thesis of the bourgeois revolution, which requires it. It is not an obstacle to the explanation of the national struggles themselves, because the cultural and political "renaissance" may well be supported on a proto-industrial economic "basis." The means that are absolutely necessary to finance the national processes come in this case—as they did in reality—from the more traditional crafts, trade, decentralized forms of capitalist enterprise, and pre-modern forms of capitalism (usury, tax farming, state deliveries for the Ottoman court and army). A considerable economic upsurge, such as the one that occurred after the 1820s, is, of course, a necessary precondition, but not necessarily on a modern capitalist basis.

Moreover, a certain peaceful "bourgeois transformation" of society, in the sense of the development of an urban "bourgeois" class (burghers, urbanites), may take place on such an economic basis. It need not present the grand and violent type of "bourgeois revolution" and bourgeois takeover of power imaged by Marxist historians on the model of the French Revolution (in its Marxist interpretation). Finally, the fact that the national struggles are hardly the exemplary "bourgeois revolution" does not preclude the "bourgeoisie" (artisans, shopkeepers, traders, etc.) taking part in the national struggles personally, or "represented" by its younger male generation (in addition to financing them). Together with the disgruntled intelligentsia (mostly of bourgeois descent), the "bourgeoisie" was actually the most active element in the Bulgarian national efforts.

A major problem for the thesis of a "bourgeois revolution" based on capitalist development is not only the absence of advanced capitalism during the Bulgarian Revival but the absence of development (and even the economic regression) long after independence, whereas the revolution was supposed to open space for it in both industry and agriculture. But this is usually disregarded by the historians of the Revival, who conveniently stop at the liberation. (Even those who work on the post-liberation period usually start "anew," that is, without the ideas and schemes that prop the previous period.) One may find some awareness of the problem in a work on "primitive accumulation" by Zhak Natan, who acknowledges that the process of accumulation was interrupted for a time after the liberation by the agrarian revolution (which had to accelerate it!) and that it was only at the end of the nineteenth century that "all necessary preconditions for the complete victory of the new capitalist relations of production were created."[72]

One can mention in this context the revisionist work of the British economic historian Michael Palairet, who argues (on the basis of extensive data) that a long phase of economic decline and stagnation set in after the liberation both in the urban economy, in retreat from the proto-industrial capacity it had reached, and in agriculture, with its conversion to a largely self-sufficient economy of peasant smallholders ("Serbianization").[73] This refutes the thesis of the "bourgeois revolution" (and a capitalist "agrarian overturn"), unless one tries to rescue it by artificial means, such as assuming another long period necessary to "create preconditions." It shows that political independence by itself does not necessarily guarantee economic progress on a capitalist basis. There were a number of particular causes for that in the Bulgarian case: a narrowed market, political turbulence, uncouth government, external intervention, etc.

The absence of strong capitalist development during the Revival (and after it) is a problem not only for the concept of a "bourgeois revolution." It is also a problem for theories of the formation of the nation based on the West European experience, which connect the nation with industrialization and bourgeois transformation. In the Balkans this was hardly the case. This has been pointed out by Gale Stokes, according to whom the formation of the nations in the Balkans, in contrast to Western Europe, remained a primarily political and ideological process, not accompanied by a massive qualitative economic transition and a corresponding social (bourgeois, urban) transformation. The Balkan experience thus attests that nation and capitalism may have a separate genesis and follow a different course.[74]

In a timid way, this has been recognized by some Bulgarian historians as well. Thus Krŭstyu Manchev and Strashimir Dimitrov affirmed that the "cultural–regenerative" processes during the Balkan revival went ahead of the degree of development of capitalist relations (except in commerce). They formulated this assertion in an acceptable form by referring to statements by Marx and Engels about the "relative autonomy" of ideas, which in this case were transferred from a more developed Western social-economic milieu to a less developed Balkan society.[75]

A special piont of the Marxist (in this case Leninist) socioeconomic interpretation of the Bulgarian Revival, and one of the first to be discarded later, is the so-called agrarian thesis (and the associated idea of a "peasant revolution"). It states that the "agrarian question" (in various versions: the "loss of land" by the peasants, "hunger for land," "serfdom," or "feudal exploitation") was the basic social question during the Revival, which had to be solved by the revolution; furthermore, the peasants are described as the main driving force of that revolution. (Hence the meaning of the Russo-Turkish liberation war as, among other things, an "agrarian overturn.")

The search for the source of the agrarian thesis and the peasant revolution leads to the Communist intellectual Georgi Bakalov, after his return from Soviet Russia in the 1930s. Adapted in this thesis are Lenin's views on the Russian revolution of 1905 as a radical peasant revolution for the liquidation of the estates of the big landowners and the remnants of feudalism, and, for that reason, a "bourgeois revolution" in its goals.[76] Along similar lines, Bakalov declared the main task of the Bulgarian revolution to be "the revolutionary solution of the agrarian question, the revolt of the Bulgarian peasant masses in order to sweep away all remnants of the pre-capitalist, semi-feudal, serf-like forms of oppression and exploitation [...] It required a democratic revolution to sweep away the landowner-*beys* and to give all land into the hands of the small peasant producers, and, together with this, state power into the hands of an independent Bulgaria."[77]

Another committed adherent of the "agrarian thesis" was Zhak Natan. He also wrote about peasant serfs; large-scale transition to *chifliks*, which was accompanied by a loss of land by the peasants and "land hunger"; the turning of the peasants into agrarian wage laborers—and all this being compounded into an agrarian question, hence imparting an agrarian quality to the revolution.[78]

The agrarian/peasant thesis was ideologically imposed upon Bulgarian historical scholarship by Vŭlko Chervenkov (as head of the party and of the state) in his notorious speech of 1953 on the eightieth anniversary of the death of Vasil Levski. He postulated that the Bulgarian national revolutionary movement (and bourgeois–democratic revolution) was a peasant movement for a "merciless people's doing away with Turkish feudalism and its supporters," and for a "people's (plebeian) eradication of the ways of feudal serfdom." The leaders and ideologues of this movement are accordingly defined as "peasant revolutionaries."[79] This is reiterated in variations by Zhak Natan, Todor Pavlov, and others.

The unfortunate thesis was overcome gradually in the post-Stalinist years, or simply ignored by a number of authors. It was supported in a diluted way until very late by the historian Hristo Hristov, who had made his career on it. When writing the introduction to a volume of some of his works (mostly from the 1960s) in 1975, he still defined the agrarian question as a "basic question" of the Bulgarian national revolution, one that stands at the roots of the national liberation struggles. The peasants in their fight for land are the mass (and main) driving force of the national revolution (even though, as the author concedes, this does not turn it into a "peasant revolution").[80] A reverberation of this notion is to be found in the last word of Bulgarian official historical scholarship—the multivolume *History of Bulgaria*, in the chapter on the April uprising written by Yono Mitev (with a reference to Hristo Hristov).[81]

Linked to the agrarian thesis is the formula that the Bulgarian liberation presented, among other things, an "agrarian overturn." In fact, the occupation of the Turkish lands by Bulgarian peasants after the liberation can hardly be called thus if what is meant is economic progress and an impetus towards capitalist development. Instead, it led to the fragmentation of the land, and to the "naturalization" of the economy and its orientation primarily to self-subsistence. This actually represents a regression not only from the commercialized *chifliks* but also from the increasingly market-oriented agriculture of free smallholder peasants.[82] Desirable as it might appear from a national (or social) point of view, the agrarian overthrow upon independence may better be designated from an economic point of view as regression (in revolutionary terminology more of a "counter-revolution").

One may more properly understand by "agrarian overturn" the agrarian reforms in the Turkish empire (the revocation of the *sipahi* fiefs in the 1830s and 1840s), which led to the prevalence of the practically free small-holder agriculture of peasants taxed directly by the treasury. But this is not what the Bulgarian historians mentioned so far have in mind.

The Economic
and the National–Spiritual Interpretation

In contrast with the close relationship between the spiritual–cultural and the national meanings of the Bulgarian Revival, the national and the economic (plus social) meanings have been clearly distinguished and at times deliberately opposed, being turned into stakes in symbolic fights.[83] We have already discussed the placing of the economic process in the foreground and the imposition of the social (class) meaning, whose precedence over the national one was expressed in "substance-form" terms. The way was shown by Georgi Bakalov in the 1930s and it came to dominate the field completely during the initial Stalinist period after the Communist takeover. It should be noted that the reordering was accompanied by historico-philosophical and methodological attacks on the older authors under the sign of Marxism. These deserve some attention, the more so as they reveal the ideological climate of the times.

The precedence of the economic–social over the spiritual–national interpretation of the Revival is derived from the priority of "material" over "spiritual" factors in history in general, asserted by historical materialism. According to Dimitŭr Kosev, the Bulgarian Revival in the materialist understanding presents a stage in the "law-guided development" of Bulgarian society and it is closely linked to the development of the material forces.

The bourgeois "idealist" historians are charged with negating this historical regularity when regarding the Revival as a result of the awakening of
the spiritual forces of the Bulgarian people, for example, when they explain
it with reference to the ardent national call of Paisii.[84] (A partial exception
is made for Ivan Shishmanov, who recognized the significance of the economic factor.) "Historico-philosophical" battles of this sort were often
fought in the introductions of Marxist authors to books of older "bourgeois" scholars (which did not prevent borrowing widely from them).[85]

Where necessary, the Marxist polemicist could evoke a "dialectic" between material and ideal factors (with the retroactive action of the latter
upon the former)[86], between objective tendency and human agency, the
individual and the people (masses, society, "collective")[87], internal and
external factors, etc. to prove whatever needed. An example is provided by
Zhak Natan, who affirms that the revolutionaries were "expressive of the
needs of their time" and "only the product of certain ripe social relations
in the country," while attaching great importance to them as "accelerators
of the process of the uplifting of the Bulgarian people."[88]

The confrontation takes place at the level of methodologies as well. The
earlier "bourgeois" historians, who saw the Bulgarian Revival as a primarily spiritual and/or national process, typically speak of "preconditions"
and "factors" for it, in which the preconditions are something like favorable circumstances or contexts while the factors are more active forces.
Ivan Shishmanov, for example, pointed out the following "preconditions"
of the Revival: the uniting of the Bulgarian people under pax Ottomana,
which put an end to the old feudal anarchy and disunity; the privileges
accorded to particular categories of the subjugated populations (e.g., to
those who guarded mountain passes); the Catholicism of the seventeenth
century; the orientation of the hopes for liberation toward Russia; and the
troubles in Turkey at the end of the nineteenth century, with the unintended consequence of strengthening the Bulgarian element in the highland towns (fleeing from the villages in the plains). As "factors" of the Revival he enumerates the role of great personalities (beginning with Paisii),
of the monasteries and religion, of the economic upsurge and the formation of a well-to-do urban class, the reforms in the Ottoman Empire, and
foreign influences.[89]

In the same vein, Nikola Milev listed a number of favorable circumstances for the Bulgarians that include most of what was put forward by
Ivan Shishmanov, plus the religious tolerance of the Ottomans (in which
religious difference helped preserve the identity of the Christians) and a

considerable local (communal) self-government.[90] The already known repertoire of "factors" of the Bulgarian Revival features in Boyan Penev's treatment of the new Bulgarian literature (he supplemented it with the new secular type of education and the role of the printing press)[91], and also in a work by Ivan Ormandzhiev.[92] Hristo Gandev called an earlier book of his "Factors of the Bulgarian Revival."

One may note a relationship between conceiving of the Revival as a spiritual–cultural phenomenon and explaining it by background economic, social, political, international, etc. "preconditions" or "factors" (but also by cultural influences of the same magnitude). The language of "factors" presupposes the working of an external impulse upon what is being explained. It also implies that once launched, the spiritual or national processes automatically go further.

The post-1944 Marxist authors launched, in their turn, the language of the "laws" and "objective regularities" of the historical development in explaining the Revival. Thus Zhak Natan (who had earlier spoken in terms of "factors") recommends to younger Marxist authors that they reveal the "laws, which drive the epoch," the "laws of the development," "the actual springs of our social development," in which the material conditions of production are the "main lever" or "main spring" of the Revival.[93]

One may note again a certain "kinship" between the economic–social interpretation of the Revival and the language of "objective regularities." It is because the economic processes are thought of as most fundamental and self-propelled that the Revival regarded as in a way "self-sufficient" and "self-driven" (not in need of external impetus). Such a concept of the course of history as a quasi-automatic working of a "law" leaves little room for human agency. This, however, proves to be especially problematic for the Revival epoch, unthinkable without its heroes, who were also needed by the Communist regime for legitimating purposes. It is not accidental that the strong (quasi-natural) language of "laws" was first diluted to "objective regularities" and later abandoned in favor of "processes." Another device for introducing flexibility is to speak of "specifics" (or peculiarities) in accounting for regional divergence in historical development from supposedly universal regularities—for example, the peculiarities of (Ottoman, Eastern) feudalism, of the transition from feudalism to capitalism, of the formation of the nation, etc. This is typically preceded by the stipulation that otherwise, and in general, the development follows the "common pattern" and its regularities.

Subsequent historians prefer to describe the Bulgarian Revival in terms of "processes," which develop in succession or in parallel, interacting and intertwining. The three major revival processes were the spread of modern Bulgarian education (preceded by cultural activities of single personalities), the unfolding of ecclesiastical struggles, and the maturing of the revolutionary movement. The processual understanding of history has its assumptions and implications, too. It privileges continuity (as opposed to breaks), unity and homogeneity (in contrast to fragmentation and the heterogeneity of events), and directional flow (instead of indefiniteness of movement). As a means of exposition (in ordering the material) it renders a smooth and rounded representation, whereas discrete actions and events appear in the historical narrative as "manifestations" of a process. The processes themselves are anonymous and unfold a "logic" or a "dynamic" (at least an "inertia") of their own, though not as inexorable as a "law" or "regularity."

Coming back to the rivalry between national and social meanings, the post-Stalinist period was marked by corrections of the dogmatic theses and bolder "revisionist" attempts. The national meaning of the Revival was gradually vindicated, while the economic–social meaning was somewhat downplayed. This led eventually to a complete reversal, and the national meaning took the foreground again. Some examples mark the step-by-step evolution from social to national, for a long time the main opponents.

At the celebration of the ninetieth anniversary of the April uprising in 1966, Dimitŭr Kosev (who had contributed greatly to the imposition of the social-class interpretation) updated the tasks of the maturing revolution in the following manner. Alongside the liquidation of the existing agrarian system ("an important, but not the only task") and the liberation of the petty bourgeois urban masses from "feudal exploitation and the despotism of the sultan," there was one general and "principal" task of the revolution—the winning of national independence and political freedom. The subordination of the social to the national is argued by the absence of a Bulgarian feudal class, hence the abolition of foreign national domination would mean doing away with the feudal system all in one. The Bulgarian revolution was thus national not only in form but also in content, and the formation of the nation and its struggles were progressive and democratic in character. The merging of the social aspect into the national revolution yields the curious combination "national-democratic." To quote Kosev: "The tasks of the revolution merged into one common national-democratic task. That is why our revolution was national-democratic in its character and essence."[94]

At the same scholarly event, Goran Todorov stated still more emphatically that rather than being only a "form" of the Revival and of the bourgeois–democratic revolution, the national question was the "core of the Revival." The social question in this period was subordinated to the national question, or, more precisely, it overlapped and coincided with it. The reason is (again) that the basic class contradiction was between the foreign feudal class (Turkish *beys* and *agas*), who used the Ottoman state as an instrument of exploitation, and the Bulgarian people as a whole, the burgeoning Bulgarian bourgeoisie included (which then had the same progressive interests and goals).[95]

For Nikolai Genchev (in 1973), "the national liberation and the bourgeois overturn are two inseparable aspects of the unitary process of the Revival, with clear dominance of the national–political process."[96] The reason given is more general—the solution of the national question would set free bourgeois and capitalist development. The same author offered (in 1978) a synthesis between the spiritual–national and social–economic interpretations of the Revival pointing to the formation of the nation. He first describes the processes of change in several domains: in the economy (commodity–money relations and the emergence of capitalism), in society (the formation of a thin bourgeois society, in which small producers predominate), in the spiritual–cultural sphere (secular education, national emancipation in the struggle against the Greek Church, the formation of the nation), and in the political sphere (struggles for political independence, inspired by the bourgeois revolutions in the West). The crowning result of the economic, social, and cultural processes is seen in the formation of the Bulgarian nation.[97]

For the historian Krumka Sharova (in 1981), the Revival means a number of things, of which the transition to capitalism (she avoids saying what from) is just one, along with the "overcoming of backwardness," the linking to the European economic system (which, in her view, was objectively progressive), the development of a new consciousness and culture, and the formation of the nation (similar to other national-liberation movements in Europe).[98] The national meaning of the Revival is heard still more emphatically from Rumyana Radkova (in 1986): "The anti-feudal struggle during the Revival merged with the national–political struggle and for that reason all ideas with a bourgeois–democratic character were subordinated to the political ideas and tasks of the Bulgarian people."[99]

The same line was continued in a purer form, that is, purified of social (class) components, after Communism. But this is so only in more nationalist writings, the more so as the revision was completed even earlier.[100] Alternatively, the Revival is described primarily, and not without connection with the liberal-democratic discourse of the post-Communist transition, in spiritual–cultural terms as a Bulgarian transition to modern times (Modernity), whether by making the favorite analogies with Western epochs or using the concept of "modernization" ("Europeanization"). The national formation then comes second or is viewed as only a part of this more comprehensive transformation.

In his "lecture course" (of 1999), Plamen Mitev endorses the view of "contemporary historical scholarship" in defining the Bulgarian Revival as an epoch of transition from the Middle Ages to Modernity (or the "bourgeois epoch"), accompanied by the genesis of modern market and social relations, and points to the considerable share in this epoch of the formation of the nation.[101]

The cultural historian Raina Gavrilova treats the Revival as a transition from "traditional society" (or "folklore culture") toward a "modern society" and Modernity, during which the Bulgarians were formed as a nation (of the ethno-cultural type) parallel with the "age of nationalism" in Europe. The author avoids both the term "Middle Ages" and capitalism, while the title of the book itself (*"The Age of the Bulgarian Spiritual Revival"*) suggests a primarily cultural understanding of the revival processes (as changes in mentality).[102] Other authors, too, prefer to speak of a primarily world-view transition from the Middle Ages to Modernity, from a traditional "community" to a modern (civic) "society," instead of a transition from feudalism to capitalism.[103]

In sum, we can see that the three interpretations of the Bulgarian Revival follow a certain pattern in time. First, the cultural–spiritual meaning of the Revival was derived by the academic authors of the "old school," mixed with not so accentuated national meaning. The economic-*cum*-social interpretation appeared very early, too, as Bulgarian socialism emerged in the 1890s. But it was still moderate and in its weak form—as a recognition of the "economic factor"—it was taken into consideration by some "bourgeois" authors. The national interpretation took the foreground and sounded sharply nationalist in the 1930s, while an equally strong social (class) interpretation was polemically opposed to it by militant leftist authors. With the victory of Communist forces, and especially under the shadow of Stalinism in the early 1950s, the priority of the economic (and class) interpretation was imposed using extra-scholarly means and by the silencing of opponents. The 1960s and 1970s were marked by corrections and "revisionist" attempts, in which the national meaning of the Revival was gradually vindicated while the economic–social meaning was downplayed. The national meaning eventually took the foreground again. Finally, the spiritual–cultural meaning made a comeback, especially after 1989. Thus, assuming that Bulgarian historical scholarship started (as to emphasis only) with the cultural interpretation of the Revival, followed by an increasing stress on the national (in competition with the socioeconomic) meaning, and then by the imposition of the socioeconomic meaning in the early Communist years, we can see the historians returning first (in the course of a "revision") to the national and finally to the spiritual–cultural interpretation, thus coming full circle.

Notes

1 For example, Ivan Shishmanov, "Paisii i negovata epokha. Misli vŭrkhu genezisa na bŭlgarskoto vŭzrazhdane." *Spisanie na BAN* 8 (1914): 1–18, esp. 15–17. Also works by economic historians such as Ivan Sakŭzov, "Razvitie na gradskiya zhivot i zanayatite v Bŭlgariya prez XVIII–XIX vek." In *Bŭlgariya 1000 godini*, 685–703; and Hristo Hinkov, "Vŭzrazhdaneto i stopanska Bŭlgariya." *Otets Paisii* 11, no. 6 (1938): 201–207.

2 Krŭstyu Rakovski, "Stranitsa iz bŭlgarskoto vŭzrzhdane." In *Misŭl. Literaturen sbornik* 1 (1910): 142–173, esp. 149–151.

3 Dimitŭr Mishaikov, "Belezhki vŭrkhu domashnata shaechna industriya v Bŭlgariya." *Spisanie na Bŭlgarskoto ikonomichesko druzhestvo* 7, no. 8 (1903): 527–553.

4 Ivan Sakazov, *Bulgarische Wirtschaftsgeschichte*, 229–230.

5 Stefan Bochev, "Kapitalizmŭt v Bŭlgariya." *Spisanie na bŭlgarskoto ikonomichesko druzhestvo* 30, no. 2 (1931): 65–78, esp. 71.

6 Dimitŭr Blagoev, "Prinos kŭm istoriyata na sotsializma v Bŭlgariya." In Blagoev, *Izbrani istoricheski sŭchineniya v dva toma*. Vol. 1 (edited by Mariya Veleva), Sofia: Nauka i izkustvo, 1985, 180–556, esp. 192–199.

7 See documents of the period in *Sudŭt nad istoritsite. Bŭlgarskata istoricheska nauka. Dokumenti i diskusii, 1944–1950*. Vol. 1 (edited by Vera Mutafcheiva, Vesela Chichovska et al.), Sofia: Marin Drinov, 1995.

8 Zhak Natan, *Ikonomicheska istoriya na Bŭlgariya*. Sofia, 1938, introduction (v–vi), 163.

9 Zhak Natan, *Bŭlgarskoto vŭzrazhdane*. Sofia: Bŭlgarski pisatel, 1949 (fourth, revised edition), 22 (similar passage on p. 11). There are substantial differences between this edition and the first edition in 1939, in which the Revival is treated in a primarily national sense and the economy is just one of the "factors." Only at one point in the 1939 edition does the author affirm the economic aspect of the Revival (but precisely as one side): "Seen from a socioeconomic viewpoint, the Revival is nothing but the deep process of the disintegration of the older, natural and feudal relations and their transition to new commodity relations. This socioeconomic process in Bulgaria is intertwined with the struggle for national liberation from the Turkish yoke" (2). In what follows I will use the 1949 edition, except where the 1939 edition is specifically cited.

10 Natan, *Bŭlgarskoto vŭzrazhdane*, 73–74.

11 Dimitŭr Kosev, "Idealistichesko i materialistichesko razbirane na bŭlgarskoto vŭzrazhdane." *Istoricheski pregled* 4, no. 3 (1947/8): 317–332, esp. 320.

12 Georgi Bakalov, *G. S. Rakovski*. Sofia, 1934, 41–42, 44. (Cit. on 41.)

13 Dimitŭr Kosev, "Klasovite otnosheniya v Bŭlgariya prez Vŭzrazhdaneto." *Istoricheski pregled* 7, no. 4–5 (1951): 443–463. (Cit. on 443).

14 Stalin, Kirov, Zhdanov, *Zamechaniia o konspekte uchebnika novoi istorii, "K izucheniiu istorii."* Moscow: Partizdat, 1937. These instructions were used in *Novaya istoriya. Chast 1. Ot frantsuzkoi burzhoaznoi revoliutsii do franko-prusskoi voiny i parizhkoi kommuny (1789–1870)*, edited by E. V. Tarle, A. V. Efimov, and F. A. Heifets. Moscow: Gosudarstvennoe sotsial'no-ekonomicheskoe izdatel'stvo, 1939; *Novaia istoriia. Vol. 1, 1640–1789*, edited by V. V. Biriukovich, B. F. Porshnev, and S. D. Skazkin. Moscow: Gosudarsvennoe izdatel'stvo politicheskoi literatury, 1951.

15 See also the review of this discussion by Veselin Hadzhinikolov, "Iz zhivota na Instituta za bŭlgarska istoriya." *Izvestiya na Instituta za bŭlgarska istoriya* 1–2 (1951): 351–386, esp. 363–376. The statement of Todor Pavlov, then president of the Bulgarian Academy of Sciences, is cited at the end to the effect that "the most responsible" comrades should come together to prepare a summary of the discussion, but the "final word" on periodization would be said when the projected history of Bulgaria was subjected to discussion. ·

16 Zhak Natan, "Po vŭprosa za periodizatsiyata na nashata istoriya." *Istoricheski pregled* 6, no. 2 (1950): 210–216. In the discussion, this opinion was shared by Raicho Karakolov.

17 Natan, *Bŭlgarskoto vŭzrazhdane*, 492–496.

18 Dimitŭr Kosev, "Kŭm vŭprosa za periodisatsiyata na Novata bŭlgarska istoriya." *Istoricheski pregled* 6, no. 3 (1950): 360–366.

19 Dimitŭr Kosev, "Kŭm izyasnyavane na nyakoi problemi ot istoriyata na Bŭlgariya prez XVIII i nachaloto na XIX vek." *Istoricheski pregled* 12, no. 3 (1956): 26–62, esp. 26–27.

20 Hadzhinikolov, "Iz zhivota na," 369–370.

21 Hristo Gandev, "Kŭm vuprosa za periodizastiyata na bŭlgarskata istoriya." In Gandev, *Problemi na bŭlgarskoto*, 501–514, esp. 512–513 (first published in 1951). In his review, Hadzhinikolov modifies Gandev's opinion of a "victory" of capitalist relations during the Revival, in the sense that the Bulgarian lands in the 1830s and 1840s not only became a sphere of operation of capitalist states but were themselves entangled in bourgeois–capitalist relations. See Hadzhinikolov, "Iz zhivota na," 370–371.

22 Natan, *Bŭlgarskoto vŭzrazhdane*, 495.

23 Thus, according to Tsvetana Georgieva, the big stock raisers of the eighteenth century were neither Bulgarian feudal lords nor members of the Bulgarian bourgeoisie, but they carried "potentially" in themselves the "progressive bourgeois tendencies" of the development of Bulgarian society. See Tsvetana Georgieva, "Za genezisa na burzhoaznite elementi v sotsialnata struktura na bŭlgarite." *Istoricheski pregled* 33, no. 2 (1977): 87–90.

24 Natan, *Ikonomicheska istoriya*, 150–153.

25 Natan, *Ikonomicheska istoriya*, 152.

26 The author deploys similar logic elsewhere: "It is wrong to think that most of the land on the eve of the Russo-Turkish war was in Bulgarian hands. If this were the case one would have to assume that the agrarian question had been solved, but this would leave unexplained why the peasants revolted against the Turks during the April uprising." See Natan, "Kŭm vŭprosa za pŭrvonachlnoto natrupvane na kapitala v Bŭlgariya." *Isvestiya na ikonomicheskiya institut* 1–2 (1954): 13–46, esp. 18–19.

27 Natan, *Ikonomicheska istoriya*, 153. Also Hristo Hristov, "Nyakoi problemi na prekhoda ot feodalizma kŭm kapitalizma v istoriyata na Bŭlgariya." *Istoricheski pregled* 17, no. 3 (1961): 83–107, esp. 107.

28 Gandev, "Kŭm vŭprosa za periodizatsiyata"; Gandev, *Aprilskoto vŭstanie, 1876*. Sofia: Nauka i izkustvo, 1974, 32–38.

29 Natan, "Kŭm vŭprosa za pŭrvonachalnoto," 13–46. The author assumes the necessity of a stage of the "primitive accumulation" of capital as a precondition for the development of capitalism. This was later contested by Nilokai Todorov because of the absence of most classical Marxist ways of primitive accumulation in the Ottoman Empire, which was itself subject to semi-colonial exploitation from outside. See Todorov, "Po nyakoi vŭprosi za ikonomicheskoto razvitie i za zarazhdaneto na kapitalizma v bŭlgarskite zemi pod tursko vladichestvo." *Istoricheski pregled* 17, no. 6 (1961): 87–105, esp. 105.

30 Nikolai Genchev, *Bŭlgarsko vŭzrazhdane*, 82–83, 125, 147–148.

31 Gandev, "Kŭm vŭprosa za periodizatsiyata."

32 Michael Palairet, *The Balkan Economies c. 1800–1914. Evolution without Development*. Cambridge University Press, 1997, 52–57, 81–82. Palairet also denies that the Bulgarian proto-industries had declined before the liberation. See, also, John Lampe, "Imperial Borderlands or Capitalist Periphery? Redefining Balkan Backwardness." In *The Origins of Backwardness in Eastern Europe*, edited by Daniel Chirot. Berkeley–Los Angeles–Oxford: University of California Press, 1989, 177–209. Lampe agrees (with local Marxist authors) that Ottoman hegemony was mostly to blame for hampering development in the Balkans and adds to that his idea that the situation as "imperial borderlands" and as the arena for wars between the Ottoman and the Habsburg Empires exerted a delaying impact.

33 Hristo Gandev, "Kŭm istoriyata na promishleniya kapitalizŭm u nas prez Vŭzrazhdaneto." In Gandev, *Problemi na bŭlgarskoto*, 426–460 (first published in 1954).

34 Stefan Tsonev, "Kŭm vŭprosa za razlozhenieto na esnafskite organizatsii u nas prez perioda na Vŭzrazhdaneto." *Trudove na Visshiya institut za narodno stopanstvo v grad Varna* 1 (1956): 3–80, esp. 55–57. Nikolai Todorov, *Balkanskiyat grad XV–XIX vek*. Sofia: Nauka i izkustvo 1972, 197–294, esp. 226–229, 293–94, 432–434.

35 Dimitŭr Kosev, *Lektsii po nova bŭlgarska istoriya*. Sofia: Nauka i izkustvo, 1952, 58–60. Also Hristov, "Nyakoi problemi," 83–107.

36 Blagoev, "Prinos kum istoriyata," 193, 199–200. Zhak Natan, "Otnovo po vŭprosa za klasite i klasovite otnosheniya v Bŭlgariya prez Vŭzrazhdaneto." *Istoricheski pregled* 7, nos. 4–5 (1951): 467–469; Hristov, "Nyakoi problemi na prekhoda," 86, 98–99, 103, 107. On the universal transition to *chifliks* and the loss of land by the peasants, see also the Russian historian N. G. Levintov, "Agrarnye otnosheniia v Bolgarii nakanune osvobozhdeniia i agrarny perevorot 1877-1879 godov." In *Osvobozdenie Bolgarii ot turetskogo iga. Sbornik stat'ei*. Moscow, 1953, 139–221, esp. 145, 151–157,164, 185, 199. The author describes the transition from *sipahi* fiefs to *chifliks* as a transition from one feudal form of land ownership to another, namely, to a kind of "*pomeschichestvo*" (i.e., similar to the Russian "*pomestie*" estates). To account for the small number of *chifliks* on the eve of the liberation, he affirms that the *chiflik* system entered a crisis immediately after its formation and began to disintegrate after the Crimean War.

37 Vasilii Konobeev, "Genezisŭt na kapitalizma v Bŭlgariya." In Konobeev, *Bŭlgarskoto natsionalno-osvoboditelno dvizhenie. Ideologiya, programa, razvitie*. Sofia: Nauka i izkustvo, 1972, 7–58.

38 Hristo Gandev, "Turski izvori za agrarnata istoriya na Bŭlgariya prez Vŭzrazhdaneto."

Istoricheski pregled 10, no. 2 (1954): 120–127. Instead of challenging the old views directly, the author documents the dismantling of the fief system in the 1830s and 1840s. See also Strashimir Dimitrov, "Kŭm vŭprosa za otmenyavaneto na spakhiiskata sistema v bŭlgarskite zemi." *Istoricheski pregled* 12, no. 6 (1956): 27–58, esp. 55–58; Dimitŭr Kosev, "Kŭm izyasnyavane na nyakoi," 52. In fact, in as early as 1951, the author spoke of a gradual transition of the land in the hands of Bulgarian peasants and an increase in the number of independent peasant smallholders. See Kosev, "Klasovite otnosheniya." Finally Todorov, "Po nyakoi vŭprosi."

39 Hristo Gandev, "Zarazhdane na kapitalisticheski otnosheniya v chiflishkoto stopanstvo na Severozapadna Bŭlgariya prez XVIII vek." In Gandev, *Problemi na bŭlgarskoto*, 271–394 (first published in 1962).

40 Strashimir Dimitrov, "Kŭm vŭprosa za otmenyavaneto," 27–58; Dimitrov, "Chiflishkoto stopanstvo prez 50-te i 70-te godini na XIX vek." *Istoricheski pregled*, 11, no. 2 (1955): 3–34. On the limited role of the *chifliks* in the Ottoman agrarian economy, see also Fikret Adanir, "Tradition and Rural Change in Southeastern Europe During Ottoman Rule." In *The Origins of Backwardness*, 131–176.

41 Strashimir Dimitrov, "Chiflishkoto stopanstvo," 34.

42 Konstantin Kosev, *Kratka istoriya na Bŭlgarskoto vŭzrazhdane*. Sofia: Marin Drinov, 2001, 51–52.

43 Franklin Mendels, "Proto-industrialization: The First Phase of the Industrialization Process." *Journal of Economic History* 32, no. 1 (1972): 241–261; Sidney Pollard, *Peaceful Conquest. The Industrialization of Europe 1760–1970*. Oxford University Press, 1981, 63–78. For the application of this idea to the Bulgarian case, see Palairet, *The Balkan Economies*, 50–57, 81–84, 171, 174, 186–202, 367–369. John Lampe and Marvin Jackson also prefer to speak of proto-industrialization rather than of capitalism. See John Lampe and Marvin Jackson, *Balkan Economic History, 1550–1950. From Imperial Borderlands to Developing Nations*. Bloomington: Indiana University Press, 1982, 139–145.

44 Palairet, *The Balkan Economies*, 81–82, 171, 201–202.

45 Svetla Yaneva, "Pŭtishta na industrializatsiyata: protoindustriite v Evropa i v bŭlgarskite zemi (XVIII–XIX â.)." *Istoricheski pregled* 56, nos. 5–6 (2000): 99–118.

46 Dimitŭr Kosev, "Aprilskoto vŭstanie – vrŭkhna tochka na bŭlgarskata natsionalno-demokraticheska revolyutsiya." In *Aprilskoto vŭstanie, 1876–1966*, edited by Ivan Undzhiev et al. Sofia: BAN, 1966, 7–17, esp. 8, 11; Hristo Hristov, "Kŭm vŭprosa za zarazhdaneto na kapitalizma i obrazuvaneto na bŭlgarskata natsiya prez Vŭzrazhdaneto." In *Bŭlgarskata natsiya prez Vŭzrazhdaneto*, edited by Hristo Hristov. Vol. 2. Sofia: BAN, 1989, esp. 11–12.

47 Halil Inalcik, "L'Empire ottoman." In *Actes du premier Congrès International des Études Balkaniques et sud-est Européennes*. Vol. 3 (Histoire). Sofia, 1969, 75–103, esp. 99–103; Inalcik, *The Ottoman Empire. The Classical Age 1300–1600*. London: Weidenfeld and Nicolson, 1973, 12–13, 107–113. As pointed out by the author, the *sipahi* in the centralized system resembles a state official. Also Inalcik, *The Ottoman Empire: Conquest, Organization, Economy. Collected Studies*. London: Variorum Reprints, 1978, 211–224. John Lampe and Marvin Jackson also prefer to speak of the Ottoman Empire in terms of "centralized rule," "bureaucracy," or "command economy" rather than feudalism, and point out that only the decline of the Ottoman system brought about feudal traits, alongside the burgeoning market economy and traditional peasant agriculture. See John Lampe and Marvin Jackson, *Balkan Economic History*, 12–13, 23–35.

48 Hristo Hristov, "Kŭm vŭprosa za klasite i klasovite otnosheniya v bŭlgarskoto obsh-

testvo prez Vŭzrazhdaneto (proizkhod, sotsialna prinadlezhnost i rolya na chorbadzhiite)." *Izvestiya na Instituta po istoriya*, 21 (1970): 51–85, esp. 63; Bistra Tsvetkova, "Promeni v osmanskiya feodalizŭm na balkanskite zemi prez XVI-XVIII v." *Istoricheski pregled* 27, no. 4 (1971): 55–73, esp. 57; Fani Milkova, *Pozemlenata sobstvenost v bŭlgarskite zemi prez XIX vek.* Sofia: Nauka i izkustvo, 1969, ń. 14.

49 For a Russian discussion of the "Asiatic mode of production" see *Obshtee i osobennoe v istoricheskom razvitii stran Vostoka: Materialy diskusii obshtestvennyh formatsiyakh na Vostoke*, edited by G. Kim. Moscow: Nauka, 1966. The discussion is mentioned by Nikolai Todorov, *The Balkan City, 1400–1900*. Seattle and London: University of Washington Press, 1983, 3–4.

50 Vera Mutafchieva, *Agrarnite otnosheniya v Osmanskata imperiya prez XV-XVI vek.* Sofia: BAN, 1962; Bistra Tsvetkova, "Prinos kŭm izuchavaneto na turskiya feodalizŭm v bŭlgarsite zemi prez XV-XVI vek." *Isvestiya na Instituta za bŭlgarska istoriya* 5 (1954): 71–153; Tsvetkova, "Promeni v osmanskiya feodalizŭm," 55–73; Strashimir Dimitrov, "Za agrarnite otnosheniya v Bŭlgariya prez XVIII vek." In *Paisii Hilendarski i negovata epokha, 1762–1962*, edited by D. Kosev et al. Sofia: BAN: 1962, 129–165; Strashimir Dimitrov and Krŭstyu Manchev, *Istoriya na balkanskite*, 61–70, 75–78; Genchev, *Bulgarsko vŭzrazhdane*, 53–57, 69–72.

51 Karl Marx, *Capital. A Critique of Political Economy*. London: Penguin Books, 1981. Vol. 3, 927. For an application of this approach to Eastern feudalism, see K. Hvostova, "Sotsiologicheskie modeli Zapadn'ye i vostochn'ye tip'y obshtestvenn'yh otnoshenii." In *Obshtee i osobennoe*, 202–212, esp. 204–206. Most Bulgarian authors speak rather mechanically of the "centralized rent" collected by the state as "collective feudal," and as an expression of its "feudal ownership" of the land. For a more theoretical but rather dogmatic discussion, see Fani Milkova, *Pozemlenata sobstvenost*, 22–25.

52 Vera Mutafchieva, *Agrarnite otnosheniya*, 15, 21, 44–48, 66, 212–221, 248. She is the only Bulgarian author to mention "feudalization" (248). On the permanent struggle between the state and individuals for ownership of the land, see also Inalcik, *The Ottoman Empire*, 107–111. See also Strashimir Dimitrov and Krŭstyu Manchev, *Istoriya na balkanskite*, 75–77.

53 This is the description in Tsvetkova, "Prinos kŭm izuchavaneto," esp. 71–73. The period from the end of the sixteenth to the mid-eighteenth century is described as the decline of Turkish military (*sipahi*) feudalism with the penetration of commercial and usurious capital, followed by disintegration in the second half of the eighteenth century under the impact of market commodity relations and semi-capitalist or capitalist forms of exploitation of the subject population.

54 Vera Mutafchieva, *Agrarnite otnosheniya*; Mutafchieva, "Otkupuvaneto na dŭrzhavnite prikhodi v osmanskata imperiya prez XV-XVII v. i razvitieto na parichni otnosheniya." *Istoricheski pregled* 16, no. 1 (1960): 40–74; Mutafchieva, "Za roliata na vakŭfa v gradskata ikonomika na Balkanite pod turska vlast, XV-XVII v." *Izvestiya na Instituta po istoriya* 10 (1962): 121–145; Strashimir Dimitrov, "Za agrarnite otnosheniya," 129–165; Nikolai Todorov, "Po nyakoi vŭprosi"; Tsvetkova, "Promeni v osmanskiya," 55–73.

55 Mutafchieva, *Agrarnite otnosheniya*, 248; Mutafchieva, *Kŭrdzhaliisko vreme*. Sofia: Nauka i izkustvo, 1987, esp. 16–24. The author points out that military-fief feudalism is just one of the forms of Ottoman feudalism; moreover, it is an earlier and less evolved form. A later and more developed feudal Ottoman institution are the *ayans*, that is, local notables who prevailed in the provinces and ruled the towns (as against the officials sent by the center) during the eighteenth century. The outcome was a form of feudalism, decentralization, and finally the feudal anarchy of the "times of

kŭrdzhalii." See, in this sense, Halil Inalcik, "L'Empire ottoman," 99–103. Bernard Lewis also speaks of the feudalization of the Ottoman Empire in the eighteenth and beginning of the nineteenth centuries: Lewis, *The Emergence of Modern Turkey.* London–New York–Toronto: Oxford University Press, 1965, 438–442.

56 Vera Mutafchieva, "Po nyakoi sporni vŭprosi iz osmanskata sotsialno-ikonomicheska istoriya." In Mutafchieva, *Osmanska sotsialno-ikonomicheska istoriya.* Sofia: BAN, 1993, 435–448.

57 The well-known Ottomanist Bernard Lewis considers the agrarian reform, along with the revocation of the *timars* in 1831, under the title "The Abolition of Feudalism" and describes it as the "liquidation of the last vestiges of feudalism." See Lewis, *The Emergence of Modern Turkey*, 89–90.

58 Strashimir Dimitrov, "Chiflishkoto stopanstvo," 6–7.

59 Hristov, "Nyakoi problemi na prekhoda," 100. Also Natan, "Otnovo po vŭprosa," 467. The author considers the *chifliks* as a feudal form of land ownership. In the same sense, see the Russian author Levintov, "Agrarn'ye otnosheniya." See also A. D. Novichev, *Istoriya Turtsii. Vol. 2, Novoe vremya. Part 1 (1793–1834).* Izdatel'stvo Leningradskogo univeriteta, 1968, 232. Novichev asserts more generally that the agrarian reform did not destroy feudalism in Turkey.

60 Gandev, "Turski izvori." The carrying out of the agrarian reform in the northwestern Bulgarian lands, and the peasant revolts there, are also researched by Halil Inalcik, "Application of the Tanzimat and its Social Effects." In Inalcik, *The Ottoman Empire,* chapter 16, 1–33.

61 E.g. Strashimir Dimitrov, "Za agrarnite otnosheniya," 158–159; Dimitrov, "Kŭm vŭprosa za otmenyavaneto," 45, 51; Milkova, *Pozemlenata sobstvenost,* 36; Hristo Hristov, *Agrarniyat vŭpros v bŭlgarskata natsionalna revolyutsiya.* Sofia: Nauka i izkustvo, 1976, 263–268. According to Gandev as well, after the transformation of the agrarian system toward free private property and a capitalist way of management, the old feudal rent was preserved in the form of a state tithe as a "feudal element" in the agrarian system. See Gandev, *Aprilskoto vustanie,* 9. In the work of Nikolai Todorov, the revocation of the *sipahi* fiefs did not abolish feudalism but only weakened its material base and led to further bureaucratization and the parasitic existence of the Ottoman dominant class through the instrument of the state. Todorov, "Po nyakoi vŭprosi," 87–105.

62 Bernard Lewis argues that the situation of the peasants even worsened after the abolition of feudalism, that is, of the *timar* system. See Lewis, *The Emergence of Modern Turkey*, 438–442.

63 Georgi Pletnyov, *Midhat pasha i upravlenieto na Dunavskiya vilayet.* Veliko Turnovo: Vital, 1994.

64 Bakalov, *G. S. Rakovski,* 41.

65 Bakalov, *Hristo Botev.* Sofia, 1934, 11–13, 70–71.

66 Natan, *Bŭlgarskoto vŭzrazhdane,* 375. A similar statement can be found on 27–28.

67 A similar operation is performed on the French Revolution by French Marxist historians such as Albert Soboul, when they interpret the whole of the eighteenth century as a time of "crisis," disregarding the evidence. See François Furet, *Interpreting the French Revolution.* Cambridge, Cambridge University Press, 1981, 90–92 (original: *Penser la Revolution Française.* Editions Gallimard, Paris, 1978).

68 Natan, *Bŭlgarskoto vŭzrazhdane,* 375.

69 Todor Pavlov, "Kŭm vŭprosa za nashata nauchna istoriya i po-spetsialno za istoriyata na Aprilskoto vŭstanie." In Pavlov, *Izbrani proizvedeniya.* Vol. 3, Sofia: BAN, 1960, 278.

70 Konstantin Kosev, *Za kapitalisticheskoto razvitie na bŭlgarskite zemi prez 60-te i 70-te godini na XIX vek*. Sofia: BAN, 1968, esp. 175–183.

71 An instance of similar circular reasoning by Zhak Natan was cited in the first part of this chapter.

72 Natan, "Po vŭprosa za pŭrvonachalnoto," 42.

73 Michael Palairet, *The Balkan Economy*, 50–57, 63–64, 81–84, 171–174, 198, 201–202, 323–324, 361–370.

74 Gale Stokes, "Introduction: In Defense of Balkan Nationalism." In *Nationalism in the Balkans. An Annotated Bibliography*, edited by Gale Stokes. New York and London: Garland Publishers, 1984, vii–xvii. In explaining nationalism without capitalist development, Stoke cites the existence of the European state system and of the ideal of (social) justice and political sovereignty (owing to the French Revolution), which was translated in the Balkans as independence from foreign domination. See also Stokes, "Dependency and the Rise of Nationalism in Southeast Europe." In Stokes, *Three Eras of Political Change in Eastern Europe*. Oxford University Press, 1997, 23–35. Ernest Gellner also recognizes that the formation of the Balkan nations presents a problem for the theory which links nationalism with industrialization and modernity (by the way, for his own theory), and that it requires additional explanation. Gellner offers, by way of explanation, the coincidence of the usual unrest on the periphery of an agrarian empire in a moment of weakness with the fact that the rebels were Christians, which served as a conductor of Western Enlightenment and Romantic influences and turned them into ideological rebels, that is, nationalists. See Gellner, *Nationalism*. London: Weidenfeld & Nicolson, 1997, 41–43.

75 Strashimir Dimitrov and Krŭstyu Manchev, *Istoriya na balkanskite*, 136–137.

76 Vladimir Lenin, "Agrarnaia programma sotsial-demokratii v pervoi russkoi revoliutsii 1905–1907 godov." In Lenin, *Polnoe sobranie sochinenii*. Moscow: Gosudarstvennoe izdatel'stvo politicheskoi literatury, 1961. Vol. 16, 193–413; Lenin, "Agrarny vopros v Rossii k kontsu XIX veka." In Lenin, *Polnoe sobranie suchinenii*. Vol. 17, 57–137. Both works were written in the aftermath of the Russian revolution of 1905. In Lenin's opinion, the bourgeois revolution in the agrarian sphere, which clears the way for capitalism, may take the form of either a "*pomeschiki*-bourgeois" overthrow (in which the land of the *pomeschiki* is dearly paid by the richer peasants, who also occupy communal land) or of a "peasant bourgeois revolution" with the confiscation and dividing of the lands of the *pomeschiki* or a preceding municipalization or nationalization. Lenin opts for the peasant revolution in the name of the interests of the working class and the Social Democratic Party.

77 Bakalov, *Hristo Botev*, 3. Blagoev was the first to speak of a "serfdom" of the peasants. But one should be aware of the largely metaphoric use of the word "serfdom" as dependence and exploitation in general.

78 Natan, *Bŭlgarskoto vŭzrazhdane*, 165–166. This is stated still more pointedly in Natan, "Otnovo po vŭprosa za klasite," 467–471.

79 Vŭlko Chervenkov, "Kŭm 80-godishninata ot gibelta na Levski." *Novo vreme* 29, no. 2 (1953): 32–37, esp. 32–33. (The speech was first published in *Rabotnichesko delo*, no. 49 (18 February 1953).

80 Hristov, *Agrarniyat vŭpros*, 8, 10–11; Hristo Hristov, *Paisii Hilendarski*. Sofia: Nauka i izkustvo, 1972, 314. The author continued to publish as late as 1989 about the serfdom of the peasants during the Revival (until the cancellation of the *sipahi* military-feudal system in the 1830s), and the "struggle for land" and for emancipation from feudal exploitation. See Hristov, "Kŭm vŭprosa za zarazhdaneto," 11–12.

81 *Istoriya na Bŭlgariya v 14 toma*. Vol. 6, Sofia: BAN, 1987, 412.

82 For a description of the decline in productivity and the naturalization of Bulgarian

agriculture after the liberation, and an analysis of the causes, see Palairet, *The Balkan Economies*, 63–64, 173–186, 201–202, 361–367.

83 The economic and class treatment of the Bulgarian Revival is unambiguously opposed to its treatment as a process of cultural–educational development by "bourgeois historical scholarship" in debates on the "reorientation" of historical scholarship in 1948, for example in Pantelei Zarev's comment on the report by Tushe Vlakhov on the state and tasks of Bulgarian historical scholarship. See *Sŭdut nad istoritsite*, 335.

84 Dimitŭr Kosev, "Idealistichesko i materialistichesko," 317, 328.

85 For example, Dimitŭr Kosev, "Uvod." In Petŭr Nikov, *Vŭzrazhdane na bŭlgarskiya narod*.

86 Natan, *Bŭlgarskoto vŭzrazhdane*, 509–510; Dimitŭr Kosev, "Idealistichesko i materialistichesko," 317–332.

87 Georgi Bakalov, *Zavetite na bŭlgarskoto Vŭzrazhdane*. Sofia, 1937, 11–12. The author affirms that the mightier the support of the masses, the bigger the feats of the heroes.

88 Natan, *Bŭlgarskoto vŭzrazhdane*, 56–58, 497–498. Ironically, the author criticizes right-wing historians for creating a cult around the personalities of the Revival during the Communist "cult of personality" epoch.

89 Shishmanov, "Uvod v istoriyata," 36–53.

90 Nikola Milev, "Faktorite na bŭlgarskoto vŭzrazhdane." In *Sbornik v chest na prof. Ivan Shishmanov*. Sofia, 1920, 129–157.

91 Boyan Penev, *Istoriya na novata*. Vol. 3, 3–211; Penev, *Nachalo na bŭlgarskoto vŭzrazhdane*. Sofia: T. Chipev, 1929 (first edition 1918), 3–8.

92 Ormandzhiev, *Nova i nai-nova istoriya*.

93 Natan, *Bŭlgarskoto vŭzrazhdane*, 498, 508–509. For the various factors of the Revival, starting with the economic, see 33–74.

94 Dimitŭr Kosev, "Aprilskoto vŭstanie–vrŭkhna tochka," 11.

95 Goran Todorov, "Sotsialno-politicheskata obuslovenost na Aprilskoto vŭstanie. Otzvukŭt na Aprilskoto vŭstanie v Rusiya." In *Aprilskoto vŭstanie, 1876–1966*, 117–130, esp. 117.

96 Nikolai Genchev, *Levski, revolyutsiyata i bŭdeshtiya svyat*. Sofia: OF, 1973, 117.

97 Genchev, *Bŭlgarsko vŭzrazhdane*, 9–11; Genchev, *Bŭlgarskata kultura*, 175–176.

98 Sharova, "Problemi na bŭlgarskoto," 5–16.

99 Radkova, *Bŭlgarskata inteligentsiya*, 286–287.

100 An example is Todev, *Novi ochertsi*, 10–65; Konstantin Kosev, *Kratka istoriya*, 15, 50. The Revival is defined by the author as first and foremost a "Bulgarian national revolution" expressed in the formation of the nation and its claims for independence, though the transition from the Middle Ages to Modernity is added (on p. 50). Still, this work is not nationalist.

101 Plamen Mitev, *Bŭlgarsko vŭzrazhdane. Lektsionen kurs*. Sofia: Polis, 1999, 5–7.

102 Gavrilova, *Vekŭt na bŭlgarskoto*, 5–8.

103 E.g. Strashimirova, *Bŭlgarinut pred praga*, 8–11, 105.

Excursus on Periodization

The Bulgarian Revival elaborated into a historical epoch has a certain duration with a beginning and an end, and it is divided internally into sub-periods. It stands between the first centuries of Ottoman rule (emotionally described as "yoke") and independence. It forms the last century or so of the Ottoman period for the Bulgarians. The preceding period has often been depicted as "dark ages," a regression from the glories of the medieval kingdom into a state of debasing submission, in which the Bulgarians suffered under double oppression—Ottoman political domination and the "spiritual" or cultural domination of the Greeks (through the agency of the Greek Patriarchy). Deprived of their aristocratic ruling class and educated priests, they sank into ignorance and became predominantly peasant. The earlier historians Nikola Zlatarski and Dimitŭr Mishev in particular darkened the colors in their picture of physical terror long after the initial conquest, with the persecution of Bulgarian priests and teachers, the burning of Bulgarian manuscripts, the introduction of Greek in the "cell" (monastic) schools to the churches, the paralysis of cultural activities, etc.[1] Although this was subsequently criticized as resting on scanty evidence and misrepresenting the realities (or even as a "myth"[2]), a residue still persists in popular versions of Bulgarian history in textbooks and school teaching, in historical fiction, etc.[3] At the other end, the Revival is clearly delimited by the fact of liberation. It is contrasted in substance, too, by pointing out that the (disinterested) national ideals of the Revival were overshadowed during the post-liberation epoch by the murky "primitive accumulation" of capital and unscrupulous political struggles (known in Bulgarian as "*partizanstvo*").

The Bulgarian Revival has been dated in various ways both as to external boundaries and internal sub-division. As mentioned previously, some contemporary activists put the beginning of the Revival in the 1820s, with the reforms of the Ottoman Empire initiated by Sultan Mahmud II and continued under his son Abdul-Mecid. The reason for making the Bulgarian Revival coincide with the reforms is that by allowing the building up of churches and schools with teaching in the native language, and by proclaiming rights and guarantees in general, they facilitated the national upsurge and gave the formal possibility for raising the "Bulgarian question" before the Sublime Porte, of which the Bulgarian activists took advantage.[4]

With his reputation as the first Bulgarian professional historian, Marin Drinov shifted the beginning of the Revival back to the year 1762, when Paisii Hilendarski finished the manuscript of his *Istoriya Slovenobolgarska* ("Slavonic-Bulgarian History"), considered as a kind of national manifesto.[5] Other authors (Ivan Shishmanov at first) have argued that a single personality or event cannot be taken as the beginning of a new epoch as they do not come into being in a vacuum.[6] Marxist scholarship, with its economic tenets, was particularly loath to date a period by a personality. The beginning of the Bulgarian Revival was thus moved further backwards toward the beginning of the eighteenth century on the assumption that an economic upsurge began then.[7] However, this dating is quite preconceived and the tension becomes stronger given the effort to detect parallel "revival" phenomena and changes in all spheres: the economy, social life, culture. The a priori logic that there must have been economic "preconditions" for what came later is not borne out by the insufficient and uncertain data, which leave the impression of an artificial adjustment.[8]

A period of "early Revival" as far back as 1600 to 1830 (or, in another version, 1700 to 1830) was defined by Hristo Gandev in his early works published before Communist rule. In his view, the Revival starts with the beginnings of the new Bulgarian language and ends with the formation of an organized society and a cultural nation. The eighteenth century in particular is characterized as the beginning of the modern period in Bulgarian history.[9] Gandev portrays the early revival as a primarily native (local) social and cultural process that was self-promoted and almost independent of external European forces and influences.

The idea of an early initial boundary of the Revival is shared by some earlier literary historians such as Benyu Tsonev, and partly Ivan Shishmanov, with regard to literary development. The appearance of the *damaskini* from the beginning of the seventeenth century is arguably the beginning of the new Bulgarian literature, on the grounds that they were written in a purer Bulgarian vernacular.[10] This view was criticized and subsequently rejected by the literary scholars Aleksandŭr Balan and Boyan Penev on account of the still religious character of the *damaskini*.[11] The significance of the time from the beginning of the seventeenth century to the middle of the eighteenth century (i.e., until Paisii) was later restored (first by Emil Georgiev) under the label of "proto-revival" (or "early revival") marked by the appearance of writers of a new type.[12]

The best-known Bulgarian "bourgeois" literary scholar Boyan Penev puts the beginnings of the new Bulgarian literature (and, together with it, of the Revival) in the middle of the eighteenth century on the grounds that it was then that the new national and national-educational spirit began to spread. The synchronization between literary and social–political history is argued by Boyan Penev with the existence of an intimate relationship between literature and social–political conditions in the period before independence, when the creative personality served the needs of the milieu, merging individual with public ideals (in contrast to the subsequent period, when literature became the expression of mostly individual aspirations and acquired a purely aesthetic value). The beginning of the 1870s, with the solution of the "church question," presents, in Boyan Penev's view, an important dividing line in the evolution of both Bulgarian literature and public life, which then entered the phase of political struggles for liberation (reflected in the revolutionary literature of Lyuben Karavelov and Hristo Botev, preceded by Georgi Rakovski).[13]

The highly regarded literary historian Petŭr Dinekov, who began his career before 1944 but had to reorientate himself to Marxist positions afterwards, had the unseemly task of criticizing the periodization and partly the concept and method of Boyan Penev, and to replace them with the "correct" view. This again happens to be a synchronization of literary development with the "total-historical" development (as with Penev), but with greater regard to the revolutionary movement. The basic internal divide then became the 1850s (instead of the 1870s), with reference to the Crimean War (1853–1856) that was followed by deep economic, social, and political changes, and the rise of the bourgeois–democratic revolution.[14]

There are different views as to the end of the Revival as well. Some authors (Petŭr Nikov, Ivan Shishmanov) put it at the year 1870, when an autonomous Bulgarian Church or Exarchate was established (by a Turkish *firman*) that meant, in effect, official recognition of the Bulgarian nation.[15] But the majority of authors (especially later authors) regard the Russo-Turkish liberation war of 1877–78 as the end of the Revival, thus including into it the last decade of revolutionary struggles. Some historians (e.g. Nikolai Genchev) make the reservation that the Revival continued until World War I in Macedonia under Ottoman rule, on the grounds that a strong Bulgarian self-consciousness survived there and the efforts for uniting continued.[16]

The end of the Revival is also put at World War I by the historian Mikhail Arnaudov (in a work of 1938), who included the processes taking place in Bulgaria itself as well. The author thus added to the usual periodization a "late Revival" from the liberation to World War I, reasoning that the winning of independence did not break with the general trends of the national Revival and with the ideal of uniting all Bulgarians, and that the processes of national formation continued under the auspices of the nation state.[17] This brings the understanding of the Revival as a nation-building process to its logical consequence. Later on, when Macedonia was joined as a fruit of the pact between Bulgaria and Nazi Germany, Mikhail Arnaudov carried the end boundary further on to World War II, on the grounds that the national unification processes were then completed (a view endorsed by Georgi Konstantinov).[18]

The internal sub-division of the Bulgarian Revival has also been the subject of controversies. The literary scholar Ivan Shishmanov, followed by Boyan Penev, divided it into a "spiritual revival" proper (reminiscent of the Italian Renaissance in some respects), which ended with the establishment of the Bulgarian Exarchate in 1870; and the "political revival" of secret committees and revolts, which began in 1860 with Rakovski's efforts to transform the armed bands (*cheti*) of outlaws (*haiduti*) into revolutionary units and ended with the liberation.[19] Mikhail Arnaudov in his turn subdivided the Revival into four phases: an "early revival" from Paisii (1762) to the peace treaty of Edirne at the exit of one Russian–Turkish war (1829); the "revival proper" from 1829 to the Crimean War (1853–1856); a "high revival" from the Crimean War to liberation (1878); and the already-mentioned "late revival" from liberation until the wars (the Balkan wars and the First World War). The Revival starts with symptoms of national regeneration under the sign of the historical past, and love for the mother tongue and the idea of the motherland; national efforts accelerate to reach a peak in the "high revival"; the impulse continues after liberation but gradually abates.[20] Wars again serve to mark the sub-periods (five in number) in a periodization proposed recently by Plamen Mitev.[21]

The widely accepted periodization of Nikolai Genchev advances three sub-periods of different economic, social, and political description: an "early revival" (the entire eighteenth and the beginning of the nineteenth centuries) characterized by the spread of market relations, the appearance of a Bulgarian bourgeoisie and the birth of the national idea; the 1820s through the 1850s (until the Crimean War) under the sign of the reforms in the Ottoman Empire, the formation of a weakly developed Bulgarian bourgeois society, the deepening of the revival processes and the beginning of national movements for modern Bulgarian education and for church independence; and a final period from the Crimean War to liberation in 1878, marked by the failure of the liberal bourgeois reforms in Turkey, the completion of the cultural revival, and the achievement of autonomy of the Bulgarian nation (recognized officially in 1870), as well as by an organized national liberation movement.[22]

The periodization of the Bulgarian literary (and cultural) development is also of interest, especially when it deviates from the "total-historical" periodization. Boyan Penev's view has already been considered. The reputed linguist and literary scholar Emil Georgiev sets apart a period of Enlightenment (or Renaissance-Enlightenment) from Paisii to the 1820s, followed by a period of national romanticism until liberation. According to this author, the first period set the tasks of the Revival (by calling on the people to wake up), to be realized during the second period.[23]

After Communism, the literary scholar Docho Lekov argued for the autonomy of the literary evolution vis-à-vis the total-historical development (i.e., social–economic and political in the main) and offered the following explicitly literary periodization: "literature of the transition" (from the beginning of the seventeenth century to the 1820s); the "period of schooling" (the 1820s and the 1830s); the first period of literature proper (from the 1840s to the 1860s); "literature of the revolutionary élan" (the 1870s); and "literature of the liberated society in the 1880s."[24] As can be seen, he restores Boyan Penev's emphasis on the significance of the 1870s.

Now that literary scholars have become increasingly sensitive to the autonomy of the literary processes, Svetlozar Igov has proposed another periodization reminiscent of Emil Georgiev (in the naming of the periods, if not the exact dating) but explicitly argued as "purely" literary in contrast to "total-historical." It includes a period of "Enlightenment" (the middle of the eighteenth century to the mid-1840s), "Romanticism" (until the end of the 1860s), followed by "Realism" as a "post-revival" literary formation (from the 1870s to the end of the century).[25]

Whatever the differences, all periodizations have in common that they include a certain "core" (sub)period, namely, from the peace treaty of Edirne (1829), marking the beginning (or intensification) of reform in the

Ottoman Empire, to the establishment of the Bulgarian Exarchate (1870) or to the liberation (1878). They differ mostly in the preceding and the subsequent periods that are being added to this "revival proper" that forms the essence of the epoch, when the economic, social, educational, church and revolutionary activities were in full sway. This also justifies the opinion of the activists of the Revival.

It can be noted most generally that just how the boundaries of the Bulgarian Revival are placed depends on what is considered as its main contents, though this is not always made explicit. If the spiritual–cultural (ideological) component is in the foreground, the initial *terminus* looks particularly fluent and hard to pinpoint or has a "pre-beginning" as all literary scholars insist. The tendency in general is then to shift the boundary backwards ("downwards") to earlier times or to isolate a period of an "early revival" (or "proto-revival"). Still, there is one date of undisputed importance—the appearance of Paisii's *History* in 1762.

If the greatest attention is paid to social–economic development, the upsurge becomes more noticeable only from the second decade of the nineteenth century (after the "Time of Troubles" were over), but dating so far has deferred to the postulate of economic materialism (that requires a "basis" for the phenomena in the "superstructure") or to the patriotic desire for an earlier progress of the nation in general, hence dating from the beginning of the eighteenth century (or its middle).

If one takes the formation of the nation as a main reference point, Paisii's *History* (1762) has a strong claim to be a beginning. But it is quite "symbolic" because the book (a manuscript with restricted circulation) had a weak impact in its times while education and the periodic press that popularized the national ideas got under way later. After the isolated early national beginnings, things were taken up in earnest only from the end of the 1820s with the upsurge in educational activities and the church movement, then passed through the acknowledgment of the nation (the Exarchate in 1870) as an epochal date, and were crowned by the establishment of a Bulgarian nation state. An entirely consistent position on this count would carry the revival processes until the wars (as does Mikhail Arnaudov), because the idea of the nation was still being hammered upon the minds of the people (and maybe more intensely than before) by way of education, conscription, and the periodical press in the nation-state.

To sum up, periodization appears differently depending on the area under inspection. The overlapping of economic, social, "spiritual" (i.e., worldview, intellectual), national, and revolutionary processes alongside a certain length of the Bulgarian historical time axis ("high revival" or "revival proper") makes a consensus among historians possible. Conversely, the absence of such a synchronization for other time intervals introduces disagreement—it is not by chance that the initial date of the Revival has been most disputed and remains problematic to this day. Things become especially fuzzy given the "totalitarian" desire for a total-historical periodization to include all or many aspects of the development, which do not move necessarily in synchrony and at the same pace. Hence the difficulties of a "total-historical" periodization that attempts to force the various processes into a "parallel" course. What is actually achieved in this way is a periodization that looks unitary (mostly under the sign of "national formation") but uses different criteria and reference points in isolating sub-periods.

The following description seems plausible. Obviously things had started to change in the minds (of some individuals) much earlier than the clear manifestation of any material progress and before a national stirring began in earnest. That is why the earlier periods of the Revival have been articulated with spiritual (intellectual) criteria in mind, the appearance of the national idea at a certain point included. But only as an "idea." Economic and social processes followed suit in the nineteenth century, carrying on their wings the broadening national processes with their "dual" ideological and material–organizational aspect (schools, churches, printed media), and ending in political liberation struggles. The going ahead of the processes in the mind (not least because of foreign influences), in comparison with the economic–material "basis," is a major problem for Marxist historians who feel under pressure to shift the initial date backwards (with a mistaken economic and social *rationale*) but even thus are not able to catch up with the literary and cultural historians who run still further backwards with their "early periods." The "unevenness" of development in the various spheres levels out only as we move toward the last decades prior to liberation when economy, society, ideology, and politics work in tune. Maybe even this presents an exaggeration as to the grip of the national processes and goals on the Bulgarian "society" of the time.

Something should be said at this point in favor of a more "fragmented" understanding of the Revival as composed of different parts, that is, different not only in chronology but in content as well. Rather than picturing the development as parallel processes running through different phases, we should rather see it as different processes at work in successive periods with only partial overlapping. This was the view of Ivan Shishmanov, Boyan Penev, Emil Georgiev, and others, who differentiated between an earlier "spiritual" revival and a later "political" revival (or, alternatively, an "Enlightenment" period followed by national romanticism). This is also the view of foreign historians such as Richard Crampton, who writes of a cultural revival followed by, and transformed into, a political or national one (the latter accompanied by an economic recovery or "revival").[26] The political revival or phase can be dated (and has been dated) either in the last pre-liberation decade of organized armed struggles or to include more broadly the educational efforts and church struggles of the previous decades, which have been "politicized" as well. The point is that these periods should be regarded as different in many respects, the mass national movement with its various expressions appearing relatively late. The Revival thus lumps together two distinct epochs with different contents and meanings rather than presenting a preordained continuity of national processes.

In general, it is better to resist the "totalitarian" desire for unitary periodization and not to look for synchrony where it does not exist but to allow for partial periodizations valid for certain domains or certain purposes only. One has to live with the inevitability of different and various periodizations, because these are, in the end, no more than a convenience in ordering the historical evidence.

Notes

1 Mishev, *Bŭlgariya v minaloto*, 194–199; Mishev, "Nachalo na bŭlgarskata probuda," 4–5. Also Nikola Zlatarski, *Nova politicheska i sotsialna istoriya na Bŭlgariya i Balkanskiya poluostrov*. Sofia, 1921, 140–143. It is possible that the source of this view goes back to the history of Bulgaria by Konstantin Jireček, cited by Mishev. See Jireček, *Istoriya na bŭlgarite*, 478–479, 550–551. The author calls the period under Ottoman rule until the national Revival "the saddest and darkest period" in Bulgarian history and writes about Greek persecutions and the burning of Slavic manuscripts.

2 See the critique in Gandev, *Faktori na bŭlgarskoto*, 61–72, 179. More importantly, the "dark" picture issues from an idealization of the earlier medieval past. This is implicitly recognized by authors who stress pacification under the Ottomans and the end of feudal anarchy as among the positive factors for the Bulgarian Revival and nation building. See notes 89 to 92 in the previous chapter.

3 See a recent description of the Ottoman period in the spirit of a "dark ages" in Konstantin Kosev, *Kratka istoriya*, 23–25, 28, 31–32. The author speaks of mass Islamization, religious and ethnic discrimination, the absolute dependency of the peasants on the *sipahi*, tax increases every year, and the fact that even the common Muslim could encroach on the life, the property, and the honor of non-Muslims, etc. This comes from an established professional historian.

4 Aprilov, "Dopŭlnenie kŭm knigata," 152–153. Georgi Rakovski, "Bŭlgarskii za nezavisimo"; Rakovski, "Bŭlgarskii naroden vŭpros"; Balabanov, "Bŭlgarskii napredŭk," 328.

5 Drinov, "Otets Paisii," 25-26. This opinion was shared by Ivan Shishmanov (initially), Boyan Penev, Mikhail Arnaudov, etc. See Arnaudov, *Bŭlgarsko vŭzrazhdane*, 5-6.

6 Shihmanov, "Paisii i negovata epokha," 12-17. The author admits that he first thought of Paisii as a "demiurge," who resurrected his people. But he later came to the conclusion (as a result of his work on the Italian Renaissance and his reading of Jakob Burkhardt) that the Revival is the outcome of a preceding economic and social development. On the other hand, Shishmanov points out the economic weakness and degraded social status of the Bulgarians as an impediment to an earlier revival "collectively as a people" prior to the peace of Edirne in 1829, in spite of individual manifestations of national consciousness.

7 Genchev, *Bŭlgarsko vŭzrazhdane*, 6-7; Virdzhiniya Paskaleva, "Predpostavki i nachenki na rannoto Bŭlgarsko vŭzrazhdane." *Istoricheski pregled* 34, no. 2 (1978): 83-98. This dating is also followed in the academic *Istoriya na Bŭlgariya v 14 toma*, vol. 5, 13-14. The reservation is here made that the "beginnings of the Renaissance," that is, the emergence of new traits, is most difficult to ascertain.

8 See Plamen Mitev, *Bŭlgarsko vŭzrazhdane*, 8-9.

9 Gandev, *Faktori na bŭlgarskoto*, 9, 179-185; Gandev, *Ranno vŭzrazhdane*. The author dates the "high" or proper revival from 1830 to the liberation.

10 Benyu Tsonev, "Novobŭlgarska pismenost predi Paisiya." *Bŭlgarski pregled* 1, no. 8 (1894): 80-94; Tsonev, "Ot koya knizhovna shkola e izlyazŭl Paisii Hilendarski." *Slavyanski glas* 10, nos. 5-6 (1912): 165-174; Ivan Shishmanov, "Koga se nacheva novobŭlgarskata literatura." *Rodna rech* 1, no. 3 (1928): 98.

11 Penev, *Istoriya na novata*. Vol. 1, 53-66; Aleksandŭr Balan, "Pochetŭk na stara i nova bŭlgarska knizhnina." *Uchilishten pregled* 20, nos. 1-3 (1921): 1-18; Balan, "Otkoga da zapochvame novata si knizhnina." *Bŭlgarska misŭl* 8, no. 1 (1933): 51. See also Petŭr Dinekov, *Vŭzrozhdenski pisateli*. Sofia: Nauka i izkustvo, 1964, 8-9.

12 Georgiev, "Bŭlgarsko predvŭzrazhdane." In Georgiev, *Bŭlgarskata literatura v obshtoslavyanskoto*, 116-148; Georgiev, *Obshto i sravnitelno*, 78-82. But the author is careful to point out that the new ideological (Renaissance and Enlightenment) phenomena were restricted to single personalities and groups closely connected with neighboring or Slav peoples, and that their feeling of belonging to their people was very close to the religious identity and was not yet a truly national feeling.

13 Penev, *Istoriya na novata*. Vol. 1, 65-82, 101-103.

14 Dinekov, *Vŭzrozhdenski pisateli*, 18-29.

15 Nikov, *Vŭzrazhdane na bŭlgarskiya*, 40; Shishmanov, "Uvod v istoriyata," 33-34.

16 Genchev, *Bŭlgarsko vŭzrazhdane*, 7-8.

17 Mikhail Arnaudov, "Dukh i nasoki na bŭlgarskoto vŭzrazhdane." In *Prez vekovete*, edited by Krŭstyu Mitev. Sofia: Bŭlgarska istoricheska biblioteka, 1938, 190-191.

18 Arnaudov, *Bŭlgarsko vŭzrazhdane*, 6; Georgi Konstantinov, *Vŭzrazhdaneto i Makedoniya*. Sofia, 1943, 34. This periodization was strongly opposed by Marxist authors, e.g. by Zhak Natan, as the idealization of the deeds of the Bulgarian chauvinists and fascists by presenting them as a continuation of the deeds of the men of the Revival. See Natan, *Bŭlgarskoto vŭzrazhdane*, 498.

19 Shishmanov, "Uvod v istoriyata," 33-34; Penev, *Istoriya na novata*. Vol. 1, 81-82.

20 Arnaudov, "Dukh i nasoki," 190-191.

21 Plamen Mitev, *Bŭlgarskoto vŭzrazhdane*, 9-10. The divisions of his five periods are the end of the seventeenth century; the 1760s (i.e. Paisii); the Russo-Turkish war of 1806-1812 (Bucharest peace treaty); the Russo-Turkish war of 1828-1829 (peace treaty of Edirne); the Crimean War of 1853-1856; and the Russo-Turkish war of 1877-1878 (Berlin peace treaty).

22 Genchev, *Bŭlgarsko vŭzrazhdane*, 7–9. This periodization has recently been endorsed by Ivan Stoyanov, *Istoriya na Bŭlgarskoto*, 45–46.

23 Georgiev, "Tipologichen relef," 237, 242; Georgiev, "Bŭlgarskoto literaturno i obshto-istorichesko," 204; Georgiev, "Renesansovo-prosveshtenskiyat," 83; Georgiev, "Romantizmŭt v yuzhnoslavyanskata literaturna obshnost." In Georgiev, *Obshto i sravnitelno*, 91.

24 Docho Lekov, *Literatura, obshtestvo, kultura. Literaturno-sotsiologicheski i literaturno-istoricheski problemi na bŭlgarskoto vŭzrazhdane.* Sofia: Narodna prosveta, 1982, 76–84; Lekov, *Bŭlgarska vŭzrozhdenska literatura.* Vol. 1, Sofia: Universitetsko izdatelstvo "Kliment Ohridski," 1993, 24–38.

25 Igov, *Kratka istoriya*, 25–27, 178–179, 184. See the description of these epochs on 191–192, 221–223, 244–245.

26 Richard Crampton, *A Concise History of Modern Bulgaria.* Cambridge University Press, 1977, 46–86; Crampton, *A Short History of Modern Bulgaria.* Cambridge University Press, 1987, 9–20.

CHAPTER THREE

Classes and Class Struggles

Some of the earlier authors showed considerable interest in the social structure of Bulgarian society during the Revival, especially in the urban "estate" and its contribution to the national revival. Just as with the development of the economy, a well-to-do class was considered as a precondition and a factor of the (cultural–national) revival, that is, as its sponsor, and as a recipient of the national ideas. The social (class) structure of Bulgarian society during the Revival epoch became a major, perhaps *the* major, topic for Marxist authors both before and after 1944. Besides describing the social structure itself, they used class as an instrument of analysis of political trends and ideologies, and as a hero or villain of the historical narrative of the Revival in general. Taking the views of the older authors as a point of departure, I will come to constructs of class under the sign of Marxism, and their subsequent revision, as the actual subject of this chapter.

The Urban "Estate" and Social Struggles in Older Historiography

In his small but influential work dated 1910, Krŭstyu Rakovski portrayed the social outlook of the purely Bulgarian highland towns. These swelled as a consequence of the troubles in the Ottoman Empire during the second half of the eighteenth century (the "times of the *kŭrdzhalii*"). Another unintended effect was the reinforcing of the belligerent tradition of outlaws (*haiduti*), which proved important for the political awakening of the Bulgarians. The author singles out as the main precondition for the national revival the growth of a well-to-do and autonomous "urban class" (or bourgeoisie), initially composed of collectors of the tax on sheep (*beglikchii*) and traders in sheep (*dzhelepi*), and later supplemented by craftsmen, shopkeepers and traders. Leaning on its economic power and growing social importance, this class succeeded in shortening the distance to the Turkish masters. It began to claim rights and took the lead in public struggles. Based on the example of the town of Kotel, Krŭstyu Rakovski depicts the first social struggles within Bulgarian society itself. The ascending "party of *esnafi*" (guilds), made up of craftsmen and shopkeepers, began to contest the power of the old notables who made their wealth in the sheep trade. The author likens the local urban struggles in the Bulgarian towns with those in the medieval Italian city-republics and points out their importance in schooling activists for the national struggles.[1]

The two most influential literary historians of the "bourgeois" period, Ivan Shishmanov and Boyan Penev, agree on the importance of the economic upsurge and the formation of an independent "urban estate" that embraced the national idea and thus became a major factor of the Bulgarian Revival. This was preceded by the strengthening of the Bulgarian ethnic element in the highland towns on both sides of the Balkan range and in the Rhodopes, and the transformation of former peasants into craftsmen and traders. Boyan Penev differentiates between a "middle estate" of artisans, shopkeepers and traders, which he compares to the West European bourgeoisie of the eighteenth century, and an "upper estate" of notables (*chorbadzhii*) as a kind of Bulgarian "aristocracy" of owners of money and property, composed initially of collectors of the sheep tax and traders in sheep.[2] The self-willed old *chorbadzhii* followed their personal whims and interests but did something for the population at large, too. With the emergence of the new social forces of craftsmen organized in guilds (*esnafi*) and the intelligentsia of teachers in the main, these came into conflict with the *chorbadzhii*. The struggles centered on the control of the town councils or communes (*obshtina*) and the management of school and church affairs. In towns where the craftsmen were better organized, they were able to assert their economic and social predominance. The struggle between the middle and the upper urban "estates" is likened by Penev to earlier struggles between the aristocracy and the bourgeoisie in the West, with the reservation that "bourgeoisie" is meant in the sense of "urbanites" or the urban "middle class," not as a modern bourgeoisie. Being at the same time struggles for "a democratic rule," they contributed to the civic education of the Bulgarians. (The contest between the Conservatives and the Liberals after the liberation is seen as their continuation.)[3]

The social-economic processes are analyzed in greater detail by Hristo Gandev in his books published before the Communist takeover.[4] The author places strong emphasis on the process of the Bulgarianization of the highland towns during the second half of the eighteenth century as a side effect of the troubles in the empire, which made many Bulgarian peasants take refuge from the brigand raids in the plains. He stresses the cultural contrast between the original population of the towns, led by its traditional notables and prone to Greek influences, and the new settlers who were strongly attached to their customs, not susceptible to Greek influence, and distrustful of the urban "patricians." The migrants underwent a slow process of transformation into urbanites. The most active among them became artisans and were associated in guilds. They eventually grew rich and began to play an important public role. They launched the struggle against the "regime of the *chorbadzhii*," who collected the taxes and spent the communal resources without control.[5] By the 1860s, they had succeeded in establishing their prevalence and laying down the principles of a new "civic and moral order."[6]

The above descriptions of social groups and struggles during the Revival contain some similarities with descriptions produced under the sign of Marxism, but the overall picture is different. First of all, they center upon the formation of Bulgarian towns and of an urban "class" (in contrast to the almost entirely peasant population before), which is taken for granted in most Marxist accounts. They also point to cultural and ethnic differences and strife in the process—between newcomers to the towns and old urbanites, people with Bulgarian self-consciousness, and Greeks or Bulgarians trying to assimilate as Greeks. Society is presented in terms of dynamics. First comes the process of urbanization, followed with the change of generations by the social conflict between the old-style notables and the organized craftsmen over the management of the communes and the spending of their resources for various purposes. The comparison with the Western "bourgeoisie" is very cautious, and refers to its earlier (burgher) phase. Finally, there is a preference for the self-designations of the epoch, such as organized craftsmen (*esnafi*), traders in sheep (*dzhelepi*), collectors of the tax on sheep (*beglikchii*), etc., the effect of which is to keep close to the historical realities. This strikes a contrast with the a priorism of the early Marxist social schemes, with their abstract and formalistic social categories (such as big, middle and petty bourgeoisie), presumed as ready-made from the beginning.

Bourgeoisie and Notables
in Earlier Marxist Controversies

Bulgarian Marxist and Communist authors distinguish three or four basic social classes in the Bulgarian society of the Revival epoch—the big (commercial and industrial) bourgeoisie, petty bourgeoisie (of artisans and petty traders), and peasants. The traditional notables (*chorbadzhii*) are presented as a separate class by some authors, while others see them as part of the big bourgeoisie. The priests and the secular intelligentsia do not qualify as a class from the Marxist point of view as they are not connected with "means of production"; they are only social "layers" or groups.[7] Let us consider in more detail the largely ideological constructs and controversies over classes and their political role during the Revival.

The founder of the Bulgarian Socialist Party, Dimitŭr Blagoev, differentiates between three classes: the bourgeoisie, the *chorbadzhii* (described as big landowners—incorrect, as it will turn out—merchants and usurers), and the peasants. In his view, the bourgeoisie fulfilled a progressive economic role, and to a large extent a progressive political role, too. It was the bearer of the national ideas and it successfully carried out the "peaceful urban bourgeois revolution," that is, the opening up of schools, the publishing of books and newspapers, and the uplifting of the national spirit through these means. The commercial-industrial (bourgeois) class also stood in the vanguard of the struggles for an independent Bulgarian church. According to Blagoev, it was only after the establishment of the Bulgarian Exarchate that there occurred a split between "evolutionists" (the conservative circle around the Exarchate, *chorbadzhii* close to the Turkish authorities, and part of the bourgeois class), and "revolutionaries" coming from radical bourgeois milieus (especially a declining petty bourgeoisie in emigration).[8]

A peculiar version of the social structure and its evolution was advanced by Georgi Bakalov in his works of the 1920s. He wrote of a heterogeneous and quite undifferentiated "third estate" (by analogy with the French Revolution) that included the bourgeoisie as one of its components. The upper layers of the third estate consisted of notables (*chorbadzhii*), dealers in sheep, merchants, purveyors to the Turkish court and state, usurers, high civil servants, bishops, etc., all hostile to the revolutionary movement. (On other occasions, Bakalov excludes the *chorbadzhii* from the third estate and places them among the supporters of the Turkish monarchy, against which the third estate was waging a battle.) The middle layers of the third estate consisted of petty bourgeois craftsmen and better-off peasants; they engendered an intelligentsia, which supplied the revolution with ideologues and leaders. Finally, the third estate included ruined artisans and peasants, outcasts and exiles (*hŭshove*), from whom the rank and file of the revolution was recruited (and who stood for the future proletariat). While the class struggle during the Revival was waged between the "third estate" and the *chorbadzhii*, the historical task consisted in the liberation of the third estate as a whole from foreign oppression.[9] (A "third estate" of peasants, craftsmen, and traders would appear again after 1989 in a work by Konstantin Kosev.[10])

The Marxist historian Zhak Natan, who started publishing before World War II and who was very influential in the initial decade of the Communist regime, follows Blagoev in his concept of the social structure and in differentiating between the bourgeoisie and *chorbadzhii* in particular. For him as well, the commercial–industrial bourgeoisie was the major progressive social force—organizer of new methods of production, agent of capitalist market relations, and promoter of material progress. Called the urban or civic class (*grazhdanstvo*) by older authors, it played a leading role in public life and in the peaceful struggles for modern education, schools, books and an autonomous church. The traditional *chorbadzhii* are considered by Natan as a class of their own, connected as a whole with the feudal type of property relations and the Ottoman feudal system, and engaged in tax farming and usury as "pre-capitalist forms of capital." They served as a broker between the Bulgarian population and the Turkish feudal system, and thus profited from Ottoman domination. It was against this class and its "party" that a struggle was eventually launched by the ascending artisans organized into guilds, the so-called Young. Finally, the peasants as a class suffered most under the Turkish yoke and the feudal system, hence they fought for a radical solution to the agrarian question.[11] (As mentioned previously, Natan was a believer in the agrarian thesis.)

The political role of the various social classes is described by the author in the following way. The peasants were the major driving force of the political struggles during the entire Revival epoch, both in the struggle for church independence and in the revolutionary struggles (supplying the rank and file during the April uprising). The urban craftsmen present another major driving force. However, the role of *hegemon* of the national revolution was assumed by the newly formed commercial–capitalist group, which initially played a progressive role and rallied the people in the peaceful struggles for schools, books, and an independent church. When the higher stage of the national struggles—that of armed revolution—was reached, this group became divided; some could go only as far as a "dualist" solution (i.e., the idea of a Turkish–Bulgarian state), but its "progressive part," and especially the "middle classes," which gave rise to a numerous people's intelligentsia, continued to play an important role in the revolutionary struggles. In contrast, the *chorbadzhii* formed part of the apparatus of the Ottoman state and were supporters and instruments of Turkish rule. They were the only ones to oppose the national revolution in all its manifestations openly and to the end, and to play, as a group, a "traitorous and anti-people role" in spite of a few positive examples of participation in the church struggles.[12] Thus for Zhak Natan it is the class of notables that betrayed the revolution, while the bourgeoisie is viewed more favorably (in contrast to the thesis that prevailed later).

The Soviet historian and academician Nikolai Derzhavin published a *History of Bulgaria* in 1948, in which he identifies the *chorbadzhii* with the commercial bourgeoisie and ascribes to them a leading role in the church struggles. (He might have been influenced by Ivan Shishmanov, who described the *chorbadzhii* as a "big bourgeoisie" of merchants and usurers.[13]) Apart from this class, Derzhavin also differentiates between the middle and petty bourgeoisie, impoverished peasants and craftsmen, and "working intelligentsia."[14] We will come back to his views, which had a considerable impact in Bulgaria during the Stalinist years.

A discussion, or rather coordination, of the views on the classes and their political role took place among Bulgarian historians at the beginning of the 1950s, and was published in the professional journal *Istoricheski pregled* (Historical review).[15] A central issue and point of contention was the economic character and the political behavior of the *chorbadzhii* as traditional notables, on the one hand, and of the ascending bourgeoisie as bearer of new economic relations, on the other. In the debate, Zhak Natan advocated (on the defensive) his above-mentioned view that these were different classes, the former tied to the old feudal order and the latter connected with the new capitalist relations.

Dimitŭr Kosev, a historian of the next generation of Marxist scholars with a bright future in store, launched an attack citing Derzhavin's thesis that the *chorbadzhii* were actually not a separate class, and not a class of feudal landlords, but the upper layer of the bourgeoisie forming a "big commercial–*chorbadzhii* bourgeoisie." They were engaged in trade and usury but also in putting-out industries, and only a few possessed land estates (*chifliks*). The "big bourgeoisie" of merchants plus *chorbadzhii* played a reactionary role during the entire Revival, even before the Crimean War (1853–1856) but especially after it. There existed in the Bulgarian society of the Revival a thin layer of middle commercial–industrial bourgeoisie of traders and owners of putting-out factories, and a numerous petty commercial–industrial bourgeoisie of craftsmen, shopkeepers (*bakali*) and ambulant traders (*kiradzhii*). Finally, the majority of the population consisted of peasants.[16] According to Kosev (an opponent of the "agrarian thesis"), the tendency in agrarian relations was for the land to pass into the hands of Bulgarian peasants, who possessed the bulk of the land even before the liberation and were thus independent smallholders while only a fraction were dependent peasants or "serfs."[17]

In his answer, Zhak Natan made the following points. There existed no industrial capitalism in the Bulgarian lands before the Crimean War, hence there was no real capitalist class (and no proletariat) but only craftsmen, owners of putting-out enterprises, and traders. The *chorbadzhii* class consisted of big landowners, who bought land with money earned in trade and usury, and of owners of capital from commerce and usury. They were all connected with the feudal order, the *chifliks* being, according to the author, a feudal form of land ownership, and capital from commerce and money lending being, similarly, a primitive feudal form of wealth. However, with the spread of commodity-money (i.e., market) relations after the Crimean War, some *chorbadzhii* transformed themselves into a bourgeoisie by investing into, and becoming organizers of, capitalist forms of production. Thus there occurred a rapprochement and a merging of the interests of the *chorbadzhii* and the upper bourgeois layers. As for the peasants, Natan repeats his affirmation that the bulk of the land was concentrated in the hands of Turkish *beys* and Bulgarian *chorbadzhii*, hence scarcity of land was the central question for the peasants; moreover, a substantial part of the peasants were "serfs" (i.e., constrained to corvée work), another part found themselves in peasant communities, while a minority were autonomous smallholders.[18]

Finally, a compromise position (already outlined by Natan) was elaborated by some participants in this debate (e.g., Mikhail Dimitrov, and Yono Mitev, who was at that time a colonel). According to this view, the *chorbadzhii* emerged historically in feudal conditions and were favored by the Turkish feudal system as brokers between the Ottoman authorities and the population, and as Turkish "agents" among the Bulgarians, but they did not enjoy feudal privileges nor did they use corvée labor in the capacity of *chiflik*-owners. Some of them eventually became involved in bourgeois–capitalist relations.[19]

The systematization thus yields three positions, espoused by other authors later on: 1) the *chorbadzhii* are clearly distinguishable from the bourgeoisie, the big bourgeoisie included, and form a separate "feudal class," either as part of the Ottoman "feudal" system (as brokers between the authorities and the population) or directly as big feudal landowners (D. Blagoev, Zhak Natan, Todor Pavlov); 2) the *chorbadzhii* cannot be differentiated from the big commercial and money-lending bourgeoisie as to occupation and sources of wealth but are part of it, nor are they "feudal" (Dimitŭr Kosev, Ivan Snegarov, later Georgi Todorov[20], Virdzhiniya Paskaleva[21], and in part Georgi Pletnyov[22]); 3) the *chorbadzhii* should be considered in dynamic terms, in which part of those who derived profits in traditional ways under the protection of the Ottoman order underwent a process of "bourgeois transformation" (*"embourgeoisement"*) after the Crimean War and undertook modern capitalist pursuits (Zhak Natan's rejoinder, with its insistence on the "feudal" quality of the earlier condition, Yono Mitev, Mikhail Dimitrov, later Nikolai Genchev[23]). One can clearly see the role of terminology, and especially of the term "feudal," in the entanglement of this controversy, which becomes easily solvable if one uses the term "traditional" or pre-capitalist instead. The main difference is whether the *chorbadzhii* were primarily big landowners (as Zhak Natan repeats mistakenly after Blagoev), or not.

This controversy contains a strong ideological element connected with the search for an enemy class, even though the scholarly debate (in 1951) somewhat preceded the abrupt turn of 1953. However, clouds were already gathering over the heads of the bourgeoisie, as attested by a paper by Vasil Kolarov (a prominent Komintern functionary, then president of the Bulgarian National Assembly) in as early as 1945.[24] The ideological element added fuel to the controversy quite independent of historical veracity; it also made the problem more intractable and introduced an element of casuistry. Scholars continued to take a stand on the issue individually for decades afterwards. Finally, and quite regrettably, one can see that not only factual untruths but also factual truths (contained in virtually all opinions on the subject) lend themselves to ideological manipulation. To clarify the situation, a small digression is necessary.

The *chorbadzhii* were placed in the role of a traditional collective "enemy of the people" by the revolutionaries during the Revival epoch itself.[25] The most radical forces then succeeded in discrediting and tarnishing in the press rich notables who were not as enthusiastic about the revolution or who denied them sponsorship. The attitude of the organized artisans and of the intelligentsia (mainly teachers) toward the traditional *chorbadzhii* was also negative. It is hard to judge the extent to which the allegations, mostly regarding the appropriation of communal funds, were justified, in the heat of local power struggles between *chorbadzhii* and *esnafi* (or between "old" and "young" in the somewhat patriarchal terminology of the times). Alongside rightful protests there were certainly cases of sheer slander.[26] The following words of Ivan Shishmanov (written in 1930) reveal the forces and passions that were instrumental in shaping the largely negative image of the *chorbadzhii*, and point to the injustice of the generalizations:

"That is why to declare the whole class of *chorbadzii* inimical to national affairs, especially during the Revival epoch, is a glaring historical injustice. There were, of course, in earlier and in later times, monsters and national apostates among them as well, but they were not the rule. [...] The later humiliation of the word "*chorbadzhiya*," which came to stand for bloodsucker and traitor, is largely due to the class struggles between the petty and the big bourgeoisie, and to the political struggles between evolutionists and revolutionaries, between old and young, conservatives and radicals, and it carries with it the traits of every impassioned social ferment, namely, subjectivity and excess."[27]

The negative image of the *chorbadzhii* was taken up after the liberation by the activists of the popular Liberal Party (especially former revolutionaries such as Zakhari Stoyanov) and carried further by the socialists (Dimitŭr Blagoev, Georgi Bakalov, etc.) as a label for their respective enemies. These symbolic struggles will be dealt with in another chapter.

For Marxist historians in particular, connecting the *chorbadzhii* with the "feudal" order makes them more suitable for the role of retrograde class (in addition to being a national enemy), while the blurring of the boundary dividing them from the "progressive" new capitalist forces creates a problem. The reverse of the coin is the idealization of the bourgeoisie as a new and "progressive" class, unblemished by the Turkish order with its *chorbadzhii* supporters, and a driving force in economic–social development. Cast in such neat and idealized (or stigmatized) images, the bourgeoisie and the *chorbadzhii* hover above the ever mixed and changing historical realities.

At a certain moment, however, a new view interfered with the clear-cut opposition between the *chorbadzhii* and the bourgeoisie, in which the former stand for reaction and the latter for progress. The Communists in power, engaged in taking revenge upon their bourgeois enemy, projected their attitude backwards onto the past. The bourgeoisie of the Revival was then portrayed as no less an enemy than the antiquated *chorbadzhii*. This is the context, quite independent of historical truth, of the amalgamation of the bourgeoisie with the hated *chorbadzhii* in the scholarly controversy.[28] In the same context a somewhat paradoxical thesis was formulated—that of the betrayal of the bourgeoisie of its own revolution.

The thesis of the betrayal of the bourgeoisie as a whole, and not only of the big bourgeoisie, was declared by Vŭlko Chervenkov (as general secretary of the Bulgarian Communist Party) in his notorious speech in 1953.[29] It was then phrased in even stronger words by the Communist Party intellectual put in charge of the Academy of Sciences, Todor Pavlov: the bourgeoisie rejected the role of *hegemon* in its own revolution and turned "against the people and into an anti-democratic and anti-patriotic class." While it is true that during the church struggles it played a certain progressive role and was even a leader, afterwards it gradually transformed itself into an "opportunistic, compromising, educationalist (*prosvetitelska*), traitorous, and in the end monarcho-fascist bourgeoisie."[30] (The end is characteristic of the liaison between the bourgeoisie of the Revival and the bourgeoisie of the 1930s and 1940s.)

Though politically traitorous, the bourgeoisie in Todor Pavlov's view is economically more progressive as a bearer of new capitalist relations than the *chorbadzhii*, who are discredited by their connection with the archaic "feudal order." The latter exploited the laboring urban and rural masses "in a typically non-capitalistic, medieval-feudal manner," besides being a "product, appendage, instrument and servant of the Turkish feudal lords, local and central"; hence, they are conservative and reactionary, and a traitor and enemy of the people. Pavlov considers the possibility of the *chorbadzhii* "growing" into a bourgeoisie, but even then they could not become, according to him, "true and typical bourgeois-capitalists" because of their descent and their organic ties with the Turkish feudal authorities.[31]

With publicistic rapture, the warrior journalist–historian Vladimir Topencharov carries the betrayal of the bourgeoisie back to its very inception. To cite a few characteristic passages by this author, the national apostates that Paisii had in mind when calling upon them to come to their senses (in 1762) were the "fathers of the young Bulgarian bourgeoisie, which betrayed its mother tongue and its people while still in diapers" and was "in complete accord with the Turkish feudal assimilators and the Greek bedpans of the assimilators." And again:

"This is an innate deformity that will accompany it all its way. The national liberation movement will have to take the bourgeoisie in tow in its own revolution to the very end."[32]

Toward Rehabilitation

Thanks to the efforts of a number of historians, the above-mentioned "thesis" was overcome in the course of time and the bourgeoisie was gradually vindicated (and, to a certain extent, the *chorbadzhii* as well). It is interesting to see how this was done. The breakthrough, at least officially, occurred during the celebration of the hundredth anniversary of the April uprising in 1966. The "amnesty" ran along several lines. The suspicion of betrayal was first lifted from the petty and the middle bourgeoisie, that is, the comparatively mass layer of craftsmen, shopkeepers, and petty traders.[33] Another line of vindication (apart from "caliber") took time into consideration—the progressive role of the bourgeoisie of any size was acknowledged for the period before the Crimean War (1853–1856), that is, before the appearance of the radical revolutionary trend (thus restoring the older socialist ideas of Blagoev in particular). In fact, the positive role of the bourgeoisie for the earlier part of the Revival had not been disputed even before, but now it came to be emphasized as an important merit. Finally, and following from the previous point, the merits of the bourgeoisie in the educational and church struggles were recognized, as well as some services for the revolution performed by individual activists, and by the class as a whole in the capacity of a genitor of revolutionaries.[34] This presents, of course, an implicit retreat from the extreme revolutionary ("Jacobean") viewpoint as a criterion for assessment.

It should be noted that when a certain social stratum is vindicated, it is considered implicitly as entirely "progressive" ("revolutionary," or generally "good") and not investigated further for "traitors." Once the progressive role of the petty bourgeoisie, and later of the middle bourgeoisie, was accepted, nobody looked for "traitors," "opportunists," "wavering" or simply indifferent people in their milieus. There are only positive and negative classes, and collective heroes and villains in the Marxist narrative of the Bulgarian historical drama.

The slight irony of these observations is not meant as an underestimation of the revisionist efforts. Under the conditions of totalitarian rule and strong ideological control, the revision involves an element of civic courage in challenging the dinosaurs of Stalinism and the ever vigilant party censorship over scholarship. But things are not that simple either, and it is not easy to see who was standing for what in such controversies. What matters is not just what is new in them, but also who is advocating it, and for what reasons. A certain knowledge of the institutional structures of both the scholarly bureaucracy and the ideological party organs at the time (admittedly, inter-penetrating) is required in order to see who had the "authority" to state a certain view or thesis (whatever its content), and who was in disfavor and came under attack whatever he or she suggested. One can note most generally that, as in the Soviet Union, the "reformed" Academy of Sciences (and the Institute of History in particular) were used as instruments for the transformation of the field of history in the desired direction. The creation of "collectives" to work on an official "academic" history of Bulgaria was another means. Furthermore, dogmatic authors also revised the old theses from time to time and rearmed themselves with new ones; new doctrinaires fought with old ones for a place under the sun (and may even have felt like combatants for the Truth). Finally, personal qualities also matter, sometimes a great deal. It may happen that a person occupying a high scholarly–administrative office and in charge of the "official line" is quite tolerant of other opinions (and even protective of their proponents), as the "doyen" of historians, Dimitŭr Kosev, seems to have been.[35] It is very hard indeed, and sometimes quite impossible, for a later observer to ascertain under such conditions the source (and priority) of a new idea in the scholarly exchange, much of which, to complicate things even further, remained oral.

Unfortunately, most of the scholarly tenets in these debates, together with their corrections, seem too doctrinal to a freer scholarship. This is partly due to the rather general and formulaic style of expression (e.g., as when classes are ascribed attitudes and behavior as a "collective subject"), partly to the strong evaluative element, but also, partly, because the corrections acquire full significance only given an obligatory initial tenet or way of posing the problem, and remain somehow tied to it, being more correct in relation to it. The debates are also marred by the assumption of a single and unitary historical Truth on each question, and by intolerance to considerable "deviations" in opinions and even more to the posing of the problem in other ways. Conceiving of the truth as "objective" in the flat epistemological sense of somehow coinciding with historical realities, hence unambiguous and independent of the position of observation, only adds to the bitterness of the debates. There is hardly any understanding of the influence of the (social or political) perspective and of the theoretical frame upon the representation and the assessment, rarely any problematization of the basic operational concepts that carry value judgments (e.g., the notion of "bourgeoisie" or "revolution"), and self-reflexivity, too, is in short supply. Still, one may observe a considerable degree of sophistication, especially in later debates, and a rhetorical and casuistic quality that comes from arguing one's own historical picture as the "true" one, without revealing the assumptions and biases of one's position.

The reappraisal of the big bourgeoisie, and of its directly political role in particular, continued into the 1970s. One can point to the preceding revisionist efforts of Nikolai Genchev, Hristo Gandev and others. According to Gandev the very fact of foreign domination made the Bulgarian big bourgeoisie more patriotic and democratic in its attitudes. It stood at the head of its people in a position of political authority and took part in the national liberation movement, though to varying degrees and with different approaches. The bourgeoisie was represented in the whole range of political trends, the most "leftist" included, on a more massive scale by its younger generations as well as by individual bourgeois intellectuals who had chosen the calling of revolutionary leaders, such as Rakovski, Karavelov, and Botev.[36] Such a notion of "representation" is a great advance on the previous *en bloc* treatment of the bourgeoisie or of its breaking down into smaller blocks (big, middle, petty bourgeoisie) with homogeneous behavior.

An important landmark is the discussion of the political attitudes of the bourgeoisie, published in *Istoricheski pregled* in 1977. "Stimulated" from above as every such discussion, it had the purpose of updating the field and consolidating a mainstream opinion. I will consider this debate in more detail as it demonstrates not only the changing views but also the structure of arguments and the way of thinking.

The signal was given with a paper by Yono Mitev (a colonel turned historian), which aimed at correcting the thesis of the "counter-revolutionary role" of the big bourgeoisie during the April uprising—previously advocated, by the way, by him.[37] As the author points out, the Bulgarian big bourgeoisie was not particularly favored under Turkish military-feudal despotism and was actually treated badly; it suffered from the general state of lawlessness (brigandage, bribery and the arbitrariness of officials), which hindered its capitalist activities. Thus its interests dictated the overthrow of foreign domination and the establishment of a state of its own, where it would be the ruling class. Yono Mitev then proceeds to enumerate the services to the armed struggles performed by the big bourgeoisie in emigration, and especially by the conservative "Old" from the émigré colonies in Bucharest and Odessa, for example, material support for dispatching armed *chetnik* bands into the country, etc. As for the big bourgeoisie living in the Ottoman capital Istanbul, he separates the group of "counter-revolutionaries" (i.e., those who took a stand against the April uprising) from those who had views similar to those of the "Old" in Bucharest. The foreign political orientation of the "Old" toward Russia can hardly incriminate the big bourgeoisie (besides, the national revolutionaries also counted on Russia). The conclusion of the author is that, with the exception of the one sub-group in Istanbul, the others played "generally speaking" a positive role, and "objectively speaking" assisted the national revolution.[38] Yono Mitev's paper is a good example of a dogmatic way of fighting dogmatic tenets (in this case, his own).

The debate on his paper was opened by the very prominent and "authoritative" Dimitŭr Kosev, who insisted on his previous view that the big bourgeoisie took part in, and led, the peaceful legal struggles but took a stand against the "underground" armed political struggles of the 1870s and promoted the ideology of "educationism" (*prosvetitelstvo*), that is, development by peaceful means, and by education in particular. While Kosev takes care to disagree with the "counter-revolutionary role" of the big bourgeoisie, he also reacts against the methods of refuting his standpoint, namely, by citing isolated counter-examples of the big bourgeoisie assisting the revolution.[39] Among other things, this presents us with a chance to see how "rule" and "exceptions" function in proving a given thesis, with examples figuring on one side or the other according to convenience (and there is the possibility for them to change places "dialectically," with the exceptions being elevated to a rule, while instances of the previous "rule" are degraded into "exceptions").

One can see this same strategy applied by Veselin Traikov in the same discussion in favor of the "good cause," that is, provided we accept as good the dissenting idea that the big bourgeoisie was also patriotic and nationalist. The author cites a number of examples from various Balkan peoples, where bourgeois circles connected with the economy of the Ottoman Empire, and even with backward forms of this economy such as tax farming, were not necessarily enemies of the liberation movement.[40]

Rumyana Radkova points to another "positive link" (though mediated) between the bourgeoisie and the national revolutionary movement. This is, namely, the Bulgarian secular intelligentsia, which originated mostly from the burgeoning bourgeoisie and was also dependent on its material support for receiving education and for the funding of its subsequent activities. In its turn, the intelligentsia became the creator and disseminator of the national ideology and supplied the national liberation movement with leaders. The author points out that the ideological differentiation among the intelligentsia was not a function of descent alone but of a multitude of factors that could send descendants of the big commercial–industrial bourgeoisie into the revolutionary–democratic camp.[41]

Another participant in the discussion, Krumka Sharova, expressed her dissatisfaction with (Yono Mitev's) posing the question of the role of the bourgeoisie as an alternative—as either revolutionary or counter-revolutionary. She argued against "going from one extreme to the other" and put forward the third possibility of it being non-revolutionary without being counter-revolutionary. According to her, the differences in views among the bourgeoisie depended not so much on place of residence (within the country or abroad) as on internal social differentiation. The various layers exhibited different attitudes because they did not suffer to the same extent from Ottoman domination. The *chorbadzhii* (considered by the author as part of the big bourgeoisie) were actually in a privileged position and opted for the status quo; the rest of the big bourgeoisie had a stable economic position and profited from the markets of the empire, hence it did not take part in revolutionary activities (though it took the lead in previous educational and church struggles); the middle and the petty producers and traders were in a more precarious position and were accordingly most radical in their political ideas.[42] To sum up a long argument, taking the tripartite scheme of the bourgeoisie as a given, the author exploits to the full the possibilities of differentiating between attitudes and roles in the various domains of the national effort in accordance with the "caliber" of the bourgeoisie.

When summarizing the debate in another paper in search of a consensus, Krumka Sharova adds a time dimension as well, taking into still finer focus the attitudes of the big bourgeoisie before the Crimean War, during the 1860s and 1870s. The conclusions are that on the earlier stage of the national revolution, the big bourgeoisie took part in the liberation movement (wars, revolts, conspiracies, etc.), while in the 1860s it opted for a peaceful "evolution" and diplomacy, and in the 1870s it betrayed outright the revolution "in some places" (i.e., in some localities of the April uprising). Concerning the middle bourgeoisie, the author makes the telling reservation that it took part in the revolutionary movement of the 1870s "only to an extent."[43] (The petty bourgeoisie had long been acquitted and seen as revolutionary.) The problem with predicating political attitudes entirely on class status here and in similar attempts is that it is largely preconceived and contains an a priori revolutionary bias in favor of the lower classes (while, empirically, those in a more precarious position may be less revolutionary). Not that empirical "examples" are lacking, but they are highly selective and easily manipulated in the "rule" and "exception" fashion mentioned above.

In still another turn of the debate, after expressing his disagreement with the total "amnesty" (the term is his) of the big bourgeoisie, Hristo Hristov used the occasion partially to exculpate the *chorbadzhii* to the point of affirming their participation in some revolutionary activities. He sounds, somewhat paradoxically, as if cleansing the *chorbadzhii* from the bad reputation of the bourgeoisie (instead of vice versa).[44]

One can note the inflation of the term "bourgeoisie" in this controversy and in Bulgarian Marxist historical scholarship in general. This occurs by an imperceptible gliding from the older and more traditional (early modern) meaning of "town dwellers" (urban class, burghers), consisting of artisans, shopkeepers, traders, etc., to a modern notion of "bourgeoisie" implying industrial production and modern conditions of life in general. The substitution is all the easier as "industry" (*promishlenost*) also has an older and more traditional (proto-industrial) meaning in Bulgarian. This amounts to thinking of an earlier (less developed) society in terms of a later (more developed) one—an obvious "modernization." Moreover, a Marxist usage of "bourgeoisie" introduces inadequate theoretical constructs and value attitudes to the study of the Bulgarian Revival.

Tsvetana Georgieva is among the few historians who questioned the criterion of belonging to the bourgeois class. She notes that one can speak of a real bourgeoisie in a Marxist sense only where a bourgeois type of property is available (she probably has full and guaranteed private property in mind) and super-value is extracted by the exploitation of free waged labor. Given that, the majority of the Bulgarian peasants until the liberation, hence the majority of the population, did not constitute a bourgeoisie both because of the character of their property (supposedly "feudal") and because peasants did not exploit anybody except themselves. But the author stops short of applying the definition to the Bulgarian town dwellers of the nineteenth century. She is satisfied with tracing the descent of the revival bourgeoisie (after Krŭstyu Rakovski) to the big stock-raisers of the eighteenth century, who contained "potentially" the "progressive bourgeois tendencies" of Bulgarian society.[45]

Hristo Hristov also posed disturbing questions about the class structure of the Bulgarian society of the Revival, for example, whether the peasant majority represented a petty bourgeoisie; whether the big bourgeoisie was capitalist (in the Marxist sense of enriching itself on super-value); whether the Bulgarian society as a whole was bourgeois in its character; and where, in that case, is the antagonistic working class.[46] The very fact that such questions were posed from a doctrinal author with simple ideas about class makes the implied negative answers still more alarming. In his frank response Hristov emphasized the predominantly pre-modern (commercial and usurious) character of the Bulgarian bourgeois class, the fact that it was not connected with "only" a capitalist mode of production, that the capitalist elements had just sprung into existence, and that the society as a whole was still not bourgeois. But he does not draw inferences for the "bourgeois revolution."

How is a "bourgeois revolution" possible in the absence or weakness of a modern bourgeoisie?[47] Some authors were aware of the problem and tried to deal with it. In a different context, Nikolai Genchev explains the failure of the April uprising by referring to the "anemia" of the bourgeoisie (although the uprising is, for him, an attempt at national liberation in the first place, and only then a "bourgeois revolution").[48] More generally, one can blame the failure of the "bourgeois revolution" on the weakness of the bourgeoisie. The point is that in so doing one does not put the existence of a "bourgeois revolution" in doubt.

Konstantin Kosev seems to have wrestled more desperately than any other historian with the problem of a bourgeois revolution in an economically and socially underdeveloped society. His original "solution," mentioned in the previous chapter, effected a logical inversion: instead of proving the development of capitalist relations (and of a strong bourgeoisie) in order to explain the revolution, he inferred capitalism and the bourgeoisie from the revolution (itself taken as a fact); the failure of the revolution in the form of the April uprising shows simply that the bourgeoisie was still not strong enough.[49]

In a recent book, Kosev makes yet another *coup de force* in treating the question of social structure during the Revival. In his view, the bourgeoisie was the only class formation in Bulgarian society comprising, in fact, the bulk of the people with the exception of a layer of "pauperized elements" (agricultural laborers, apprentices, journeymen, hired workers, the poor).

Like the "third estate" on the eve of the French Revolution, Bulgarian
society consisted of peasants, craftsmen and traders, who "acquired a
qualitatively new essence under the impact of the growing bourgeois tendencies"—namely, they lost their medieval character and swelled the ranks
of a bourgeoisie in the process of formation.[50] We are thus left with a magical and logically tautological bourgeois transformation under the pressure
of "bourgeois tendencies."

The widely accepted formula that the Russo-Turkish war (of 1877/8)
played, for the Bulgarians, the role of a bourgeois revolution (besides
bringing liberation) makes, in fact, the "bourgeois revolution" do without a
bourgeoisie. The thesis of the "betrayal" by the bourgeoisie of its revolution and the taking up of the task by other classes says the same in another
way. According to this solution, it is left to other forces to accomplish the
work of "progress." No attention is given to the fact that the whole retro-
spective interpretation of the Revival as an epoch of the maturing of the
bourgeois revolution becomes unconvincing.

The controversies regarding the bourgeoisie considered so far were par-
alleled by a reappraisal of the role of the traditional notables in public life
during the national revival. Instrumental in normalizing the views was the
more neutral conceptualization of the *chorbadzhii* as a primarily administrative (instead of class) category—persons fulfilling an office in the Bulgarian communal councils (*obshtina*). It was introduced, or rather reintro-
duced, by Hristo Hristov. It thus became possible to account for the fact
that the *chorbadzhii* were socially heterogeneous; that they were sometimes
connected with the older "feudal" activities (i.e., the collection of taxes,
usury) and sometimes belonged to the new bourgeois classes; that they
expressed the interests of various social groups and, alongside those
("Old") who were loyal to the Turkish authorities and to the Greek Patriarchy, there were also "new" *chorbadzhii* recruited from among the artisans
and traders who headed the struggles for Bulgarian bishops; that the rural
chorbadzhii were simply richer peasants; that although the *chorbadzhii*
mediated between the Turkish authorities and the population, as functionaries of the local self-government, they supported the national revival (by
taking care of the schools and churches, though rarely by taking part in
armed struggles); that the *chorbadzhii* played a different role before the
Crimean War and in the changed conditions of the national movement
afterwards, etc.[51]

The lawyer Stefan S. Bobchev, himself the descendent of a *chorbadzhii*
family, was the first to consider systematically (in 1938) the various mean-

ings of the word *chorbadzhi* and to describe the activities of these notables. He points to a generalized and metaphoric meaning of the word, that is, a well-to-do and influential person, a notable, elder, and, most broadly, head (master) of the house, who hosted the Turkish civil servants touring the country; this meaning derives from the soup (*chorba*) cook in the Turkish army. The author also points to a later, narrower meaning, namely, a person fulfilling a public (communal) function and acting as a broker between the Turkish authorities and the population, being responsible for the collection of taxes and the allotment of corvée tasks in particular. As pointed out by Bobchev, the *chorbadzhii* were a motley bunch of people. Some defended the population before the Turkish authorities and did charitable work for the poor and for people in distress. There were those among them who performed great services in "people's affairs" (i.e., the national cause), for example by making donations to schools and churches, taking part in the church struggles, etc. But there were also unworthy people who mismanaged communal affairs and misused their position for personal gain. Still, the vilifying of the *chorbadzhii* as "bloodsuckers" of the people, first by Rakovski and then by other revolutionaries, was an injustice. It was justified to an extent with regard to *chorbadzhii* with public functions, who confused tax accounts—whether on purpose or by mistake—especially after the Crimean War, when the population was burdened with many new or emergency taxes. But it was easier to blame the mediators than to protest directly against the Turkish authorities.[52]

Coming back to the Communist period, the partial "amnesty" of the *chorbadzhii* was greatly helped by considering the services and merits of particular personalities in particular places. This is the strategy employed by Georgi Pletnyov in his numerous works on the *chorbadzhii* in the region around the town of Tŭrnovo. The author reveals the great role of notables in organizing the military defense of the communities (back in the "Time of Troubles") and in protecting the population from Turkish arbitrariness, as well as in setting up schools and churches, and participating in conspiracies and armed revolts (especially before the Crimean War, when they constituted an undisputed local elite).[53]

The *chorbadzhii* are presented in a still more sympathetic light by the same author in a book that appeared after 1989 under the telling title *The Chorbadzhii and the Bulgarian National Revolution*. The author regards them (following Hristo Hristov) as cross-class, socially motley functionaries of the local self-government. He considers their contribution to the various currents of the "national revolution"—education, church struggles, and

armed revolts—and gives them a generally high grade, though differentiated as to period and lower for the time after the Crimean War, when many
of them succumbed to "Turcophile" (i.e., pro-Turk) ideas, and to legalism
(or sultan legitimism). Characteristically, the author puts himself in the
shoes of the *chorbadzhii* in order to explain why, from their point of view
(as communal functionaries and rich people), the revolt was unnecessary
and harmful, and only the reform of the empire was good; moreover,
(peaceful) "evolutionism" is presented as a more realistic assessment of the
balance of forces. Now that high class status is no longer incriminating, the
chorbadzhii are identified again to a great extent with the big (and middle)
bourgeoisie in a social sense and as to political preferences (evolutionism,
reliance on Russia for liberation).[54]

The vindication of the *chorbadzhii*, especially in the role of communal
functionaries, is carried still further by the sociologist Milena Stefanova.
Their role prior to the Crimean War is judged as indisputably positive,
although less so afterwards, when they were attacked by the new social
forces—craftsmen, the intelligentsia of teachers, and the revolutionaries.
The defense of the *chorbadzhii* includes sympathy with their delicate position as mediators between the Ottoman authorities that required legitimism, and the growing claims of the local population—rather like being
"between hammer and anvil." A separate chapter is devoted to the treatment of the *chorbadzhii* in the Revival newspapers, which the author finds
generally unjust. Finally, she recommends that the "institution" of the
chorbadzhii be regarded as a forerunner and antecedent of the institution
of mayor, a valuable source of knowledge about the tradition of Bulgarian
self-government that has become very relevant in view of democratization
after 1989. To cite her words sounding as a "policy recommendation":

"In the present period it might not be superfluous to cast a glance
backwards to history in order to draw a lesson from the will of our forefathers in preserving the Bulgarian spirit. And we should know that they
were realizing their plans in the framework of the Bulgarian communes.
The Bulgarian *chorbadzhii* were among the major actors in the communes.
Let us draw a lesson from them. For good and for bad."[55]

Ironically, the *chorbadzhii*, so hated before, end up as a positive example
of self-government functionaries in today's democratizing society.

The *chorbadzhii* pose an important methodological problem: can they
be conceived of as a social group or class, implying at least a common outlook and common interests, if not group loyalties, solidarity and a degree
of cooperation? One pole is presented by the Marxist approach of aggregat-

ing individuals in large groups (classes) and of exaggerating supra-local homogeneity, cohesion, and group solidarity. This also satisfies the need for a clear-cut class enemy. However, the *chorbadzhii* are a very strange class precisely from a Marxist point of view, given the heterogeneity of their economic basis and the fact that they cannot easily be distinguished from the bourgeoisie. They have also been presented as a social stratum, that is, something "less" than a class, for example, by Nikolai Genchev.[56] The (consciously sought for) effect of this treatment within the Marxist framework is that it somehow downplays the significance attributed to them.

At the other pole is the approach that presents the *chorbadzhii* as separate individuals with little in common, as in the following statement (from the pre-Communist epoch) by Dimitŭr Strashimirov:

"There is no such thing as an estate of *chorbadzhii*. This is a category of separate individuals that occupied a position in accordance with the local conditions in a bigger or smaller town, or in a village, everyone according to his bad character or his personal preferences. This is a dispersed and local element. Nothing but isolated persons."[57]

As has been demonstrated, *chorbadzhii* is actually an umbrella concept that covers figures from various epochs and of different description: the older self-willed sheep dealers (collectors of the tax on sheep, owners of large sheep flocks, traders in sheep), with their armed retinues and bravado gestures; authoritative elders and self-willed local dignitaries in a patriarchal society; the functionaries of the communes following the introduction of a measure of local self-government by the Ottomans; and, most generally, influential rich people (regardless of how they made their wealth and of their personal qualities and public merits).[58]

The word *chorbadzhiya* has been the subject of an evolution, in the course of which it has pointed to different referents and absorbed corresponding value attitudes. It is precisely the lack of clarity and the elasticity of meaning that have made the word so convenient as a stigma. Leaving aside historical veracity, the *chorbadzhii* have taken the role of enemy of the nation, the people, the poor, etc. in the discourses of revolutionaries, populists, and socialists (and even today the word is used in everyday life to refer to a person, somewhat ironically, as a "big shot"). This is a prime example of a "historical term" not extinguished by time but dragged along and implicated in present-day realities, epoch after epoch. Later discourses are modeled on earlier ones, already divorced from realities, but with a stigmatizing effect. For this reason it is hard to neutralize and use the term in historical scholarship, which has itself misused the word grossly while claiming a "scientific" status. Even when such an attempt is made, as in some of the recent works cited, one can hardly accept it without irony, knowing its "career." It would be better to replace the term with a more neutral one, such as "notables" or "elders," but the clarification would refer back to the previous regrettable state of affairs. Maybe one should just leave it to the pragmatic influence of the new market and democratic conditions to "rehabilitate" the term from negative connotations, or at least restore the ambivalence accompanying the bearers of wealth and power in the midst of a generally poor and egalitarian public.

The Peasants

The vast majority of the Bulgarian population during the epoch of the national revival were peasants. While "bourgeois" authors were not very much interested in the peasants, they are reserved a special place in the Marxist schemes of the 1930s and the 1950s. They are the collective (somewhat anonymous) hero that suffered most severely under Turkish feudal oppression, both under the earlier feudal fief system and on the big land estates (*chifliks*). In some versions, the peasants feature as serfs until very late (up to the abolition of the fief system in the 1830s). According to the agrarian thesis considered previously, on the eve of the liberation they were in a process of losing their land, or were experiencing "land hunger." From their being most oppressed, the role of the peasants as the "main driving force" in the national revolution is inferred (first by Georgi Bakalov and Zhak Natan).[59] The Communist general secretary Vŭlko Chervenkov defined the bourgeois–democratic revolution itself as peasant because of the betrayal of the bourgeoisie, which made the peasants stand out as the "main driving force," led by the "people's intelligentsia," of peasant descent itself.[60]

The years of the "cult of personality" were crowned by an academic two-volume "*History of Bulgaria*" (1954), for which a special "model" was first worked out under the guidance of Todor Pavlov in the capacity of president of the Bulgarian Academy of Sciences. Contained within it is a phantasmagoric description of the unbearable situation of the peasants under the feudal oppression of the Turkish military fief owners (*sipahi*) during the eighteenth century. According to the authors, the peasants had to pay at least 41 taxes to the *sipahi*, the local administration, the treasury, and the

Greek Church. Besides, they were subject to total arbitrariness and severe repression by tax collectors, as well as arbitrary mobilization and requisitions in times of war.[61] The unbridled imagination of the authors was ironically assisted by the Communist repression of the peasants during the ongoing "collectivization" and the forced deliveries and requisitions.

There were, however, different opinions around that time as well. Thus we have seen Dimitŭr Kosev earlier holding to the view (in the discussion in 1951) that the peasants were personally free in their majority, and that they possessed land of their own and were actually smallholders. Views on the peasants became realistic in the works of Hristo Gandev and of the Ottomanist scholars Vera Mutafchieva, Strashimir Dimitrov, and Bistra Tsvetkova.[62] The main points already mentioned in another context are hereditary land tenure; the possibility for the peasant to sell his land and move to another place; practically no serfdom (some corvée work but no personal dependence); the development of big, semi-capitalist land estates during the nineteenth century alongside the conditional *sipahi* fief, but only in some regions; the revocation of the *sipahi* fiefs from 1832 onwards through the 1840s, resulting in the predominance of free peasant land ownership; the passing of the greater part of the land into the hands of the Bulgarian peasants who cultivated it; the movement of Bulgarians down from the mountainous regions where they had previously found refuge into the plains in the last decades prior to the liberation, etc.

The Intelligentsia

The intelligentsia receives an occasional mention by earlier authors. Literary historians were primarily interested in outstanding personalities—monks, priests, writers, and eventually teachers as a professional group, although they rarely treated the intelligentsia as a whole. The question of the public role of the intelligentsia is of special significance, all the more so as the idea of a national mission was widely shared by the men of the Revival itself. A number of earlier authors recognize the prominent public role and national leadership of the intelligentsia. Stefan Bobchev, for example, enumerates the major driving forces of the struggles of the Revival in the following succession: from the *chorbadzhii* through the priests to the craftsmen with their guilds, and finally to the teachers.[63] The intelligentsia is defined in terms of its public role and its duty to guide and enlighten the people by authors under the influence of Russian populism (*narodni-*

chestvo). Some contrasted the intelligentsia of the Revival, unified by the national ideal, with the division of the post-liberation intelligentsia between parties and ideologies.[64] The nationalist Right in the 1930s evoked the image of the intelligentsia as a (spiritual) leader of the Bulgarian people during the Revival in their calls for a "new Revival."[65] The idea that the intelligentsia provided the national revolution with leadership was also expressed by the leftist sociologist Ivan Hadzhiiski in a work on the April uprising.[66]

In a popularizing history of Bulgaria published in 1947, Hristo Gandev presents the young Bulgarian intelligentsia descended from the middle and lower classes, and especially the teachers, as the main revolutionary force in the end phase of the Revival. Its radicalization is explained by the author with reference to its more developed political consciousness but also to its material hardship and proletarianization, and the absence of conditions for applying its qualifications in the Ottoman Empire—hence the attraction of the ideal of an independent Bulgarian state with administrative, economic, and cultural institutions of its own. The "materialistic" explanation here sounds stronger than the "idealistic" one. A second revolutionary group in this account was formed by the political émigrés, who worked together with the intelligentsia of teachers to organize politically the peasants and the lower urban strata.[67]

The intelligentsia posed a special problem for Stalinist (Chervenkovist) historians. While it was clear that the intelligentsia (educated priests included) took the lead in the educational and church struggles, there was the all-important question of its participation in armed revolutionary struggles. That it had a very important contribution in that respect, too, was not doubted. But the doctrinal problem is that, not constituting a basic class (or a "class" at all), it can hardly be the hegemon (the leading force) of the revolution. Besides this scholastic consideration, it would be embarrassing for a Communist regime, deriving its legitimacy from the "working class" (or the "people") and viewing the intelligentsia with (Leninist) distrust, to laud it too much. Interestingly, Vŭlko Chervenkov allowed the intelligentsia to stand at the head of the national "peasant revolution," but by default—as a result of the betrayal of the bourgeoisie, the absence of a working class with a party, and the insufficiently organized artisans—and he took additional care to describe it as "the most progressive part" of the "people's intelligentsia," itself of peasant stock.[68]

In his work on the April uprising many years later (1975), Hristo Gandev touched upon the relationship between the intelligentsia and the revolution again. He pointed to the fact that many Bulgarian professional revolutionaries came from the intelligentsia, recruited in its turn from the younger male generations of craftsmen and traders. In the April uprising in particular, the bourgeoisie was represented by its younger educated generations, who actually "made the events."[69] Similar views, though less generalized and explicit, can be found in certain works on the teachers and their role in the national revolution.[70]

The Canadian historian Thomas Meininger is the author of a sociological–historical work on the Bulgarian intelligentsia of the Revival. He made a sociological profile of it by studying the background, place of origin, occupation, age, sex, etc. of a sample of several hundred educated people. Bringing in psychology, he linked the revolutionary missionary attitude of the young Bulgarian intelligentsia, especially those educated abroad, with their idealistic upbringing and their frustration at the humiliating conditions around and the indifference of the peasant masses, and, last but not least, their resentment at the absence of opportunities for professional realization in the Ottoman Empire.[71] (In fact, a similar observation was made by Ivan Hadzhiiski in his work on the "psychology" of the April uprising, published in 1940.[72])

The thesis that frustrated young and educated people are more prone to "radicalization" is quite convincing and can be empirically confirmed. It is interesting that orthodox Bulgarian Marxists, always on the lookout for class struggle and conflict in general, refused to find them here, maybe because they did not recognize the intelligentsia as a "class" or because they could not admit such a motivation for class struggles, or simply because the struggles of "the young" and of "educated people" did not qualify as sufficiently serious. A more differentiated social description of the revolutionaries, including (besides "class") also age, sex, profession, civil status, place of residence, etc., would portray them as primarily younger people, males, unmarried, emigrants, coming from just a few localities, etc. But in leading away from what they considered important, and in revealing a comparatively narrow recruitment ground for the revolution, such an approach would have seemed crudely "reductionist" to the masters of reductionism.

The interest in the intelligentsia as a separate and very important social group increased especially in the 1980s, probably stimulated by a growing self-consciousness and the critical attitude of some historians and humanitarians (e.g., Nikolai Genchev, Toncho Zhechev, and the writer Georgi Mishev), who may have felt like heirs and successors to the intelligentsia of the Revival, with its exalted sense of public mission.[73] Works by Rumyana Radkova are also devoted to this theme,[74] as are works by Angel Dimitrov (on the teachers in particular)[75], as well as publications resulting from comprehensive research on the intelligentsia of the Revival under the direction of Nikolai Genchev.[76] Various aspects of the intelligentsia were studied, such as its social and economic background, education, professional structure and employment, social status, and diverse public activities. Its role in the national struggles attracted special attention. There is, in all these works, a characteristic emphasis on the missionary national role of the intelligentsia (idealized to a point), and one may sense a certain empathy on the part of the authors.

The Class Struggles between the Social and National

The social struggles in Bulgarian society, identified by non-Marxist authors (Boyan Penev, the early Hristo Gandev), were considered at the beginning of this chapter. Social struggles were of special importance for the Marxist interpretation of the Revival, being ascribed the role of an engine of progress. But it is here that the greatest problems arose.

There were, of course, classes in the Bulgarian society of the Revival epoch, in spite of its social leveling, as in every society with a certain complexity and a degree of social differentiation. But social difference, and even social "contradictions," do not necessarily result in struggles, especially in a predominantly traditional, patriarchal society (the relation between masters and apprentices is paradigmatic). And, most importantly, the fact of foreign domination entangles the social with the national aspect as it placed all Bulgarians in a subordinate position (as a *reaya*, i.e., flock) and reoriented their grievances toward the Ottoman rulers. The national mobilization also overshadowed and blurred the existing social contradictions and displaced them toward the national plane.

In the end, the idea of a (more serious) class struggle could only be rescued by taking it out of Bulgarian society proper and applying it to relations between the Bulgarians as a subordinate "class" (*reaya*) and the Turks (actually, the Ottoman elite) as a politically dominant master "class," and between Bulgarians and Greeks (the Greek Patriarchy as a tax-collecting authority, and the rival Greek bourgeoisie). Inter-ethnic relations are then interpreted as class relations. This is not without justification, though somewhat strange for the usual (intra-ethnic) Marxist interpretation. The Bulgarian *chorbadzhii* appear as an "exploiter class," but again only in so far as they supported the foreign masters and profited from their protection. The difficulties of a "classical" class interpretation can be illustrated with a few examples that characteristically mix social and national antagonism in various doses.

According to Georgi Bakalov, Bulgarian history presents a history of "class struggle," in which only classes and circumstances are subject to change. In his view, the class struggle in Bulgarian society before the liberation was waged between the "third estate" of artisans, petty traders, peasants, and the newly created intelligentsia on the one hand, and the "*chorbadzhii*," that is, usurers, big landowners, merchants, and bureaucrats, supported by the Ottoman authorities, on the other. But even he admits that the "historical task" of the epoch consisted in the liberation of the "third estate" from foreign domination, hence the organization of a revolutionary movement for political independence.[77]

Another militant Marxist author (Zhak Natan) tried to solve the issue of class struggle by differentiating between its form and content—national form, social content. To cite a passage by him:

"The group struggle during this epoch, from its lowest to its highest forms, assumed, and could not but assume, a national scope and a national character. The struggle of the peasants against the fief holders (*sipahi*) and the *chorbadzhii*, and the struggle of the artisans (*esnafi*) against the *chorbadzhii*, were simultaneously struggles against foreign domination, against the domination of the Ottomans. The struggle of the Bulgarians against Turkish domination was a social struggle in its content, national in its form."[78]

The interethnic aspect, that is, Bulgarian peasants against Turkish fief holders, thus becomes part of the social conflict while being also a struggle against foreign domination. Moreover, purely Bulgarian struggles, for example, Bulgarian peasants and artisans against Bulgarian *chorbadzhii*, are fitted into the national format by stressing that the latter were supporters of foreign rule among the Bulgarians.

The social contradictions and struggles are interpreted by Goran Todorov very clearly as contradictions between opposing ethnic–religious groups, in which the Bulgarians as a whole are in the position of a subordinated "class":

"The basic class contradiction was the contradiction between, on the one hand, the foreign feudal class—the Turkish *beys* and *agas*, whose chief instrument of exploitation was the Turkish state, and the Greek Patriarchy, which, during the nineteenth century, was the conductor of the interests and the assimilation aspirations of the Greek bourgeoisie; and, on the other, the mass of the Bulgarian people—all categories of peasants, craftsmen, factory owners, and traders. The revolution had to solve exactly this class conflict. In this period the burgeoning Bulgarian bourgeoisie was part of the people's masses in a sociopolitical sense."[79]

This author is fully consistent in pointing out that the class contradictions within Bulgarian society itself remained relatively underdeveloped and played a subordinate role during the entire Revival epoch.[80]

Among the Bulgarians themselves, social (class) struggles were waged between the traditional local *chorbadzhii* and the ascending artisans, shopkeepers, and petty traders for the control of the communes and the management of schools and churches, that is, local struggles in purely Bulgarian towns during the last decades of the Revival. These struggles were largely exaggerated and generalized in the writings of the Stalinist period. An example is provided by Dimitŭr Kosev. Not satisfied with the struggles between the "big commercial–*chorbadzhi* bourgeoisie" and the artisans organized in guilds (*esnafi*), he searched painstakingly for contradictions within the "petty commercial–industrial bourgeoisie" itself, for example, between masters, journeymen and apprentices.[81]

Leaving aside such fictitious clashes between masters and apprentices, and the talk about "proletariat" (later replaced with the more realistic "pre-proletariat" or "urban poor"), the urban struggles were not as neat and structured around principles, as pointed out by a number of researchers (Georgi Pletnyov, Virdzhiniya Paskaleva, and Hristo Hristov).[82] At the beginning, and until quite late, these struggles were being waged between the "parties" of adherents of different *chorbadzhii*, and eventually between "old" and "young" *chorbadzhii* with a different outlook and style, while the artisans entered the public arena at a later date (around the middle of the nineteenth century). In addition, the power struggles had a strong personal aspect and often damaged the conducting of public affairs. Finally, the Bulgarian "self-government" was actually restricted when formally arranged during the era of the Ottoman reforms and especially by the law on the *vilayet*s (large administrative units) of 1865. The latter aimed at incorporating the Christian population into an ethnically mixed and centralized administrative system and discredited the local self-government from a national(ist) point of view.

The sociologist Milena Stefanova has given recently a still more defocused and sociologically neutralized picture of the struggles in the communes.[83] After the initial strife between factions of different *chorbadzhii* for the local self-government, their power was contested in the last pre-liberation decades by the new social forces—the artisans and the intelligentsia (mainly teachers). The conflict basically concerned the management of the communal finances, now provided mainly by the artisans; the fulfillment of the fiscal functions (the allotment and collection of taxes); but also activities in the educational field and the church question. While the *chorbadzhii* were more "conservative" as a rule and wanted things to go in the old ways, the new forces should not be idealized as entirely principled either; the struggle included a natural striving for power and profit, and recourse to dubious means—unsubstantiated accusations, newspaper campaigns to discredit opponents in public opinion, etc. In the author's opinion, these struggles on a local level for the "democratization of society" do not warrant accusing the *chorbadzhii* of the betrayal of "people's interests."

Especially arbitrary is the idea of a peasant class struggle against Turkish fief holders (*sipahi*) and big Bulgarian landowners (of which there were few). Revolts by Bulgarian peasants in the northwestern Bulgarian lands during the first half of the nineteenth century are often cited as forms of peasant class struggle. The problem is that they were closely associated with local peculiarities, such as local separatism, the refusal of the governor to undo the *sipahi* system, the encroachment of influential persons upon peasant lands, and the exaction of additional taxes, in addition to being connected with external instigation (on the part of Serbia) in order to qualify as the generalized class conflict with clear-cut fronts usually imagined by doctrinal Marxists.[84] Considerable stretching and twisting is necessary in the effort to make the local into the national or to give to a particular economic grievance the meaning of a class or national struggle. A typical means of rescuing the idea of class struggle in such dubious cases has been to define them as "spontaneous" forms of social protest.

Hristo Gandev is, once again, the author of a realistic account of the issue of classes and class contradictions. He points to the subjugation of the Bulgarian people as a whole and to the common liberation objective as factors of social and political rapprochement and solidarity between the bourgeois circles and the lower strata of Bulgarian society; the metaphors of "pressing," "flattening out" and "cohesion" are used to describe this situation. Such conditions are rarely found among free peoples living in a polity of their own (e.g., the Russian big bourgeoisie was alienated from both the Russian peasants and from the intelligentsia). To argue his point, Gandev also stresses the close economic ties of the big bourgeoisie with crafts and retail trade, as well as its recent descent from artisans and peasants and its nearness to them in habits, morals, knowledge, and prejudices.[85]

The issue of class struggle was thus deflated in the last Communist decades. Not surprisingly, it was tacitly dropped from works on the Bulgarian Revival written after 1989, in parallel with the emphasis on the national meaning.

Vulgar Marxist Sociologism and Its Abandoning

A vulgar sociologism under the sign of Marxism thrived in the initial decades of Communist rule in Bulgaria, in which the political trends or ideological views of a given national activist were linked with class status and supporting "social basis." Taking reductionism to its extreme, the political groupings express totally and exclusively class interests, while the particular activists are guided in their views and political activities by class motivations alone. In its turn, class (defined mostly in terms of property) is linked "one to one" with political parties and ideological programs in such a way that a given class stratum champions distinct ideological views and supports one particular "party."

The founder of the Bulgarian Socialist Party, Dimitŭr Blagoev, set the pitch with the following description. After the success of the church struggles the radical part of the bourgeois class, and especially the impoverished petty bourgeoisie in emigration, embarked upon a course of revolutionary struggle toward political liberation. This resulted in a split between "evolutionists" (persons around the Exarchate, *chorbadzhii* close to the Turkish authorities, part of the bourgeois class), and "revolutionaries." Within the "revolutionary party" itself a further differentiation of ideological trends occurred—into "radicals" (led by Lyuben Karavelov), who expressed the interests of the "more well-to-do petty bourgeoisie and the revolutionary part of the commercial–industrial class and the peasant classes" on the one hand, and, on the other, "communards" (led by Hristo Botev) from the "impoverished and proletarianized petty bourgeois and peasant masses."[86]

The a priori logic here (and in Marxist authors to follow) is that the poorer and more impoverished a certain social layer, the more radical and revolutionary it will be; the poor and déclassés (the contemporary term was *hŭshove*) are the revolutionaries par excellence. It is interesting to note a paradoxical agreement on this count between socialist authors and the most conservative "bourgeois" authors. The difference is that the latter thought of sinking to a lower class status as negative, while the former hailed the "proletarianized" people as a recruiting ground for their future army.

Zhak Natan presents the class underpinnings of the political factions in the following way. After the Crimean War the party of the "Young" (meaning the organized artisans) and the party of the "Old" (meaning the *chorbadzhii*) engendered four political trends: Turcophiles (pro-Turks, i.e., those who wanted the preservation of the Ottoman Empire); dualists (i.e., those in favor of a dualist Turkish–Bulgarian monarchy); Russophiles (pro-Russians, i.e., those expecting liberation to come from Russia); and revolutionaries. The Turcophiles were *chorbadzhii* and the upper commercial-industrial class; the dualists were big and middle traders and craftsmen inside and outside the country; and the Russophiles were big émigré merchants and owners of land estates in Romania. Finally, the revolutionaries were a new emigration composed of impoverished artisans and landless peasants, chased out of the country for their revolutionary activities but finding support within the country among the artisans and peasants as well as among the liberal fraction of the traders and industrialists and among the people's intelligentsia.[87]

The Soviet academician Nikolai Derzhavin detailed the class interpretation of the Bulgarian Revival to an absurd degree in his *History of Bulgaria* (published in 1948). This scheme is also interesting for its transcription of Bulgarian political trends in terms of the French Revolution.[88] According to the author, the church struggles were led by the commercial bourgeoisie. After the winning of church autonomy, it did not want to go further and the banner of the class battles was taken up by the revolutionary-minded part of the middle and petty bourgeoisie, the impoverished peasantry, the impoverished part of the urban artisans (in the process of being ruined), and the working intelligentsia. These classes began to struggle not only against the semi-feudal Turkish bureaucracy and the Greek priests and merchants, but also against their own commercial–money-lending exploiter bourgeoisie—the *chorbadzhii*. This marks a split in the "third estate," which, until then, had presented a united bourgeois front comprising various social strata under the guidance of the commercial bourgeoisie against foreign domination. The split (into rich and poor, exploiters and exploited) was the result of growing class contradictions within the Bulgarian bourgeoisie itself, under the impact of advancing capitalist relations in the 1860s. Rakovski was the first organizer of the petty bourgeoisie, that is, of a block of unemployed workers from the putting-out (decentralized) enterprises, impoverished peasantry, artisans, petty traders and laboring intelligentsia, who all became class aware (as a "class for itself") and began to oppose the *chorbadzhii*. Thus Rakovski became the first leader of the Bulgarian revolutionary democracy and he also worked out new tactics for revolutionary activities in the form of organized guerrillas (*chetnitsi*) to conduct the armed struggle against foreign political domination and the feudal order.

Toward the end of the 1860s, there were three political factions among the Bulgarian emigration in Romania: the group of the big financial-commercial bourgeoisie around the "Benevolent Society" (*Dobrodetelna druzhina*) on the right-wing flank; the petty bourgeois revolutionary group of Rakovski, composed of guerrillas and *hŭshove* (i.e., outcasts, and the hungry, homeless poor) on the left-wing flank; and the petty bourgeois opportunistic group of Ivan Kasabov around the newspaper "*Narodnost*," which presented in essence "the swamp of intelligentsia." Expressed in the language of the French Revolution, the right-wing group were the Bulgarian *Feuillants* and *Girondists*, the group in the middle were the Bulgarian *Jacobins-Dantonists* (the *Dantonists* being the opportunists in this block); and the group on the left were the Bulgarian left *Jacobins*, which united at this stage the Bulgarian *Robespierrites* (i.e., better-off petty bourgeois elements) and *Hébertists* (i.e., impoverished layers of the petty bourgeoisie).

The active role in the further deployment of the Bulgarian bourgeois revolution passed to the left wing of the Bulgarian *Jacobins*, which evolved from the group of Rakovski. His death left the Bulgarian bourgeois revolution temporarily without a leader until it found new leaders in the persons of Levski, and his friends Karavelov and Botev. They brought the revolution to a climax, when the extreme leftist and revolutionary elements of the petty bourgeoisie—the left wing of the Bulgarian *Jacobins*—took over the arena. The revolution then became a revolution of the whole people, the expression of mass heroism against foreign political domination and against all social exploitation.

The "Jacobin revolution," in the form of the April uprising, was defeated. After the liberation of Bulgaria the reactionaries seized political power and grew stronger due to the rapid process of capitalist industrial development. But a new enemy of the bourgeoisie, in the shape of the working class, sprang up with the development of the forces of production and the sharpening of class contradictions. The new *Jacobin* forces heroically carried the banner of the social revolution until the moment when they were able (together with the impoverished laboring peasantry) to win the final battle. The victory of the Bulgarian Communists, directed by their leader Georgi Dimitrov, over the fascist clique on 9 September 1944, marked the happy beginning of a solution to the social problem, one that Levski and Botev could only dream about. Thus far Nikolai Derzhavin.

As one can see, the projecting of the French Revolution (in its extreme left, "Jacobin," interpretation) on the Bulgarian national revolutionary movement results in the caricature of a primarily social revolution with preconceived social and political articulations. The whole construction is guided by the logic of revolutionizing in stages, which begins from the rich upper layers, who then lead a block of all classes below them (still unaware of their own class interests), and goes all the way down through the middle, lower-middle and petty bourgeois strata to the most impoverished and downtrodden, who are the last to manifest class consciousness of their own. Thus an incessant class (and, together with it, political) differentiation takes place, in which the "block" of the previous stage disintegrates into its social components in the next stage. The banner of class struggle passes to ever lower classes, and, along with this, there occurs a broadening of the front of the struggle, so that an ever growing number of classes or strata higher up are included among the enemy. The "good ones" here are the poorest and socially lowest classes, finally the déclassé and proletarianized elements, which are supposedly greater in number and in that way "democratize" the struggle, carrying it furthest (in fact, against all the rest). By the same token, social justice is extended to the lower classes, bringing a permanent solution to the "social question." It should also be noted that the social revolution, thus represented, only begins during the Revival but continues after the (national) liberation until the Communists finally ascended to power.

Another instance of the class analysis of political trends and struggles during the Bulgarian Revival is provided by Dimitŭr Kosev. While it is not difficult to recognize the influence of Derzhavin, the connection with Bulgarian realities is closer. According to the author, the class struggle was waged between the big bourgeoisie, composed of merchants and *chorbadzhii* (a combined commercial–*chorbadzhii* bourgeoisie) on the one hand, and the petty commercial–industrial bourgeoisie on the other. They fought over the management of the communes, schools and reading rooms (*chitalishte*), as well as over the orientation of the national liberation movement. The last decade of Ottoman rule saw the formation of the so-called Old Party, advocating the interests of the big bourgeoisie and *chor-badzhii*, and of the Young Party, which expressed the interests of the petty bourgeoisie (and the peasants). Politically, one part of the Old Party (the Turcophiles) favored moderate bourgeois reform and the preservation of the empire, while another part (the Russophiles) relied on Russia in winning autonomy for Bulgaria under the supremacy of the sultan; both were against a revolution. The "Young" took part in the church national struggles during the 1860s but then split into two—a "moderate, opportunistic" wing that expressed the vision of the middle and ascending petty commercial–industrial bourgeoisie, and a "revolutionary–democratic" wing that reflected the aspirations of the declining petty commercial–industrial bourgeoisie and of the peasants, whose ideal was a revolution and a democratic republic. In its turn, the revolutionary–democratic wing split in the second half of the 1860s into a moderate and an extreme wing.[89]

The detailing of the last-mentioned revolutionary wing by the same author reveals the following émigré formations (in Romania) in the 1860s: the Bulgarian Secret Central Committee (*Bulgarski Taen Tsentralen Komitet*), made up of persons posing as "Young" and revolutionary but who were, in fact, opportunists and preferred a compromise with the sultan (as attested by their memorandum in favor of dualism); and a revolutionary group of the true "Young" headed by Rakovski, reflecting the aspirations of petty bourgeois milieus that felt threatened by the crisis in the Bulgarian handicrafts and saw their salvation in the national democratic revolution alone (this group would pass successively under the leadership of Karavelov, Levski and Botev). Alongside these moderate and radical factions within the revolutionary–democratic current, there existed in Bucharest a formation of the "Old"—the so-called Benevolent Society (*Dobrodetelna Druzhina*), composed of the big commercial bourgeoisie with a Russophile orientation, which was against acting without external help.[90]

The extremes of the interpretation in terms of social class were overcome in the course of time by the moderation of class determinism, and later by refusing even to make a direct connection between classes and political trends. The extreme revolutionary bias that went together with it was also softened and attenuated in various ways, for example, by taking circumstances and tactics into consideration. In a further and more radical form of reappraisal, various trends were treated in a conciliatory spirit in the interests of the common goal—liberation. In this way they were relativized and put on an equal footing.

The first to write in this sense was, to my knowledge, Hristo Gandev, in his work on the April uprising (the revised version of 1974). He rephrased the account of the national struggles in the following manner. While the church struggles were carried out by a "broad popular movement"– democratic and liberal–several views emerged later within Bulgarian society concerning the ways and means of achieving political liberation. There was, first, the revolutionary–democratic trend, supported to varying degrees by the peasants, artisans, petty traders, intelligentsia, and the urban poor. It created a team of professional revolutionaries and a mass organization, and reached its most mature revolutionary concept in the ideas and activities of Levski–namely, an internal uprising, organized by a network of "committees" and facilitated by the wars of external allies. The liberal-bourgeois intelligentsia took part in the revolutionary movement and even led its leftist wing, as attested by the political activities of Rakovski, Karavelov, and Botev, all of them "bourgeois intellectuals who had voluntarily taken the road of people's tribunes and revolutionary leaders." There was also the "bourgeois–liberal" concept of the liberation, with more supporters among bourgeois milieus. It relied upon concerted action with the already free Balkan states, but mostly on the power and assistance of Russia, although on some occasions it supported revolutionary initiatives congruent with its combinations. The broad popular opinion also saw Russia as a great and favorable force for solving the Bulgarian question. Gandev speaks here of a "Russophile bloc" between the Bulgarian bourgeoisie and the mass of the people (which "tacitly" supported this view). Although, on one occasion, a dualist project originated from this trend (in connection with the Paris Conference of 1868), Russian help was its permanent position.

The two concepts of the way to liberation, with their different emphases (one on internal uprising with independent leadership, the other on liberating action by external powers) ran parallel but could merge or clash, even in the behavior of a single person, depending on the conditions at a given time. The wavering between different positions on the part of the bourgeois politicians was due to their being on the lookout for better prospects and to their placing their hopes in one power or another. However, in public affairs in the towns, in the educational field, and in church affairs, the two trends cooperated and worked in common toward a single objective. The revolutionary–democratic trend, which was engaged entirely with achieving liberation, had a less clear vision about the future nation state than the liberal–bourgeois one, with its greater diplomatic and political experience.

Still, according to Gandev, the dividing line between the two concepts was not an expression of class differences, nor were the existing differences due to any "basic contradictions"; such were formed only after the liberation, when the effect of the "pressing and cohesion" of the social layers under foreign rule vanished.[91]

The normalization of historiography on the Revival as regards classes and political trends was continued by Nikolai Genchev (in 1978). He refrains from tying up political trends with classes, apart from the general role of the bourgeoisie. The church movement is characterized as "the most popular and most comprehensive Bulgarian movement during the nineteenth century," which established the hegemony of the bourgeoisie in the national movement. All trends within the church movement—those favoring radical national action, the moderates seeking a compromise with the Greek Patriarchy, the Turcophiles and those oriented to the West—were united by their Bulgarian patriotism and the desire to solve the church question in the interest of the nation.[92] Later during the 1860s, when the church question was solved, the forces of the national revolution realigned. There emerged two main trends—the movement for cultural–spiritual progress (of "educators–church activists"), and the political movement for liberation (of "politicians–revolutionaries"). But according to Genchev the division is "only relative," as there were reformers and revolutionaries in both camps. The views depended not so much on the social-class status of the activists but on whether they lived in the country or outside it (which made them more radical), on the foreign influences upon them, and on purely accidental factors. As a result, activists with a similar social standing often found themselves in opposing political camps. In sum, the formation of the "parties" and of the ideological trends in the "Bulgarian revolution" cannot be derived mechanically from "social motives" because this was primarily a national revolution taking place under the impact of strong foreign influences.[93]

An awareness of the role of circumstances on the political orientation of the revolutionaries is also present in its treatment by Krumka Sharova (in 1981). The author stresses the importance of the particular historical moment and how it was assessed by the revolutionary activists and organizations when advocating a certain view or undertaking a certain political action—for example, "pro" or "contra" union with Serbia and Greece; "pro" or "contra" all-Balkan cooperation and a Balkan federation against the Ottoman Empire; attitudes toward Russia or toward a certain Western great power, etc. As Sharova points out, these attitudes were dictated by the moment and should not be judged from the point of view of which one proved to be "historically correct." She probably meant to say (but could not say at the time) that the views and attitudes of the revolutionaries should not be compared with the current "politically correct" standpoint (as was the practice), for example, the attitude of the Communist regime toward the Soviet Union, Yugoslavia, or toward the idea of a "Balkan union," etc., projected back and applied in assessing the activists of the Revival.

While political circumstances changed dynamically, affecting the views and strategies of the revolutionaries (Sharova also allows for the effect of social status), they were united by a common goal—the liberation of the Bulgarians. To cite her: "According to their social position and the political circumstances they reached a different solution, but to one and the same question."[94] The emphasis here is characteristically on the common national goal in contrast to the emphasis on the revolutionary means by the hard-line Marxists considered earlier. And the effect is unifying rather than divisive, as when means matter most.

In sum, from an all-important determinant of ideological–political views, class became one among a number of others: residence, political moment, tactics, influences, etc. One can perhaps note a shift in the social empathy shown by the historian, from identification with the lowest social strata (the impoverished, déclassé, and proletarianized) to sympathy with more well-to-do layers up the social ladder, though not the richest.[95] But social empathy in general receded into the background. Political views were endorsed for their own merits by historians under the sign of an active patriotism (nationalism). This led to a reappraisal of the political trends to include increasingly moderate and "legalist" ones, so that the various branches of the national movement became equal in importance. The change of attitude in historical scholarship toward the one-time "evolutionists" and "revolutionaries" will be considered in more detail in the next chapter.

Notes

1 Krŭstyu Rakovski, "Stranitsa iz bŭlgarskoto," 146–153, 172. Krustyu Rakovski became prominent in the international socialist movement and in the Russian Bolshevik revolution.

2 Shishmanov, "Uvod v istoriyata," 43–45; Shishmanov, "Paisii i negovata epokha," 15–17; Penev, *Istoriya na novata*. Vol. 3, 3–59.

3   Penev, *Istoriya na novata.* Vol. 3, 42–43, 55–57.
4   Gandev, *Ranno vŭzrazhdane,* 53–92; Gandev, *Faktori na bŭlgarskoto,* 149–176.
5   For a colorful description of the early *chorbadzhii* and their arbitrary ways, see Gandev, *Ranno vŭzrazhdane,* 53–75.
6   Gandev, *Ranno vŭzrazhdane,* 89–92.
7   Hristo Hrisrov, *Bŭlgarskite obshtini prez vŭzrazhdaneto.* Sofia: BAN, 1973, 21–22, 31.
8   Blagoev, "Prinos kŭm istoriyata na sotsializma," 194–199. Blagoev distanced himself from the "theory" of the revolutionaries that divided the Bulgarian people into two classes—people and *chorbadzhii* (201–207).
9   Georgi Bakalov, *Nashite revolyutsioneri. Rakovski, Levski, Botev.* Sofia, 1924, 3–5, 13–15, 26–27.
10 Konstantin Kosev, *Aprilskoto vŭstanie-prelyudiya na Osvobozhdenieto.* Sofia: Hristo Botev, 1996, 39.
11 Natan, *Bŭlgarskoto vŭzrazhdane,* 196–241.
12 Natan, *Ikonomicheska istoriya,* 166–173.
13 Shishmanov, "Uvod v istoriyata," 43–45. The author puts the "estate of *chorbadzhii*" in inverted commas, implying that he thinks of it as a popular designation for merchants and usurers.
14 Derzhavin, *Istoriia Bolgarii.* Vol. 4, 65, 72.
15 See also the information about this discussion in Hadzhinikolov, "I zhivota na instituta," 376–386.
16 Dimitŭr Kosev, "Klasovite otnosheniya," 453–454, 463. See also Kosev, *Lektsii po nova bŭlgarska,* 61–63.
17 Dimitŭr Kosev, "Klasovite otnosheniya," 455–457. Ivan Snegarov was of a similar opinion in the discussion.
18 Natan, "Otnovo po vŭprosa za klasite," 464–482.
19 See Hadzhinikolov, "Iz zhivota na instituta," 382–383.
20 Goran Todorov, "Sotsialno-politicheskata obuslovenost," 119–120, 122–123.
21 Virdzhiniya Paskaleva, "Razvitie na gradskoto stopanstvo i genezisŭt na bŭlgarskata burzhoaziya prez XVIII vek." In *Paisii Hilendarski i negovata epokha,* 71–126, esp. 124.
22 Georgi Pletnyov, "Proizkhod i sotsialna prinadlezhnost na chorbadzhiite ot Turnovsko." *Trudove na Velikotŭrnovskiya universitet "Kiril i Metodii"* 9, no. 2 (Istoricheski fakultet),1971–1972, Sofia, 1973, 69–104, esp. 75, 103; Pletnyov, Sotsialnata prinadlezhnost na kotlenskite chorbadzhii prez Vŭzrazhdaneto." *Istoricheski pregled* 31, no. 2 (1975): 69–74.
23 Genchev, *Levski, revolyutsiyata,* 33. Genchev, *Bŭlgarsko vŭzrazhdane,* 146–147.
24 Vasil Kolarov, "Vŭrkhu Aprilskoto vŭstanie." In Kolarov, *Izbrani proizvedeniya.* Vol. 3, Sofia: BKP, 1955, 180–190 (first published in 1945). In this paper he puts part of the big commercial–industrial bourgeoisie in the bad camp of supporters of the Ottoman state (as profiting from its markets), together with the *chorbadzhii* as a "product of the decaying Turkish Asiatic feudal system." The paper is portentously couched as a critique of Zhak Natan on some counts.
25 On the representation of the *chorbadzhii* in the press during the Revival, see Milena Stefanova, *Kniga za bŭlgarskite chorbadzhii.* Sofia: Izdatelstvo na Sofiiskiya universitet "Kliment Ohridski," 1998, 124–136.
26 Stefanova, 69–79.
27 Shishmanov, "Uvod v istoriyata," 45.
28 This has been pointed out in retrospect by Nikolai Genchev, according to whom the interpretation of the *chorbadzhii* as part of the bourgeoisie discredited the latter as

traitorous. See Genchev, *Bŭlgarsko vŭzrazhdane*, 147; Genchev, "Sotsialnata struktura na bŭlgarskoto obshtestvo prez Vŭzrazhdaneto" *Sotsiologicheski problemi*, no. 6 (1980): 3–13. A similar observation has been made recently by Todev, *Novi ochertsi*, 91.

29 Chervenkov, Kŭm 80-godishninata, 32–33.

30 Todor Pavlov, "Za marksicheska istoriya na Bŭlgariya." In Pavlov, *Izbrani proizvedeniya*. Vol. 3, 355–356, 362; Pavlov, "Za sŭdŭrzhanieto i formata na istoricheskiya protses." In Pavlov, *Izbrani proizvedeniya*. Vol. 3, 405, 407, 410. (cit. on 362).

31 Pavlov, "Za marksicheska istoriya," 359–362.

32 Vladimir Topencharov, *Portretŭt na Paisii*. Sofia: Narodna Mladezh, 1959, 51–55.

33 For a rehabilitation of the middle bourgeoisie (in 1966), see Goran Todorov, "Sotsialno-politicheskata obuslovenost," 123–125. The "betrayal" of the bourgeoisie is here ascribed only to its upper *chorbadzhii* stratum.

34 A landmark on the path towards the exculpation of the bourgeoisie is a work by Dimitŭr Kosev from 1962, in which he argues its positive role in the beginning of the bourgeois–democratic revolution, namely, in the church and educational efforts, and consigns the betrayal of the bourgeoisie, the big bourgeoisie in particular, to the third (but most important) phase—the struggles for political independence. See Kosev, "Za ideologiyata na Paisii Hilendarski." In *Paisii Hilendarski i negovata epokha*, 20–21, 27–28. See also Kosev, "Aprilskoto vŭstanie—vrŭkhna tochka" In *Aprilskoto vŭstanie*, 12–16. Kosev is of the opinion that the bourgeoisie betrayed the April uprising.

35 Vasil Vasilev, "Akademik Dimitŭr Kosev kakŭvto go vidyakh i zapomnikh." *Istoricheski pregled* no. 1 (1997): 105–129. The idea of the paper is to show how tolerant the academician was toward his colleagues and how he maintained a more balanced scholarly climate at the academic Institute of History in spite of the great institutional power concentrated in his hands in the historical "guild" and in making contact with the Central Committee of the Bulgarian Communist Party. While assuming that this was so, a different reading of the paper suggests other thoughts. One can see the ideological motives for establishing the various units of history research, the censorship and disciplinary authority exercised by "coordinating" and supervising units, and the mechanisms of "agreeing" an official view on various issues and enforcing "scholarly politics" concerning the past. See also the commemorative publications, on the fiftieth anniversary of the setting up of the Institute of History, by Veselin Hadzhinikolov, "Nachalni godini na Instituta po istoriya." *Istoricheski pregled* 53, no. 4 (1997): 130–154; Vasilka Tŭpkova-Zaimova, "Nachaloto." *Istoricheski pregled* 54, nos. 1–2 (1998): 51–62. The authors describe the early "cadre" politics and the strongly ideologized discussions at the time, the direct political interference of Vŭlko Chervenkov and Todor Pavlov, the work on the two-volume *History of Bulgaria*, preceded by the preparation of a "model" of crude postulates (taken to the Soviet Union for "consulting"), etc.

36 Gandev, Aprilskoto vŭstanie, 46–48, 58–61, 69, 77–78.

37 *Istoriya na Bŭlgariya v tri toma*. Vol. 1, Sofia, 1961, 469. This is a revised postChervenkov edition of the previous two-volume edition of the "academic" history. There he cited Chervenkov in affirming the counter-revolutionary role of the bourgeoisie as a whole (amalgamated with the *chorbadzhii*). See *Istoriya na Bŭlgariya v dva toma*, edited by D. Kosev, D. Dimitrov, Zh. Natan, H. Hristov, and D. Angelov. Vol. 1, Sofia: Nauka i izkustvo, 1954, 471.

38 Yono Mitev, "Dvizheshti sili na bŭlgarskata natsionalna revolyutsiya s ogled uchastieto na burzhoaziyata v neya." *Istoricheski pregled* 33, no. 1 (1977): 105–116.

39 Dimitŭr Kosev, "Misli po diskusiyata za rolyata na bŭlgarskata burzhoaziya v natsionalno-osvoboditelnoto dvizhenie." *Istoricheski pregled* 33, no. 1 (1977): 103–105.

40 Traikov, Veselin. "Dva aspekta za rolyata na burzhoaziyata v bŭlgarskoto natsional-noosvoboditelno dvizhenie." *Istoricheski pregled* 33, no. 2 (1977), 82–90.

41 Rumyana Radkova, Za vrŭzkite mezhdu inteligentsiyata i burzhoaziyata v bŭlgarskoto osvoboditelno dvizhenie." *Istoricheski pregled* 33, no. 2 (1977): 90–93.

42 Krumka Sharova, "Bŭlgarskoto natsionalnorevolyutsionno dvizhenie i edrata burzho-aziya." *Istoricheski pregled* 33, no. 2 (1977): 71–80.

43 Krumka Sharova, "Nauchni rezultati ot diskusiyata za rolyata na burzhoaziyata v bŭl-garskoto osvoboditelno dvizhenie i predstoyashti izsledovatelski zadachi." *Istoricheski pregled* 34, no. 1 (1978): 93–102, esp. 96–99.

44 Hristo Hristov, "Za rolyata na bŭlgarskata burzhoaziya v natsionalnata revolyutsiya." *Istoricheski pregled* 33, no. 3 (1977): 91–97.

45 Georgieva, "Za genezisa na burzhoaznite," 87–90.

46 Hristov, "Za rolyata na bŭlgarskata," 92–93.

47 The question is all the more relevant as even the French Revolution is hard to ac-commodate within the concept of a "bourgeois revolution" (and a radical transforma-tion from feudalism to capitalism) for a number of reasons: the integration of the bourgeoisie into the "ancien régime," the mostly pre-modern forms of wealth such as rent, the buying of offices, etc. and the absence of a radical economic break long after the revolution, the participation of various classes in it, etc. See Furet, *Interpreting the French Revolution*, 92–93, 120–122.

48 Genchev, *Bŭlgarsko vŭzrazhdane*, 392, 395, 399–400. Virdzhiniya Paskaleva attributes the economic weakness and political impotency of the Bulgarian bourgeoisie to the slow and painful transition to capitalism. See Paskaleva, "Razvitie na gradskoto," 126.

49 Konstantin Kosev, *Za kapitalisticheskoto razvitie*, 175–183.

50 Konstantin Kosev, *Kratka istoriya*, 69–70.

51 Hristo Hristov, *Bŭlgarskite obshtini prez Vŭzrazhdaneto*. Sofia: BAN, 1973, 20–32, 194–195; Hristov, "Kŭm vŭprosa za klasite," 51–85; Hristov, "Za rolyata na bŭlgar-skata," 94–95. For a review of the concept of *chorbadzhii*, see Georgi Pletniov, *Chor-badzhiite i bŭlgarskata natsionalna revolyutsiya*. Veliko Tŭrnovo: Vital, 1993, 4–11; Stefanova, *Kniga za bŭlgarskite*, 47–51; Elena Grozdanova, *Bŭlgarskata selska obshtina prez XV–XVIII vek*. Sofia, 1979, 83–84.

52 Stefan Bobchev, "Elensko prez vreme na turskoto vladichestvo." In *Elenski sbornik*. Vol. 2. Sofia, 1938, 1–108, esp. 20–45, 75–87. The second part of the work has the ti-tle "The *chorbadzhii* as a public service institution under Ottoman rule."

53 On the contributions of the *chorbadzhii*, see Georgi Pletnyov, "Rolyata i myastoto na chorbadzhiite ot Tŭrnovsko v prosvetnoto dvizhenie prez Vŭzrazhdaneto." *Trudove na Velikotŭrnovskiya universitet "Kiril i Metodii."* Vol. 10, no. 2 (Istoricheski fakultet) 1972/3, Sofia, 1973, 53–83; Pletnyov, "Chorbadzhiite ot Tŭrnovsko v natsionalnoos-voboditelnoto dvizhenie." *Istoricheski pregled* 33, no. 3 (1977): 105–109.

54 Pletnyov, *Chorbadzhiite i bŭlgarskata*, 126–127, 185–187, 195. An assessment of the activities of the *chorbadzhii* in the various trends of the national revolution is made in the summary (215–221).

55 Stefanova, *Kniga za bŭlgarskite*, 138–139.

56 Genchev, *Bŭlgarsko vŭzrazhdane*, 146–147.

57 Strashimirov, "Komitetskoto desetiletie," 856. For a similar view, couched in some-what pretentious sociological jargon, see Stefanova, *Kniga za bŭlgarskite*, 56–57.

58 Hadzhiiski, Ivan. *Sŭchineniya v dva toma*. Vol. 2 (Bit i dushevnost na nashiya narod) Sofia: Bŭlgarski pisatel, 1974, p.197, 390–391.

59 Natan, *Bŭlgarskoto vŭzrazhdane*, 518–521; Natan, "Otnovo po vŭprosa," 467–471.

60 Chervenkov, "Kŭm 80-godishninata," 32–33, 36. These postulates entered *Istoriya na Bŭgariya v dva toma*. Vol. 1, 311–506.

61 *Istoriya na Bŭlgariya v dva toma*. Vol. 1, 311–312.

62 Vera Mutafchieva, *Agrarnite otnosheniya*, 181–250; Mutafchieva, "Kategoriite feodalno zavisimo naselenie v nashite zemi pod turska vlast prez XV–XVI vek." In *Izvestiya na instituta po istoriya*. Vol. 9 (1960): 57–90; Strashimir Dimitrov, "Za agrarnite otnosheniya," 130–133, 154–161; Dimitrov, "Kŭm vŭprosa za otmenyavaneto," 55–58; Gandev, "Turski izvori," 120–127. See, also, a summary of the developments in Bulgarian Ottomanist scholarship in Genchev, *Bŭlgarskoto vŭzrazhdane*, 50–83, 122–130.

63 Bobchev, "Elensko prez vreme," 43–44.

64 Nikola Gabrovski, *Nravstvenite zadachi na inteligentsiyata*. Sofia, 1889, esp. 21–24, 42–43; Todor Vlaikov, "Sluchaini belezhki. Po vŭprosa za inteligentsiyata ni." *Demokraticheski pregled* 8, no. 1 (1910): 99–106; Vlaikov, "Nashata inteligentsiya." *Demokraticheski pregled* 18, no 5 (1926): 289–309. On the post-liberation Bulgarian intelligentsia, see Roumen Daskalov, "Transformations of the East European Intelligentsia: Reflections on the Bulgarian Case." *East European Politics and Societies* 10, no. 1 (1996): 46–84, esp. 62–71.

65 Some historians developed the theme, most notably the medievalist Petŭr Mutafchev. See "Kŭm novo vŭzrazhdane." *Otets Paisii* 8, no. 1 (1935): 3–9; Mutafchev, "Deloto i primerŭt na Paisiya." *Otets Paisii* 8, no. 7 (1935): 333–337.

66 Ivan Hadzhiiski, "Psikhologiya na Aprilskoto vŭstanie." In Hadzhiiski, *Sŭchineniya v dva toma*. Vol. 1. Sofia: Bŭlgarski pisatel, 1974, 318–319 (first published in 1940).

67 Hristo Gandev, *Kratka bŭlgarska istoriya. Populyaren ocherk*. Sofia, 1947, 99–103.

68 Vŭlko Chervenkov, "Kŭm 80-godishninanata."

69 Gandev, *Aprilskoto vŭstanie*, 30–31, 77, 178. After Communism, Plamen Mitev stressed the young average age of the revolutionaries, and of the organizers of the April uprising in particular. See Mitev, *Bŭlgarsko vŭzrazhdane*, 128.

70 For example, Dimitrov, *Uchilishteto, progresŭt*. The author devotes a special chapter to the contribution of the teachers to the national revolution.

71 Thomas Meininger, *The Formation of a Nationalist Bulgarian Intelligentsia, 1835–1878*. New York and London: Garland Publishing, 1987, 394–398. The thesis is endorsed by M. Palairet, who adds the alienation of the intelligentsia from the "business community" of craftsmen. See Palairet, *The Balkan Economies*, 162–163.

72 Hadzhiiski, "Psikhologiya na Aprilskoto," 318–319.

73 Genchev, *Bŭlgarskata vŭzrozhdenska*.

74 Radkova, *Bŭlgarskata inteligentsiya*.

75 Angel Dimitrov, *Uchilishteto, progresŭt*.

76 This research resulted in an encyclopedia of the Bulgarian intelligentsia of the Revival epoch, *Bŭlgarskata vŭzrozhdenska inteligentsiya. Entsiklopediya*, edited by Nikolai Genchev and Krassimira Daskalova. Sofia: Petŭr Beron, 1988. It contains about 10,000 entries (names). The data are used by Daskalova, *Bŭlgarskiyat uchitel*; and Kuyumdzhieva, *Intelektualniyat elit*.

77 Bakalov, *Nashite revolyutsioneri*, 3–4.

78 Natan, *Ikonomicheska istoriya*, 160–161.

79 Goran Todorov, "Sotsialno-politicheskata obuslovenost," 117.

80 Goran Todorov, "Sotsialno-politicheskata obuslovenost," 118.

81 Dimitŭr Kosev, *Lekstii po nova bŭlgarska*, 61–64, 144–145.

82 Georgi Pletnyov, "Borba za obshtinskata vlast prez vŭzrazhdaneto." *Trudove na Velikotŭrnoskiya universitet "Kiril i Metodii."* Vol. 8, no. 2 (Istoricheski fakultet), 1970/71, Sofia, 1973, 163–191, esp. 177–178, 185; Virdzhiniya Paskaleva, "Za samou-

pravlenieto na bŭlgarite prez Vŭzrazhdaneto." *Izvestiya na Instituta po istoriya*. Vols. 14–15 (1964): 69–84, esp. 82–83. Hristov, "Kŭm vŭprosa za klasite," 65, 70–71, 82.

83 Stefnova, *Kniga za bŭlgarskite*, 69–79.

84 For an account of these revolts, see Inalchik, Halil. "Application of the Tanzimat."

85 Gandev, *Aprilskoto vŭstanie*, 45–47, 60–61, 77–78; Gandev, *Ot narodnost kŭm natsiya*, 26–29.

86 Blagoev, "Prinos kŭm istoriyata," 201–217.

87 Natan, *Bŭlgarskoto vŭzrazhdane*, 223–232.

88 Derzhavin, *Istoriia Bolgarii*, 72, 114, 128, 137–138, 146.

89 Dimitŭr Kosev, *Lektsii po nova bŭlgarska*, 145–146, 159. In Constantinople the "Old" were Gavril Krŭstevich, the Turkish spy Ivancho Penchovich, and Chomakov, while the "Young" were led by Pencho Slaveikov. They existed in Bucharest, too.

90 Dimitŭr Kosev, *Lektsii po nova bŭlgarska*, 171.

91 Gandev, *Aprilskoto vŭstanie*, 48–78.

92 Genchev, *Bŭlgarsko vŭzrazhdane*, 205, 298–299.

93 Genchev, *Bŭlgarsko vŭzrazhdane*, 341–343. Similarly, Traikov, *Ideologicheski techeniya i programi*, 11. The author explains the shifting of ideological orientation with reference to the "unstable Balkan situation" and the pragmatism of the Balkan political activists.

94 Sharova, "Problemi na bŭlgarsoto," 29.

95 Somewhat belatedly Konstantin Kosev ridicules the apologists of the "proletarian revolution" with their beloved pariah hero and speaks fondly of the "middle class" of urban and rural bourgeoisie as the hero of the revolution. See Kosev, *Kratka istoriya*, 17–18.

CHAPTER FOUR

Paths of the Revival and National Heroes

The Bulgarian Revival began with monk Paisii's *Slavonic-Bulgarian History*, completed in 1762 in the monastery of Zograph, which attests to the first stirrings of national feeling. Several decades of activities on the part of solitary "awakeners" ensued, after which the national endeavors intensified and branched off into separate fields: education, struggles for church autonomy (as a preliminary to national autonomy), and armed actions. With the emergence of an organized revolutionary movement in the last pre-liberation decade, known as the "decade of committees" (i.e., units of secret organization), there began an embittered polemic in the periodical press on the means and paths of the national movement. The three currents of national efforts were then reduced to two—reliance on peaceful, legal means, known as "evolutionism" (in the sense of gradualism), and the way of "revolution" (i.e., uprisings). The latter, especially, produced Bulgarian national heroes. I will consider here the debates on the currents and heroes in the historical scholarship.

Paisii as a Problem

A vast amount of literature is devoted to the founder (or precursor) of the Bulgarian Revival—the monk Paisii of Hilendar. It ranges from scholarly books through popularizing brochures to fiction, as well as celebratory speeches. Paisii has been mentioned in earlier chapters when discussing the Enlightenment and romanticism among the Bulgarians. Here we will be concerned more centrally with problems of the interpretation of his epoch and his oeuvre.

The importance of Paisii for the Bulgarian Revival was already recognized in the final phase of the Revival. Marin Drinov was the first to place him at its beginnings. After that, Ivan Shishmanov and Boyan Penev worked out important issues in the understanding of Paisii and suggested major lines (and contexts) for his interpretation.

Ivan Shishmanov, the first great Bulgarian literary historian of the "bourgeois" (pre-Communist) epoch, ascribed to Paisii enormous importance as the progenitor of the Revival and compared him with the great men of the Renaissance. Initially he was fascinated by the great personality, capable, so it seemed, of working miracles "ex nihilo." But influenced by Jacob Burkhardt's work on the Italian Renaissance, he came to recognize the role of the economic factor and of the social ascent of an urban bourgeois (burgher) class in preparing the ground for the spiritual advance. Within the spiritual revival itself he became aware of forerunners of Paisii, whom he now began to regard as "a great link in a long causal chain," while defining the Revival itself as a "collective work, not of Paisii personally but a product of a more or less slow social evolution." Shishmanov thus posed the ("historico-philosophical") theme of the relationship between personality, society, and economy that would concern subsequent researchers of Paisii. Finally, Shishmanov regarded Paisii as a historical personality that belongs to the whole nation, since he had shown the way to national formation before the split in views and ideas that occurred later.[1]

The other major Bulgarian literary historian of the "bourgeois" epoch, Boyan Penev, pointed out that it was Paisii's already formed national self-awareness, a fellow feeling for the suffering of his people, and faith in its future that sets him apart from all his forerunners. There were, according to Paisii, three necessary preconditions for the awakening of the Bulgarian people: becoming aware of the importance of the native language as against the danger of Greek assimilation; becoming cognizant of the native land; and becoming aware of the Bulgarian historical past, which, in turn, justifies aspirations toward spiritual and political independence. Consequently, Paisii saw as his task the awakening of a feeling for the Bulgarian language, and for the native land and its history as major attributes of the nation. Boyan Penev notes that the political tendency in Paisii's work, that is, the denunciation of Turkish oppression, is weakly developed; it is implied indirectly through the comparison between the glorious past and the unfortunate present, which might have suggested the thought of political freedom to the readers. The primary goal of Paisii had been to expose the Greek spiritual domination and to incite his compatriots against it by creating Bulgarians out of them.[2]

The national message of Paisii's oeuvre stands out more intensely in the historiography of the 1930s, no doubt under the influence of the new nationalism that was the spirit of the times. It left a trace even in serious historical scholarship, for example in a work by Mikhail Arnaudov published in 1942, in this case less in the content (the author renders Paisii's ideas quite faithfully with a sense for his epoch) than in his empathy and expressive style.[3] The national message of Paisii is central to the more secondary historian Ivan Ormandzhiev, who puts the (implicit) political element of that message into deep relief. Interestingly, the author makes Paisii's appeals sound trans-historical and merges them with his own vision of the "all-Bulgarian ideal" of political liberation but also "unification" (with the *irredenta*).[4]

The proliferation of shorter essays and articles of a popularizing nature should also be mentioned. They are expressive, metaphoric, and lofty in style, and sound emotionally and even ecstatically tense. The words of Paisii are not just rendered but freely interpreted, messages are read into them, and lessons are drawn. The voice of the particular author becomes merged with the voice of Paisii as a kind of "extension" and prolongation of his views or intuitions under new historical circumstances. The message itself acquires a crystal-clear nationalist meaning and sounds like a prophesy or warning addressed to the future nation. Old-fashioned cultural notions of "people" are modernized in tune with newer state nationalist ideas and theories.[5]

In the official state propaganda, Paisii became subject to still greater distortion not only in a nationalist but also in a clerical and monarchical sense. He was enlisted into the service of an authoritarian state under a monarch, and for a new attempt at national unification during World War II. Here is an example from a speech broadcast on Radio Sofia by Boris Yotsov, on Father Paisii's Day (27 September) in 1942:

"He clarifies indirectly, with all the strength of his being, the idea of the nation as the strongest shield for defense and thrust forward. [...] With the wisdom of an oracle he suggests the idea of the state, of the Bulgarian state, which, according to him, finds its embodiment in the figure of the pious and devout Czar, the guarantor of its strength and of its greatness. The state is unthinkable without the Czar and its destinies are linked to Him."[6]

The Marxist interpretation of Paisii developed in parallel to the nationalist trend and continued to develop afterwards, but posed entirely different questions. Central to it is the question of class: For whom did Paisii speak? Whose interests did he express? In what relation did he stand to the bourgeoisie that would become the leader of the national movement? And, concerning the content of his message: What does Paisii say directly and indirectly? Let us consider in more detail the answers given to these questions.

According to Georgi Bakalov, Paisii expressed the interests of the peasants and the artisans and his protest against Grecophilia was addressed to Bulgarian traders in the towns, who wanted to pass for Greeks and whom he tried to persuade to come to their senses. Thus he is the ideologue of the common people against oppression by the Phanariots (i.e., rich and influential Greeks from the Phanar district in Istanbul) but also against the Bulgarian renegades. Although in an indirect way, by extolling the old Bulgarian statehood, Paisii raised hopes for future independence. He stands at the beginning of both lines of the Bulgarian Revival—that of the Church and the educational struggles, as well as that of the political (revolutionary) struggles.[7] (Bakalov follows Ivan Shishmanov in this respect.)

The Russian historian Nikolai Derzhavin treated Paisii (during the Stalinist 1940s) in crude a priori class terms as an ideologue of the young, ascendant, still progressive Bulgarian bourgeoisie in its struggle for national–cultural self-determination against the Greek bourgeoisie and the rule of the sultan. According to him, Paisii created the first political program of the bourgeoisie and formulated the main tasks of the national liberation movement—a national language, national church, and national state.[8]

Bulgarian historians followed suit. Dimitŭr Kosev considered Paisii's work (in 1952) under the rubric "the beginnings of bourgeois ideology," and affirmed that it was the expression of the attitudes and aspirations of the burgeoning Bulgarian bourgeoisie; Paisii himself is characterized as its first ideologue, who addressed the bourgeoisie of artisans and traders in particular.[9] (Ten years later, Kosev partially corrected his view in order to take into account the absence of a bourgeoisie in the time of Paisii, and defined his oeuvre as the "first manifesto of the Bulgarian national revolution" to be implemented by the Bulgarian bourgeoisie later on.[10])

An extreme example of distortion and "modernization" in the spirit of Stalin's precepts on the "national question" is presented by the Russian historian Vasilii Konobeev (in a work published as late as 1972 already quite outdated). According to the author, the idea of national liberation and the "call for the demolition of the Turkish feudal regime" found their first expression in Paisii's work. The latter elaborated the first Bulgarian

national program by setting the following objectives for the national liberation movement, "whose bourgeois–democratic character is self-evident."
First, cultural–national revival and a struggle for national education,
whereby he gave expression to the ideas of the progressive young Bulgarian
bourgeoisie but also to the "objective needs of capitalist development."
Second, the winning of church-national independence as a precondition
for the spiritual emancipation of the Bulgarian people from the Greek
Patriarchy. Third, a struggle for political independence (in contrast to
authors who stress the primarily anti-Greek tendency of his work). In addition, Paisii demonstrated, in a peculiar form, the great potential of the
Bulgarian lands for economic development by calling them "good and
plentiful," as if suggesting to the reader to ponder over the problem "What
impedes the economic progress of the country?" Finally, Paisii's ideology
was objectively anti-feudal, being the first attempt to reveal the economic
essence of the Turkish national oppression and the degree of exploitation
of the Bulgarians.[11] An outright falsification like this one somehow discred-
its any "moderation" that may come along the same lines.

The treatment of the ideology of Paisii as bourgeois was interrupted for
a time by the thesis of the betrayal of the bourgeoisie, projected backwards
to the beginning of the Revival. Todor Pavlov, then in charge of the Bulgarian Academy of Sciences, rejected (in 1952) the idea that Paisii's work was
written for the nascent bourgeoisie and affirmed instead that it was addressed to the Bulgarian urban and peasant folk—simple ploughmen, dig-
gers, and craftsmen. He characterized Paisii's oeuvre in propaganda terms
as "a model of goal-oriented, passionate, ideologically and politically
pointed work," a "mighty instrument for the awakening, organization,
mobilization and activation of the revolutionary national and democratic
consciousness of the Bulgarian people," and, among other things, as "a
model for the application of the party principle in the field of history writing."[12]

Following in his steps, the party propagandist turned historian, Vladimir
Topencharov, affirmed (in 1959) that Paisii had addressed his call to the
peasants and handed them "the rapier of the revolutionary struggle" (since
the bourgeoisie betrayed its people). The national movement that began in
the times of Paisii was grounded in the peasants, not in the bourgeoisie,
and expressed their protest against feudalism and Turkish rule; Paisii's
slogan of national self-determination and sovereignty was a peasant slogan
in the first place.[13]

Topencharov places Paisii at the source of the "people's line" of the national–liberation movement only (in contrast to the bourgeois line of "infamous compromise" with feudalism and Turkish rule), to be continued subsequently by the "revolutionary party" of Levski, Botev, and the revolutionary democrats in general.[14] Hristo Hristov is another author who reserves Paisii for the "combative-democratic trend," contrasted with the "liberal-reformist, compromising ideology of the Bulgarian commercial–money-lending and entrepreneurial bourgeoisie."[15] Thus we have Ivan Shishmanov and Georgi Bakalov regarding Paisii as a founder of both lines of the Bulgarian Revival, while for Topencharov and Hristov he was the founder of only the combatant-revolutionary line. (The opinion that he represents primarily the evolutionist trend was voiced by Mikhail Arnaudov in his book of 1942, argued with reference to the absence of conditions for revolutionary propaganda.[16])

The intrusion of the "peasant thesis" was repelled by Dimitŭr Kosev, who restored the "bourgeois" interpretation of the ideology of Paisii in 1962 in a volume (from a conference) dedicated to an anniversary of Paisii's oeuvre. According to the author, Paisii expressed the interests of the peasants, craftsmen, traders, and the patriotic part of the Bulgarian bourgeoisie. His "ideology" has an anti-feudal, bourgeois–democratic character (still in the absence of antagonism between the nascent bourgeoisie and the peasants). Its main goal was to contribute to the formation of the Bulgarian nation.[17] In defining Paisii's "ideology" as bourgeois-democratic, and in the enumeration of the various interests he is supposed to "express," one can see a conciliatory mediation between bourgeoisie and "common people." At the same time, the "bourgeois" character of his ideas is affirmed.

This reasoning is made even more explicit by Goran Todorov (in 1968). He stated the bourgeois character of the "ideology" of Paisii, qualifying it further as bourgeois–democratic, and, given the underdevelopment of class relations in eighteenth-century Bulgarian society, as having, in fact, an all-people's character.[18] The same line was taken up further by Nikolai Genchev, who argued (in 1978) that while Paisii was a herald of bourgeois ideas in the early times of the Bulgarian Revival, this reflected the general needs of social development at the time as well as the interests of the entire society in national emancipation. The bourgeois ideology of Paisii thus became a national ideology, an ideology of the whole society in its struggle for spiritual and political liberation.[19] In the line traced by these three authors, both the nature of the ideas and the social addressee of Paisii glide from the bourgeoisie through the "people" (in a more or less inclusive sense) to the "nation" of all Bulgarians (whereby the class meaning is muted). One can see how a way was found to reconcile "bourgeoisie" and "people" by the extension of the "social base" of the ideas. In short: from (one) class via people to nation.

To the by now traditional question "Of which social strata was Paisii the ideologue?" (and whose interests did he express?), the literary scholar Velcho Velchev replied (in 1981) in contemporary socialist jargon—"Of the common toiling people, the immediate producers of goods," of "the exploited and oppressed laboring people" who fought against feudal exploitation and who were concerned with material progress and national formation.[20] This can be seen as an attempt to reactivate the "populist" interpretation (though not in a peasantist form), as against the already accepted bourgeois, gliding into the all-national, one. It is tempting to see in the debates on Paisii's ideas and his "social base" a reflection of the games of social inclusion/exclusion played under the Communist regime (by way of their displacement toward history).

Another issue to attract attention from early on and to demand explanation is the connection between Paisii and the world around him. The puzzle is that the oeuvre of Paisii (in 1762) stands in isolation, being some sixty years ahead of Bulgarian development, both social-economic advance and the spread of national ideas. As already mentioned, Ivan Shishmanov stated that the oeuvre of Paisii should be regarded as a result of a social evolution and as a link in a causal chain, but he did not study it; nor did he prove the existence of the economic and social "factor" he believed was there. A similar problem emerged for Marxist authors when they conceived of Paisii's ideas as expressive of bourgeois interests in the absence of a developed bourgeoisie in his times.

Dimitŭr Kosev admitted the substantial interval between Paisii and the deployment of revival processes on a massive scale. At first he simply attributed "great historical acumen" to Paisii, who was able to perceive the "incipient trends of the historical development" that became evident only in the third and fourth decades of the nineteenth century.[21] In addition, he posited a nascent Bulgarian bourgeoisie as Paisii's audience. Later he proposed a better solution, in which Paisii was the originator of a national ideology, which was taken up by the bourgeoisie only after a time.[22] In that case it is not necessary for Paisii to express contemporary social interests or attitudes, bourgeois ones in particular, and his ideas may connect to real social forces later on. But then an orthodox Marxist interpretation has to confront a problem that flows from its own premises: how to explain the emergence of an ideology that goes ahead of its own economic and social "base."

Dealing with a similar problem, Iliya Konev registered the interesting fact that in the Bulgarian case, and in Southeast Europe in general, phenomena from the ideological superstructure (national and Enlightenment ideas in particular) went ahead of the social base, that is, of socioeconomic changes in the direction of a bourgeois "formation"; in fact, they even stimulated their advent.[23] The same was noted with regard to the Balkan revivals by Strashimir Dimitrov and Krŭstyu Manchev, who explained it by the "relative autonomy" of the ideas (in this case, coming from the outside).[24] When speaking more generally about the formation of the nations in the multinational empires in Central and Southeast Europe, the Russian historian Ilya S. Miller observed that this took place in conditions of underdeveloped capitalism and uncompleted bourgeois revolutions.[25] In contrast, for a more doctrinaire author such as Hristo Hristov, such an incongruity, whereby ideas overtake the state of the society, is not possible (and he cites the copies made of Paisii's work as a proof of the existence of social needs).[26]

Another attempt to place Paisii more comfortably in his contemporary social context and to explain the ideas in his work by contemporary social conditions (not later ones) was made by Hristo Gandev. According to him, the *Slavonic-Bulgarian History* was written with regard to the self-conscious Bulgarian majority in the towns. The strong anti-Greek attitude expressed its discontent with the fiscal policies of the Patriarchy but also the rivalry between the new urban population (that had migrated from the villages to the towns) and the original inhabitants of the towns who readily assimilated as Greeks. In Gandev's view, Paisii's work reflects the social attitudes of socially equalized peasants, artisans and petty traders, united before a common evil, a kind of "people's front of the laboring classes" (the author was perhaps making ironic use of the Communist newspeak) to fend off the alien influence. To that, Gandev adds the strong impact upon Paisii of more advanced national movements, especially the Greek one.[27] Here is a more sophisticated version of a social explanation that replaces a bourgeoisie proper with an earlier (pre-bourgeois) social situation of oppression and rivalry.

The well-known American Balkanist scholar James Clarke also remarks on the considerable time gap between the writing of Paisii's *History* and its reception. He attributes that partly to isolation and the absence of a printing press in the Ottoman Empire at that time, but also to the absence of cultural centers and people ready to accept Paisii's ideas. The author speaks of a misfit between Paisii and his contemporaries: when they were ready for him, the medieval monastic tone of his work already sounded antiquated, in spite of the secular content. Clarke admits that Paisii had a prophetic vision in grasping the danger of denationalization (assimilation) and in providing means for fighting it through his super-patriotic work, otherwise devoid of originality or scholarly quality (on that he is in accord with Boyan Penev and in disagreement with some patriotic Bulgarian authors). Clarke then puts forward the very provocative view that this work is not enough to qualify Paisii as the "author" of the movement that led to the liberation of the Bulgarians, even though he had followers such as Sofronii of Vratsa (to supply the link).[28] This statement, sounding, as it does, as anathema to Bulgarian historical scholarship, can actually be argued if assigned a proper meaning, that is, the lack of direct and personal continuity, and the differentiation between being the progenitor of the Bulgarian national ideas and being the initiator of the national movement itself.

An altogether different solution to the paradox of Paisii's "overtaking" his times has recently been proposed (at least indirectly) by the Bulgarian historian Elka Drosneva. The author approaches Paisii's "historicism" through the study of the intellectual conditions in which he found himself and of what was, or could have been, available to him at the time (apart from the well-researched foreign sources of his work). What she seems to suggest is that, leaving his patriotic appeals aside, his *History*, and the world-view it expressed, were, in fact, very well grounded in the circumstances of his times and milieu and, for all their innovation, did not depart from them radically. Thus he borrowed pieces of information and his style of presentation from folklore and from the Bible, as well as from available Bulgarian hagiographies and short inscriptions in books (*pripiski*) in particular, though he wrote a true history and not a medieval chronology. Standing on the threshold between medieval and modern times, he combined elements of both, being actually a "transitional" figure.[29] This also sounds as a word of caution against the patriotic exaggerations so typical of many writings on Paisii.

The work of the Russian literary historian and Slavist Andrei N. Robinson on Paisii is of great interest, with its rejection of vulgar sociologization and distorting "modernization." According to him, the *Slavonic-Bulgarian History* should not be interpreted as an articulation of an ideology for the still weakly differentiated social layers, or as an expression of their presumable "aspirations." One can only say that Paisii's appeals and his polemical historical oeuvre were addressed to the Bulgarian people as a whole, in an all-inclusive sense; it is another matter that half a century later they began to harmonize with certain interests and views of the bourgeois–democratic forces, who took advantage of them in a selective manner. Robinson also rejects connecting Paisii with the Enlightenment. His oeuvre contains no ideas for a revival of Bulgaria upon new social and political foundations similar to the bourgeois–republican, philosophical–materialist, or natural–scientific ideas characteristic of the contemporary West European movements. What it contains are calls for a revival of what was lost by the Bulgarians as a result of the Turkish conquest and of the Greek influence.[30]

Robinson insists that Paisii's oeuvre should be read in connection with its sources and against the background of a common (shared) historiographical trend of "Slavic revivals" in particular. According to him, the "ideology" of Paisii took shape gradually on the basis of his own social experience (which nurtured his political sense and keen national feeling), mediated by his historiographical knowledge, hence the possibility to go considerably ahead of his times. Characteristic of the common Slavic tradition of history writing from which he drew are a strong civic education feeling, a patriotic national concept, and the ascription of public functions to historical knowledge, so that the writing of history assumes a programmatic–ideological character. Characteristic of it, furthermore, is a strange and contradictory mixing of scholarship with religion, history, sermonizing and moral exhortation, and political journalism. These common traits, and the common device of using history writing to influence public life, were taken up one after the other by every Slavic people that stepped on the road of national development and acquired a peculiar national coloration.[31] (It should not be forgotten that, among Bulgarian authors, Emil Georgiev likewise treated the Paisii phenomenon as part of the "South Slav revival" in its first "Renaissance-Enlightenment" period, bringing him out of his isolation.[32])

In the same vein, the historian Plamen Mitev recently rejected any claims that Paisii had foreseen the historical tendency of the future and had formulated its programmatic tasks. He argues that the oeuvre of Paisii had a different meaning in its own times, though he is not specific on this point (apart from affirming that it was built upon the principles of Enlightenment rationalism with some purely patriotic elements). The nineteenth century, which brought about the emergence of the educational movement and of the church question, gave a new meaning to Paisii's oeuvre and it began to sound like a conscious national platform. The rare direct appeals of the author to his compatriots to get to know and treasure the Bulgarian language, history, and culture, and the suggested "otherness" based on them, then worked toward enhancing the self-awareness of the Bulgarians as a separate national community.[33]

Robinson's idea that Paisii was selectively used by various forces and read in the light of subsequent experience can in fact be generalized beyond the Revival activists to later "readings." As shown before, the interpretative process continued in professional historical scholarship and it was given free rein in nationalist and Communist propaganda writings. Depending on the contemporary context the "exegesis" went to the extremes of attributing a lucid nationalist message to him and even of hearing a revolutionary clarion call, of discovering monarchism or of taking a populist stance (appeals to the "common people"). Guided by various interests, Paisii's text proved very elastic indeed. At a certain point one leaves the terrain of "reception theory," concerned with the spontaneous (unguided) understanding of the text by different readers in various contexts, to enter more or less purposeful ideological manipulation.

It is curious to note that Paisii's oeuvre was recently mobilized again at the service of the national idea by a historian. In the strongly nationalistic reading of Iliya Todev, his own attitude blends with the nationalism of Paisii. We are reminded that the latter took upon himself the task of showing to the Bulgarians to which nationality they belonged, of teaching them their history, and of making them love their identity. He wanted to safeguard the Bulgarian *ethnos* from its "most dangerous denationalizer" at the time—the Greek language and culture propagated by the Greek Patriarchy. The author then presents his reflections on the theme of the Bulgarian "national nihilism," "national apostasy," "self-rejection," "adoration of others," etc., and lauds the prophetic gift of Paisii to see through these traits of the "innermost Bulgarian essence" and to counter them with his passionate nationalism. This, according to Todev, bestows on his oeuvre actuality in all times.[34]

One can guess why the author deemed it necessary to actualize the call of Paisii in Bulgarian post-Communist conditions. The fall of the barriers and the opening up of the country to the outside world, accompanied by massive emigration, brought about renewed fears of "adoring others," giving up the national identity, and de-nationalization. While Paisii may be a reference in such times, this clearly goes beyond the scholarly stance.

Evolutionists and Revolutionaries

Bulgarian historical scholarship often takes up and replays the strife between the "parties" and the activists of the last decade of the Revival,
sometimes taking sides with one camp against the other.[35] The basic contemporary controversy was that between "evolutionists" and "revolutionaries," that is, those who believed that gradual development would in the end
lead to national liberation, and those in favor of urgent revolutionary action. In what follows I will consider the debate not during the Revival itself,
but in the historiography (and in public polemics). Its symbolic stakes are
made intelligible in connection with the historical moment and the social–
political context.

In his treatment of the April uprising in the early post-liberation years,
Zakhari Stoyanov (himself one of its organizers) glorified the way of revolt
and ridiculed and devalued all other ways and means. The national poet
and novelist Ivan Vazov did his best to immortalize the armed struggles
and the revolutionaries. The historian of the April uprising, Dimitŭr
Strashimirov, extols the activities of the members of the secret revolutionary organization (called *komiti* or *komitadzhi*, from the word "committees") as the greatest achievement in the civic life of the Bulgarian people
under the Ottomans and as the apex of the Revival.[36]

The unsuccessful attempts at national unification during the Balkan
wars (1912–1913) and World War I, participation in which was motivated by
the objectives and the ideals of the Revival, led to a reappraisal of the Revival epoch. The ways and means of the Revival were rethought polemically, and even such sanctified events as the April uprising and the Russo-
Turkish war of liberation were problematized with regard to their outcome,
namely, the partitioning of ethnic Bulgarian territories. The other path–of
"evolution," that is, graduality–acquired credibility all of a sudden. It is
somewhat ironic that its affirmation took place after one series of military
adventures and on the eve of another. Here are a few examples.

Cultural activities were emphasized in opposition to revolutionary
"adventures" by Boris Yotsov, in a paper dedicated to the scholar and phi-
lanthropist of Bulgarian education Vasil Aprilov.[37] According to this
author, had there appeared in Bulgaria after Aprilov "not ten prominent
revolutionaries" but "five modest educators like him in shape and spirit,"
and had they set up schools such as the one opened by him in Gabrovo, the
Bulgarian people would have perhaps remained united instead of being
partitioned by the Berlin Congress in 1879.[38] The author argues in another

paper for the way of education as the basic component of the Bulgarian Revival, which, in his view, "begins with education, follows its course in education, and ends with education." This is contrasted with the revolutionary struggles, "otherwise splendid and heroic" but with dubious consequences. In a rhetorical move Yotsov finds the "cult of the revolutionaries" somewhat far-fetched and one-sided, and quite disparaging towards the creators of Bulgarian education and culture. He appeals to the readers to learn to appreciate "cultural feats" as befits a "cultural people" and not to think that "only revolt is a people's virtue." The advocacy of the peaceful, cultural feat and its personality is supported by the typical association between Slavdom and peace, and Slavdom and culture. (Ironically, a few years later, as minister of education, the same author would draw militant lessons from the Revival.)

At around the same time (1936), the well-known liberal intellectual and political activist Todor Vlaikov voiced his doubts about the April uprising, again with regard to the consequences. Pondering upon the more distant causes for the national catastrophes (in the Balkan wars and in World War I) he went back to the April uprising. He then put forward the hypothesis that, were it not for the uprising, one could "assume with a great degree of probability" that the Russo-Turkish liberation war would not have taken place and thus there would have been no Berlin Congress. According to Vlaikov, the uprising should not have taken place and it was a mistake, in spite of the patriotism and self-sacrifice of its leaders. The revolutionary movement in general was transplanted to Bulgaria from the émigrés in Romania and it presented a "diversion" from the "straight and beaten track" followed from the beginning of the Revival, namely, the path toward the awakening of the national consciousness, cultural–educational uplifting, and the uniting of all Bulgarians under "the motherly roof" of the autonomous Bulgarian Church. Had this "normal" way of economic, social, and educational–cultural development been pursued further, one can "assume with all probability" that, after a time, the Bulgarian people would have achieved great progress and would have occupied a prominent place in the Turkish state, and that it would then have won autonomy "one way or another" without giving grounds for its partitioning.[39] Vlaikov thus repeats the arguments of the "evolutionists" in a counter-factual and hypothetical way, that is, after history had run its course.

Other authors are even more harsh in their judgment of the revolutionary trend of the Revival. They blame the revolutionaries for the adventurism that led to the dismemberment of the Bulgarian lands, calling them fantasists, adventurers, and revolutionary romantics. They regret the revolutionary mentality of haste and rashness that took the upper hand in contrast to the moderation and tact of the cultural activists and educators. The "evolutionary" path is described as slower but posing no risk to unity, as well as more independent of external forces.[40]

The advocacy of the revolutionary path in the inter-war period was typically undertaken by Marxist authors, whereby the Communists identified themselves with the revolutionaries of the Revival and claimed their legacy. Georgi Bakalov, in particular, reacted against the "cutting off" of the revolutionary branch from the Revival, and claimed the revolutionary legacy for the Communists. The lines of the status quo and the dualist proposals are ridiculed by him as merely waiting for liberty to come from the sultan, while the ideal of combat is called "the true bequest of the Revival." The author unmasks those in favor of proceeding gradually (by "evolution") as people in possession of capital who had an interest in preserving the markets of the Turkish empire and who, for that reason, became reconciled with the status quo (or proposed a dualist program of semi-autonomy).[41]

However, only a few years later the Communists would have to fight on two fronts, as the revolutionary legacy of the Revival would be claimed by militant right-wing nationalist forces, and the joining of Macedonia in World War II would be presented as a completion of the ideals of the Revival. The Communists were then left with the rather weak option of differentiating between the (good) patriotism of the activists of the Revival, and the (bad) nationalism of the contemporary bourgeoisie, defined by Bakalov as the "aggressive chauvinism of the imperialist bourgeoisie in decay," aimed at instigating a militant mood among the masses in the preparation for war.[42]

The Communists, who seized power in Bulgaria in September 1944 by "revolutionary" means (backed by the Soviet army), continued to see the revolutionaries of the Revival as their forerunners. The "evolutionism" or "educationalism" of those in favor of peaceful means was then condemned as reformism, conformism, compromise, and, in the end, the betrayal by the bourgeoisie of its own revolution. To cite the major ideologue of the Stalinist years Todor Pavlov, while the bourgeoisie played a certain progressive role in deciding the church issue, and was even a leader, it later turned into an "opportunist, compromising, traitorous, educationalist, and, in the end, monarcho-fascist bourgeoisie."[43]

For quite some time, the revolution took the field entirely for itself to the point that earlier education and church efforts became confounded

with later "evolutionism" and "educationalism" (i.e., a reliance on education in particular); at the same time, the "revolution" was traced almost
as far back as Paisii. Dimitŭr Kosev claims credit for differentiating between the two, whereby only the ideology and politics of the liberal bourgeoisie of the 1860s and 1870s is a (reprehensible) rejection of revolution
and "evolutionism."[44] In the academic *History of Bulgaria* of the "personality cult" period, the "educationalism" (*prosvetitelstvo*) of the 1860s and
1870s is defined as the ideology of the bourgeoisie (its commercial part
in particular), who relied on external interference or on Turkish–
Bulgarian dualism, and who had a demobilizing impact on the national
liberation struggles.[45] The underestimation of the "legal path" was present
in an attenuated form until quite late, as attested by the foreword (in 1972)
to the memoirs of one of the Bulgarian national activists who lived in Istanbul.[46]

Aleksandŭr Burmov made his reputation with research into the revolutionary movement (his first book appeared in as early as 1943). He is
known for his meticulous archival studies of the various problems and
events of the revolutionary movement and the verification of numerous
dates, names, personal relations, organizational affiliations, etc. But beyond the factual style and the claims to have found out the truth about
various issues, one can identify the vantage point from which the revolutionary movement, its ideas and organizations are being observed and their
evolution traced. This is consistent revolutionism and the concept of the
internal organization and independence of the Bulgarian revolution from
external powers, advocated by Burmov no less than by their famous expo-
nent Levski. The dynamics of the revolutionary movement itself are characteristically presented as a process of purification and of maturing toward
"ideological–revolutionary clarity."[47] In successive studies the author traces
the evolution of the "Young" in Bucharest (of middle and petty bourgeois
origin), who held democratic views as a whole, but some of whom were
"liberal bourgeois" while others were staunchly "revolutionary–democratic." The picture looks as follows: the "Young" first formed the organization "Bulgarian Society" (around Ivan Kasabov) and the "Young Bulgaria" group; next, the Bulgarian Revolutionary Central Committee was
formed in their midst, with Lyuben Karavelov as its chairman. After initial
mutual compromises with "bourgeois liberalism" and "reformism," there
began a struggle for "ideological–revolutionary purity." Finally, the idea of
an internal revolutionary organization (i.e., inside the country) was conceived, which had a certain prehistory but which was realized by Levski.

The highest standard for measuring ideas and personalities—unwavering revolutionism and the "internal revolution"—was thus set up. Opportunism, reformism, and bourgeois liberalism are lower notches on the measuring-stick of the revolution, while evolutionism does not belong there. The special sympathy toward the armed "revolution" in the past (quite natural for the Communists while struggling for power) looks somewhat strange in the context of a totalitarian Communist government, which tried to preserve once and for all the newly established order and its own domination; so was the spectacle of official historians in state service praising revolutionaries (misrepresented as social combatants). In fact, gradually and quietly the revolutionaries of the Revival again assumed nationalist and state legitimating functions, just as during the right-wing authoritarian regimes of the 1930s and early 1940s, namely, to provide positive examples of patriotism, necessary for the national upbringing of the youth and for reinforcing the loyalty of the citizens to the regime. For a number of reasons the Communist regime evolved toward nationalism.

Coming back to the two paths of the Revival, there were from the very beginning attempts to avoid opposing them and to achieve reconciliation, in the sense that both had contributed equally, though in a different way, to the national cause. Such attempts are not necessarily value neutral. They may carry a certain message or at least some value "overtones" beyond what they literally say, depending on the context and the intention of the authors.

From the post-liberation (i.e., post-1878) period there stem several descriptions in a balanced, impartial tone, and from a certain distance. They affirm the merits and deserts of both trends for the people's cause and differentiate between them only as to the means but not the objective or the patriotic feeling. One such early characterization of the "two patriotic parties in their times," the "church activists" and the "rebels," is provided by Stoyan Zaimov (himself among the organizers of the April uprising).[48] The historian Dimitŭr Mishev also sounds neutral and reconciliatory. According to him, the church movement and the political movement had apostles and a rank and file of their own; their centers and headquarters were often in conflict "not about the goals but about the methods and the means."[49]

Boyan Penev wrote in a balanced and distanced style, too. In his view, the two trends had the same final objective—national liberation (spiritual and political), but they had a different conception of the means to achieve it: the legal means of the church struggle and education, on the one hand, or violent revolutionary means on the other. This was conditioned by differences of temperament among their activists but also by different conditions of existence, inside the empire (and in the capital city Istanbul) or in emigration in Vallachia (Romania).[50]

The harnessing of the two strands together brings an altogether different sound—that of a rallying call—under the sign of the newly actualized national ideal during World War II. According to Mikhail Arnaudov, the "two methods" (education and revolution) have "equal merits" for the creation of national consciousness and collective will among the Bulgarian people.[51] They both stand under the sign of the national idea, "bequeathed" by the Revival as an ideal "capable of reconciling separate views, so that even when the camps and schools of the increased warrior brotherhood contend between themselves, still some great issue takes the upper hand in accordance with the imperatives of the moment, and the most important groups rally around it. The educational, the revolutionary, and the church slogans serve, in the end, the self-determination dear to us all. Conceived of in this way, the revival means a close rallying around the new ideas of liberty and honor, of cultural and civic progress. It impresses us with the readiness of leaders and followers to make incredible sacrifices under the sign of a fanatic patriotism unknown before."[52]

Though not as characteristic, the spirit of reconciliation between the two lines of the Revival may issue from the political Left (Zhak Natan in 1939), in this case attributing a manifestly revolutionary character to both (the peaceful struggles included).[53]

The spirit of the reconciliation of the two strands of the national Revival acquired yet another meaning in the context of the Communist regime, namely, as a normalizing revision of the extreme revolutionism and national "nihilism" imposed by the regime in its initial decades. The beginnings of this revision were traced down to Hristo Gandev, Nikolai Genchev, and Krumka Sharova in another context in the previous chapter. Thus Gandev lessened, in practice, the dramatization of the opposition between revolutionaries and others with his "two concepts" of liberation: "bourgeois–liberal" (relying on external powers), and "revolutionary–democratic" (geared toward internal uprising); he made a further rapprochement by pointing out that the former was supported by the broad Russophile popular masses, while the latter welcomed foreign diplomatic and military help. In his turn, Nikolai Genchev worked out the differences between the two trends but then affirmed that the very division into "educators–church activists" and "politicians–revolutionaries" is relative, because there were reformers and revolutionaries in both camps; besides, all were united around the idea of liberation "regardless of whether they worked in the field of education or in political and public organizations."[54]

In fact, a reasoning of this kind has an antecedent as early as 1910. In the preface to his famous book on the post-liberation epoch, Simeon Radev laid out a division of the national movement into "nationalists" and "Old" (meaning *chorbadzhii* and Russophiles). While the nationalists favored active struggle and relied on the people's potential, the "Old" relied on foreign help; the revolutionaries were "nationalists of the political struggles" but there were "nationalists of the church struggles," too.[55]

A more or less open advocacy of the "evolutionists" would be the next step. The book by the literary scholar Toncho Zhechev, *The Bulgarian Easter or the Bulgarian Passions* (1975), deserves special mention in this respect. It enjoyed great success among the critically minded Bulgarian public at the time and was received as bordering on dissidence. What made such an iconoclastic impression at the time was the rendering of tribute, as equally patriotic, to the conservative (moderate, "opportunist") political line of legal means and the "compromise" of some church activists from Istanbul (e.g., Todor Ikonomov and the pragmatic Dragan Tsankov), and even the vindication of figures previously condemned as "Turcophiles" (e.g., Prince Stefan Bogoridi and Gavril Krŭstevich). By putting himself in their shoes, the author in fact reproduces the previously suppressed arguments of the "evolutionists" against rash actions and the warnings of the dangers of partitioning, as well as the speculation of the 1930s about unrealized possibilities.[56] The book is permeated throughout with the patriotism of the author, who was, in his own words, obsessed with the idea of "keeping the candle burning and not letting the fire of the national spirit die." Hence the hesitancy of the Communist authorities (among whom there were persons who actually shared the feelings of the author) to ban the book and persecute an authentic patriot.[57] (As can be expected, this book would later become a point of departure for the "neo-evolutionist" attack.)

The ideological vigilance over scholarship during the Communist era forced historians to take indirect routes, sometimes stretching and turning around the accepted notions in expressing unorthodox thoughts. Such a concealed revisionist strategy was employed by Zina Markova in her work on the church movement before the Crimean War, in which she vindicated it as an equally valuable manifestation of, and a necessary stage in, the national and bourgeois–democratic revolution.[58] When the "revolution" alone is legitimate, it can be stretched elastically to accommodate within itself all other national struggles—church struggles and education efforts. Hence the somewhat oxymoronic expression "a peaceful stage of the national revolution" (or "peaceful revolution").[59]

The author pushed further with her "breakthrough" in another book (published in 1989) on the Bulgarian Exarchate in the 1860s and 1870s. There she emphasized the useful "nation-consolidating" functions of this institution in a period when it was not "on the crest of the wave of the national revolution" and had steered a "conservative course." She used the occasion to vindicate legal "evolutionism" in general. The "legalists," as she perceptively puts it, had advanced economically and socially and stood to lose in a revolutionary struggle. They were patriotic, too, and aspired to liberation but did not believe that this could be achieved through open struggle and alone. Rather, they wanted to proceed in the direction of the widening of internal autonomy within the Ottoman Empire through the Exarchate and thus preserve Bulgarian national unity against the appetites of others. The reformist illusions "foundered on the April uprising," in the ambiguous expression of the author.[60]

A similar strategy of extending the term "revolution" was applied by Angel Dimitrov as regards the movement for education.[61] As a result of revisionist attempts of this kind, the notions "revolution" or "liberation movement," which were restricted initially by militant Communist historians to armed action alone, became generalized to cover all trends of the Revival. A systematization of the political trends by Angel Dimitrov in late socialism characteristically presents the two basic trends—the reformist and the revolutionary—as two parts of the national liberation movement. The revolutionary movement in the third quarter of the nineteenth century is itself subdivided into "revolutionaries–democrats" and "revolutionaries–liberals," differing as to their consistency in the revolutionary activities and their attitude toward the role of the broader masses in the national revolution. The reformist strand is subdivided in turn into groups according to foreign political biases and orientation, that is, into Russophiles, pro-Westerners, Turcophiles, and persons with wavering orientation.[62] It should be noted that in this re-classification of the trends, and of the groups within them, all are subsumed under the rubric "national liberation movement," and even "Turcophiles" are included in contrast to the earlier stringent opposition to them and their exclusion.

The dualist project (inspired by the Austro-Hungarian model) and its potential for solving the Bulgarian national question are discussed earnestly by Hristo Gandev in his (1974) work on the April uprising.[63] The author also ascribes greater significance (than usual) to the reforms in the Ottoman Empire. The standard presentation underlines their insincerity (under external pressure), their half-way character, and the fact that they were scarcely implemented.[64] According to Gandev, the reforms were an expression of a sincere desire for change on the part of certain Ottoman circles, but they had the paradoxical effect of discrediting Turkish rule because they revealed how far it was from the civilized standards of advanced states, and because of local resistance to their implementation. Here is an example of the well-known paradox of a backward empire's attempts at reform undermining an order previously endured with greater resignation.[65]

That all trends and "parties" are parts of the national liberation movement became an accepted truth as a result of the "revision" that started at the end of the 1970s and ran its course during the 1980s. After the fall of Communism, there was no need for them to branch off from the revolution (inflated as it had become); now they could be viewed as equivalent under the "unity of the Revival processes" and directed toward the common national task and goal. This is, in fact, the idea behind the formula of the "tri-unity" of the movements for national education, church autonomy, and political liberation elaborated by Krumka Sharova. According to the author, the tri-unity finds expression in the simultaneity of the movements (from the very beginning onwards), their mutual reinforcement, and their interlacing within the same personalities. In support of her own "tri-unity theory" on the interrelation between the various strands of the liberation movement, Sharova adduces the ideas of the national revolutionary Lyuben Karavelov (whom she studied extensively), summarized as follows: knowledge leads to political consciousness, which leads to liberation action. As a proof that knowledge (underestimated before as passive "educationalism") leads to action under certain conditions (such as foreign rule), the author cites the strong political activism of the Bulgarian intelligentsia, which would otherwise (in the nature of its function) have engaged in peaceful intellectual activity; under the given conditions even educational–cultural activities acquired a patriotic and political meaning.[66]

The reappraisal of the various "evolutionist" alternatives and their adherents continued after Communism, not surprisingly as further reordering and re-classification. Plamen Mitev voiced his dissatisfaction with the division into conservatives, liberals, and revolutionaries (or revolutionary democrats) because of the absence of clear criteria as to "who was what," and because the strategies and tactics often changed. He proposed instead the restoration of the designations that the activists of the Revival had given themselves, namely "Old" and "Young" (implying generation differences). The "Old" from the "Benevolent Society" (*Dobrodetelna druzhina*) in Bucharest and the "Board of Trustees in Odessa" (*Odesko nastoyatelstvo*) advocated moderate forms of struggle (not armed action), worked out reformist projects, and committed themselves to Russia. The "Young" around Rakovski and the secret committees favored radical action against Turkey—armed bands (*cheti*), revolts, and all-nation insurrections.[67]

Another revision of the received revolutionary nomenclature was undertaken by Iliya Todev.[68] He criticizes (somewhat belatedly) the narrowing of the concept of "revolution" to armed action alone and assigns to it the (actually Marxist) meaning of "change of formation," that is, from feudalism to capitalism. It follows that all activists of the Revival were "bourgeois revolutionaries," or, more precisely, "bourgeois national revolutionaries" in so far as they fought for a Bulgarian state. Todev then subjects to criticism the inherited labels such as reformists, conservatives, (bourgeois) liberals, radicals, revolutionaries, etc., as infelicitous transcriptions of the political realities of the Bulgarian Revival into European political terminology. In his view, the term "revolutionary democrat," which is the central positive term for Marxist authors, is particularly infelicitous because of its association with the Russian populists (*narodniki*) and with utopian socialism; according to him, in the Bulgarian case it can be properly applied only to Botev.

Todev puts forward as the main dividing line the judgment by the national activists of the autonomous (purely) Bulgarian potential for achieving independence (possibly under Gandev's influence). Along this divide the basic parties in Bulgarian society of the 1860s and 1870s were either adherents of "independent action" or adherents of "non-autonomous (dependent) action." The usual opposition "educationalism—revolt" (or "reform"—"revolution") is taken as a subsidiary criterion in further subdividing the "independents" in particular into revolutionaries and reformists. We thus obtain the following tripartite scheme: "independents"-revolutionaries (with Levski as their leader), "independents"-reformists (represented most notably by Stoyan Chomakov), and "dependents," that is, those who relied on some external power. As will be seen, the reordering operation aims at crediting (after due eulogy of Levski) the doctrine of Stoyan Chomakov with capturing the Ottoman Empire "from within" without destroying it. In addition it allows for the scorning of the "party of national impotence," especially those who relied on Russia.

In a recently published book Konstantin Kosev considers the "so-called evolutionists" and the "so-called revolutionaries" as representatives of two variants of the liberation movement in the unfavorable conditions after the Crimean War. The former had as its major drawback the indefiniteness of the liberation, while the latter had the disadvantage of the inevitable interference of the great powers in deciding the fate of the Bulgarians.[69] In fact, Kosev follows, without mentioning it, authors of the 1930s and especially Todor Karayovov, according to whom the "evolutionary school" had the flaw of keeping the Bulgarian people under Turkish domination for an indefinite time although this was offset by remaining united while the revolutionaries pushed towards a quick solution at the risk of foreign interference and territorial claims by neighbors, as actually happened.[70]

Curiously enough, the term "Bulgarian national revolution" (and national liberation movement) was broadened by Konstantin Kosev to absurdity. The revolution becomes all-inclusive in his formulation, covering not only all educational and church struggles but also the economic and social development, and even human reproduction and population increase, to become explicitly synonymous with the Bulgarian Revival.[71] If this logic is to be consistently followed, the peasant working his land, the artisan bent over his material, and the childbearing mother would all be national revolutionaries or at least their assistants. Such an understanding is all the more curious as it comes in a time of free scholarship, with no need for terminological stretching.

In the post-Communist times many of the previously underrated (and disparaged) trends and emblematic figures found their advocates, for example "revolutionary liberals" such as Ivan Kasabov (founder of a "Young Bulgaria" society inspired by Mazzini), the theoretician of "educational-ism" Gavril Krŭstevich, and Prince Stefan Bogoridi (a Bulgarian who served in the highest administrative positions in the Ottoman Empire without losing his Bulgarian self-consciousness).[72] Dualistic projects such as the "memoir" issued in 1866 by the Secret Bulgarian Central Committee, which previously received only a brief mention, are now being considered on an equal footing with the other projects and accorded serious treatment.[73]

The dualist idea has recently been advocated most vigorously by Iliya Todev. He praised Stoyan Chomakov as the leader of the "party of independent action" of an evolutionary type and as a staunch champion of the idea of development within the Ottoman Empire until the Bulgarians seized the opportunity to secede in their entire ethnic and territorial scope. Todev explains Chomakov's support for the French–Ottoman idea of abolishing the *millet* system (of representation by religion) and the formation of a unitary Ottoman nation with ambitious imperial schemes on his part (reminiscent of the Greek Phanariots), and the hope that the Bulgarian element would take the upper hand and capture the empire "from within," Christianizing it in the process.[74] One gets the impression that the authors are competing in vindicating increasingly evolutionist and dualist (previously condemned as compromising and outright "Turcophile") projects, circles, and persons.

The swinging of the pendulum to peaceful "evolutionism" at the expense of the revolution went so far that Krumka Sharova felt obliged to defend the revolutionary struggles from defamation. Choosing, emblematically, the "eulogy of evolutionism" by Toncho Zhechev as her target, she pointed out that the negation of the armed efforts with the argument that, were it not for them, the Bulgarians would gradually have achieved autonomy and independence, presents a "futurology projected in the past." It does not take into account the historical realties of Turkey and the fact that no Balkan people has won independence by peaceful means alone and without foreign support, but only by way of revolts and foreign intervention.[75]

Not as provocative as the "neo-evolutionist," but definitely innovative, are some works by Ognyana Madzhrakova-Chavdarova on the "legal political struggles"—a concept aimed at underlining that the Bulgarian activists did not only do politics by way of arms. The author broadens these struggles to include, alongside struggles for church autonomy (with their national goal), the previously neglected struggles for civic and political, as well as "minority" (national), rights, stimulated by the Ottoman reform acts in a bourgeois–liberal spirit (the *Hatt-i Sherif* and the *Hatt-i Humayun*). Among the proclaimed civic rights and liberties that met with strong conservative resistance and that could only be made effective through struggle were guarantees of life and property, of the right to bring petitions and complaints, of the right to association and meetings, and to representation in local government, etc. The effective advocacy of civic rights (that empowered "nationalities") required institutional props. Hence the efforts of the influential bourgeoisie to ensure some kind of "national representation" of Bulgarian interests before the Porte (preceded by similar initiatives on the part of single activists and émigré organizations before the international world[76]), as well as wider Bulgarian representation in the local authorities and the broadening of communal self-government. What is new here is the positive appreciation of liberal politics in making use of the proclaimed rights of Ottoman "subjects" (an advance on the concept of "*reaya*," meaning "flock"), and it is not by chance that the author refers to similar, though more manifest and more successful, struggles of subject peoples in the Habsburg Empire.[77] This also means a certain recognition of liberalism for it own sake (not just as an accompaniment to nationalism).

The reappraisal of the variants of "evolutionism" ran parallel with the problematization of independent (self-reliant) armed action in the national revolution, regarded previously as the apex of the national programs (ironically, under an entirely dependent Communist regime). Hristo Gandev is probably the first to accentuate (in as early as 1974) the role of the "external factor" in the plans of even the most committed revolutionaries. As shown by him, the principle of the independence (self-reliance) of the Bulgarian mass uprising, raised by Levski to an absolute precondition, did not exclude but actually sought to combine the Bulgarian liberation effort with other anti-Turkish armed initiatives (reminiscent of the Italian unification simultaneously "from below" and "from above").[78] Already after Communism, Plamen Mitev expressed doubts about the "uncritical absolutization of the self-reliance of the Bulgarian national liberation movement and of the advantages of the all-people's revolution."[79]

One can cite in the same context the interesting observation by Iliya Todev that reliance on one's own strength actually draws toward the legal forms of struggle, while orientation toward armed struggle (given the negligible prospects of success) runs into the need for foreign help; thus the organizers of the April uprising simply had to rely on Russia.[80] In fact, a similar point was made already in the 1930s by Todor Karayovov.[81] But in the new context it destroys the association made by Marxist historical scholarship between self-reliance and armed action in addition to crediting the evolutionists with the much praised advantage of self-reliance.

Finally, this line of reasoning necessarily leads to a reassessment of the relative weight of the "internal factor" and the "external factor" in the Bulgarian national revolution. The initial militant Communist scholarship accentuates the "internal factor" and privileges the internal perspective on affairs. The importance of outside forces was formally acknowledged, but the interest focused on the internal developments and the wider picture was lost. There occurred in the course of time an increasing recognition of the dependence of the "Bulgarian question" on the politics of the great powers, defined by their geopolitical interests in the Balkans. Nikolai Genchev, for example, showed a keen sense for the entanglements of the "Eastern question" and the controversial interests of the European great powers in the Balkans, in which Russia was the active side in her thrust toward the Straits, and keeping this in check preserved the status quo for a long time.[82] The Bulgarian émigré social philosopher Stefan Popov pointed to the unfortunate fact that the "Bulgarian question" could not be internationalized as a Bulgarian question but only linked to Russian aspirations and the Russian–European controversies, hence its solution could not but do harm to Bulgarian interests.[83]

The crucial importance of international politics in resolving the Bulgarian national question stands naturally in the foreground in works on international diplomacy, for example the book on Bismarck by Konstantin Kosev.[84] The author recently firmly stated the dependency of the Bulgarian liberation cause on "great politics." Only by hitting upon an (internationally) favorable moment could internal action lead to a successful outcome, itself negotiated between the great powers without Bulgarian participation.[85] In some of his recent essays Iliya Todev goes to the extreme of geopolitical determinism regarding Bulgarian development, modern as well as medieval.[86]

To sum up, the "evolutionists" versus "revolutionaries" controversy shows that the national point of view shared by historical protagonists and historians alike is rather ambiguous. Today as during the Revival it defines the goal alone but allows for different options as to the ways and means of its achievement. The various options are taken up and replayed in thought experiments by historians speculating about unrealized alternatives. For a time under Communism one option—that of armed uprising—was imposed as the right one. Then, in the course of a revision that started in the 1970s, the field began to open up again for debate. Initially this assumed the form of the more or less open "rehabilitation" of various trends and figures to reach the point of direct debate on the relative merits of the options they favored. Beyond an assessment of the historical realities, there is ample space here for personal preference and for the working of the internal dynamics of the field (in the form of reaction against previous "dogma").

Methodologically, the controversy attests to the difficulties of a more distanced, "objectivized" treatment of historical happenings that have had important longer-range consequences for the national community to which the historian belongs. It is only with the fading of the consequences (or their acceptance as definitive) that the controversy can "cool down" and become "purely academic," and that the identification of the historian with the protagonists may weaken. Regarding the Bulgarian Revival this is still not in view. What can be observed is rather a movement in a direction opposite to the theses that were dominant under Communism, though these were not static but subject to continuous change, too (with pressure for consensus at a given moment). In any case, the very fact that it is now possible to consider and discuss the alternatives freely not only shatters the truths of earlier historical scholarship but reflects back on the new theses, relativizing them in the interests of problem-oriented and poly-variant scholarship.

The Hierarchy of National Heroes: Rakovski, Karavelov, Levski, Botev. Reappraisals and Reshuffling

First Zakhari Stoyanov and Ivan Vazov, and then the historian Dimitŭr Strashimirov glorified the revolutionaries of the Bulgarian Revival as national heroes, thus laying down the foundations of the national pantheon. At work here was a patriotic ethos and an admiration for the great personalities and the self-abnegation of the heroes rather than an orderly system built upon principles. There are eventually some personal preferences in favoring one hero above the others, but no system. A cult of Paisii (and the other early "awakeners") also evolved, most emphatically in the 1930s.

The Communist historiography and hagiography of the 1920s through the 1960s proceeds in a different manner. It accords the foremost place to the revolutionaries, too, but by ordering them in a hierarchy in accordance with certain ideological (and class) criteria. The classification is guided by such principles as, in particular, how radical the revolutionary was (the more so, the higher the grading), how consistent and permanent his views were (whether he wavered, at a certain point rejecting the revolution), and how close he came to a social (not only a national) view of the struggle. As additional criteria are his attitude toward the *chorbadzhii*, that is, how much he hated them as a measure of the class interests he advocated; whether he relied entirely on the strength of his own people for the liberation or leant on foreign forces (the less so the better, but in the event that he did, better on Russia); what form of future government he preferred (in descending order: democratic republic, republic, monarchy); and what his thoughts were on the issue of a Balkan or Slav federation, and, if he was in favor, whether he envisioned a federation "from below" or "from above" (i.e., created by the peoples themselves or by the governments).

With these criteria in mind, the grading becomes straightforward and predictable. To take just the four most famous revolutionary leaders, Lyuben Karavelov is at the bottom of the hierarchy because, toward the end of his life, he allegedly turned to passive "educationalism"; higher up is Rakovski, consistently revolutionary and anti-*chorbadzhii*; still higher is Levski, totally devoted to the revolution to his end as a martyr, and relying on the people alone (not on foreign help); on top is Botev, with his utopian socialist views and extreme radicalism, besides being a poetic genius.

The particular labels/evaluations of the revolutionaries in ascending order are as follows: "revolutionary–liberal" (in other versions "liberal–democrat" or "bourgeois radical" and occasionally "radical–democrat"), "revolutionary democrat" (with "consistent" as the highest degree), and finally "revolutionary democrat and utopian socialist."[87] Karavelov is revolutionary-liberal. Rakovski is the first national revolutionary leader and a staunch revolutionary democrat. So are Levski and Botev, both of the consistent type, and if they stand higher it is because of the advantage of coming later and carrying the revolution further (to fruition). Botev is, in addition, a utopian socialist, which places him on top. But the actual apex of the hierarchy is an implicit one—scientific socialism. None of the revolutionary leaders of the Revival has reached it because the epoch was not yet "mature" for a socialist revolution. This gives a kind of superiority of the militant Communist historians over the revolutionaries of the Revival (expressed in their position of sitting in judgment).

This classification scheme can also be applied to revolutionaries of lesser stature, though with diminishing returns, reaching zero with the rank and file. But it is not meant at all for national activists who were educators or church activists. The education and church struggles being lower stages of the national movement (and a pre-stage of the revolutionary movement), their activists have to content themselves with the generally lower status of "awakeners," "Enlighteners," "educators," "scholars," "church activists"; and politically (where applicable) "reformists" and "bourgeois liberals" at best, and "conservatives," "dualists" or "Turco-philes" at worst.

There is the special case of Petko R. Slaveikov, who enjoys exceptionally great prestige for his contributions to education, journalism, and the church struggles, where he occupied the radical position, but who lacks the revolutionary credentials of the émigré activists. His various merits, and being among the most prominent post-liberation Liberals and one of the fathers of the Constitution, have earned him the (somewhat populist) title of a prototypical "people's activist"—meant broadly and without degrading qualifications. He is thus positioned foremost among the non-revolutionaries. In what follows I will consider the symbolic fights around only the greatest revolutionaries, renouncing in advance any claim to comprehensiveness.

For Marxist and non-Marxist authors alike, Georgi Sava Rakovski (1821–1867) is the founder or "patriarch" of the revolutionary movement. He effected the transition from armed bands (*cheti*) to an organized revolutionary movement.[88] It is exactly this quality of a "first revolutionary" within a situation of not quite differentiated "fronts" that contains the potential for various interpretations; moreover, his authority may be evoked against his successors. Thus Dimitŭr Strashimirov refers to this "father figure" in an attempt to reconcile his revolutionary progeny and to condemn the party divisions and internecine strife both before and after the liberation. In his view Rakovski is a "patriarchal," "pre-party" and "above-party" patriot who gathered around himself all sorts of rebellious elements: church activists, émigrés, outlaws (*haiduti*), etc. Being a revolutionary did not make him an enemy of the church activists, and being an émigré did not alienate him from the patriots inside the country acting within the law; he was with them all. The division into parties began after Rakovski's death, and those who came after him, especially Karavelov and Botev, started the division into camps and the political strife in pursuit of a particular political ideal or program to the detriment of the revolutionary unity.[89]

As a "pure" national revolutionary without strongly expressed social views, Rakovski presented a problem for the early socialists who claimed his symbolic capital. Georgi Bakalov had to fight (in the 1930s) against the "epigons of nationalism" who had succeeded in "appropriating this revolutionary titan and concealing the misery of their reactionarism behind the aura of his fame." The author proceeded by establishing a line of revolutionary continuity, both personal and ideological, from Rakovski through the other revolutionaries (who thus appear as good disciples of Rakovski rather than leaders of warring factions) right to his own times.[90]

It is not my task here to trace in detail or even in outline the evolution of the interpretation of Rakovski under Communism. It can only be noted that from the extreme Left field he was later gradually restored to the all-national Center of the terrain. In Nikolai Genchev's treatment (reminiscent of Strashimirov) Rakovski is indivisible among "parties" and classes—first ideologue and leader of the national revolution, a (consistent) revolutionary democrat, and standing for the interests of the whole nation; his bourgeois–democratic platform became the ideology of the nation.[91] The "patriarchal" status of Rakovski is self-evident for most of the authors to follow.

Luyben Karavelov (1834–1879) is not an easy case to assess from an extreme revolutionary position because his biography is marred by his alleged turning away from the revolution toward the end of his life and his devotion to "educationalism." (As will be seen, it is also marred by conflict with Botev, whose unjust accusations were long taken by historians at face value.)

The founder of Bulgarian scientific socialism, Dimitŭr Blagoev set the tone in underrating Karavelov, whom he described as a "progressive liberal, whose views do not go further than political radicalism." A "liberal" is presented here as a person who seeks progress in the gradual development of science, trade, and industry but does not ascribe great weight to the change of economic conditions and the relations between the classes; who considers knowledge as a necessary precondition for the advance of society; and who has as his political ideal a communal self-government like that in Switzerland, Belgium, or the United States of America. All this is meant disparagingly and contrasted with the credo of a socialist revolutionary (such as Botev) that aims at the undoing of economic subjugation and holds that until this is the case, all efforts to educate the people will remain vain.[92]

Karavelov does not qualify as consistent revolutionary democrat such as Levski or Botev (and Chernishevski and Dobrolyubov among the Russians) for Todor Pavlov. But he is not "at the lower points of the revolutionary wave" either, having been, after all, a combatant against the Bulgarian *chorbadzhii*, the big bourgeoisie, and "the opportunists, traitors, and defeatists" in general. With his ideology, and his revolutionary and literary oeuvre he thus stands somewhere in the middle of the revolutionary wave, nearer to its crest than to its base, being a "bourgeois radical" or "bourgeois liberal." Having said that, in a display of generosity Todor Pavlov proffers the following evaluation:

"Lyuben Karavelov remained in essence, in spite of all wavering, compromise, and errors, in the position of a revolutionary democrat rather than in the position of a bourgeois–liberal or a bourgeois–democrat, though without the utopian socialism of Botev and the entirely consistent revolutionary democratism of Levski."[93]

Whatever the particular evaluation, this kind of treatment is characteristic of the Stalinist period, when the historian in the role of ideologue (or an ideologue posing as a historian, as in this case) was supposed to sit in judgment and pass verdicts. Later on, this would be mitigated to making presumably "objective" assessments and only much later would the historian describe and try to understand rather than evaluate. A value element may, of course, be contained in what seems a "pure" description but this is finesse compared to the kind of direct categorical judgment just mentioned. The "objectivist" language in which the evaluations were proffered and made to appear "in the nature of things," quite at odds with their position-related nature, should also be noted. Ideology posed here as positivist scholarship, all the more easily as the latter was the dominant concept of Bulgarian history writing inherited from the "bourgeois" epoch (when it evolved under strong German influences).

An evaluation of Karavelov's "class position" and political views by Dimitŭr Kosev reads: "an ideologue of the petty bourgeoisie," and, more precisely, a "petty bourgeois radical-democrat with considerable wavering to the left or to the right toward the moderate bourgeois liberals."[94] This provides us with a refinement of the scale of evaluation, where "bourgeois liberal" is politically to the right of "radical democrat." Karavelov is seen as representative of the moderate wing in the Bulgarian national revolutionary movement of the 1870s. His (presumable) retreat from the revolutionary movement is explained by class commitments deriving from his class status as a "representative of the Bulgarian petty commercial–industrial bourgeoisie, which preferred that liberation from the Turkish yoke be achieved with foreign help instead of suffering heavy losses itself."[95] In a similar (class) vein, and with greater hostility, Karavelov has been qualified by militants as a "cabinet revolutionary," "renegade," "liquidator," the one to blame for the split in the revolutionary organization, etc.[96]

Karavelov had to wait for Krumka Sharova in 1970 (after an initial moderate advocacy by Nikola Kondarev) for a higher evaluation of his deeds, though issuing from the same standard. Her vindication consists in the recognition (empirically buttressed) that he, too, was a consistent revolutionary, akin to the Russian "revolutionary democrats" Alexander Herzen, Nikolai Chernishevski, and to Pisarev both during his more dubious (from a revolutionary point of view) period in Serbia and during his period in Bucharest when he became the principal organizer and head of the Bulgarian Revolutionary Central Committee.[97] Thus Krumka Sharova pulled Karavelov out of the ranks of suspicious "liberals."

In a more radical way, Nikolai Genchev vindicated (in 1978) the whole

trend represented by Karavelov. Not only was he "a committed revolutionary activist and thinker, a proponent of the liberal and national liberation
ideas of the nineteenth century," but the contradictory evaluations of him
resulted from the unscholarly characteristics of bourgeois liberalism as a
non-revolutionary trend in the Bulgarian liberation movement in general.[98]

A special note was added in the 1970s by Hristo Gandev in describing
(the intellectual and man of letters) Karavelov, and also Rakovski and
Botev, as "bourgeois intellectuals" (*intelligenti*). This was meant as a justification of the bourgeoisie that supplied the revolution with its ideologues
and leaders.[99] Following up this line Plamen Mitev recently explained the
"hesitations" and wavering of Lyuben Karavelov with reference to his intel-
lectualism, which is ascribed a positive meaning in contrast to the typical
revolutionary disparagement of intellectual hesitancy. To cite him:

"Karavelov is, in fact, one of the few intellectuals of subjugated Bulgaria, and this explains best his at first sight complicated and contradictory
political path. In contrast to the rectilinear émigrés, who followed the chosen objective without deviation, Karavelov took things to heart, experienced doubts, looked for a compromise, tried to sense alternative opportunities, and it is precisely this that makes him into a personality of national
stature."[100]

Vasil Levski (1837–1873) is least disputed among the national revolutionaries, not least because of his exceptional character and (saintly) lack of
personal flaws.[101] His major and generally recognized contribution is the
transfer of the center of gravity of the revolutionary activity from emigration to the interior of the country and the setting up of a network of secret
revolutionary "committees." He is thus commonly described as an organizer and "practical worker" of genius but also as a strategist and tactician
of the revolution. The debate concerns only his contribution to the development of the revolutionary ideas and his education. It should be noted
that this debate is not constituted along ideological lines but is of a more
"technical" nature. The way Levski was drawn into the ideological field (of
contesting current political realities) is different, namely, as a (mostly implicit) counterpoise in greatness to the utopian socialist Botev.

The evaluation of Levski by Dimitŭr Blagoev (founder of the Bulgarian
Socialist Party) reads: "practical genius, genius organizer," "a pure, bright
figure" without blemish.[102] In the same vein Dimitŭr Strashimirov (not a
socialist) calls Levski a "mighty architect" and builder of the internal organization (the idea is ascribed by him to Karavelov), "soul of the revolution," its genius and "highest judge."[103]

In a work of 1924, the Communist intellectual Georgi Bakalov calls
Levski a "genius of revolutionary organization and practice" but expresses
doubts as to his education and "theoretical preparation." Still, owing to his
"sound common sense" and the fact that he was able to pass the "school"
of Rakovski, Karavelov, and Botev, he managed to raise himself to the level
of his contemporary revolutionary ideas and apply them in a creative manner.[104] In a later work of his (of 1938) Bakalov acknowledges Levski's priority in conceiving of the idea of internal organization besides putting it in
practice.[105] By describing Levski's rules and the arrangement of the secret
committees, the author was actually suggesting the way to organize the
underground activity of the Communist Party and to train a cadre of professional Communist revolutionaries.[106]

In his work on Levski (published in 1946) Hristo Gandev reveals the
sources of Levski's idea for a self-reliant popular revolution, namely, the
ideas of Mazzini and of the political movement "Young Europe" mediated through the Bulgarian émigré group of Ivan Kasabov. Levski does
not look here as isolated and "self-taught" as he is presented by many
later authors. Moreover, as pointed out by the author, Mazzini's teaching
uses an undifferentiated concept of "people" and puts forward the ideals
of a people's freedom and equality, and a "sacred republic" (as with
Levski), but does not operate with classes and class struggle. Gandev also
emphasized the crisis of the revolutionary movement following the capturing and hanging of Levski—a fact that the militant Marxist historians
just emerging on the scene would jump over in their heroic image of the
revolution as a continuous escalation.[107] It is hardly surprising that the
book came under severe attack by Bulgarian and Soviet authors (Ivan
Undzhiev, Nikola Kondarev, Mikhail Dimitrov, Dimitŭr Sheludko) and
that for a long time the possibility of even hinting at Levski's "Mazzi-
nism" disappeared (along with any interpretation of Ivan Kasabov in the
spirit of revolutionary nationalism, as if "liberal nationalists" were not
revolutionary).[108]

Levski, in Dimitŭr Kosev's description, is a consistent democrat and national revolutionary, to whom it was clear, firstly, that liberation from
Turkish domination should be realized with exclusive reliance on one's
own strength; and secondly, that in order for the people to take to arms en
masse, determined and systematic organizational groundwork among the
masses was necessary—and, as a "man of deeds," he undertook it. But having "insufficient education" and "weak theoretical preparation," Levski
was prevented from emerging as a leading publicist and from giving a more

definite shape to his political views.[109] Here again is the intellectually condescending attitude.

Nikolai Genchev, the brightest dissident historian in the last decades of Communist rule, wrote his most inspired book about Levski. He resolutely rejected the presentation of Levski as just an organizer and a man of practical deeds, implementing the ideas of others but not quite educated and lacking theoretical knowledge. In contrast, he stressed precisely his political views (elaborated mostly in letters), especially his ideas of self-reliant revolutionary organization as well as his pronouncements on the "sacred and pure" future democratic republic.[110] This book defied censorship and the authorities on a number of points. Firstly, there was the elevation of Levski to the highest position in the national pantheon—as the greatest Bulgarian, eclipsing both Botev and later Communist heroes. Second was the idea that every political force attempts to appropriate Lesvki for its own purposes by falsifying him (with the implication that the Communists did so as well). Third, there was the reading of Levski's ideas for a future Bulgaria that implies that his "pure and sacred" republic is the opposite of the Communist regime (in the direct reference transparently masked as "totalitarianism"[111]). Finally, Nikolai Genchev (and Gandev after him) opposed, more or less explicitly, Levski's concept of organization to the more "anarchistic" Botev, thus revising the hierarchy established by the Communist regime.[112] Genchev's book on Levski was an act of defiance, and it was received as such by the regime, even though it managed to find its way into print (unlike other works by the same author that were banned from publication or confiscated once published).

In a later version of his book on Levski (in 1987), Genchev included an important second part, in which he discussed Levski's presence in the Bulgarian "historical memory," especially in memoirs, fiction, art, and historical scholarship, as well as his "canonization" in the popular memory. In the review of the scholarly writings on Levski, he demonstrated how views have changed over time and in particular conjunctures, ranging from "negation" to a "competition for the appropriation of his immortality" and a "share in the partition of the historical legacy of Levski."[113] It is worth noting that in spite of his defense of Levski from "encroachments" from various quarters, by his admiration Genchev contributed greatly to the setting up of a cult of Levski, initially strongly personal and opposed to the authorities but then, with the growing publicity of the author, receiving wide public acclaim (an indication, among other things, of the evolution of the Communist regime itself in a nationalist direction).

Unlike the saintly Levski, Hristo Botev (1847–1876) was strongly contested and admired from various quarters during his own lifetime and afterwards—contested for his fiery temper and admired for his poetic and journalistic genius. He has been portrayed variously as a social revolutionary and forerunner of Bulgarian socialism, an ardent patriot and nationalist, an indomitable rebel in the tradition of the Balkan outlaws (*haiduti*), a rootless cosmopolitan, and even as an irresponsible rogue and socially subversive atheist.[114]

Botev was the absolute favorite of the Communists both before and after World War II. Dimitŭr Blagoev styles him as "socialist, even extreme socialist," committed to destroying the economic subjugation of the people; leader of the extreme left wing of the revolution, that of the "Communards."[115] Blagoev could not miss the opportunity for mobilizing Botev's authority in favor of the socialist cause:

"An organized socialist movement now exists in Bulgaria, which is not only a continuation of Botev's trend and Botev's spirit but an improvement that left out everything transitory in Botev, everything in his tactics and struggle that was transitory and dictated by the conditions then, hence necessary at the time but incongruous with today's conditions of the struggle, and with today's state of development."[116]

The line of socialist (Communist) researchers into Botev goes through the more or less academic Mikhail Dimitrov and Ivan Klincharov, who stressed the influence on him of the Russian utopian socialism (in its revolutionary variety represented by Chernishevski, Herzen, and Dobrolyubov), of Bakunin's anarchism and the populist (*narodniki*) movement of the late 1860s and early 1870s; Ivan Klincharov even implies that Botev was beginning to be acquainted with the scientific socialism of Marx.[117]

More of a propagandist, Georgi Bakalov resolutely claimed Botev for socialism, the proletariat and the Communist Party. Still, he acknowledges that Botev was not an ideologue of the Bulgarian proletariat, non-existent in his time as a class, and that his views were not those of the scientific socialism of Marx and Lenin. Ideologically, Botev was connected with Russian revolutionary populism and its petty bourgeois utopian socialism (his faith in the people's originality, the vaguely expressed idea of decentralized communes). He was especially a disciple of Chernishevski and Bakunin and a "great revolutionary democrat" (as Lenin praised Chernishevski). Botev was expressing the interests of the class of petty producers in a kind of peasant democracy, while he understood the proletariat as a parasitic and pauperized class in the sense of antiquity rather than the contemporary proletariat as the basis of production.[118]

It is interesting to note that the interpretation of Botev's utopian socialism opened internal debates between Marxist authors, who thus formulated their own views about the varieties of socialism, the Russian populists
(*narodniki*), the Russian revolutionary democrats of the 1860s, etc., and
their relation to "scientific socialism."[119]

At the same time Botev was claimed by the Bulgarian anarchists in polemics with the Communist authors. This interpretation stressed the anarchist strand in Botev's ideas under the influence of Bakunin and Proudon,
namely, his extreme revolutionism, his rejection of any authority, his pronouncements for decentralized communes and true federalism and against
private property, etc., while the influence of the Russian populists and of
utopian socialism (Chernishevski) was downplayed.[120]

Finally, one may cite Boyan Penev's attempt (in 1926) to "integrate" the
personality of Botev, claimed, contested and divided into ideological
strands. The author points to the underlying unity of Botev's passionate
"nature," governed by a (romantic) love of freedom in all senses—
individual, national, and social. Hence he was attracted to any teaching
that has at its root the notion of freedom: individualism (the widest personal freedom though stopping short of egotism), socialism (the freedom of
the toiling people and of the proletariat from social subjugation), nationalism (as an ardent Bulgarian patriot suffering with his people under foreign
rule), and internationalism (sympathy with all suppressed peoples). Because of his impatience and dedication to revolutionary activities, these
remained little elaborated in his writings and some are contradictory if
considered as doctrines; still, they combine in his passionate drive for freedom.[121] Clearly, Penev does justice to the various sources of Botev's views,
and, hence, the various interpretations, while affirming a deeper binding
element that relativizes any single interpretation. But for the exponents of
the various doctrines Botev was needed in ever partial (and skewed) portraits to concord with their own ideas and lend them his aura.

Todor Pavlov's speech (on the celebration of Botev's day, 2 June, in
1945) already represents the triumphalist and mandatory appropriation of
Botev by the victorious Communists. Though Botev's Bulgaria was on the
eve of a bourgeois–democratic transformation, Botev was not a "great
bourgeois democrat" (this is already a stigma) but a leader of the "leftmost
revolutionary wing"—of the Communards. Under the conditions of his time
he could not evolve as an accomplished scientific socialist, Marxist, and
dialectical materialist, but remained a utopian socialist with "intuitions of
dialectical materialism." He was also a patriot, in fact an "accomplished"

and "great" patriot, not a false patriot or "chauvinist," besides being a "great internationalist."[122]

In the early Communist years, and in Botev's canonized case until quite late, the official view flowed directly into historical scholarship. In Dimitŭr Kosev's description, Botev is the apex of the Bulgarian revolutionary-democratic ideas before the liberation. Besides being a revolutionary of the most consistent type, he is a utopian socialist (in his views on the future of the society), though not a Marxist and only to an extent under the influence of scientific socialism, but rather under the impact of the Russian populists, of the utopian socialists, and of the petty bourgeois anarchism of Proudon. He "paid little attention to the propaganda of socialism" and more to the propaganda of revolutionary-democratic ideas. This is explained by Kosev by the fact that a "deep and penetrating mind" such as Botev's "saw very clearly that a national-democratic (not socialist) revolution was imminent in Bulgaria." Botev was also a champion of the idea of a "brotherly union" between the Balkan peoples, not by way of agreement between governments (which did not then express the will of their peoples) but as the Balkan peoples themselves fight their way into a union.[123] (Botev thus appears as a forerunner of the inter-war and immediate post-war Communist thesis for Balkan federalism "from below," understood as a federation of Balkan peoples led by their Communist parties.)

These were the general lines of Botev's interpretation, followed by numerous authors afterwards alongside the accumulation of empirical findings and the writing of a comprehensive biography.[124] In fact, the case of Botev shows clearly that an interpretation is only to some extent dependent on empirical findings and that a preconceived scheme may accommodate various facts. Thus (apart from cruder attempts to align Botev with Communism) it was a question of "politics" to stress the impact upon him of utopian socialism, and of populism, rather than of anarchism or of Western liberalism.

Nikolai Genchev was probably the first to cast doubts on the revolutionary precedence of Botev, both indirectly by extolling Levski, and directly by downgrading his view of a spontaneous people's revolution (plus an Aesopian hint at his socialist utopianism, with which Levski was not "infatuated").[125] Such ideas could be elaborated more explicitly only in the free post-Communist conditions. Thus according to Ivan Stoyanov, Botev retreated from the positions reached by Levski because he did not pay attention to the necessity of preparing the people for an uprising but relied (anarchistically) on its revolutionary instinct. Also, in contrast to Levski, who put the emphasis on a mass people's uprising, Botev was in favor of "combined tactics"—uprising plus the dispatching of bands (*cheti*) from neighboring states (another drawback). When considering Botev's views the author enumerates populism, anarchism, bourgeois liberalism, and utopian socialism already on an equal footing, of which Botev sought "the most appropriate for the Bulgarian conditions." Interestingly, Botev's utopian socialism, which previously served to legitimate the Communist order, is now itself in need of justification, namely, that it had nothing in common with the "familiar socialist reality."[126]

Speaking of the historical revolutionist narrative in general, one should add that the heroes are typically introduced in an ascending gradation. The value hierarchy is thus reinforced by presentational means: plotting, sequencing, moving toward denouement, etc. Every revolutionary does something but everyone lacks something and is superseded by the next (and overtaken in merits). The revolution is thought of as a relay race, in which the baton is passed on to increasingly radical personalities until the culmination is reached, that is, Botev and the organizers of the April uprising.[127] With the appearance of more radical persons and ideas, all the rest become anachronistic and drop out of the race. To use another metaphor, the revolutionaries are imagined as climbers on a steep rock who are stuck at different points, destined to remain where they are. The unconquerable peak they are climbing is called socialist revolution and the equipment necessary to reach it—scientific socialism.

The treatment of the Bulgarian revolutionaries by Zhak Natan provides an illustration. Rakovski is a "revolutionary democrat," a father of the Bulgarian revolutionary ideology, but his ideology was still not quite lucid and complete. Karavelov is a "great revolutionary democrat," the first among the Bulgarian revolutionaries to create a system with a "broad revolutionary democratic character." But he was not able to assimilate the critical revolutionary teaching of the Russian social philosophers Belinski, Herzen, Chernishevski, and Dobrolyubov. He came to the idea of a revolution by way of a mass popular uprising, but it was Levski who realized it. Besides, he did not adhere to the revolutionary tenets to the end but passed to evolutionism and educationalism, being in fact a "bourgeois radical." Levski, in his turn, elaborated an "accomplished and broad national-revolutionary ideology that lifts him to the highest peak of the ideological trends of the epoch." He is distinguished by a "lucid and consistent democratism, nationalism and patriotism" and is "the most consistent Bulgarian revolutionary democrat" and most able organizer of the national

revolution, who introduced into it the principle of methodical organizational work. But he, too, did not surpass the framework of his epoch. Botev
elaborated a theory of revolution by way of mass popular uprising, although as an organizer he lags behind Levski. He fought not only for the
national liberation of the people but also for social liberation and for a
brotherly union between the Balkan and South Slav peoples. His views
represent a mixture of the ideas of the utopian socialists, the petty bourgeois anarchism of Proudon, the scientific rationalism of the eighteenth
and the nineteenth centuries, and the ideas of the Russian revolutionary
democrats. He is a "great revolutionary democrat and utopian socialist,"
the highest peak of Bulgarian revolutionary ideology during the Revival,
and the only one who managed to exceed the limits of his epoch and become a "forerunner of scientific socialism." But (as implied) he, too, was
neither a Marxist nor a scientific socialist.[128]

The reappraisal of the revolutionaries that began somewhat "underground" in the 1970s continued after Communism. The central figure in
this reappraisal is Krumka Sharova, who based her inferences on extensive
research, in contrast to the lovers of bombastic revisionist statements. Her
interest is focused on the crisis in the revolutionary movement following
the death of Levski, and the conflict between Karavelov and Botev that led
to the split in the Bulgarian Revolutionary Central Committee in Bucharest (headed by Karavelov) and to the founding of a new revolutionary
formation, the so-called Bulgarian Revolutionary Committee of 1875. The
previous interpretation (of Aleksandŭr Burmov) had showed the new organization as a natural continuation of the older one and the conflict between Botev and Karavelov as a fight between the consistent revolutionary
forces around Botev and the liberal-bourgeois (and educationalist) tendencies. However, the conflict and the split that followed are shown in a very
different light by Krumka Sharova. She portrays the impulsive, touchy, and
intolerant Botev as the more active in this quarrel, incited by persons who
wanted the removal of Karavelov from the leadership. There were also
disagreements in terms of principles. Botev was breaking the principles
established in Levski's time when insisting upon a more active role for the
émigrés in organizing armed bands from outside instead of the careful
preparation of an uprising from within (as he believed the people were
ready to rise at any time). Again in violation of the established rules he
imagined the revolutionary organization as decentralized on the model of
the underground Russian socialist and other circles, in contrast to the
existing subordination and discipline, and he relied too much and quite

unrealistically on the intervention of neighboring states (especially Serbia and Montenegro). Botev's views were embodied in the new Bulgarian Revolutionary Committee (of 1875), created (as Sharova says) as a "separatist organization" by a small group of people around him, not especially prominent and authoritative and without the support the majority of the émigrés and of the internal activists.

Finally, based on a number of facts, Krumka Sharova categorically rejects the standard accusation against Karavelov (made first by Botev and later taken up by historians) of retreating from the revolutionary movement and devoting himself entirely to peaceful "educationalism." The conflict in the revolutionary movement appears thus to be not between the liberal-bourgeois tendencies and the resolute revolutionaries, but within the committed revolutionary movement itself, between disciplined and consistent activists on the one hand, and rash and anarchistic ones on the other hand. The committee of 1875 did not exist long and its plans and actions were ill-conceived and adventurous. It was succeeded by the so-called Committee of Gyurgevo (a Romanian town), created again by associates of Botev, who undertook the preparation of the April uprising by sending emissaries into the country (in a return to Levski's views). Botev was in Russia when this was taking place and his feat of entering the country at the head of an armed band (*cheta*) to join the uprising (which had already been suppressed), as well as his heroic death, are consistent with his views.[129]

Plamen Mitev is another historian who recently sided with Karavelov (in agreement with Krumka Sharova) in his conflict with Botev. He pointed out that it was actually Botev who retreated in 1875 from a number of hard-won views on the revolutionary struggle, such as preparation of the uprising from within the country (and the priority of the internal organization), the need for centralized leadership, the anachronism of fighting by dispatching bands from outside, apart from the fact that the organizational legitimacy in the conflict was not on his side.[130] Interestingly, Plamen Mitev devotes little space in his published "lectures" to Botev, who is reduced in stature to a "most active follower" of Levski after his death (it is worth remembering that, for earlier authors, it was Levski who learned from Botev).[131] The newer interpretation thus not only performed a U-turn to take the side of Karavelov against Botev, of the disciplined national revolutionary against the anarchistic social revolutionary, but this led to a reshuffling in the national pantheon. Botev will remain the greatest national poet, but not the greatest national revolutionary or the most saintly figure.

Beyond the empirical highlighting of what was going on within the revolutionary movement in 1875, the reappraisal implicitly reaches further. To begin with, one becomes aware of how small the group of radical activists that organized the April uprising was, even within the context of the revolutionary movement itself—a handful of people taking the initiative and steering the national movement upon the fateful path of mass uprising. This destroys the fiction of a smooth, conflict-free continuity and shatters the assurance that the most radical activists necessarily have "right" and "far-sightedness" in history on their side (and that there is something "most advanced" in this respect), bringing back an awareness of alternatives and of historical "contingency." This somehow raises doubts about the course of action taken, this time not by comparing it with the "evolutionist" alternative, but by considering the revolutionary trend from within.

Notes

1   Shishmanov, "Paisii i negovata epokha," 88, 92.
2   Penev, *Paisii Hilendarski*, 9–11, 97–98; Penev, *Istoriya na novata*. Vol. 2, 226–233, 252–253, 322–325.
3   Mikhail Arnaudov, *Paisii Hilendarski (1722–1798)*. Sofia: Hemus, 1942, 42–60.
4   Ivan Ormandzhiev, *Otets Paisii i epokhata na Vŭzrazhdaneto*. Sofia: Kazanlŭshka dolina, 1938, 19–23.
5   Examples are Georgi Konstantinov, "Po sluchai 175 godini ot napisvaneto na negovata istoriya." *Otets Paisii* 10, no. 7 (1937): 259–270; Boris Yotsov, "Bŭlgarskata istoriya, neinata razrabotka do Osvobozhdenieto i znachenieto i za probudata na bŭlgarskiya narod." *Otets Paisii* 6, nos. 8–9 (1933): 6–11; Nikola Aleksiev, "Obrazŭt na ottsa Paisiya." *Otets Paisii* 12, no. 10 (1939): 444–446.
6   Boris Yotsov, "Paisii Hilendarski." *Uchilishten pregled* 41, no. 7 (1942): 838–841, cit. 839–840. See also "Den na Ottsa Paisiya." *Uchilishten pregled* 40 (1941): 1008–1111.
7   Georgi Bakalov, "Otets Paisii. Deloto na Paisii." In Bakalov, *Izbrani istoricheski proizvedeniya*. Sofia: Nauka i izkustvo, 1960, 33–37.
8   Derzhavin, *Istoriia Bolgarii*. Vol. 4, 70–95, esp. 70–72, 94; Derzhavin, "Paisii Hilendarski," 65, 102–103, 106–107.
9   Dimitŭr Kosev, *Lektsii po nova*, 22–23.
10 Dimitŭr Kosev, "Za ideologiyata na Paisii Hilendarski." In *Paisii Hilendarski i negovata epokha*, 7–30, esp. 12–13.
11 Vasilii Konobeev, "Za klasovoto sŭdŭrzhanie na ideologiyata i programata na Paisii Hilendarski." In Konobeev, *Bŭlgarskoto natsionalno-osvoboditelno dvizhenie. Ideologiya, programa, razvitie*. Sofia: Nauka i izkustvo, 1972, 59–79.
12 Todor Pavlov, "Bezsmŭrtnoto delo na Paisii Hilendarski." In Pavlov, *Izbrani proizvedeniya*. Vol. 3, 7–14, cit. on 9 (first published in 1952); Pavlov, "Za marksicheska istoriya," 354. Todor Pavlov was professor of dialectical materialism at the Institute of Red Professorship in Moscow (1932–1936), president of the Bulgarian Academy of

Sciences (1947–1962), and a member of the Central Committee and Politburo of the Bulgarian Communist Party (1954–1976). His major task was the Communist reorientation of Bulgarian science and culture. See the entry in *Entsiklopedia Bŭlgariya.*

13 Topencharov, *Portretŭt na Paisii,* 50–57. Topencharov was director of the press in the Ministry of Information and Arts (which was actually a ministry of propaganda and censorship) between 1945 and 1947, and professor of "general history" at Sofia University (1949–1964). He was awarded the title of academician. See the entry on him in *Entsiklopedia Bŭlgariya.*

14 Topencharov, *Portretŭt na Paisii,* 57–58.

15 Hristo Hristov, *Paisii Hilendarski,* 284–287, 292; Hristov, "Paisii Hilendarski i Bŭlgarskoto vŭzrazhdane." In *Paisii Hilendarski i negovata epokha,* 33–69, esp. 62–63, 66.

16 Arnaudov, *Paisii Hilendarski (1722–1798),* 61.

17 Dimitŭr Kosev, "Za ideologiyata na Paisii," 30.

18 Goran Todorov, "Istoricheskite vŭzgledi na Paisii," 160–162. The author adduces Lenin's view that in the transition from feudalism to capitalism even the peasant revolution is "objectively" bourgeois in character.

19 Genchev, *Bŭlgarsko vŭzrazhdane,* 91–92.

20 Velcho Velchev, *Paisii Hilendarski. Epokha, lichnost, delo.* Sofia: Narodna prosveta, 1981, 127, 129.

21 Dimitŭr Kosev, *Lektsii po nova,* 27.

22 Dimitŭr Kosev, "Za ideologiyata na Paisii," 12–13.

23 Konev, *Bŭlgarskoto vŭzrazhdane.* Vol. 1, 29.

24 Strashimir Dimitrov and Krŭstyu Manchev, *Istoriya na balkanskite,* 136–137.

25 Ilya S. Miller, "Formirovanie natsii. Mesto problemy v sovokupnosti protsessov perekhoda ot feodalizma k kapitalizmu v stranakh tsentral'noi i iugovostochnoi Evropy" *Sovetskoe slavianovedenie,* no. 6 (1975): 93–98.

26 Hristov, "Kŭm vuprosa za zarazhdaneto," 24–25.

27 Hristo Gandev, "Kŭm ideiniya razbor na Paisievata istoriya." In Gandev, *Problemi na bŭlgarskoto,* 166–177 (first published in 1946).

28 James Clarke, "Father Paisii and Bulgarian History." In Clarke, *The Pen and the Sword,* edited by Dennis Hupchick. East European Monographs. Boulder, New York: Columbia University Press, 1988, 87–111, esp. 92–94.

29 Elka Drosneva, *Folklor, Bibliya, Istoriya. Kŭm 230-godishninata na "Istoriya Slavyanobulgarska."* Sofia: Universitetsko izdatelstvo "Kliment Ohridski," 1995.

30 Andrei Robinson, *Istoriografiia Slavianskogo Vozrozhdeniia i Paisii Hilendarski.* Moscow: Izdatel'stvo Akademii nauk SSSR, 1963, esp. 93–96.

31 Robinson, *Istoriografiia Slavianskogo,* 94, 96, 133–139.

32 Emil Georgiev, *Obshto i sravnitelno,* 83–90.

33 Plamen Mitev, *Bŭlgarsko vŭzrazhdane,* 33–34.

34 Iliya Todev, "Paisii–avtor na bulgarskata," 23–34, esp. 27–29.

35 As François Furet asserts, this is the stance of most historians of the French Revolution, who show their own royalist, liberal, or Jacobin views when discussing it. See Furet, *Interpreting the French Revolution,* 1–2, 10–11.

36 Strashimirov, "Komitetskoto desetiletie," 787; Strashimirov, *Istoriya na Aprilskoto.* Vol. 1, 4.

37 Boris Yotsov, "Pŭt na bŭlgarskoto vŭzrazhdane." *Rodna rech* 8, no. 5 (1935): 197–204.

38 Boris Yotsov, "Vasilii Aprilov." *Prosveta* 1, no. 2 (1935): 129–139, cit. on 135.

39 Todor Vlaikov, "Ako to ne beshe stanalo." *Prosveta* 1, no. 5 (1936): 528–532.

40 Petŭr Mutafchiev, "Dukh i zaveti na Vŭzrazhdaneto." *Otets Paisii* 7, no. 10 (1934): 199; Ormandzhiev, *Nova i nai-nova istoriya*, 299; Todor Karayovov, "Prosvetiteli i revolyutsioneri." *Prosveta* 4, no. 4 (1938): 400–412.

41 Georgi Bakalov, *Zavetite na bŭlgarskoto*, 13. Bakalov, *Bŭlgarskoto natsionalno-revolyutsionno dvizhenie*. Ocherki, Sofia, 1937, 3–7.

42 Bakalov, *G. S. Rakovski*, 10, 44.

43 Pavlov, "Za marksicheska istoriya," 362.

44 Dimitŭr Kosev, "Aprilskoto vŭstanie–vrŭkhna tochka," 12.

45 *Istoriya na Bŭlgariya v dva toma*. Vol. 1, 402–403. For a more cautious expression, see Natan, *Bŭlgarskoto vŭzrazhdane*, 245–253.

46 Strashimir Dimitrov, "Foreword." In Stambolski, *Avtobiografiya. Dnevnitsi, Spomeni*, 5–15.

47 Aleksandŭr Burmov, "Bŭlgarskoto natsionalno-revolyutsionno dvizhenie i bŭlgarskata emigratsionna burzhoaziya prez 1867–1869 g." In Burmov, *Izbrani proizvedeniya*. Vol. 2, 140–164 (first published in 1961); Burmov, "Borba za ideino-revolyutsionna chistota v BRTsK v Bukuresht (1869–1871)." In Burmov, *Izbrani proizvedeniya*. Vol. 2, 201–218 (first published in 1966); Burmov, "BRTsK (1868–1877)." In Burmov, *Izbrani proizvedeniya*, 9–114 (first published in 1943).

48 Zaimov, *Minaloto*, 48–52.

49 Mishev, *Bŭlgariya v minaloto*, 408–409.

50 Penev, *Istoriya na novata*. Vol. 4, part 1, 182–203.

51 Arnaudov, *Bŭlgarskoto vŭzrazhdane*, 55. Still, at the end of this book Arnaudov seems to take sides with the "evolutionists" (182–183).

52 Mikhail Arnaudov, *Paisii Hilendarski (1722–1798)*. Sofia: Hemus, 1942, 6. The passage appears in a slightly modified form, avoiding the nationalist idiom, in a later edition: Arnaudov, "Paisii Hilendarski." In Arnaudov, *Tvortsi na bŭlgarskoto vŭzrazhdane*. Vol. 1, Sofia: Nauka i izkustvo 1969, 7–61, esp. 7–8 (first edition in 1942.). See also the earlier work of Arnaudov, "Dukh i nasoki," 191–192.

53 Natan, *Bŭlgarskoto vŭzrazhdane*, 75.

54 Genchev, *Bŭlgarsko vŭzrazhdane*, 342.

55 Simeon Radev, *Stroitelite na sŭvremenna Bŭlgariya*. Vol. 1. Sofia, 1910, VIII–X, XIV–XV. The more extreme activists of the church struggles (Stoyan Chomakov, Todor Ikonomov, Petko Slaveikov, Dragan Tsankov) are described as "nationalists of the church struggle."

56 Zhechev, *Bŭlgarskiyat Velikden*, 100–115, 330–379. Todor Ikonomov enjoys the special sympathies of the author, who calls him a revolutionary among the church activists and who describes his life after the liberation (when he was badly treated by the Liberals) in order to exemplify the difficulty of advocating moderation in the prevailing conditions.

57 In his postscript to the post-Communist edition of the book, the author describes the aura of dissidence around it even before publication because of the neglect of the "heroic" and the interest in clerical affairs. The Bulgarian émigré dissidents Petŭr Uvaliev from the BBC and Georgi Markov from Radio Free Europe expressed an interest in the book, but then the Bulgarian Communist authorities decided to allow it and praise it in order to preempt and baffle "Western propagandists." However, after the initial benevolence of the regime there followed attacks on the part of hard-line former anti-fascist activists, who saw it as reneging on the revolutionary line. See Zhechev, *Bŭlgarskiyat Velikden*, 441–461.

58 Markova, *Bŭlgarskoto tsŭrkovno-natsionalno*, 192–195. The author tactically cited, in support of her view, revolutionary authorities from the Revival such as Rakovski and

Karavelov, and explained the strongly negative attitude of Botev by the anachronism of the church question once it was solved.

59 Markova, *Bŭlgarskata Ekzarkhiya*, 27.
60 Markova, *Bŭlgarskata Ekzarkhiya*, 5–30, 315–323.
61 Angel Dimitrov, *Uchilishteto, progresŭt*. The last chapter treats the contribution of the education struggles to the national revolution.
62 Angel Dimitrov, *Uchilishteto, progresŭt*, 152–153.
63 Gandev, *Aprilskoto vŭstanie*, 73–75.
64 Though factually true, such a representation contains a dose of insincerity because a full implementation of the reforms and a stabilization of the Ottoman Empire on the basis of civic equality and administrative integration would have been rejected by the nationalist movements that wanted to destroy it (and the same is true of the national historians).
65 Gandev, *Aprilskoto vŭstanie*, 40–42. Interest in the Ottoman reform continued after Communism, e.g., Ivan Stoyanov, *Istoriya na bŭlgarskoto*, 55–58, 64–65; Pletnyov, *Midhat pasha*.
66 Krumka Sharova, "Vzaimodeistvie na dvizheniyata za natsionalna kultura, tsŭrkva i politichesko osvobozhdenie prez Vŭzrazhdaneto." In *Kultura, tsŭrkva i revolyutsiya prez Vŭzrazhdaneto*, edited by Krumka Sharova. Sliven, 1995, 11–39.
67 Plamen Mitev, *Bŭlgaskoto vŭzrazhdane*, 109–110. Before Mitev, the terms "Young" and "Old" were employed by Aleksandŭr Burmov, but with a strong revolutionary bias.
68 Iliya Todev, "Partiite v bŭlgarskoto natsionalno dvizhenie i osbobozhdenieto." In Todev, *Novi ochertsi*, 66–82.
69 Konstantin Kosev, *Aprilskoto vŭstanie–prelyudiya*, 60–63. Also Kosev, *Kratka istoriya*, 111–112, 170–171. The author pays due attention to political groups other than the extreme revolutionaries (120–127).
70 Karayovov, "Prosvetiteli i revolyutsioneri," 403–404.
71 Konstantin Kosev, *Kratka istoriya*, 15–16.
72 Vera Boneva, *Istoricheski etyudi po Bŭlgarsko vŭzrazhdane. Veliko Tŭrnovo*, 1997, 5–11, 23–31,59–69.
73 Ivan Stoyanov, *Istoriya na bŭlgarskoto*, 174–183.
74 Iliya Todev, "Dr. Stoyan Chomakov ili ot osvoboditelen kŭm imperski natsionalizŭm." In Todev, *Kŭm drŭgo minalo*, 149–164; Todev, "Kŭm problema za genezisa"; Todev, "Partiite v bŭlgarskoto," 71–73, 78–79; Todev, "Dualizmŭt kato dŭrzhavnostroitelna initsiativa v Bŭlgarskoto vŭzrazhdane. Begŭl pogled ot 1992 g." In Todev, *Novi ochertsi*, 123–136.
75 Sharova, "Vzaimodeistvie na dvizheniyata," 32–36.
76 Alongside the national efforts for education, church, and state, Krumka Sharova subsequently formed into a separate (fourth) trend the international initiatives of the activists of the Revival for engaging Europe with the "Bulgarian question." See Sharova, "Vzaimodeistvie na dvizheniyata," 11.
77 Ognyana Madzhrakova-Chavdarova, "Predpostavki i nachalo na legalnata politicheska borba na bŭlgarskiya narod prez Vŭzrazhdaneto." *Istoricheski pregled* 48, no. 7 (1992): 3–29; Madzrakova-Chavdarova, "Bŭlgarskoto narodno predstavitelstvo–idei i opiti za sŭzdavaneto mu (40-te–60-te godini na XIX vek)." *Istoricheski pregled* 49, no. 2 (1993): 3–35.
78 Gandev, *Aprilskoto vŭstanie*, 51–54.
79 Plamen Mitev, *Bŭlgarskoto vŭzrazhdane*, 120–121.
80 Todev, *Kŭm drugo minalo*, 228–229; Todev, *Novi ochersti*, 118, 121. A similar conclu-

sion is reached by Konstantin Kosev when assessing the disadvantages of the "violent variant," namely, that it presupposes "the inevitable interference and the crucial role of the great powers in the final denouement of the events." Kosev, *Kratka Istoriya*, 170–171.

81 Karayovov, "Prosvetiteli i revolyutsioneri," 403–404. According to the author, the evolutionists "held their fate in their own hands" while the revolutionaries placed the solution of the Bulgarian question at the mercy of the will and appetites of others.
82 Genchev, *Bŭlgarsko vŭzrazhdane*, 13; Genchev, *Bŭlgarskata kultura*, 257–266.
83 Stefan Popov, *Bŭlgarskata ideya*. Munich, 1981, 114–116.
84 Kosev, *Bismarck, Iztochniyat vŭpros i bŭlgarskoto osvobozhdenie, 1856–1878*. Sofia: Nauka i izkustvo, 1978.
85 Kosev, *Aprilskoto vŭstanie–Prelyudiya*, 20–25, 148–149; Kosev, *Kratka istoriya*, 21–22, 171–172.
86 Todev, *Kŭm drugo minalo*, 233–244; 245–254.
87 In this terminology liberal is more to the right than (bourgeois) radical. "Revolutionary democrat" is Lenin's definition of a person with populist and utopian-socialist views, such as Herzen, Dobrolyubov and Chernishevski.
88 Blagoev defines Rakovski simply as a patriot. See Blagoev, "Prinos kŭm istoriyata," 207. For a recent biography of Rakovski in English, see Mari Firkatian, *The Forest Traveller. Georgi Stoikov Rakovski and Bulgarian Nationalism*. New York: Peter Lang, 1996.
89 Strashimirov, "Komitetskoto desetiletie," 854–855.
90 Bakalov, *Nashite revolyutsioneri*, 12–13.
91 Genchev, *Bŭlgarsko vŭzrazhdane*, 330–332.
92 Dimitŭr Blagoev, "Hristo Botev." In Blagoev, *Za Bŭlgarskoto vŭzrazhdane*, edited by D. Raikov. Sofia: Partizdat 1982, 86–103, esp. 89–92 (the work is dated 1887).
93 Todor Pavlov, "Po vŭprosa za ideologiyata na Lyuben Karavelov." In Pavov, *Izbrani proizvedeniya*. Vol. 3, 81–90, cit. on 89.
94 Dimitŭr Kosev, *Lektsii po nova*, 193–194. Kosev actually follows Derzhavin, *Istoriya Bulgarii*. Vol. 4, 114, 137–138.
95 Dimitŭr Kosev, *Lektsii po nova*, 193–194, 216.
96 By, for example, Mikhail Dimitrov, Zhak Natan, Pantelei Zarev, Aleksandŭr Burmov, Mikhail Arnaudov, Ivan and Tsveta Undzhievi, etc. See the reviews of the opinions on Karavelov in Krumka Sharova, *Lyuben Karavelov v bŭlgarskoto osvoboditelno dvizhenie, 1860–1867*. Sofia: Nauka i izkustvo, 1970, 7–23; Plamen Mitev, *Sŭzdavane i deinost na Bŭlgarskiya revolyutsionen komitet–1875*. Sofia: LIK, 1998, 16–21.
97 Sharova, *Lyuben Karavelov v bŭlgarskoto*, esp. 22–23, 406–411.
98 Genchev, *Bŭlgarsko vŭzrazhdane*, 370. A belated and already anachronistic reverberation of the struggle around Karavelov is to be found in Ivan Stoyanov, *Istoriya na bŭlgarskoto*, 235.
99 Gandev, *Aprilskoto vŭstanie*, 60.
100 Plamen Mitev, *Bŭlgarskoto vŭzrazhdane*, 120.
101 For a somewhat romantic description of the life and deeds of Vasil Levski in English, see Mercia MacDermott, *The Apostle of Freedom. A Portrait of Vasil Levsky*. Sofia Press, 1979.
102 Dimitŭr Blagoev, "Iz Vŭtreshen pregled." In Blagoev, *Za Bŭlgarskoto vŭzrazhdane*, 146–150 (first published in 1898).
103 Strashimirov, *Istoriya na Aprilskoto*. Vol. 1, 95.
104 Bakalov, *Nashite revolyutsioneri*, 25.
105 Bakalov, *Bunt protiv Levski*. Sofia, 1938, 28–29.

106 Zhak Natan, "Predgovor." In Georgi Bakalov, *Izbrani istoricheski*, 13.
107 Hristo Gandev, *Vasil Levski. Politicheski idei i revolyutsionna deinost*. Sofia, 1946, esp. 30–31, 35–39, 77, 80, 97–99, 111–112, 125–126.
108 Vera Boneva, "Ivan Kasabov kato teoretik na vŭzrozhdenskiya revolyutsionen liberali- zŭm." In Boneva, *Istoricheski etyudi*, 59–69.
109 Dimitŭr Kosev, *Lektsii po nova*, 186–187, 193.
110 Genchev, *Levski, revolyutsiyata*, esp. 11–15, 28–34, 41–52, 96–97; Genchev, *Bŭlgarsko vŭzrazhdane*, 360, 366–367. On the personality and the oeuvre of Nikolai Genchev, see the special issue of *Studia culturologica*. Vol. 1, spring 1992.
111 Genchev, *Levski, revolyutsiyata*, 112.
112 Genchev, *Levski, revolyutsiyata*, 110–111, 116–118; Genchev, *Bŭlgarsko vŭzrazhdane*, 374–375; Gandev, *Aprilskoto vŭstanie*, 49, 55.
113 Nikolai Genchev, *Vasil Levski*. Sofia: Voenno izdatelstvo, 1987, esp. 129–218.
114 On the various portraits of Botev and the polemics around him, see Evgeni Volkov, *Hristo Botev*. Sofia, 1929, 13–22. Botev was portrayed as only a patriot and nationalist by Zakhari Stoyanov, Stoyan Zaimov, and the intellectual and poet Pencho Slaveikov in the 1880s and 1890s. A certain Makdŭf produced the most negative writing on Botev, attacking his personal qualities, socially subversive ideas and atheism. See Makdŭf, *Chii e Botev? Nravstveniyat lik na taya zloveshta lichnost*. Sofia: Armeiskiya voenno- izdatelski fond, 1929. The author opposes the modest and presumably God-fearing Levksi to Botev.
115 Blagoev, "Hristo Botev," 89–92; Blagoev, *Prinos kŭm istoriyata*, 209–210.
116 Dimitŭr Blagoev, "Hristo Botev kato poet i zhurnalist." In Blagoev, *Za Bŭlgarskoto vŭzrazhdane*, 129–145, cit. on 144 (first published in 1897).
117 Mikhail Dimitrov, *Hristo Botev. Idei. Lichnost. Tvorchestvo*. Sofia: Novo Uchilishte, 1919; Dimitrov, *Lichnostta na Botev*. Sofia, 1938; Ivan Klincharov, *Hristo Botev. Zhivot i dela*. Sofia, 1926, esp. 74–75.
118 Bakalov, *Hristo Botev*, 3–5, 58–79.
119 On such debates see Zhak Natan's introduction to Bakalov, *Izbrani istoricheski*, 14–19. Natan's own view of Botev is stated in Natan, *Bŭlgarskoto vŭzrazhdane*, 378, 383, 414– 419. The author insists that Botev is a "forerunner" of scientific socialism but not a scientific socialist, i.e., that there is no direct line between him and the later Commu- nists.
120 I. Pravdolyubov, *Hristo Botev ne e marksist*. Sofia, 1933, esp. 91, 158–163, 167. During the Communist regime the book was placed in the classified section in the Bulgarian National Library, and access to it was denied.
121 Boyan Penev, "Hristo Botev." In *Hristo Botev. Po sluchai petdeset-godishninata ot smŭrtta mu*. Sofia, 1926, 81–115, esp. 86–87.
122 Todor Pavlov, "Hristo Botev i nasheto vreme." In Pavlov, *Izbrani proizvedeniya*. Vol. 3, 41–51, esp. 44–45 (this is a celebration speech in 1945).
123 Dimitŭr Kosev, *Lektsii po nova*, 220–222.
124 Ivan Undzhiev and Tzveta Undzhieva. *Hristo Botev. Zhivot i delo*. Sofia: Nauka i iz- kustvo, 1975.
125 Genchev, *Levski, revolyutsiyata*, 110–111, 116–118; Genchev, *Bŭlgarsko vŭzrazhdane*, 374–375.
126 Ivan Stoyanov, *Istoriya na bŭlgarskoto*, 237–241.
127 In fact, this metaphor occurs explicitly, as in the following citation from Undzhiev's book: "Having taken the revolutionary relay baton from Rakovski, the combatants from Botev's generation were filled with the proud awareness of their historical mis- sion." In Ivan Undzhiev and Tzveta Undzhieva, *Hristo Botev. Zhivot i delo*, 202.

128 Natan, *Bŭlgarskoto vŭzrazhdane*, 250–399, esp. 396–399.
129 Sharova, "Bŭlgarskiyat revolyutsionen komitet—1875." In *Bŭlgarsko vŭzrazhdane. Idei. Lichnosti. Sŭbitiya.* Sofia: Obshtobŭlgarski komitet "Vasil Levski" i Universitetsko izdatelstvo "Kliment Ohridski," 1995, 42–128, esp. 113–123.
130 Plamen Mitev, *Sŭzdavane i deinost*, 21–22.
131 Plamen Mitev, *Bŭlgarskoto vŭzrazhdane*, 122–123.

CHAPTER FIVE

The April Uprising, the Russo-Turkish Liberation War, and the Revolution

The 1876 uprising of the Bulgarians (known as the April uprising), organized by a group of Bulgarian revolutionary émigrés in Romania, was the greatest Bulgarian national uprising toward the end of the Ottoman domination. It was severely suppressed in what became known in Western Europe as "the Bulgarian horrors." In its aftermath, a conference of the ambassadors of the great powers was convened in Constantinople (Istanbul) to work out a scheme of reforms. Turkey hastened to proclaim liberal reform and a constitution (in 1876) in order to preempt external interference, but did not agree to European inspection of the reforms. Russia then took the initiative and declared war on the Ottoman Empire (1877–78), which ended with the establishment of a Bulgarian state. The preliminary peace treaty (of San Stefano) envisioned a greater Bulgaria, to include all territories with Bulgarian population (roughly the territories under the Exarchate), but the final Berlin Congress of the European great powers (1–13 July 1878) divided it into the autonomous Kingdom of Bulgaria and the self-governing Eastern Rumelia under the authority of the sultan, while Macedonia remained under the Ottomans. We will consider now how these events are accounted for in Bulgarian scholarship on the Revival.

The April Uprising and the Russo-Turkish War

The April uprising of 1876 generated debates and interpretations in historical scholarship for a number of reasons. To begin with, the military inadequacy of the uprising imparts to it an air of adventure. Rather than a serious military undertaking it appears as a vast massacre of civilian population. The very plan of the organizers and leaders was to urge outside intervention by provoking the Turks into bloodshed. This creates a moral problem: were the organizers justified in consciously leading militarily inexperienced people to their deaths? By unleashing a causal chain of events through the Constantinople Conference of the great powers and the Russo-Turkish war in 1877–78, the April uprising actually "led" toward liberation. This is its great merit and achievement. But the Bulgarian state established by the Berlin peace treaty did not unite all lands populated by Bulgarians and fell short of the national consolidation achieved during the national revival. Here arises the problem of the balance between what was gained and what was lost, hence whether the path of the uprising was the right one. Moreover, the "incomplete liberation" predetermined the irredentist goals of the Bulgarian state in the subsequent period, the pursuit of which ended in catastrophe. These longer-range "consequences" cannot but affect the assessment of the uprising. The treatment of the April uprising in historiography may be considered a way of coping with the above-mentioned problems.

There is, to begin with, the glorification of the April uprising in verse and prose. Ivan Vazov, the emblematic "people's writer," created a heroic and glorious image of the uprising in his poetry (the "The epic of the forgotten" cycle) and in the novel *Under the yoke*. The darker aspect—of "shame" and "infamy" from the panic and the betrayal—finds its way into some of his poems,[1] and the novel stops where the uprising begins. Zakhari Stoyanov, one of the "apostles" of the April uprising (as the organizers were named) and a leading public figure after the liberation, contributed most to the heroization and sanctification with his *Notes on the Bulgarian uprisings*. These were, according to him, "the most glamorous pages" of modern Bulgarian history. Though he admits that the uprising had weaknesses and that, viewed critically, it was not well prepared and not practical, he justifies it by pointing to the "sacred goal and the noble intentions" of the organizers; he also argues against the "prudent worshippers of reason" and those who put their faith in "Enlightening" and education.[2] Spelling out his own biases, Zakhari Stoyanov was the first to blame the better educated and the well-off for staying away from the uprising and even creating obstacles. While an analysis of the data on the members of the secret committees does not support such an inference, it suited very well Chervenkov-Pavlov's thesis of the "betrayal of the bourgeoisie" in the 1950s.

In his monumental study of the April uprising (published in 1907), Dimitŭr Strashimirov presented a mass of empirical data and took a stand on the contemporary debates. He rejected the view coming from so-called Russophobes that the uprising was the result of Russian scheming and instigation, notwithstanding the drive of Russia toward the Straits, the widespread belief of the Bulgarians in its liberating mission, and the hopes placed in her by the revolutionaries themselves. In contrast, he affirms the independence of the undertaking, which issued from the inner conviction of the revolutionaries and set its own objectives (to provoke intervention from Europe, Russia included). Although in the opinion of the author (who refers to the "practical genius" of Levski) more years were necessary in order to prepare a mass popular rising, he considers the organizers fully justified in risking this desperate venture with faith in the European intervention, because their calculations proved right and "History vindicated them." Strashimirov, too, does not believe in waiting and "evolution," that is, in the road of gradual reform. As he puts it emphatically, there was no other way, the situation "dictated" the choice of this path.[3]

The author expresses the outcome of the uprising in the form of an oxymoron: it had the extraordinary fate of succeeding in its very failure; it was a failure "altogether," but a complete success as to its objective.[4] The liberation came out of the "ashes" owing to Europe's intervention. Research on the social composition of the insurgents led him to the conclusion that the uprising was embraced only by the industrial urban centers and that while the "rich class" in general was against risky ventures, so was the mass of the peasants.[5]

Defeat in the Balkan wars (1912–13) and in World War I, conducted by Bulgaria with irredentist purposes, brought about a reappraisal of Bulgarian history. Todor Vaikov, a well-known Bulgarian intellectual and political activist, raised once again in the 1930s the fundamental question of the "justification" of the April uprising, that is, of how necessary or reasonable it was, especially in view of the consequences. What is meant here is the fact that the events resulted in the establishment of a small Bulgarian state (due to Western opposition to Russia). The author takes up the arguments of the "evolutionists" in hypothesizing that a liberation under different circumstances, after more time and after achieving greater economic and social progress, would have led "one way or another" to a more felicitous solution to the "Bulgarian question," that is, without the partitioning of the Bulgarian lands that "conditioned" the irredentist wars afterwards.[6] (But he does not consider the blunders of the Bulgarian leadership in the wars.)

The April uprising became a source of pride and identification for the Bulgarian Communists. Writing in 1938, Georgi Bakalov defines it as "the most heroic page in our modern history" and "the highest point of the

Revival." Responding to charges of weak preparation (and unconcerned with empirical truth) he describes it as "a mass rising of the popular strata, prepared by way of continuous methodical propaganda and agitation by a widespread revolutionary organization." Bakalov closes up the debate with the deterministic *ultima ratio* that the uprising was a "historical necessity" and a "historical inevitability" along the road to liberation of the Bulgarian people. Although it proved to be a failure, it was important as a combat experience and as a "preparation for historical life."[7] As can be seen, from this perspective no justification of the uprising by the subsequent liberation is needed, because being a revolutionary act, it is self-sufficient *per se*.

In fact, the historians are unanimous in characterizing the April uprising as the climax of the revolutionary efforts and of the national revolution, and most of them consider it as "justified" both with regard to the effects (the Russo-Turkish war and the liberation) and in itself—as a deed of valor, a paragon of heroism. The difference is only that hard-line Marxist authors insist on the mass dimensions of the heroism, and the fact that it was displayed by both the popular strata and their leaders.[8] Heroization in general nourishes national self-confidence and pride, which is exactly what many national historians regard as their task. It should also be noted that heroism somehow takes the question of meaning out of the discussion. Alternatively, one may say that heroism makes the event meaningful in itself, without regard to previous plans and to the immediate or longer-range effects.

The heroic interpretation encounters one major problem. The very facticity of the uprising, which was drowned in a blood-bath by Muslim irregulars, makes the balance between heroism and suffering precarious. The emphasis on the Turkish atrocities and the number of victims arouses pity and leaves the victimizing impression of a massacre. (The participation of Bulgarian Muslims—"*pomaks*"—in putting down the revolt and committing the greatest atrocities is the nationally awkward moment that rarely receives mention in the historical narrative.) A way out of this unfortunate situation is to interpret the April uprising as a moral "expiation" ("redemption") of Liberty with the blood of the victims, which now seems morally deserved and not offered as a free gift by Russia.[9] This interpretation of course applies a rather general pattern with a religious provenance. There is, in addition, the possibility of combining a heroic interpretation with a sense of tragedy, for example by treating the uprising as a "heroic deed driven by desperation," a combination of passion and reason.[10]

A reappraisal of the April uprising in the freer post-Communist epoch broke the taboo that surrounded the "mass heroism" and put the emphasis on martyrdom (derived from the Christian faith). Especially the massacre of Batak, where the insurgents gave away their weapons only to be massacred by the thousands while paralyzed with terror, is interpreted in this vein.[11]

A special problem in the interpretation of the April uprising is presented by the intentions of the organizers (as attested by major figures[12]) to provoke Turkish atrocities and thus attract the attention of "Europe." While most historians admit that the uprising was ill-prepared and uncoordinated, the open statement of the leadership's strategy appears morally problematic, especially when coupled with lack of faith in the success of the venture itself from the very beginning. It is for that reason that the eulogy of the "desperately brave strategy of the apostles" by the leftist sociologist Ivan Hadzhiiski (in the early 1940s) sounds somewhat unconvincing. In spite of the efforts of the author, the leader of the uprising Georgi Benkovski does not occupy the highest place in the Bulgarian national pantheon and is sometimes characterized as "adventurous" (in contrast to the brave but prudent Levski).[13] Hadzhiiski himself shows little compassion for the "human material of the uprising" composed primarily of "petty owners" (peasants and artisans). These are characterized by him as "natural opportunists," wavering and bending to circumstances, so that the leaders had to take recourse to some "noble lies" and psychological tricks in order to persuade them.[14] (Conscious of the problem of how this would be received, Hadzhiiski charges the "bourgeois" researchers of the uprising and their "bourgeois public" with cowardice, philistinism, and intellectual hesitancy.)

One can also mention a recent attempt to ease the moral tension of the recognized and clearly stated ethical problem—"Did the organizers consciously lead the people into massacre?"—by saying that, while they had expected and even programmed it, they never envisioned "such a bloody bacchanalia."[15] Others would simply disregard the inconvenient facts and flatly state that the leaders of the uprising believed in its success.[16] But more common than a direct confrontation with the ethical problem (and the consequent soul-searching) is the already-mentioned emphasis on heroism and self-sacrifice in a kind of national apotheosis, adding, eventually, that such undertakings are unpredictable in principle and there is no guarantee for success.

The sheer number of the victims and the ruthlessness of the retribution make the doubts about so much suffering sound like sacrilege. The uprising cannot be interpreted—psychologically as well—as meaningless. The victims, even more than the heroism, give the event a meaning (or block reflection on the meaning). But above all, with national liberation as the supreme goal, any price or "cost" in terms of human life seems acceptable and justified. This is premised on the system of values shared by the national historians and their nationally formed public. Hence the *ultima ratio* of justification that closes up the debate is the pure and simple identification of the April uprising with liberation, and of its "negation" by advocacy of the Turkish "yoke."[17]

For the Communists, the April uprising has an additional meaning in that it led to the first liberating intervention of Russia, which prefigures the second "liberation" that brought them to power. It is worth noting that the tendency in this case is to reduce the uprising to a mere "ground" (or pretext) for Russian intervention, a prologue to the war, regarded as an automatic consequence, and idealized (especially in popular versions) as disinterested help. By ignoring not only the goals of the Russian empire in the Balkans but also the complex configuration of circumstances that led to Russia's (apparently reluctant) intervention, such writings suggest that she had only waited for an appropriate moment in order to rush into liberating her Slav brothers. The more scholarly formula for this (in the "high" historical narrative) states that the April uprising "provided Russia with the moral right and strong political and diplomatic grounds to declare war on Turkey."[18]

Above and beyond any particular meaning, the April uprising is presented by Communist scholarship as the culmination of a revolution (national and social), in its turn metaphysically perceived as a task set by History. I will return to this point later. Suffice it to say here that this makes the participants in the uprising into a "driving force" of the revolution rather than mere insurgents, while the organizers are indicative of its social "hegemon" (i.e., leader-class). In so far as the nature and character of the revolution (peasant, bourgeois, bourgeois–democratic, etc.) presented an a priori construction decreed by the political authority, this was simply projected onto the April uprising. But even later the changing notions of the character of the revolution were forced upon the uprising as its goals or "social character," instead of defining the revolution on the basis of the uprising (which would compromise the apriorism, as actually happened in empirical studies). Without going into details, I will indicate how the interpretation of the April uprising was tailored to the changing notions of the revolution and its "hegemon" (but also of its "traitors").

The meaning of the April uprising/revolution was firmly set by the head of the Bulgarian Communist Party and head of state Vŭlko Chervenkov in 1953. The revolution was defined (actually decreed) as being bourgeois-democratic (in goals) and peasant (in driving force), while the bourgeoisie was declared a traitor to the revolution. In its absence it was the people's intelligentsia (of peasant descent) that had to take the leading role. Not having, among other things, the right leadership, the Bulgarian bourgeois-democratic revolution could not succeed as a peasant revolution in the form of the April uprising; it could only achieve success with outside help.[19]

The concept of (the uprising as a) "peasant–bourgeois" revolution went into the academic *History of Bulgaria* of 1954, together with the counter-revolutionary role of the bourgeoisie. In the revised edition of 1961 the uprising was already modified as a "national, bourgeois–democratic revolution," while the counter-revolutionary enemies of the uprising were reduced to the *chorbadzhii* and the big bourgeoisie.[20] The "predominantly peasant" character of the uprising was to be sustained in a diluted form to the very last (even in the 1980s) by academician Hristo Hristov, for whom the peasants played the role of "main driving force," even though artisans, petty traders, the urban poor, and the intelligentsia also participated, which gave the uprising a democratic and all-national character.[21]

The ninetieth anniversary of the April uprising in 1966 became the occasion to spell out the revisions that had been under way for quite some time and to assert more forcefully the new tenets. Dimitŭr Kosev argued for the bourgeois democratic character of the revolution but still thought that the bourgeoisie betrayed the national (armed) revolution, that is, the April uprising.[22] Goran Todorov defined the April uprising as a national and bourgeois revolution (not a peasant or plebeian one) that had to solve the basic class contradictions between the Turkish rulers (and their state) on the one hand, and the Bulgarian popular masses on the other. According to the author, the participants in the uprising were primarily peasants, and especially the freer petty bourgeois peasant stratum, but also the petty and middle urban bourgeoisie while it was led by the people's intelligentsia (of teachers, priests, educated traders and artisans).[23] The revolution was thus "all-national" (with the characteristic absence of the big bourgeoisie).

A book on the April uprising co-authored by Konstantin Kosev and Nikolai Zhechev (in 1966) already points to the middle and petty commercial–industrial and rural bourgeoisie as the "hegemon" of the revolution; moreover, it admits the financial contributions of representatives of the "big commercial–moneylending bourgeoisie" (thus prefiguring the debate on its role in the 1970s).[24] The April uprising itself is interpreted in a buoyant revolutionary spirit as "the most important and crucial moment" in the Bulgarian national democratic revolution, a "natural consequence and a glorious finale of the revolutionary wave that gradually grew up in strength and might in order to fall down with a roar upon the rotten foundations of the feudal-despotic Turkish empire."[25]

In his 1974 book on the April uprising Hristo Gandev put forward a number of new propositions and elevated the discussion to a higher level of sophistication in general. He describes the April uprising as the deed of professional revolutionaries who originated in different social layers, thus avoiding the ideologized debates on the role of the different social classes as classes. As the author points out (in a conciliatory spirit), this was an "all-people" (nation-wide) uprising with the participation of peasants and urban poor, artisans and petty traders (i.e., the petty bourgeoisie), but also well-to-do (middle and big bourgeois) "elements" and especially the intelligentsia of teachers, priests and educated young people of various descent, who cooperated closely with the professional revolutionaries. The bourgeoisie was represented by its younger generation in the uprising. While a great part of the big bourgeoisie inside and outside the country showed reserve for economic reasons or due to closer ties with the Turkish authorities, or simply to save their lives, hesitancy cannot be ascribed to the middle and big bourgeoisie alone. Peasants, artisans and the urban poor, but especially uneducated people isolated in small places, were also afraid and stood back. Concerning the character of the uprising, Gandev puts the emphasis on national liberation while the bourgeois–democratic revolution comes second. It was he who coined the formula of the April uprising as providing moral justification as well as political and diplomatic grounds for the Russian military intervention. This, in his view (as in Strashimirov's), vindicates the insight of the revolutionaries as to the necessity of the uprising in order to achieve freedom.[26]

An interesting turn in the interpretation of the April uprising is presented by Nikolai Genchev (in 1978). He directly affirms that the bourgeoisie was the major revolutionary element, as attested by the social composition of the revolutionary committees. Instead of presenting the usual technical and organizational explanations for the failure of the uprising, the author adduces the weakness of the bourgeois class, which he derives from Bulgarian economic development during the eighteenth and nineteenth centuries. Thus, if the failure of the uprising can be blamed upon the bourgeoisie, it is not because of betrayal or non-participation but due to weakness (hardly a fault of its own). Collective betrayals of the uprising were committed by some urban or rural notables (*chorbadzii*), while peasants and shepherds, "brutalized by the conditions of the yoke" were guilty of grave individual betrayals (although, as the author ironically points out, one should hardy infer from this a "betrayal by the peasants").[27]

Genchev finds a round-about but very effective way of expressing his opinion about the uprising, namely, by comparing it to the ideas of the greatest Bulgarian national revolutionary Vasil Levski. Contrary to his ideas, the April uprising was not well prepared, not nation-wide, and lacked the necessary coordination; it was rather a "spontaneous revolt without a strategic perspective," governed by the idea of forcing the attention of Europe on the Bulgarian question by the spilling of blood.[28] The contrasting of the uprising with Levski's ideas cannot but cast a shadow of doubt upon it, although the author balances this by calling the uprising a "great feat of despair" and saying that "negating" it is tantamount to advocating a form of Asian despotism. While making a causal link between uprising and liberation, he also points to such negative consequences of this path of liberation as the dismemberment of the Bulgarian lands and the loss of political prestige by the Bulgarian bourgeoisie (thus covertly agreeing with Vlaikov's arguments).

The 1980s brought about a kind of "synthesis" that reconciled a high evaluation of the role of the bourgeoisie with praise of the revolutionaries and of the people, and an emphasis on the significance of the uprising *per se* with its role as a crucial factor for international intervention (while moderating the pro-Russian propaganda). The section on the April uprising in the new official multi-volume *History of Bulgaria* (authored by Yono Mitev again) presents an example of profaning hard-won theses through dogmatic recitation, apriorism and "modernization." The uprising, in this official narrative, took place with the participation of "all classes and estates" of the Bulgarian society—artisans, traders, peasants (most numerous), the proto-proletariat and the people's intelligentsia (especially active); only the traditional *chorbadzii* remained outside the "general enthusiasm." The big bourgeoisie, too, had an interest in the success of the national revolution because of the prospects of taking a leadership position in the future state, and only a small group based in the Ottoman capital Istanbul was against. The uprising presents the apex of the national revolution, which also aimed (in a social sense) at the "toppling of the dominant Turkish feudal class" and its supporters. Still, the major goal of the revolution was to overthrow the foreign oppressors and to restore the Bulgarian state, which "according to historical law-like necessity," had to be a bourgeois one, hence the revolution had a "national bourgeois–democratic character." The peasants were the mass element in the revolution because they saw the "chasing away of the Turkish *beys* and *chiflik*-owners" as the only way to solve the agrarian question. Thus the bourgeois revolution had to fulfill the role of an agrarian overturn by abolishing the supreme property rights of the Ottoman state over the land. The leaders of the uprising were ideologically influenced by the revolutionary–democratic trend, which expressed the aspirations of the petty bourgeoisie and of groups in the process of proletarianization for a "democratic republic" with a "people's government."[29]

A curious attempt to revert to blaming the bourgeoisie was offered by one author on the occasion of the 110th anniversary of the April uprising (in 1986).[30] According to Evlogi Buzhazhki, even the patriotic bourgeoisie first reacted against the uprising. But when it broke out the bourgeoisie exploited it politically by taking the initiative to secure liberation with foreign help and to gain the upper hand in the process. In order to realize its plans, it presented the uprising as a falsification, that is, invented by the Turks as justification of atrocities committed upon the peaceful civilian population. The idea of a "feigned uprising" was indeed circulated in the aftermath when looking for help from Europe (by sending delegations, inviting commissions, etc.), but here it appears as a display of class selfishness on the part of the bourgeoisie, and one can feel the indignation of the author about the "stolen" revolution as the bourgeoisie first "betrayed" it and then hurried to collect its fruits (and, according to him, only in this way assumed its normal leadership role in the national liberation movement).

Already after Communism Konstantin Kosev explained the political success of the uprising (in contrast to its military failure) by considering how it managed to insert itself in the *haute politique* of the great powers. The uprising broke out precisely when Germany was trying to push Russia into war with the Ottoman Empire in order to isolate her from the French–German conflict that had resulted from German unification. The Bulgarian national revolution that had been "frozen" together with the Eastern question after the Crimean War (1853–1856) now hit the right moment and acquired a mighty pull by a political effect far exceeding Bulgarian military capacities.[31] The same author gives to the self-abnegation and self-sacrifice demonstrated during the uprising (and during the Revival epoch in general) a strangely rationalizing turn, namely, as a "strategy" of the radical liberation activists and a "necessary precondition for political dividends."[32]

A "postmodern" treatment of the April uprising by the literary scholar Inna Peleva deserves a special mention. The author is interested in its literary existence in texts, both history works and fiction, as it is here that the transformation of the uprising into a central national myth at the heart of Bulgarian national ideology takes place. How is this achieved? Among the various versions of the April uprising (including the affirmation that it actually did not happen), one particular version is selected as the "true" one. This is the most glamorous and heroic account, which reinterprets the defeat as glory, and turns the suffering into aestheticized pathos. The selection is governed by the need for a positive self-portrait of the national community so that it might love its own collective self. Conversely, versions that do not accord with this positive image are displaced and muted. One example is an authentic contemporary text (*"In the Dungeon"*) by a participant in the uprising who was beset by doubts on the eve of the uprising. In a sudden "sobering from the intoxication," Konstantin Velichkov saw it in an altogether different light—as the assuming of grave responsibility with preparations that looked no more than a "childish game" and that would bring about bloodshed and destruction, a sin rather than a feat. Not only were such texts eliminated but the very texts accepted in the "cannon" are read selectively and in a deliberate manner, for example Vazov's great novel *Under the yoke* (where there is less "yoke" than freedom, and less "revolution" than "theater"), and even parts of Zakhari Stoyanov's *Notes on the Bulgarian Uprisings*, where Turkish rule does not appear as the heaviest and most arbitrary.

According to Peleva, the need to work out a "justification" of the uprising leads to the search for reasons for regarding it as necessary that thus balance out the bloody consequences. Hence the notorious "unbearable situation of the people" (heavy taxes, violence, murders), which is rather at odds with the reality as described in numerous contemporary testimonies[33] and with the peaceful pictures prevailing in Ivan Vazov's novels *Uncles, New land*, and even *Under the yoke*. As observed by the author, alongside the explanation of the uprising by pointing to its causes stands another understanding of it—as a sudden miracle, an "explosion in the historical order." And it is actually the miracle rather than the causality that makes up the myth of 1876 as the "most authentic Bulgarian time," a unique event that could happen just once, the highest soaring of the Bulgarian national spirit.[34] One can see here the breaking of a new ground—an explo-

ration of how events are set in texts, and, together with that, insights into
the selective, goal-oriented, and here nation-bound, reading of such textual-
ized events. This "deconstructionist" approach contains great desacralizing
potential; and in any case offers a new understanding of History as Text
(and Story).

We now pass to a consideration of views on the Russo-Turkish war
(1877–1878) that brought about liberation for the Bulgarians. From a
Marxist perspective this is not just a "liberation war" but has another basic
meaning as well—that of a "revolution." Since the revolution (social and
national), in the form of the April uprising, failed, it fell to the war to fulfill its function, or, to be more precise, to bring it to completion. The war is
thus defined as a "revolutionary war," that is, a revolution and a war in
one, a sort of continuation of the national liberation movement (also literally, in so far as Bulgarians took part in the war as volunteers).[35]

Since the revolution was social and national in one, so must the war
have been. Its outcome was defined as a radical social transformation in
the sense of a bourgeois (or bourgeois–democratic) revolution, which abolished the remnants of Turkish feudalism and cleared the way for the development of capitalist relations. It brought about a radical agrarian overturn
in particular, understood variously as the passing of Turkish properties
into Bulgarian hands, the breaking up of the *chiflik* estates, or the abol-
ishment of the "feudal" land rent, that is, the taxes paid to the Turkish
treasury. The thesis of the Russo-Turkish war as being simultaneously a
liberation war, an (anti-feudal) bourgeois–democratic revolution, and a
radical agrarian overturn proved to be one of the most stable in Communist historical scholarship from its very beginning to the fall of the regime,
and occasionally after Communism.[36] The validity of the thesis about the
socioeconomic (bourgeois–capitalist) transformation has been discussed
above. It is enough to recall here that independence as such did not give
the decisive impetus for a capitalist development of the country in either
industry or agriculture, and that there followed decades of stagnation and
even regression before capitalism (and the market economy in general)
could make progress. Here I will consider the unproblematic liberation
function of the Russo-Turkish war and its ideological mis/use by the Communist regime.

To begin with, the disinterested help of the "brotherly" Russian people
was the focal point in all jubilee presentations of the liberation, which
underplayed—or omitted to mention—the imperial aspirations of the Russian tsars toward the Straits. (Ironically, the founder of socialism in Bul-

garia, Dimitŭr Blagoev, having suffered persecution for his activities while in Russia, was especially negative about the goals of Russian tsarism.) This was part of the efforts to cultivate love and gratitude toward the liberator among the (generally Russophile) Bulgarians and toward its successor, the Soviet Union. More "serious" historical scholarship, however, differentiates between the aggressive goals of "official Russia" and the help and suffering of "the Russian people" in winning Bulgarian liberty. Moreover, a difference is made between "subjective" (tsarist) goals and the "objective" outcome of the war. It is pointed out that, notwithstanding the expansionist goals of the Russian empire (still stopping short of territorial occupation— as if this were a matter of choice), the war objectively had a "progressive" character because it led to the destruction of the Turkish feudal order and the establishment of an independent Bulgarian state. The unjust Berlin peace treaty, which superseded the preliminary Treaty of San Stefano and thwarted Bulgarian expectations of forming a state to include all compatriots, is entirely blamed on the Western great powers, especially Britain, Germany, and Austria–Hungary.[37]

The liberation of Bulgaria by Russia had another more important function for the regime, and for Communist historical scholarship. It was a first liberation, which created an independent Bulgarian state, and was followed by a "second liberation," this time from fascism, resulting in the establishment of Communist rule. What is implied is that these are similar events, thus identifying liberation from foreign domination with "assistance" in installing a puppet totalitarian regime in a (nominally) sovereign state. The legitimacy and prestige of the first (national) liberation is thus being projected onto the second "liberation" and actually conceals the loss of national sovereignty, that is, its exact opposite. The struggle against (German and Bulgarian) fascism is the link that allows for the substitution to be effective under the same label of "liberation." To cite a post-war Communist historian (Zhak Natan):

"Just as the liberation after the April uprising came due to the intervention of the Slav brothers from the East, so now again the chasing away of the Germans and the second liberation of the country came about due to the intervention and assistance of the great Russian Red Army."[38]

Gratitude to the "double liberator" and "eldest brother" is expressed in jubilee papers on anniversaries of the Russo-Turkish liberation war, as in this example by an authoritative historian: "When the ideas of the Great October triumphed in our country as well, again with the crucial help of the descendants of our former liberators, this friendship became eternal and indissoluble, an eternal and indestructible union between the peoples of Bulgaria and of the Soviet Union."[39]

As can be seen, the liberation from the Turks by Russia, and the supposed precedent it established, became an important symbolic resource for the Communist regime for its own legitimation. Its founding myth was the "struggle against fascism," in which the crucial help of Russia (the Soviet Union) became once again indispensable. This also explains why every attempt to give a more realistic account of Bulgarian fascism met with bitter resistance until the very end of the regime. But this is another topic that cannot be dealt with here.

The Revolution

The ideas and activities of the revolutionaries, the April uprising, and the Russo-Turkish war are merged into one revolutionary block—the Revolution. The uprising is the culmination of the revolution. It did not succeed by itself but set in motion a causal sequence, usually presented as automatic (and stripped of intermediate links), toward the Russo-Turkish war, which ended in liberation. The Russo-Turkish war is thus the denouement of the evolving revolution and the ending of the April uprising, as in the following passage by Todor Pavlov:

"Certainly, under the objective historical circumstances then prevalent, the April uprising could not evolve into a socialist or into a similar popular-democratic revolution. Actually, it ended in the Russo-Turkish war and the establishment and further development of our bourgeois state and a bourgeois, capitalist social formation."[40]

What we have here is a continuity of the revolution that not only embraces the April uprising and the Russo-Turkish war but also prefigures a later revolution (socialist, popular–democratic). As for its beginning, the revolution (a conflation of a national and a social one) goes as far back as Paisii of Hilendar (i.e., the mid-eighteenth century), at least according to Todor Pavlov.[41]

Professional historians following in his steps, most notably Dimitŭr Kosev and Konstantin Kosev, also imagine the revolution as maturing from the very beginning of the Bulgarian Revival and as preconditioned and determined by developments in every sphere—economic, social, and cultural. Kostantin Kosev in particular recently went to the extreme of explicitly considering the term Bulgarian Revival as identical with, and equivalent to, "Bulgarian national revolution," which, in addition to armed action, the educational–cultural movement, and the movement for church independence, also includes social–economic development, demographic growth, etc.[42]

Here we have a truly Hegelian–Marxist teleology of historical development with a preconceived end goal (in this case a national one). It turns out that the epoch of the Bulgarian Revival as a whole, from its modest beginnings onwards, in all its manifestations—to the most routine or intimate—is a national revolution. The national revolution is endowed with a supra-empirical, metaphysical essence, and at the same time it penetrates the particular historical world giving it a meaning, cohesion and direction, so that even reproduction and demographic growth acquire a goal-oriented revolutionary and liberation character. Accordingly, the revolution deploys its own dynamics, not subject to empirical causality or contingency (for that reason Konstantin Kosev flatly rejects any attempts to explain the April uprising by particular causes). True, these are only the extremes of revolutionism in Bulgarian historiography.

While the revolution is very important for the nationalist interpretation of the Bulgarian national revival, for the Communist (presumably Marxist) interpretation it is all-important. The debate here rotates around the question: What exactly is the social character of the revolution? Negatively defined it is anti-feudal. Positively defined, in various versions it is bourgeois, bourgeois–democratic, peasant, peasant–bourgeois–democratic, or popular–plebeian. The definition is in harmony with the "tasks" ascribed to the epoch and with the idea of the "hegemon" and the "driving forces" of the revolution. There is also the important question of the relative weight of the social and the national component of the revolution. Let us consider the evolution of the views in more detail.

In 1934 the Communist intellectual Georgi Bakalov defined the revolution as "objectively" a bourgeois one, directed toward the clearing of the road ahead for capitalist development. In his view the capitalist development of Bulgaria depended on the solution of the agrarian question. Hence the author points to the peasant masses (but also the artisans) as the major driving force of the revolution, rather than the "notables." According to him the peasant movement was "the deepest and broadest stream of national stirring." In so far as the land-owners were foreign, the revolutionary movement of the peasants assumed a national character; the agrarian question in the country was "putting on the costume of a national question"—that of liberation from foreign domination.[43]

The development of capitalism in the country required the liquidation of the big land estates of the (Turkish) *beys* in the first place. This could happen in one of two ways—either compromise or revolution, named by Bakalov (adapting Lenin[44]) the Prussian and the American ways. The former consisted in a slow evolution toward capitalism while preserving semi-feudal land ownership, and a corresponding adjustment of the bourgeoisie to the *ancien régime*. In native terms this translates as the "compromise way of the *chorbadzii*" taken by the Bulgarian bourgeoisie. The second (American or farmer's) possibility was that of a "revolutionary" seizure of the land of the big Turkish landowners by the Bulgarian peasants, the elimination of all "remnants of serfdom," and the subsequent rapid development of capitalism. This way was taken by the national revolutionary movement and its leaders Rakovski, Levski, and Botev.[45]

Enough has already been said to make it clear why drawing an analogy between the Bulgarian national movement and Lenin's interpretation of the Russian revolution of 1905 is patently wrong. Predominantly free peasant land ownership after the land reform (and to some extent even before), the limited spread of estates (*chifliks*), and the absence of "serfdom," hence of a peasant question, should not be forgotten here. Nor is it clear why distributing the land from the estates (already partly capitalist and market-oriented) among smallholder peasants would represent rapid capitalist "progress."

The thesis about the peasant character of the national revolution was imposed upon Bulgarian historical scholarship "from above," namely, via Vǔlko Chervenkov's notorious speech at the eightieth anniversary of the death of Vasil Levski in 1953. Some points have been reproduced in other contexts. It is the notion of the revolution that concerns us here, but also the imagery that goes with it.

The Bulgarian national revolutionary movement is defined as the manifestation of a bourgeois–democratic revolution, whose basic feature is its peasant character. Accordingly it was a peasant movement, and its leaders and ideologues, Levski and Botev, were peasant revolutionaries (and consistent "revolutionary democrats"). It was directed against Turkish feudalism and its supporters, and aimed at the eradication of feudalism and serfdom. The peasants and the artisans were the major driving force of the bourgeois–democratic *cum* national revolution, while the bourgeoisie as a class betrayed it. This made the revolution far reaching and provided the opportunity for a most radical doing away with feudalism by the people (or plebs). But the peasants alone were unable to guide the peasant–bourgeois revolution in a firm and consistent manner. Nor could the insufficiently organized artisans provide such guidance. Thus the most progressive part of the people's intelligentsia, of a mostly peasant background, had to take the lead in the revolution. But the unfortunate absence of an autonomous leader-class (given the betrayal by the bourgeoisie and the absence of a working class) determined the failure of the revolution as a peasant revolution in the April uprising of 1876.

Levski and Botev looked far into the future and prepared "to jump over the capitalist society with its evils, in addition to the plebeian elimination of feudalism and the national subjugation." But their dreams to overleap capitalism were unfeasible and utopian because the country was then living through a period of bourgeois transformation, the preconditions for anything else were lacking, and they could not change the objective economic laws of historical development. After the defeat of the April uprising, the development of the country toward capitalism took another turn, namely, liberation came from the "brotherly Russian troops" and power passed over to the bourgeois class.[46]

The concept of a "plebeian" revolution was elaborated further by Todor Pavlov. While the revolution was bourgeois in its "objective content" it assumed a plebeian–popular form that gave it a mighty impetus, and it put out "not only bourgeois–democratic and anti-feudal, but also anti-capitalist and even socialist, though utopian, slogans."[47] The deeply popular plebeian character, and hence the mighty impetus of the Bulgarian bourgeois–democratic revolution, were due to the rejection by the Bulgarian bourgeoisie (having taken part in the church struggles) of its hegemonic role "in its own revolution." In the absence of a proletariat this role was taken up by the peasants, the artisans, and the "people's intelligentsia," who thus became the major driving forces of the maturing revolution.[48]

The insistence that the "bourgeois revolution" was, in fact, "bourgeois–democratic" or even "popular" ("plebeian"), and that it set for itself revolutionary–democratic objectives, obviously stretches it toward socialism. The rapprochement is effected from the socialist end, too, if we recall that the Communist regime in Bulgaria, as in other countries in Eastern Europe, styled itself as a "people's democracy" (and not outright "dictatorship of the proletariat"). It thus became possible to draw analogies, and even to establish continuities, between the bourgeois–democratic revolution (the April uprising plus the Russo-Turkish war) and the Bulgarian "socialist revolution" of 9 September 1944. Both were effected with "crucial" Russian aid and both were profoundly popular in character, and not only that, but the first one appears as a rehearsal and as training for the second. In any case, it possessed an extreme democratic and even socialist potential (Botev), which could not then unfold, in spite of the refusal of the bourgeoisie to stand in the lead of its own revolution, because the socialist revolution was not "on the agenda" and its hegemon (the proletariat) was missing.[49]

Presenting the national revolution as a precursor (and herald) of the socialist revolution marks the extreme point of the Communist assimilation of the revolutionary legacy for its own legitimation purposes. The following lines by Moscow-trained historical materialist and dialectician Todor Pavlov can be cited:

"The historical form of our people's revolution, as every objective-real form, being defined primarily and above all by the bourgeois–democratic content of the revolution, manifested itself in addition in such a way that the revolutionary action and strivings of the people's revolutionaries, especially Levski and Botev, prepared for a long jump—beyond the plebeian doing away with feudalism and the national yoke—to overleap the capitalist yoke, with its evils already amply substantiated by Western Europe, for which the heroic uprising of the Paris Communards presented strong evidence. However, the active force of the historical manifestation of our people's revolution proved unable to effect this jump. [...] After the first liberation of Bulgaria, capitalism and the bourgeois–capitalist order in general developed in such a way that only a few years after the first general rehearsal of our new people's revolution in September [1923], the royal-fascist rule, and together with it the rule of the Bulgarian bourgeoisie, was destroyed on 9 September 1944, to be replaced by a people's democratic rule."[50]

To summarize, with a certain simplification, the people's revolution of the national revival epoch made an additional effort to jump over capitalism directly into socialism, besides doing away with feudalism and with foreign domination, which were its primary objectives. But it failed in this premature objective, which was too far ahead of its times, obstructed by the absence of a revolutionary hegemon in the form of a working class led by a socialist party. The revolution resulted only in a "first liberation" and the clearing of the way for capitalism. Already in the presence of a revolutionary hegemon there followed a "general rehearsal" for a socialist revolution in the form of the September rising of 1923 (organized by the Bulgarian Communist Party on instructions from the Komintern). Then came the event itself—the victorious socialist revolution (or Communist takeover) on

9 September 1944, with the crucial help of Soviet troops marching into Bulgaria (an ally of Nazi Germany). This presents a "second liberation" by "the same" liberator (this time from fascism).

The revolutions are like waves that follow one after another, and they only reach a different point along the way to the final goal that the authors have as their ideal—Communist rule. Moreover, each revolution-as-wave reaches a more advanced point (than actual conditions allow) and then recedes until one last wave, the socialist revolution, succeeds in retaining the foremost (and ultimate) position captured. The fact that they are all imagined as oriented towards one final goal, and all described as democratic, actually conflates them into a single (and continuous) revolution. This is why Communist authors think of even the "bourgeois" revolution of the Revival epoch as "their" revolution. In a similar way the French Revolution in Marxist interpretations remains open-ended, contains promises of the future, prefigures and assimilates new events, and is conflated with other revolutions, especially with the Bolshevik revolution (according to François Furet).[51]

The relative weight given to the national and the social components of the "revolution" of the Bulgarian national revival is a point of considerable importance. Initially, this was dealt with from a Communist point of view by differentiating between the "form" and "content" of the revolution, where the national liberation component is the "form" (with typical underestimation) and the bourgeois–democratic component is its "content."[52] But even this does not seem radical enough from the point of view of the unitary and continuous revolution as presented above, because it differentiates between the two components in the first place and thus allows for a certain autonomy of the national liberation. Thus authorities like Chervenkov and Pavlov preferred to have the national liberation struggles and the bourgeois–democratic (anti-feudal) struggles merged into one "unitary revolutionary people's struggle" or a "people's revolution."[53]

Many of the above-mentioned tenets of the Stalinist (Chervenkov) years, including the "peasant revolution" thesis, found expression in the two-volume academic *History of Bulgaria* (of 1954). One can also mention an absurd attempt by an army general turned amateur historian to present the *kŭrdzhalii* robber bands that pillaged the Balkan territories of the Ottoman Empire at the end of the eighteenth century as a mass anti-feudal peasant movement of the Bulgarian people against the Turkish feudal class and for national independence. (True, it was countered by historians, but it is indicative of the spirit of the times.)[54]

As shown elsewhere, the thesis of the peasant or "plebeian" character of the revolution was gradually overcome during the 1960s. The bourgeoisie gradually assumed its role as "hegemon" in its own revolution (lastly, in its armed forms) by a process of step-by-step vindication. The participation of the peasants was reduced to "driving force" at best, together with others (artisans, the intelligentsia, etc.). The revolution itself became more emphatically national in meaning (Dimitŭr Kosev in 1966, Goran Todorov in 1966, Nikolai Genchev in 1973, and others[55]), while the bourgeois transformation receded into the background. After Communism the latter is sometimes silently omitted as a meaning of the Russo-Turkish war of liberation (though not of the revival process).[56]

There were "residues." As late as 1972 a study by one Russian author, published in Bulgarian, dwells on the "agrarian program" in the views of the Bulgarian national revolutionaries Rakovski, Levski, and Botev.[57] The Bulgarian historian Hristo Hristov was most obstinate in tying the revolution to the "agrarian question" (and the "agrarian overturn") until the late 1970s. He pictures the Russo-Turkish war as a continuation of the revolution, which was thus spread over vast territories and included fresh peasant masses engaged in solving the agrarian question through "revolutionary" occupation of the lands in the plains and the liquidation of the Turkish *chiflik* estates.[58]

Given the great, even mythical, dimension of the revolution, whether social or national, in the historical imagination, there arises one problem: Why did so much revolutionism end in a rather modest uprising and liberation by an external force (not by one's own efforts)? The question is euphemistically addressed by Konstantin Kosev as a problem of the "relationship between internal and external factors" in the Bulgarian national liberation movement. The author explains the "inertia and timidity" of the majority of the Bulgarians (speaking of the 1860s) in spite of the "ripe social necessity" and the available revolutionary potential of the nation with the complicated international situation and the dependence of the Bulgarian national question on the "high politics" of the great European powers. To cite him: "In practice it turned out that the ripe historical necessity of abolishing the Turkish feudal-despotic system needed the crucial Russian military aid. The internal factor was conditioning and determining, but the external one, in this case Russia, was crucial."[59]

The question is not, of course, as dramatic for those who recognize from the outset the very strong, and in fact crucial, impact of external forces in solving the "Eastern question" (and the "Bulgarian question" as part of it) and who do not exaggerate the revolutionary mood of the population. The author cited above would eventually state most emphatically what he implies here, namely, the decisive role of external factors in solving the Bulgarian national question, while the role of the internal factor would be to await the appropriate moment to present it to the attention of the great powers (by way of an uprising).[60]

One may wonder why so much attention is paid here to historiographical views that are manifestly preconceived, biased, and dogmatic, and that diverge so widely from the historical evidence—besides being already "antiquated" and "overcome." It is not only the "archeological" interest and the completeness of the historiographical review that motivates me. Such views are a clear demonstration of the ideological uses of history. History was mobilized to legitimate a regime claiming a popular and revolutionary kind of legitimacy (rather than electoral votes) and styling itself as the outcome of a long process of national and social struggles going as far back as the national Revival. Schoolchildren and university students in the humanities were taught and indoctrinated by learning from the vast pseudo-scholarly literature produced by people with scholarly titles and great influence (alongside some good historical works and empirical contributions). And this literature, for example the "academic" editions of the *History of Bulgaria*, was widely circulated and in use long after it was "dated." Successive generations were thus molded to see the past in a certain way, as consisting exclusively of heroic social and national struggles represented from a certain point onwards by the working class and "its" party. No wonder one meets even now with deeply embedded public representations, which, for all their patent errors, are defended with bitterness and dogmatic self-assurance.[61]

Concerning historical scholarship itself, it is worth noting the interesting fact that views apparently proven wrong and "overcome" may preserve a certain efficacy in spite of all "revisions." This is perhaps due to the fixation of the critique on the contested point of departure, hence absorbing its initial direction and logical impetus, the inertia of the fundamental concepts and the validity of the underlying frame. To give some examples, even when overt value judgments on the national revolutionaries are no longer being made, they are again being ordered in an implicitly ascending order, as the passing of the baton of struggle in the kind of relay race described. As national heroes they are used to legitimate the new political class and form the next generation in the desired sense, emphasizing, on demand, national, social or perhaps now liberal elements (but without

giving critical thought to the function of "heroism" as a symbolic resource). The notion of revolution also carries with it an automatism of
reasoning that has outlived the more superficial debates on its "character"
and "driving forces." Whatever the relative weight of the national and social components in the revolution, the latter, as such, hovers metaphysically
over the historical realities or moves on its own, gathering force and esca-
lating to the final denouement, with little regard for empirical causality,
breaks, gaps and contingencies.[62] Historians continue to use constructions
such as "bourgeoisie," "feudalism," "capitalism," etc. with little inhibition,
as if these are "naturally given." Sympathy toward the major "revisionist"
effort to affirm the leading role of the bourgeoisie in its own revolution
should not hinder one from seeing the doctrinaire in this hard-won and
sweet fruit as well, which hangs upon a preconceived idea of "revolution"
and an undefined use of the notion of "bourgeoisie." On these more fundamental (methodological and theoretical) levels, things are changing
slowly and by no means automatically after Communism, intellectual freedom notwithstanding.

Revisions and Reappraisal

As is to be expected, the fall of Communism brought about a reappraisal of
the role of Russia, or at least the recognition of some uncomfortable facts.
An antecedent is presented by a book on Bulgarian–Russian cultural exchanges by Nikolai Genchev, published in 1975 and immediately "arrested" by the censors (to appear only after 1989).[63] A reading of this book
now reveals a number of points that explain the reaction at the time. One
is the analysis of Russian educational policies toward the Bulgarians, which
consisted in sending Bulgarian students (supported with Russian stipends)
chiefly to seminaries, preparing them to become priests and teachers ready
to spread Russian influence (in its conservative forms). Some Russian
graduates were used directly as Russian "agents" in Bulgaria (as were Bulgarian émigré organizations in Russia) to influence the Bulgarian national
movement along the lines of Russian foreign policies. As the author points
out, these were often at variance with Bulgarian interests, for example
when favoring the "unity" of Christians under the Greek Patriarchy. In
general, the Russian "propaganda" among the Bulgarians is presented as
on an equal footing with the propaganda of some Western states, which
may have infuriated the censors. The author also reveals the enormous

harm done to the Bulgarians by the exchange of populations between Russia and Turkey, in which tens of thousands of Tartars and Circassians were settled in northeastern Bulgaria and the migration of tens of thousands of Bulgarians to southern Russia (Bessarabia and Moldova) was organized. While one could level occasional criticism at tsarist Russia at that time in a fuzzy and indefinite manner, Genchev did this quite openly and clearly, supporting it with a wealth of empirical material from Russian archives and thus breaking a tacit "scholarly" taboo.

Topics that were taboo (or "discouraged") at the time are now being openly tackled. For example, the massive destruction and dislocation brought about by the series of Russo-Turkish wars, including the already-mentioned resettlement.[64] The Russo-Turkish war of 1877–78 that led to the Bulgarian liberation itself is viewed in a more critical light. Untoward aspects of it that were eclipsed in previous jubilee expositions are mentioned: grave tactical errors and failures of the Russian army; crooked dealing in food and medicines at the expense of the Russian soldiers; a disastrous sanitary and epidemic situation; an increase in casualties as the result of all this; numerous casualties among the Bulgarian civilian population; material destruction as well as the opening of a deep chasm between Bulgarians and Turks; the slowing down of economic development, etc.[65]

The idea of a great Bulgarian state encompassing all ethnic Bulgarian territories within the boundaries drawn up in the preliminary peace treaty of San Stefano is revealed as a "myth" in view of the fact that there were previous agreements between Russia and Austria-Hungary, and between Russia and Britain, which excluded such an option. It thus turns out that the Berlin peace treaty, which divided the Bulgarian lands, has to be blamed not only on the Western great powers, as was the case before, but on Russia as well.[66] The very idea that the Russo-Turkish war of 1877–78 was declared with the exclusive purpose of liberating the Bulgarians is exposed as a "myth," since Russia was rescuing the Serb kingdom in the first place (which was suffering defeat at the hands of the Ottomans at that very moment).[67]

The description of the Bulgarian national revolutionary movement now also looks different, not as monolithic and seamless as before. The expositions started paying attention to discontinuities, rifts, crises and failures, animosities between revolutionary activists that had previously been elevated to heroic status and sanctified. The important work of Krumka Sharova on the Bulgarian revolutionary committee of 1875 has already been mentioned. Leaning upon it, the younger historian Plamen Mitev

presents a rather discontinuous and conflictive account of the revolutionary movement on the eve of the liberation: a conflict between Karavelov
and Botev; the "splitting" of Botev to form the next revolutionary committee (of 1875); an abortive attempt to start an uprising in Stara Zagora; the
improvised convening of a committee in Gyurgevo (by "youngsters" prone
to resolute action) to start preparations for a new uprising; the hastily prepared April uprising of 1876, etc.[68]

Krumka Sharova was again the first to draw attention to the crisis in the
revolutionary movement, which began in 1872 with the capturing of Levski
by the Turks and continued for years after his death. Characteristic here is
the open treatment of "awkward" questions such as the use of revolutionary terror in providing the organization with money, which attracted the
attention of the Turkish authorities and led to the disclosure of the structure and functioning of the committee organization in the country and to
the capturing of its architect, Vasil Levski. Also new is the change of perspective, allowing affairs to be seen from the point of view of the Ottoman
authorities, whose energetic reaction under Midhat pasha (together with
the loss of Levski), put the underground organization in jeopardy and
deepened the crisis following the failure.[69] These inferences are reflected in
the work of other authors, who also point to the deep crisis in the revolutionary movement and the contradictions in it after the hanging of Levski,
and then again after the failure of the April uprising, that led to reliance
exclusively on external aid and especially the turning toward Russia.[70] This
is in sharp contrast with previous representations of a "revolutionary situation" growing like an avalanche until culminating in the April uprising
and the reticence about its aftermath (or the treatment of the Russo-
Turkish war as its direct prolongation and denouement).[71]

In general, the revolutionary trend with its branches and offshoots
claims less space in the expositions of the Bulgarian national revival, filled
until recently by authors with revolutionaries, revolts and conspiracies.
There have appeared a few examples of school textbooks that take the new
tendencies into account, though the inertia here is much stronger.[72] Everyday life and the various aspects of existence under the Ottomans, such
as demography and the family, social interaction, relations between the
ethnic and religious communities and between the sexes, still have a hard
time winning space for themselves within a perimeter preserved primarily
for the "trinity" of revival processes, and are offered as an appendix
at best. In historical scholarship the epoch remains under the all-
determining sign of the political revival and its struggles, even if few Bul-

garians at that time would have perceived in this way the age in which they were living.

Finally, one may pose the question as to what can be expected from the present revision of the "dogmas" and the "myths" of the historical scholarship that sailed under the banner of Marxism-Leninism (but was actually quite dynamic). Many authors act in the conviction that they are restoring the "historical truth," or even the Truth with a capital letter. After Communism the search for the scholarly Truth about the national Revival stands clearly under the sign of the national idea and (contrary to claims of "objectivity") is often strongly emotional and biased. As indicated, the national idea that serves as a guiding light is not unambiguous but lends itself to various interpretations (prefigured in the conflict between "revolutionaries" and "evolutionists" during the Revival) and generates variance and discord now as well.

One can sympathize with myth-fighting, at least initially on exiting from an ideological regime. But it is usually too self-confident and blind to its own limitations. Bulgarian historical scholarship today is developing in a normal situation (economic conditions excluded)—as a free "enterprise" in an autonomous academic community that allows for (or cannot prohibit) different views and dissent. It is not only probable but certain that the new scholarly ideas, after becoming "orthodoxy," will in their turn be subjected to doubts, criticism and reappraisal, and to displacement by new topics. This is due to the complex relationship between knowledge and the external social world, but also to the internal logic of the professional field, driven (in Pierre Bourdieu's terms) by the symbolic rewards of difference (where novelty may well be a somewhat forgotten old). Thus one may expect the revealing of aspects previously "in the shadow," or the shifting of the very focus of historical interest, that is, of what is considered "significant" and worth studying, to new phenomena (leading to a discovery of other relevant "facts"). It is true that such self-propelled processes of the development of historical knowledge are held back in a community of historians that set themselves primarily patriotic tasks, especially in the study of the national Revival, and remain methodologically committed to a version of "positivism," but they cannot be halted.

The review of previous historical ideas has an important function to fulfill in this respect. Avoiding extreme relativism or a "postmodernist" understanding of history as exchanging one myth for another, historiographical review makes one aware of the conditioning of knowledge by its context (with its current concerns) and by the "perspective" of the observer, that is, his/her values, but also the concepts and theories applied. The exposition also shows that a (unitary) Truth on matters of interpretation beyond the mere ascertaining of dates and events can hardly be the ideal of free scholarship as it may only be reached by coerced (totalitarian) "consensus."

Notes

1 For example, the poems "Kocho," "1876," etc.
2 Zakhari Stoyanov, *Zapiski po bŭlgarskite*, 29–30.
3 Strashimirov, *Istoriya na Aprilskoto*. Vol. 1, 352–355.
4 Strashimirov, *Istoriya na Aprilskoto*. Vol. 3, 358.
5 Strashimirov, *Istoriya na Aprilskoto*. Vol. 1, 351–352.
6 Vlaikov, "Ako to ne beshe," 528–532.
7 Georgi Bakalov, *Aprilskoto vŭstanie i Benkovski*. Sofia, 1938, 3–6.
8 Natan, *Bŭlgarskoto vŭzrazhdane*, 194–195; Evlogi Buzhazhki, "Burzhoazno-fashistki falshifikatsii na bŭlgarskoto natsionalno-revolyutsionno dvizhenie." *Istoricheski pregled* 8, no. 3 (1951/52): 315. See also *Istoriya na Bŭlgariya v 14 toma*. Vol. 6, 412.
9 Examples are Ormandzhiev, *Otets Paisii i epokhata*, 55; and Gandev, *Kratka bŭlgarska istoriya*, 109. For thoughts on the heroization or victimization of the uprising as a kind of "compensation," see Iliya Todev, "Problemŭt za smisŭla na Aprilskoto vŭstanie v bŭlgarskata marksicheska istoriografiya." In Todev, *Novi ochertsi*, 83–104; Konstantin Kosev, *Aprilskoto vŭstanie–Prelyudiya*, 16–22.
10 Genchev, *Bŭlgarsko vŭzrazhdane*, 390–391.
11 Iliya Todev, "April 1876 ili Bŭlgarskoto razpyatie." In Todev, *Novi ochertsi*, 105–113; Todev, "Problemŭt za smisŭla," 88–89.
12 Such as Stoyan Zaimov, Georgi Benkovski, Tsanko Dyustabanov, and Todor Kableshkov. See *Zaimov, Minaloto*, 13; Konstantin Kosev, "Kŭm vŭprosa za deistvieto i vzaimodeistvieto na vŭtreshnite i vŭnshnite faktori v bŭlgarskoto natsionalno-osvoboditelno dvizhenie prez vŭzrazhdaneto." In *V chest na akademik Hristo Hristov*. Sofia: BAN, 1976, 35–48, esp. 44–45.
13 Ivan Hadzhiiski, "Aprilskoto vŭstanie i Benkovski." In Hadzhiiski, *Sŭchineniya v dva toma*. Vol. 1, Sofia: Bŭlgarski pisatel, 1974, 344–366 (first published in 1943).
14 Hadzhiiski, "Psikhologiya na Aprilskoto," 324–337, 343. On this, see Todev, "Problemŭt za smisŭla," 95–96.
15 Ivan Stoyanov, *Istoriya na bŭlgarskoto*, 254–255.
16 Natan, *Bŭlgarskoto vŭzrazhdane*, 194.
17 For example Hadzhiiski, "Psikhologiya na Aprilskoto," 326. Also Genchev, *Bŭlgarsko vŭzrazhdane*, 391.
18 *Istoriya na Bŭlgrariya v 14 toma*. Vol. 6, 418. The formula was coined by Gandev, *Aprilskoto vŭstanie*, 180–181. But this author describes the real objectives of Russia.
19 Chervenkov, "Kŭm 80-godishninata," 36.
20 *Istoriya na Bŭlgariya v dva toma*. Vol. 1, 471, 473; *Istoriya na Bŭlgariya v tri toma*. Vol. 1, 469–470. The author, in both cases, is Yono Mitev.
21 Hristov, *Agrarniyat vŭpros v bŭlgarskata*, 196.
22 Dimitŭr Kosev, "Aprilskoto vŭstanie–vrŭkhna tochka," 11–13, 16.
23 Goran Todorov, "Sotsialno-politicheskata obuslovenost," 117–128, esp. 124–125.

According to the author, the "betrayal" of the big bourgeoisie is to be understood as a refusal to provide means and as attempting to restrict the revolutionary activities, but it, too, possessed national consciousness and dreamt of a leading role in a future national state, though it did not want to risk life and property in armed struggle.

24 Konstantin Kosev and Nikolai Zhechev, *Aprilskoto vŭstanie, 1876.* Sofia: Nauka i izkustvo, 1966, 20–23.
25 Konstantin Kosev and Nikolai Zhechev, *Aprilskoto vŭstanie,* 153.
26 Gandev, *Aprilskoto vŭstanie,* 49, 88, 176–181. But Gandev also paid tribute to Stalinism in an earlier book on the April uprising containing Chervenkov-Pavlov's theses. See Hristo Gandev, *Aprilskoto vŭstanie.* Sofia: Narodna mladezh, 1956.
27 Genchev, *Bŭlgarsko vŭzrazhdane,* 390–400.
28 Genchev, *Bŭlgarsko vŭzrazhdane,* 398. For a similar thought see Ormandzhiev, *Otest Paisii i epokhata,* 55.
29 *Istoriya na Bŭlgariya v 14 toma.* Vol. 6, 412–418.
30 Evlogi Buzhahzki, "Politicheskata formula na burzhoaziyata za 'mnimo bŭlgarsko vŭstanie' prez 1876 g." *Vekove* 15, no. 3 (1986): 5–20.
31 Konstantin Kosev, *Aprilskoto vŭstanie,* 20–25, 148–149; Kosev, *Kratka istoriya,* 19–22, 111–112, 136–141, 153–157, 171–172.
32 Konstantin Kosev, *Kratka istoriya,* 11–12, 151–153.
33 As usual in history, it was actually the more well-to-do and free people who took to arms, in this case those from the prosperous proto-industrial upland urban centers in the Balkan range and the Rhodopes, with practically no Turks in their midst. This is pointed out by Hadzhiiski when considering the causes of the April uprising. The author cites among the reasons the robberies by Circassians on passing traders and the insecurity of travel (along with the discontent, especially of younger educated people, with foreign domination, etc.). See Hadzhiiski, "Psikhologiya na Aprilskoto," 304–308, 318–319.
34 Inna Peleva, "'Pod igoto i' i bŭlgarskoto znanie za 1876." In Peleva, *Ideologŭt na natsiyata,* 89–199, esp. 180–189, 200–213.
35 *Istoriya na Bŭlgariya v 14 toma.* Vol. 6, 458. The part on the war was written by Hristo Hristov. Also, recently, Konstantin Kosev, *Kratka istoriya,* 161.
36 The "triple" meaning of the Russo-Turkish war is present in Pantalei Zarev, *Bŭlgarskoto vŭzrazhdane.* Sofia: Nauka i izkustvo, 1950; N. Levintov, "Agrarn'ye otnosheniya," 145, 151–157, 164, 185; *Istoriya na Bŭlgariya v dva toma.* Vol. 1, 505–506; *Istoriya na Bŭlgariya v tri toma.* Vol. 1. 503; *Istoriya na Bŭlgariya v 14 toma.* Vol. 6, 458. See also Dimitŭr Kosev, "Harakter i znachenie na rusko-turskata voina prez 1877–1878 g." In *Osvobozhdenieto na Bŭlgariya ot tursko igo, 1878–1958.* Sofia: BKP, 1958, 3–12, esp. 5; Kosev, "Devetdeset godini ot Osvobozhdenieto na Bŭlgariya." In *Osvobozhdenieto na Bŭlgariya, 1878–1968.* Sofia: BAN, 1970, 7–13, esp. 9, 13; Hristov, *Agrarniyat vŭpros v bŭlgarskata,* 196–197, 263–265. Even Nikolai Genchev repeats the obligatory triple formula—Genchev, *Bŭlgarsko vŭzrazhdane,* 413. After Communism the thesis appears in a reduced form (without the agrarian overturn) in Ivan Stoyanov, *Istoriya na bŭlgarskoto,* 278.
37 *Istoriya na Bŭlgariya v dva toma.* Vol. 1, 505–506; Dimitŭr Kosev, "Devetdeset godini," 9, 12; Kosev, "Harakter i znachenie," 3–4; Hristo Hristov, "Harakter i znachenie na Osvoboditelnata voina." In *Osvobozhdenieto na Bŭlgariya, 1878–1968,* 15–26, esp. 17; *Istoriya na Bŭlgariya v 14 toma.* Vol. 6, 458 (by Hristo Hristov).
38 Natan, *Bŭlgarskoto vŭzrazhdane,* 196. The citation appears also in the edition of 1947 but here it is taken out of the edition of 1949. Similarly on the "double liberator" and Bulgarian–Russian friendship, see *Istoriya na Bŭlgariya v tri toma.* Vol. 1, 506.

39 Dimitŭr Kosev, "Harakter i znachenie," 12. Similarly on friendship with the peoples of Russia, among which the Russian people is "the eldest brother," see Kosev, "Devetdeset godini," 13. The examples can be multiplied. The point is that professional historians served the regime by propagating pro-Russian sentiments.

40 Pavlov, "Za sŭdŭrzhanieto i formata," 406.

41 Pavlov, "Za marksicheska istoriya," 356–357.

42 Dimitŭr Kosev, "Aprilskoto vŭstanie–vrŭkhna tochka," 7–8; Konstantin Kosev, *Aprilskoto vŭstanie*, 16–17; Konstantin Kosev, *Kratka istoriya*, 15–17.

43 Bakalov, *Hristo Botev*, 11–13.

44 Lenin, "Agrarnaia programma"; Lenin, "Agrarny vopros v Rossii," 128–129.

45 Bakalov, Hristo Botev, 70–71; Bakalov, Georgi. "Dvete linii v Bŭlgarskoto vŭzrazhdane." In Bakalov, *Bŭlgarskoto natsionalno-revolyutsionno*, 3–7.

46 Chervenkov, "Kŭm 80-godishninata," 32–37.

47 Todor Pavlov, "Hristo Botev. Bezsmŭrten sin, uchitel i vozhd na naroda." In Pavlov, *Izbrani proizvedeniya*. Vol. 3, 62.

48 Pavlov, "Za marksicheska istoriya," 355–356; Pavlov, "Za sŭdŭrzhanieto i formata," 405–411; Pavlov, "Kŭm vŭprosa za nashata nauchna," 263–291.

49 Bakalov was the first to suggest that the most advanced revolutionaries like Botev had reached the idea of "overleaping the capitalist formation and entering directly into a higher stage of economic organization," but this was a populist utopia at the time. See Bakalov, "Dvete linii," 5–7. Similarly, Bakalov, *Nashite revolyutsioneri*, 5. The author affirms that with Botev the revolution of the "third estate" surpassed itself, and that he is the link that joins it (i.e., the bourgeois revolution) with the struggle of the proletariat. The possibility of the transformation of one type of revolution into another (peasant or bourgeois–democratic into proletarian) is obviously borrowed from Lenin.

50 Pavlov, "Za sŭdŭrzhanieto i formata," 410–411. Similarly, Zhak Natan presented the "mass anti-fascist uprising" of 9 September 1944 as a continuation of the revolutionary tradition of the Revival, and of the organizers of the April uprising in particular. See Natan, *Bŭlgarskoto vŭzrazhdane*, 195 (in the edition of 1947; the passage is excluded from the 1949 edition).

51 Furet, *Interpreting the French Revolution*, 4–7, 84–87.

52 Bakalov, *Hristo Botev*, 11–13; Bakalov, *G. S. Rakovski*, 41; Natan, *Bŭlgarskoto vŭzrazhdane*, 27–28, 375, 399.

53 Pavlov, "Za sŭdŭrzhanieto i formata," 409.

54 Shteryu Atanasov, *Koi sa bili kŭrdzhaliite i protiv kogo sa se borili te?* Sofia: Dŭrzhavno izdatelstvo, 1954. See the critique by Kosev, "Kŭm izyasnyavane na nyakoi," 52–55.

55 Dimitŭr Kosev, "Aprilskoto vŭstanie–vrŭkhna tochka," 11; Goran Todorov, "Sotsialnopoliticheskata obuslovenost," 117; Genchev, *Levski, revolyutsiyata*, 117.

56 Konstantin Kosev, *Kratka istoriya*; Plamen Mitev, *Bŭlgarsko vŭzrazhdane*.

57 Vasilii Konobeev, "Za agrarnata programa na bŭlgarskite revolyutsioneri prez 60-te i 70-te godini na XIX vek." In Konobeev, *Bŭlgarskoto natsionalno-osvoboditelno dvizhenie. Ideologiya, programa, razvitie*. Sofia: Nauka i izkustvo, 1972, 368–437.

58 Hristov, *Agrarniyat vŭpros*, 54–55, 102,196–197, 263–265, 268. The actions of the Bulgarian peasants during the war are compared with those of the French peasants during the French Revolution. For a residue of that, see *Istoriya na Bŭlgariya v 14 toma*. Vol. 6, 412, 458 (in the chapters on the April uprising and the Russo-Turkish war by Hristo Hristov and Yono Mitev).

59 Konstantin Kosev, "Kŭm vŭprosa za deistvieto," 35–48, cit. on 40.

60 Konstantin Kosev, *Aprilskoto vŭstanie*, 20–25, 148–149; Kosev, *Kratka istoriya*, 21–22, 171–172.

61 Vera Mutafchieva notes the specific ardor and the somewhat paradoxical intolerance of the Bulgarian lay public regarding questions of history (rather than the currently happening and vitally important), as well as the great assurance of individual (formed in an unclear way) opinion rather than confidence in the specialist-historian; also the refusal to admit competing views and theories in historical scholarship, in contrast to other sciences. She explains such attitudes by the long subjection to ideology and indoctrination of the public in the spirit of the Unity of Historical Truth. See Mutafchieva, "Predislovie." In *Sŭdŭt nad istoritsite*, 5–7.

62 Compare François Furet's critique of the way orthodox Marxist authors conceive of the French Revolution. Furet, *Interpreting the French Revolution*, 89, 121–122. According to the author, their concept suffers from an overdose of logic, contains "potentially" everything, and, like an unfolding metaphysical monster, strangles the historical reality in its coils; besides, it replaces causality with a teleological end goal.

63 Nikolai Genchev, *Bŭlgaro-ruski kulturni obshtuvaniya prez Vŭzrazhdaneto*. Sofia: LIK, 2002. The book was published in 1975 and immediately confiscated from the printing shop.

64 Todev, *Novi ochertsi*, 146–190.

65 Plamen Mitev, "Razmisli vŭrkhu Rusko-turskata osvoboditelna voina (1877–1878)." *Istoriya* 3, no. 2 (1994): 52–59; Mitev, *Bŭlgarskoto vŭzrazhdane*, 151–153. One can also find an earlier description of the epidemic disaster of the war in a specialized work on the history of healthcare in Bulgaria: Vera Davidova, *Istoriya na zdraveopazvaneto v Bŭlgariya. Ochertsi*. Sofia: Nauka i izkustvo, 1956 (translated from Russian), 66–83.

66 In a myth-fighting spirit, see Todev, *Novi ochertsi*, 218–224; Plamen Mitev, *Bŭlgarskoto vŭzrazhdane*, 149–150, 153; Mitev, "Razmisli vŭrkhu," 55–56. In a more conciliatory spirit, see Ivan Stoyanov, *Istoriya na bŭlgarskoto*, 267, 274–278. The diplomatic games are considered in greater detail by Konstantin Kosev, *Kratka istoriya*, 159–173. None of these authors denies the necessity of the liberation war or affirms that the liberation would have been achieved anyway.

67 Plamen Mitev, "Razmisli vŭrkhu," 53–54. This means that the massacre of the April uprising was not the major motive for the war (and the author says so).

68 Plamen Mitev, *Bŭlgarskoto vŭzrazhdane*, 109–143; Mitev, *Sŭzdavane i deinost*, 16–22.

69 Krumka Sharova, "Krizisni yavleniya v BRTsK prez lyatoto i esenta na 1872 g." *Istoricheski pregled* 47, no. 3 (1991): 3–24; Sharova, "Mithad pasha i bŭlgarskoto revolyutsionno dvizhenie prez 1972 g." *Istoricheski pregled* 47, no. 6 (1991): 3–16.

70 Ivan Stoyanov, *Istoriya na bŭlgarskoto*, 260–264; Todev, *Novi ochertsi*, 77–78; Konstantin Kosev, *Kratka istoriya*, 134–135, 157.

71 For example, the presentation of the "revolutionary situation" in Botev's times in Dimitŭr Kosev, "Aprilskoto vŭstanie–vrŭkhna tochka," 15–16.

72 One such example, albeit an isolated one, is *Istoriya za 11 klas*. Sofia: Anubis, 1996 (the lessons on the Ottoman period are written by Vera Mutafchieva, and those on the Revival by Raina Gavrilova). But most of the textbooks are more traditional. However, this is a separate topic that cannot be discussed here.

CHAPTER SIX

The Continuing Revival: Symbolic Struggles and Images

For a long time the epoch of the national revival did not recede into history but remained alive in public life and animated the political struggles in the independent state. The Constituent Assembly in Tŭrnovo in 1879 ended up adopting a very democratic constitution that rejected the "conservative" idea of a second chamber (or senate). The two major political parties that emerged from the constitutional debates took up, in their outlook and phraseology, the former enmity between the "evolutionists" and the "revolutionaries," or, more dramatically, between the *chorbadzhii* and outcasts (*hŭshove*).[1] Among the leaders of the large and popular Liberal Party were such highly regarded Revival activists as Petko Slaveikov and Petko Karavelov (brother of Lyuben Karavelov), and the revolutionaries Zakhari Stoyanov and Stefan Stambolov ("apostles" in the April uprising). In the rather embittered political strife that ensued, the Liberals undertook the advocacy of the "people" employing a strongly populist language and propaganda. The Conservatives were caricatured as "*chorbadzhii*," in particularly florid terms in the political journalism of Zakhari Stoyanov in the early 1880s.[2] This was intertwined with bitter strife between the so-called Russophiles and Russophobes, in which major former revolutionaries (who had been pro-Russian before) took a strongly anti-Russian stand in vigorous defense of the country's independence against interventions by the liberator, while most of the "Conservatives" had pro-Russian sympathies.[3]

The ideals of the Revival epoch justified and inspired the struggle against the strongly resented decisions of the Berlin Congress for the unification of the partitioned Bulgarian lands. The revolutionary trend of the Revival in particular was imitated in the preparations for the unification of the Kingdom of Bulgaria with the autonomous Eastern Rumelia (the part of Bulgaria south of the Balkans) by such activists of the April uprising as

Zakhari Stoyanov, Ivan Andonov and others, by way of setting up secret "committees" on the model of the internal revolutionary organization in Levski's times. It is true that in carrying out the Unification in 1885 the matter-of-fact official line represented by army officers and leaders of political parties prevailed, while the "romantic" revolutionary trend found some theatrical expressions.[4] The Ilinden uprising in Macedonia (1903) was also inspired by the liberation goals of the national Revival. The impulse of the Revival lasted until the Balkan wars (1912–1913) and World War I, fought by the Bulgarians for Macedonia and parts of Thrace but ending in chilling "national catastrophes."

The Bulgarian Revival with its national ideals and heroes presents a source of coveted symbolic capital. Various political forces tried to mobilize it for their own purposes, and symbolic struggles were fought between them for the appropriation of this symbolic capital and the drawing of political "dividends." This involved styling the Revival into ideologically trimmed images, suited to particular purposes. I will now consider how the prestige of the Revival was claimed by rightist (nationalist, authoritarian), liberal-democratic, and leftist (Communist) forces, and what images of it were shaped in the process.

Rightist Visions of the Bulgarian Revival

During the 1930s and into the war years, Bulgaria (as most of Central and Eastern Europe) stood under the sign of the Right, more precisely, of a new and intense nationalism, adopted as state ideology and policy. The country was ruled by an authoritarian government from 19 May 1934, first a military, then a monarchist dictatorship. A number of extreme nationalist, and a few outright fascist, organizations sprang up. The epoch of the national Revival was then mobilized for nationalist (irredentist, unification) goals and to legitimize authoritarian rule. The slogan "back to the Revival" or "for a new (second) revival" acquired wide currency, meaning a return to the spirit and the virtues of the Revival but also rallying support for a new attempt at the unification of all Bulgarians within the territories encompassed by the national Revival.

The Revival in the nationalist discourse presents a specific image and is part of a larger narrative. In the inspired visions of the medieval historian Petŭr Mutafchiev (and the jurist Lyubomir Vladikin) it appears as a time of the spiritual unity of the Bulgarians on the basis of the national con-

sciousness, the people's values, and a specific national mode of life, ce-
mented by social cohesion between the intelligentsia (as a "spiritual
leader") and the people. Development was then healthy, gradual, and
"organic," building upon a self-grown original (*samobitna*) culture that had
its seat in the people's material life, customs, world-view and artistic
achievements (and among the peasants and artisans in particular). This
spiritual unity (and healthy development) were supposedly broken after the
liberation under the storm of foreign cultural and ideological influences
and the adoption of foreign models and ideas. The polluting influences
mentioned all come from Europe, especially liberalism and the spirit of
individualism but also "extreme political teachings" that "negate the state"
(obviously Communism and anarchism). A deep rift occurred in public life
between the intelligentsia and the people as the intelligentsia embraced the
foreign influences and turned away from the people, who also turned away
from their "spiritual leader." Culture became imitative, education lost its
national meaning, the pseudo-European towns became alienated from the
traditional villages, the social classes and groups became entangled in contradictions and strife, the intelligentsia degenerated into job-hunters, and
the people lost faith in their leaders and in themselves.

The present misfortunes of the country—and the authors—are due to the
fact that the bequests of the Revival were forgotten. They required confidence in the people's spirit and the assertion of the nation, awareness of
the people's unity and of the common goal (shared equally by *chorbadzhii*
and outcasts), namely, that all lands populated by Bulgarians should be
included in the future Bulgarian state. Another bequest demanded the
moral cohesion of all strata, and the faith of the people in their leaders,
themselves inspired by patriotism and pure idealism, devoted to the service
of their people and ready for self-abnegation and self-sacrifice in the name
of the national whole.

Having diagnosed the malaise, the authors prescribe the cure. In order
to return to the healthy condition the Bulgarians should take up the Revival again or work toward a new revival by repudiating the foreign influences and by overcoming the rift between the intelligentsia and the people.
The "prodigal" intelligentsia in particular should cease negating "the native" and forgetting its own peasant and artisan background, and reunite
with the national community by embracing the people's spirit. All available
knowledge and talent should be placed at the service of the people's
(national) community. Sacrifices are required by all, and especially by
those who have taken upon themselves the duty of leadership, who should

be as disinterested and self-abnegating as the activists of the Revival. Expressed as a program, the new revival should consist in the working out of a "national ideology" on the basis of a good knowledge of the Bulgarian people, the Bulgarian land, and the problems of the life of the nation. State policies should become national, and the sovereignty of the state should come first. The people should follow their leaders as before independence. Culture should become nationalized and nothing should be accepted into it without first passing through the "furnace" of the Bulgarian spirit in order to free it from poisonous substances; this would also shorten the distance between the intelligentsia and the ordinary people. The new revival should follow the bequests of the original Revival, that is, to treasure above all the nation and its unity beyond "artificial and contingent" boundaries.[5]

The "return to the Revival" call elicited a sober response from Dimitŭr Mikhalchev, editor-in-chief of the authoritative journal *Filosofski pregled* (Philosophical review), who wrote that such a return to the "lost paradise" of the times of national awakening and general upsurge was impossible. The Bulgarian nation after liberation lived in a complicated situation of statehood and with economic and ideological contradictions that could not be eliminated.[6] To this, Petŭr Mutafchiev responded that a national regeneration movement was possible even under the new conditions because in fateful periods in their history the peoples are able to overcome economic and ideological contradictions and restore their internal unity. A "primeval instinct" for the "preservation of the species" is then aroused and the "transitory ideological ballast" falls away.[7] In other words, the national is the deepest, primary or "organic" layer, while the social and ideological contradictions are only secondary layers.

The call for a "return to the Revival" seemed not radical enough to Naiden Sheitanov, a rather curious figure and the creator of pagan, Thracian–Orphic and other indigenist phantasmagoria. He compared it to contemporary slogans and movements in other countries, especially in Italy (i.e., fascist ideas of restoring the glory of ancient Rome and its victorious legions), national-socialist Germany (the cult of pagan Germany and its heroic world-view), Hungary (the idealized pagan times of the Magyars), Greece (the calls for a resuscitation of ancient Greece and medieval Byzantium), Romania (the "Latin idea" of kinship with the Romans), Turkey (Turkism inspired by the old Turkic past), etc. According to this author, instead of evoking only the national Revival, one should better call for a (symbolic) return to the glorious Bulgarian medieval past (as did Paisii), hence the slogan should be "back to Simeon the Great," "back to Cyril and Methodius," "back to Bogomil," "back to Boyan the Wizard," or "back to Omurtag." Not satisfied with even this historical regression, Sheitanov descends to his favorite Thracians, with their musician Orpheus and the god Dionysus, and proposes the creation of "Thracism as a cultural regenerative trend."[8]

While the authors considered so far expressed themselves in more abstract terms and high-pitched metaphors, others were more explicit in setting the national goals and the desired boundaries. They urged for the fulfilling of duty to the "tribe" and the "mother tongue," referring again to the projects of the Revival activists and the span of the Bulgarian Church under the Ottomans.[9] The presumed unity of the nation during the Revival in particular was evoked in order to blunt internal social and class conflict.

The perpetrators of the military coup d'état of 19 May 1934 were guided by the idea of national regeneration by way of ending party strife, uniting the people, rationalizing the economy, tightening the administration, and strengthening the Bulgarian state. They portrayed the new order (in the organ of the military league *Narodna otbrana*—"People's defense") as the successor to the traditions of the Revival and as a new manifestation of the "people's spirit." The Bulgarian army itself began with volunteers from the Russo-Turkish war. Even the canceling of the Tŭrnovo constitution was presented as the rejection of a foreign import and as the restoring of a kind of "estate representation" similar to the role of the guilds (*esnafi*) in the urban communities of the Revival.[10] As the military was pushed aside and the regime evolved toward royal dictatorship, the emphasis fell on the monarchy while the rightist ideologists, influenced by fascism, contributed elitist and Führer tones to the propaganda.

While there were isolated anniversary celebrations of acclaimed activists of the Revival prior to World War I, annual "all-nation" holidays were introduced in the inter-war period, such as the Day of the People's Awakeners (1 November, introduced in 1922), and Father Paisii's Day (27 September, introduced in 1942). These, along with the traditional "St. Cyril and St. Methodius's Day" (24 May, elevated to a national holiday in 1916), were systematized and filled with strongly nationalistic contents during the late 1930s and early 1940s.[11] The Ministry of Education, acting as the ideological organ of the state, organized official celebrations with political propaganda speeches. In them, the deeds of the activists of the Revival epoch were presented as a striving toward a united Bulgaria, the sense characteristically shifting from "liberation" toward "unification," with the joining of

Macedonia (during World War II) appearing as its completion. The rallying
of the nation behind its leaders, a strong (authoritarian) statehood, and
monarchism are all derived from the Revival. In the following example
(one out of many) a continuity is affirmed between the efforts of the national "awakeners," the ideal of "San Stefano Bulgaria" (i.e., comprising
all territories of the Treaty of San Stefano) and the "unification" achieved
in alliance with Germany in World War II:

"The efforts of the awakeners point ultimately toward the realization of
the ideal of freedom—a liberation that is at once spiritual, economic, and
political, and is a liberation of the entire Bulgarian people within its historical and ethnographic boundaries. [...] The people's awakeners thus
startled the Bulgarian nation, made it aware of itself, and created it. Together with that, they outlined the Bulgarian fatherland, its span, its beau-
ties, and its greatness. They erected the Bulgaria of San Stefano in the soul
of their people so that she already existed before being created with blood
and the sword. [...] The unification that we are now in the process of building up is a continuation of their deeds."[12]

Paisii's personality and oeuvre (a history of medieval Bulgaria) in particular became subject to reinterpretation and falsification not just in nationalist, but in outright monarchist and even clerical keys, in tune with
the "God, King, and Fatherland" formula. Here is an excerpt from a
speech on Radio Sofia pronounced by minister Boris Yotsov on the "Day of
Father Paisii" (27 September) in 1943:

"In the national ethos of Paisii of Hilendar, there shine three political
ideas—the people, the state, and the historical personality. [...] Among the
personalities, Paisii places the person of the tsar in the foremost place. For
him, the royal authority manifests itself in one highest sense, namely, it is
predestined for [a role in] the historical development of the Bulgarian
people. That is why his fatherland can only be a monarchy with a hereditary ruler. The royal institution, the church, and the intellectual elite are
the major pillars of the state. But its greatest strength derives from the
army, which is needed in days of peace and in days of national struggles.
Thus by making use of history Father Paisii highlighted the future development of the Bulgarian people."[13]

From Paisii as a first and prototypical "awakener of the people" the interest was widened to other "awakeners" and the phenomenon (*buditelstvo*)
in general.[14] The collective image of the awakener of the people occupies a
central place in rightist writings, while the revolutionaries (even if positively viewed) are somewhat in the background as just one branch from the

thick trunk of the Revival. Not the revolutionaries but the awakeners are at the foundation of the national building.

The nationalist ideals derived from the Revival found their way into educational policies, namely, as a new and more active formative ideal in the schools that proclaimed the primacy of upbringing and the forging of "characters" over acquiring knowledge. The new *voelkisch* (*narodnosten*) ideal purported to create the "New Bulgarian" as a person in close relation to his/her people and to the state. In practice, this meant the fostering of nationalism and the application of discipline (defined in terms of duty), apparently to higher public goals, including readiness to sacrifice oneself in the pursuit of the national "ideals." The rightist ideology preached social harmony under the authority of the state, attacking the divisive or subversive leftist (Communist, anarchist) teachings. Changes were made to the curricula in order to increase the space for the national subjects (Bulgarian language, literature, history, geography and civic education) in view of achieving the national(ist) educational ideal. Again, this was often argued as a return to the true Bulgarian (people's) spirit cultivated during the Revival.[15]

One encounters directly fascist proposals to use the slogan "back to the legacy of the Revival" as a "practical program" for state building in an authoritarian spirit inspired by the examples of Fascist Italy and Nazi Germany. According to one such "policy advice," the Revival epoch, so rich in "moral titans" and in great "examples and deeds," should be used in the upbringing of activists of a new revival, understood as a new "national revolution." The latter must create a nationalist intelligentsia, beyond ideological and party differences, to be entrusted with the "spiritual leadership" of its people. The author describes the national revolution as the stamping upon the mind of the Bulgarian people of the idea of a non-party nation state and of an authoritarian (but also "social") government akin to those in Germany and Italy.[16]

To sum up, the nationalist and authoritarian forces of the 1930s and the early 1940s made use of the Revival for their own ideological–educational purposes and for political mobilization, strongly falsifying it in the process. To begin with, they created a highly simplified, harmonized, and idealized image. The Revival appears here as a unity of purpose (shared by notables and outcasts alike), in which an idealized people dutifully follows its leaders. There are no internal contradictions, no entanglement in (and "corruption" by) Ottoman rule, just a massive display of patriotism and self-abnegation. The rightist image of the national Revival is not only strongly idealized but contains outright falsifications, such as the above-mentioned authoritarian relation between "people" and "leaders" and the cult of the monarch. One should mention as another mystification the idea of absolute cultural originality or authenticity (*samobitnost*) that ignores the strong European ideological–political and cultural influences in the process of shaping national Bulgarian "high culture." This mythologized portrait of the Revival is contrasted with a darkened image of decline after the liberation, supposedly due to a retreat from the national ideals (even though in reality Bulgaria entered two wars in pursuit of them).

Transformed in such a way, the Revival functions as a model for emulation in the present. The logic is this: the people followed their leaders then, and so they should now; the leaders were united under the priority of the national goal during the Revival, and they should be united now; the nation stands above all and justifies any sacrifice, then and as well as now. In such a way the people were being mobilized for the new attempt to realize the "national ideals" (in alliance with Nazi Germany).

The recasting of the Revival epoch in the new mold was facilitated by the fact that, for all their differences, the liberal nationalism of the nineteenth century and the new militant nationalism of the 1930s shared some assumptions, such as the primacy of the community over the individual, the metaphysics of the "people's spirit," the notion of organic development and national self-realization, the idea of historical rights, etc. They also had some ideological delusions and self-delusions in common: the idea that the nation is "primordial," the idealization of the people and of popular culture, etc., and both employed a lofty metaphoric language. That is why the new nationalism could imperceptibly be substituted for the earlier one, or why they could be presented as standing in basic continuity.

But the ideas and rhetorical figures of the Revival acquired a different meaning in the new setting where they were employed to other purposes. Thus "the people" to whom the awakeners referred in their national mission (and to whom the revolutionaries referred in order to move or frighten the unpatriotic *chorbadzhii*) was directed, in the new authoritarian discourse, against social, ideological and political cleavages and contradictions. The assault was on liberalism, individualism, and the foreign influences contracted by the intelligentsia in general, presented as "unhealthy" aberrations. But the attacks against the infected intelligentsia did not prevent the mobilization of its residual prestige. The "spiritual" leadership of the intelligentsia finds itself transformed into an authoritarian leadership (on a fascist model), cultivating some kind of elitism.

The Democratic Image

Reacting against the modeling of the Bulgarian Revival in such a nationalist and authoritarian way (and against what it had to support), others derived from it a contrasting, democratic image. Ivan Hadzhiiski, a sociologist with leftist ideas, posed the following question in 1937: Which way
should Bulgaria go—the way of democracy, or the way of authoritarianism?
He then proceeded to argue, in a work characteristically called *The Historical Roots of Our Democratic Traditions*, that historical experience and continuity with the Revival require that Bulgaria takes the road of democracy.
The author detects the democratic traditions of the Revival in various
places: in the artisan guilds (*esnafi*), especially in their internal organization and struggles against the traditional notables (*chorbadzhii*) for control
of the communal self-government and of the school and church boards; in
the unfolding of wide democratic movements for secular national education and for church autonomy; and especially in the struggles for political
independence. The Ottoman domination itself is interpreted by him as a
precondition for the "democratic course of our history" because it abolished the advancing feudalization of the medieval Bulgarian state and replaced it with a different social order—without serfdom of the peasants and
without estates (and accordingly free of any "estatist spirit"). The dominant
Ottoman layer did not penetrate the Bulgarian people because of the different faith, language, and customs, but lived alongside it, hence the larger
part of the Bulgarians lived practically under self-government.[17]

Hadzhiiski had, in fact, a number of predecessors, who had pointed to
one or another democratic trait of the Bulgarian Revival. Thus the inspired historian of "the making" of Bulgaria, Simeon Radev, had pointed
in as early as 1910 to "democratic attitudes" as one of the characteristic
virtues of the Revival epoch, the others being, according to him, love for
education and national feeling. The author meant by democratic attitudes
the general striving toward freedom and equality that found expression in
the struggles against the *chorbadzhii* and the Greek Phanariots, as well as
the hostility of the people toward social and political hierarchies.[18] The
church historian Ivan Snegarov, in his turn, derives the democratic idea
from the struggles for an independent church, which led to a union of the
various social classes in the common effort, but also to the idea of equal
access to the public goods thus achieved. Hence the statutes of the Exarchate (the autonomous Bulgarian Church) provided for a wide democratic
(i.e., lay) participation in church matters, and the same democratic spirit

subsequently prevailed in the constitution of the Bulgarian state. Snegarov goes as far as to affirm that political democracy in Bulgaria was born out of church democracy. But he also pays tribute to the Bulgarian town communes and town councils as "true people's institutions," "sanctuaries of democracy," and a school for self-government.[19]

One might also mention some writings of the so-called national psychology (or national mentality) genre, problematic as any enterprise of this kind is. Thus the well-known Bulgarian literary historian Ivan Shishmanov enumerates among the moral qualities of "the Bulgarian under the Turkish yoke" a democratic attitude and a desire for progress (and, rhyming somewhat uneasily with that, patriarchal family life). According to him as well, the democratic spirit characteristic of the Revival epoch was cultivated in the milieu of the local self-government of the communes.[20] When listing the qualities of "the Bulgarian," another author specializing in "national psychology" writes down on the asset side of the national character qualities such as love of freedom, sensitivity concerning individual rights, tolerance toward foreigners, and an attitude of opposition (to authorities). On the liability side are listed such traits as inability to organize socially, distrust, intractability, and egoism. Faced with the ambiguity of qualities that appear both as good and as bad (depending on whether formulated positively or negatively), this author finds a way out in ascribing the good qualities to the times of the national Revival (and expresses the hope that they are still dormant in the souls and present a guarantee of a better future).[21]

But most of the "national psychologists" of the post-liberation times are strongly critical of Bulgarian "democratism," which, according to them, has a deformed and perverse expression as hostility toward any authority and any administrative order as such, disrespect for law, "individualism," egoism, social apathy, etc. They usually derive these attitudes from the Turkish "yoke," the Revival included (as taking place under it), but some ascribe their cultivation to the patriarchal tradition as well (within the family and in the craftsmen's guilds).[22] The deficient understanding of democracy in post-liberation Bulgaria and the distortion of democratic political practices in the absence of a true democratic "spirit" to animate the democratic institutions are the bottom line of the bitter reflections of the great Bulgarian satirical writer and social critic Stoyan Mikhailovski, who also blamed life under the "yoke" for a legacy of social immaturity and cultural backwardness.[23]

Somewhat curiously, the democratic image of the national Revival was polished anew under state socialism, which sought to present itself as a continuation and a higher level of development of the democratic traditions of the national Revival. An example is provided by the strongly ideological and very confused writings of the literary figure Marko Semov, who conceived of himself as a successor in the tradition of the "science" of national psychology (especially in the line of Zakhari Stoyanov and Ivan Hadzhiiski). The author devotes much space to Bulgarian "democratism" (i.e., democratic attitudes), dating it from as far back as the communal social order of the early Slavs (sixth to the ninth centuries). He reveals three stages in the development of Bulgarian "democratism" in modern times: during the April uprising, bourgeois democratism, and the socialist order. The "democratism" of the April uprising manifested itself in the equality of all before the "laws of the struggle"; the responsibility of the organizers ("the apostles") to the people; the rejection of "cults of personality" and of estate prejudices; comradeship, etc. Bourgeois democratism found expression in the lack of a sense of hierarchy among the Bulgarians and their critical attitude toward the state and any superiors, as well as in a certain democratization of family life (but not to the extent of "equalizing" women completely). As is to be expected, socialism is the highest form of democratism, but, as the author notes, unfortunately negative attitudes toward the state (inherited from capitalism) were not entirely overcome.[24]

Not all authors are as optimistic about the democratic traits of the Revival. Toncho Zhechev, a literary historian with a dissident aura, pointed to such "shadier aspects" of the Bulgarian democratic mentality as the envy that goes together with the democratic feeling of equity and recognizes no "aristocratic" superiority, perceiving equality in the sense of "nobody is better than me," hence nobody deserves more, etc.[25] To take another example, the historian Nikolai Genchev regards the communal self-government as a "cradle of the democratism of the Bulgarian society." In the absence of a traditional aristocracy of big inequalities and deep social cleavages, the mentality of the Bulgarian nation was shaped in accordance with democratic principles—a feeling of equality and self-respect, lack of estatist (aristocratic) prejudice, and the practice of elections in communal, cultural and political organizations. But nor does this author have a high opinion of Bulgarian democratism, which, according to him, was counteracted by the patriarchal peasant tradition and remained of "servile" quality.[26]

Generally speaking, the descriptions of the Bulgarian democratic tradition, whether in terms of national psychology or otherwise, are strongly biased and affected by the personal experiences of the author and by the attitude toward present-day realities. One can note that the democratic reading of the national Revival becomes stronger in moments of resistance against authoritarianism (e.g., Hadzhiiski, or some crypto-critical tones during state socialism). But this can also be a way to bolster national self-esteem at any time, where cheerful socialist optimism is especially characteristic. Conversely, and ironically, skepticism regarding the democratic traits of the Revival prevails under relatively democratic conditions, and the "servile vices" of the Ottoman epoch are evoked as an explanation of the political and social deficiencies of Bulgarian democracy.

The authors most critical of the Bulgarian "democratic tradition" describe it as a widely spread negative attitude toward the state and the authorities, a kind of spontaneous "opposition." A more balanced representation takes into account both the face and reverse of Bulgarian democratism. The most idealized democratic reading of the Revival understands democracy in the sense of civic self-initiative and voluntary association for various purposes, including charity (i.e., as "civic society" in the sense of Alexis de Tocqueville), rather than as liberal democracy (which is more "aristocratic" and takes individual rights seriously) and greater respect for law. Though idealized, this is consistent with the "immediate" practice of democracy on a small scale in local affairs (the community, the local church, and school, cultural associations, etc.) in the absence of a Bulgarian state during the national Revival.

The Battle of the Communists for the Legacy of the Revival

The main traits and details of the "leftist image" of the Revival formed by the Marxist interpretation with its emphasis on class divisions and class conflict, revolutionism, etc., has been outlined in various places in this book. Rather than repeating what has already been said, I will concentrate on the appropriation of the legacy of the Revival by the Communists, and the operations to which it was subjected in the process. The symbolic use of the past, and especially of the deeds of the revolutionaries, began with the founder of the Bulgarian Socialist Party, Dimitŭr Blagoev. According to him, the government that the Bulgarian people received after the liberation did not resemble the one for which Levski had fought and was hanged. The bourgeoisie—this new kind of *chorbadzhii*—crucified the newly attained freedom while the petty bourgeoisie and the intelligentsia, previously engaged in the revolutionary movement, were now in economic decline. The ideals of Levski became incomprehensible for some and contrary to the interests of others, until they were taken up by the working class and its party:

"However, another type of people emerges, another social force that remembers sincerely and with warmth such activists of the people as Levski, Lyuben Karavelov, Botev and the others. This is the working people, whose self-conscious part embraces the ideals of our revolutionaries, puts new substance into them, develops them, and fights for their realization."[27]

Georgi Bakalov, one of the next generation of Communist intellectuals and propagandists, fully recognized the stakes in the interpretation of the legacy of the Revival and its application as a weapon in contemporary political struggles. He made special efforts to gain the Revival epoch with its revolutionaries for the Communist Party by various interpretative strategies and the recasting of history. Here is his account of what happened with the legacy of the Revival upon independence. From the liberation until the unification (of the Kingdom of Bulgaria and Eastern Rumelia) in 1885, all political forces and movements referred to the Revival in its entirety. The early Liberals, who found support in the peasant masses recently liberated and provided with land, were strongly democratic and stood close to the ideals of Levski and Botev. But with the development of the capitalist system, its supporters became increasingly conservative and alienated from the great bequests of the Revival, especially those concerning the liberties of the people. At the same time, a new social element entered the public arena in the shape of the socialists, who claimed the legacy of the national revolutionary movement and stood nearer to the ideals of Levski and Botev, hence were fully entitled to carry their "banner." According to Bakalov, the threat posed by the socialists led to the emergence in the bourgeois camp of a "new theory" of the Revival. Instead of taking it in its entirety as a struggle for spiritual and political liberation, this theory cut off the branch of the political revolutionary struggles and reduced it to education alone; moreover, it claimed that the revolutionary struggles were unnecessary and even impeded the political liberation. The author, in his turn, takes a decisive stand on the side of the revolutionary trend of the Revival (in their opposition to the adherents of the status quo or of dualism) and claims the revolutionary legacy for the Communists.[28]

Actually, Bakalov's account itself should be taken with reservations. Even when polemically contrasting "evolutionists" and revolutionaries, the nationalist authors rarely ceded the revolutionary activists. This is attested by the polemics Bakalov himself had to conduct in order to reclaim the national revolutionaries for the Communist Party in the 1920s and 1930s. Quite naturally, the most direct continuity was established with Botev's brand of communism (actually, an early form of socialism, intermingled with anarchism and populism). According to Bakalov, the liberation movement of the "third estate" had an extreme leftist stream, especially among the emigration in Romania, which consisted of ruined artisans and peasants, workers without a definite profession, intelligentsia and idealistic youth inspired by "the most generous and extreme ideas." The outcast (hŭsh) was the revolutionary of the times, a "forerunner of the proletarian of today." In the figure of Botev, this stream reached out for the Communist ideal:

"In the person of Botev the revolution of the "third estate" superseded itself. Botev foresaw the future and prophesied the international social revolution of the proletariat. Thus Botev appears as the uniting link in the chain between the revolution of the third estate and the liberation struggle of the proletariat. [...] Under the cheerful banner, raised for the first time in our country by Botev, his children—the contemporary proletarians, will win the victory."[29]

In fact, the elaboration of lines of succession of "forerunners" and "successors" ("forefathers" and "heirs") became a favorite device in establishing a personal continuity between the Revival figures and the Communists, as well as the substantial continuity of the "deed."

It was not so easy to claim purely national revolutionaries as Levski and Rakovski. Writing in 1924, Bakalov argued that now that the fight over Botev had been completed successfully, the time had come to "deliver to the working people his brothers-in-arms, namely, his teacher Rakovski and his friend Levski." Applying himself to the job, the author establishes a line of continuity from the Revival to post-liberation times as regards the class struggle and the struggle against the *chorbadzhii* in particular. The scheme is as follows. After the liberation the previously revolutionary "third estate" disintegrated into the classes of the bourgeoisie, the petty bourgeoisie, and the proletariat, whereby the heirs of the old *chorbadzhii* joined the core of the bourgeoisie. By identifying the new bourgeoisie with the old *chorbadzhii* whom Rakovski had fought in his time, Bakalov wrests him away from the bourgeoisie and draws him toward the camp of the socialists. In his turn, Levski is appropriated using arguments of class descent, being presumably a "proletarian child, nurtured by a widowed mother from the distaff and the spinning-wheel."[30] One can clearly see the way of proceeding by identification/assimilation: the *chorbadzhii* of the Revival epoch = the post-liberation bourgeoisie; the people of the Revival = the proletariat after independence; the revolutionaries of the Revival = socialists (Communists).

Another characteristic polemic device applied by the socialists in appropriating the legacy of the revolutionaries of the Revival is the affirmation that, had a certain revolutionary activist lived in the contemporary conditions, he would have stood inevitably on the side of the proletariat and would have become a socialist. Conversely, contemporaries are hypothetically projected back to find analogies for them during the Revival.[31]

Bakalov was the first to encounter a problem that would be faced by all those who carried the economic and class interpretation of the Bulgarian Revival to extremes and made use of law-like historical stages. The problem is this: with a bourgeois transformation lying ahead, it follows that the "titans" of the Bulgarian national revolutionary movement strove for capitalism; they were, so to say, "combatants for capitalism." The national revolutionaries were exonerated in the following manner: in their beliefs (i.e., "subjectively") they were in favor of the "small producers" and of the "toiling people" and dreamt about the welfare of the people, so it was not their fault that the "objective" conditions of small-scale production nourished the development of capitalism. And the most advanced revolutionaries like Botev had even reached the idea of "jumping over" the capitalist stage and entering directly the higher socialist stage.[32] Of course, the basic problem with this type of deterministic thinking of history is not really solved by differentiating between "subjective" intentions and "objective" laws of development. Because if one believes in progressist, stage-like schemes, one risks seeing one's heroes fighting for something that looks anachronistic and even reprehensible two stages later.

In fact, the symbolic contests about the revolutionaries of the Revival continued throughout the inter-war period. Thus Ivan Andonov, an activist of the Revival and major participant in the April uprising, strongly objected in his memoirs (published in 1927) against the use of Botev and Levski in the Communist propaganda, pointing out that they were patriots and nationalists in the first place.[33] The nationalists of the 1920s and 1930s showed a special predilection for Botev, probably because of his fiery temperament. A major patriotic student organization (at Sofia University) named itself after him in 1920 and opposed the Communist-dominated student union. This was characteristically accompanied by the interpretation of Botev as primarily a great patriot and good nationalist who fought for the whole Bulgarian people; in addition, there is the idea that nation and humanity are in unison, and that the national movement does not exclude economic and social demands.[34]

Only after the Communist takeover (and the silencing of opponents) could the Communists assert their claims to the legacy of the Revival, revolutionary and non-revolutionary alike. Zhak Natan opened fire (in 1949) against the appropriation of the "legacy of ideas" of the Revival by "Great Bulgarian chauvinists" and "fascist historians." He declared instead the activists of the Revival to be forerunners of the "great deed of transformation" performed by the Fatherland's Front (a Communist-dominated mass anti-fascist organization). The line of succession and the fulfillment of the bequests of the Revival by the Communist regime is seen by him, ironically, in points such as the achieving of national independence by Bulgaria, the "brotherly union" between the Slavic peoples, the triumph of republican ideas, the establishment of a true "people's democracy," and the implementation of Botev's ideal of complete human freedom and social liberation, but also (and more to the point) in the hatred of the people's traitors and the enemies of the people from the "camp of the *chorbadzhii*."[35]

In fact, once the Communist regime was firmly in place, there was hardly any need for "genealogies" in order for it to establish its "kinship" with the revolutionary activists from the Revival epoch. With self-assured arrogance, it could now take over from them the leadership of the people (and even patronize them), as in the following triumphalist statement by Todor Pavlov:

"By serving objectively our bourgeois–democratic and national revolution, and by becoming ideologues, leaders and heroes of the peasant–plebeian, anti-feudal, democratic and national revolution in our country, Rakovski, Levski, Botev, as well as Paisii before them, became true people's ideologues, leaders, and heroes. For that reason they belong now to us, and only to us, and not to our traitorous, reactionary, and fascized Bulgarian bourgeoisie."[36]

The consolidation of the Communist regime in power gave it the opportunity to reach for non-revolutionary activists of the Revival as well. This is seen with special clarity in the controversy over Paisii—the progenitor of the Bulgarian Revival (and conceiver of the Bulgarian national idea). He was previously claimed by the nationalist bourgeois elites and became especially popular with the rise of the new nationalism in the 1930s (one strongly nationalist organization then assumed the name "Father Paisii").

The socialists/Communists were then in a weak position, judging from the fact that even a polemicist such as Bakalov was content to derive from Paisii "both lines" of the Revival (the peaceful and the revolutionary).

The regime applied a number of strategies in appropriating Paisii. To begin with, it made special efforts to discredit the right-wing nationalist organizations of the "Father Paisii" type as not just nationalist but outright fascist. Another device was the differentiation between patriotism (good, compatible with Communism) and nationalism (bad, bourgeois), so that now Paisii could be presented as something different from a "bourgeois nationalist," namely, a patriot of the people (e.g. by Hristo Hristov).[37]

The co-opting of Paisii to the leftist tradition had recourse to the tested way of establishing "genealogical" affiliations and "kinship" (direct or more distant). As mentioned in another place, for authors like Vladimir Topencharov and Hristo Hristov, Paisii is the founder of only the combat-ant–revolutionary trend of the Bulgarian Revival (not of the big bourgeois, liberal-reformist line), which passes through Sofronii of Vratsa and Neofit Bozveli, the peasant uprisings of the 1830s and 1840s, the outlaws (*haiduti*) and Rakovski, to culminate in the organized revolutionary movement of the 1860s and 1870s. In the absence of contesting it became possible to point even to the working class and the Bulgarian Communist Party as "successors and promoters" of the ideas of Paisii.[38]

Another way of drawing Paisii closer was by using a class approach, namely, by presenting him as a spokesman of the "democratic" classes such as peasants, artisans, shopkeepers and petty traders or the "laboring masses." The ideology of Paisii was (according to Hristo Hristov) not just about national liberation but also anti-feudal, that is, it called for social struggle in a certain sense (though only against feudalism).[39] Or, in a more populist manner, Paisii was presented as a port-parole of the interests of the whole people (now taken in Communist custody). The militant publicist Vladimir Topencharov devotes a special chapter to this idea in his work on Paisii, containing passages such as the following:

"Paisii stands there almost two centuries ago at the historical entrance hall of the struggle for the people's freedom—with all his hatred for the apostates and the traitors of the motherland, and all his love for the people and the motherland. The Bulgarian workers and laboring peasants—descendants of Paisii's ploughmen and land-tillers, shepherds and simple artisans—carried the struggle for the freedom of the people to a successful end with the Party at their head."

Despite such tours de force, the Communist regime discontinued some of the national holidays connected with the Revival, especially the Day of the People's Awakeners and Father Paisii's Day (as being associated with right-wing regimes), and instituted the commemoration of the national revolutionary heroes (the Days of Botev and Levski on 2 June and 19 February) and of events such as the April uprising and Liberation Day (3 March). It added specific meanings and emphases—thus Botev's Day became the "Day of Botev and of those fallen in the struggle against capitalism, fascism, and in the Fatherland's war" (i.e., World War II).[40] Official celebration of historical personalities and open-door historical conferences propagated this kind of historical "memory."

The ideologues of the Communist regime made increasing claims on the legacy of the Revival epoch, even on its non-revolutionary part. This was argued using the Leninist precept that the proletariat and its party are successors of all democratic traditions of the past, regardless of their origin, the progressive legacy of the bourgeoisie included. Taking this view, Veselin Hadzhinikolov criticized (in 1966) the appropriation of the legacy of the Revival by the Communists before 1944 as too narrow.[41] The blunt manner of putting things makes this a very interesting text. The author notes that from the very beginning the Bulgarian socialists paid the greatest attention to the personality, deeds, and legacy of Hristo Botev in various initiatives such as the celebration of Botev's Day (on the date of his heroic death, 2 June) and Botev's anniversaries, recitations of his poems, referring to him in party speeches and papers, using him in arguments regarding the present-day tasks of the proletariat and of the Socialist Party, naming party clubs after him, etc. Much less attention was paid to the April uprising or even to Levski. The lifting of Botev above all other Bulgarian revolutionaries by the Communist Party continued after World War I and the October Revolution, and later during the leftist-sectarian period of its history, already in competition with the bourgeois parties who tried in their turn to mobilize Botev's aura to nationalist goals. Conversely, persons, deeds and events not directly related to the proletariat and Marxist ideology were underestimated. Especially the democratic and revolutionary traditions, created by the peasants and the petty bourgeoisie, were neglected contrary to Lenin's injunction that required the inheriting of everything positive from the past, including what originated in non-proletarian laboring classes and even in "progressive and revolutionary circles of the dominant classes." The epic April uprising in particular was still being underrated.

This rather unfortunate state of affairs continued until the Seventh Congress of the Comintern (1935), when the Bulgarian Communist leader

Georgi Dimitrov (head of the Comintern at that time) stressed the need to utilize the entire positive legacy of the past for the purposes of class struggle. This was the turning point in the reappraisal of the cultural and revolutionary legacies toward "full utilization of all progressive and heroic traditions in the revolutionary upbringing and inspiring of the working classes." By way of appropriating the broader revolutionary–democratic ideas and deeds in general, the Communists spoke more of the April uprising, they organized readings of Vazov's poems from "The Epic of the Forgotten" and pilgrimages to Oborishte (where the date of the April uprising was decided), republished Zakhari Stoyanov's *Notes on the Bulgarian uprisings*, etc. Already during World War II Communist guerrilla brigades and detachments were given the names of Botev, Levski, and of heroes of the April uprising such as Benkovski, Bacho Kiro, and Kocho Chistemenski. But a battle had to be fought even around Botev, as fascist politicians and ideologues tried to present him as a nationalist and chauvinist (and a rightist student organization named itself after him). It was not before its victory on 9 September 1944 that the Bulgarian Communist Party could free itself entirely from the non-Leninist attitude toward the progressive legacy. In this, the party was supported by Bulgarian historians, who thus "directly combined scholarship with practice."

Thus far Veselin Hadzhinikolov, and there is little more to add. The more comprehensive and massive appropriation of the legacy of the Revival after 1944 coincides in a sense with the history of Bulgarian historical scholarship under Communism. As we have seen, during the Stalinist period the Communist Party and its historians made efforts to appropriate the revolutionary legacy of the Revival in the first place, while degrading the other (peaceful) Revival struggles and personalities to an inferior status. Legitimation by "revolution" and the initial need for an enemy (the *chorbadzhii*–bourgeoisie) are reflected in this limitation. It was only in the course of time that the regime, acting through the agency of historical scholarship, gradually appropriated (with grading and hierarchies) more and more of the legacy of the Revival, and the Revival as such, but not without first translating it in terms of revolution (social and increasingly national).

The history of the Revival, to be sure, became the terrain of a kind of scholarly dissent in the form of the affirmation of the "national" against the "national nihilism" of the early Stalinist years. As an epoch of national formation, the Revival seems naturally designated to that purpose. But one can note the growing comfort of the regime with a broader Revival legacy (though not everything) that went parallel with its claim for the extension of its social basis from a working class-based rule toward an inclusive all-people's (national) rule during mature socialism. Besides, the practical merger of the party with the state made the Communist regime increasingly into a bearer of the "state idea" (in contrast to the subversive identification of the earlier socialists with the revolutionaries of the Revival). The shift of the Communist regime itself toward nationalism also worked to increase the range of acceptable figures and political trends. Ironically, the "revisionist" efforts of many historians in fact brought new assets into the patrimony of the regime.

After the demise of Communism in a situation dominated by aspirations to join "Europe" and by liberal individualistic discourses, the Revival, with its collectivist national spirit, seems less appropriate (or politically correct) both as a stock of ideas and as a language. Initially, some references to it were made in the media, even calls for a "new revival," issuing mostly from marginal nationalist parties and organizations (e.g. *Mati Bŭlgaria*). Curiously, when the former king (later premier) Simeon II declared in May 2001 his intention to enter politics and run for election, he evoked the image of an economic and political revival of the country. But the tone of the post-Communist discourse in Bulgaria is different, and the national ideas are hardly compatible with the universalistic liberalism, the free-market globalism, and the open-door policies now prevailing. While it is true that the Revival can be stretched in a liberal democratic style, it is more easily adopted by hard-line nationalists. Hence one can make a guess that only a disappointment with the supra-national (a rejection by "Europe" in particular) may renew its actuality in the search for a source of reliance and self-assurance.

Notes

1 See Lyubomir Vladikin, *Istoriya na Tŭrnovskata konstitutsiya*. Sofia: Hristo Danov, 1936, 24–25; Radev, *Stroitelite na sŭvremenna*, iv–v.
2 Zakhari Stoyanov, *Publitsistika. Sŭchineniya*. Vol. 3, Sofia: Bŭlgarski pisatel, 1983, 60–69. While the Conservatives are exposed as *chorbadzhii*, the Liberals are presented as young, educated and progressive "sons" of the people.
3 On these struggles, in a Russophile spirit, see Petya Pachkova, *Ideinoto razvitie na pobornitsite sled Osvobozhdenieto*. Sofia: Nauka i izkustvo, 1988.
4 Ilcho Dimitrov, *Epokha 1885. Istoricheski ocherk za Sŭedinenieto na Severna i Yuzhna Bŭlgariya*. Sofia: Taliya, 1995 (first edition in 1985 under the title: *Predi 100 godini. Sŭedinenieto*).

5 Mutafchiev, "Kŭm novo vŭzrazhdane," 3–9; Mutafchiev, "Deloto i primerŭt," 333–337; Mutafchiev, "Dukh i zaveti," 197–200; Lyubomir Vladikin, "Natsionalizmŭt kato kulturno-politicheski faktor." *Prosveta* 2, no. 3 (1936): 289–304.

6 Dimitŭr Mikhalchev, "Mozhe li dneshna Bŭlgariya da se vŭrne kŭm dukha na nasheto vŭzrazhdane?" *Filosofski pregled* 11, no. 3 (1939): 330.

7 Petŭr Mutafchiev, "Dneshna Bŭlgariya i dukhŭt na nasheto Vŭzrazhdane." *Prosveta* 5, no. 10 (1940): 1169–1181, esp. 1178–1179.

8 Naiden Sheitanov, "Predosvoboditelno ili tsyalostno vŭzrazhdane." *Filosofski pregled* 9, no. 2 (1937): 183–191.

9 G. Genov, "Politicheskite lozungi na vŭzrazhdaneto." *Otes Paisii* 7, no. 10 (1934): 211–213; Georgi Konstantinov, "Zaveti na nashite vŭzrozhdentsi." *Otets Paisii* 7, no. 10 (1934): 209–210.

10 See the editorials in *Narodna otbrana*, no. 1724 (9 October 1934); no. 1725 (16 November 1934); no. 1758 (3 July 1935); no. 1762 (31 July 1935); no. 1765 (21 August 1935); no. 1766 (28 August 1935); and no. 1775 (30 October 1935). See also Vladimir Migev, *Utvŭrzhdavane na monarkho-fashistkata diktatura v Bŭlgariya, 1934–1936.* Sofia: BAN, 1977, 48.

11 On holidays and celebrations up to 1942, see the publication of the Ministry of Education *Sbornik ot otbrani okrŭzhni ot osvobozhdenieto do kraia na 1942 g.*, edited by Nikola Balabanov and Andrei Manev. Vol. 2, Sofia, 1943, 881–998. See also the study of the state school holidays by Ivan Elenkov, "Denyat na narodnite buditeli. Za funkstiite na uchilishtnite praznitsi vŭv vremeto mezhdu dvete svetovni voini." In *Simpozion ili Antichnost i humanitaristika. Izsledvaniya v chest na prof. Bogan Bogdanov*, edited by Violeta Gerdzhikova et al. Sofia: SONM-2000, 269–281.

12 "Den na narodnite buditeli (rechi na Boris Yotsov i na D. Dyulgerov)." *Uchilishten pregled* 40, nos. 9–10 (1941): 1230–1240, cit. on 1238–1239. Similarly "Den na narodnite buditeli (rech na Boris Yotsov)." *Uchilishten pregled* 41, no. 9 (1942): 1119–1124; "Den na narodnite buditeli (rech na Boris Yotsov)." *Uchilishten pregled* 42, nos. 9–10 (1943): 1168–1172.

13 "Chestvane na ottsa Paisiya (rech na Boris Yotsov)." *Uchilishten pregled* 42, no. 8 (1943): 998–1003, cit. on 1000–1001.

14 Boris Yotsov, "Naroden buditel." *Otets Paisii* 3, nos. 19–20 (1930): 287–295; A. Tsvetkov, "Nashite narodni buditeli." *Otets Paisii* 10, no. 9 (1937): 330–335.

15 K. Lambrev, "Bŭlgarskoto vŭzrazhdane i dneshnite uchilishtni ideali." *Uchilishten pregled* 38, no. 1 (1939): 3–18; Hristo Stoyanov, Vŭzpitanieto v svetlinata na natsionalniya ideal. Sofia, 1935, 55–59, 87–96; Marin Vlaikov, *Vŭzpitanieto v novata dŭrzhava.* Sofia, 1935, 16–19, 48–64, 74–87; S. Chakŭrov, "Novobŭlgarsko obrazovanie." *Uchilishten pregled*, 34, nos. 5–6 (1935): 545–578; Vasil Manov, *Uchilishteto i novata dŭrzhava.* Sofia, 1935; Damyan Dimov, "Narodnost, narodnosten chovek i obrazovanie." *Uchilishten pregled* 34, nos. 5–6 (1935): 521–544. For a number of official circulars of the Ministry of Education to this effect, see *Sbornik ot otbrani okrŭzhni.* Vol. 1, Sofia, 1943.

16 Hristo Boyadzhiev, "Sŭshtnost na natsionalnata bŭlgarska dŭrzhava i rolyata na uchitelya za izgrazhaneto i." *Uchilishten pregled* 41, no. 10 (1942): 1259–1273.

17 Ivan Hadzhiiski, "Istoricheskite koreni na nashite demokraticheski traditsii." In Hadzhiiski, *Sŭchineniya v dva toma.* Vol. 1, 85–99 (first published in 1937).

18 Simeon Radev, *Stroitelite na sŭvremenna.* Vol. 1, VII–XI.

19 Ivan Snegarov, *Natsionalno i obshtestveno znachenie na bŭlgarskite tsŭrkovni borbi.* Sofia: Kuzman Katsarov, 1920, 33–34.

20 Shishmanov, "Uvod v istoriyata," 69–70.

21 Konstantin Gŭlŭbov, "Psikhlogiya na bŭlgarina." *Bŭlgarska misŭl*, 9, no. 2 (1934): 109–119.
22 Penev, *Istoriya na novata*. Vol. 1,161–197; Anton Strashimirov, *Kniga za bŭlgarite*. Sofia, 1918, 98–99; Todor Panov, *Psikhologiya na bŭlgarskiya narod*. Sofia, 1914, 194–195; Nikola Krŭstnikov, *Opit za psikhologicheski analiz na nashiya obshtestven zhivot*. Sofia, 1922, 29–34; Naiden Sheitanov, "Dukhŭt na otritsanie u bŭlgarina." *Filosofski pregled* 5, no. 2 (1933): 128–141.
23 Stoyan Mikhailovski, "Kak zapadat i se provalyat dŭrzhavite." In Mikhailovski, *Neizdadeni sŭchineniya*. Vol. 1, Sofia, 1940.
24 Marko Semov, *Dushevnost i otselyavane. Razmisli za haraktera na nashiya narod*. Plovdiv: Hristo Danov, 1982, 73–132; Semov, *Bŭlgarinŭt–poznat i nepoznat*. Sofia: Voenno izdatelstvo, 68–112. Interestingly, the author points to a "capacity for survival" as the basic trait of "the Bulgarian."
25 Toncho Zhechev, "Ivan Hadzhiiski i nie." In Zhechev, *Istoriya i literatura*. Sofia: Bŭlgarski pisatel, 1982, 468–483, esp. 474–476 (first published in 1966).
26 Genchev, *Bŭlgarsko vŭzrazhdane*, 141, 318–319.
27 Blagoev, "Iz vŭtreshen pregled," 150–151.
28 Bakalov, *Zavetite na bŭlgarskoto*.
29 Bakalov, *Nashite revolyutsioneri*, 4–5, 42 (cit. on 5).
30 Bakalov, *Nashite revolyutsioneri*, 2, 13–16, 22–23.
31 Bakalov, *Nashite revolyutsioneri*, 29.
32 Bakalov, "Dvete linii," 5–7. Also Natan, in his foreword to Bakalov, *Izbrani istoricheski*, 19–20.
33 Andonov, *Iz spomenite mi ot tursko*, 6–7.
34 For example, Kosta Veselinov, *Bortsi za natsionalna svoboda*. Sofia, 1940, 19–24.
35 Natan, *Bŭlgarskoto vŭzrazhdane*, 483–489.
36 Pavlov, "Za marksicheska istoriya," 356–357.
37 Hristov, *Paisii Hilendarski*, 305.
38 Dimitŭr Kosev, "Za ideologiyata na Paisii," 30.
39 Hristov, *Paisii Hilendarski*, 310, 316.
40 On public (or in fact state) holidays under socialism, see the strongly ideological account by Petko Yanev, *Traditsionni i novi praznitsi*. Sofia: OF, 1970, 53–54; Nikolai Mizov, *Praznitsite kato obshtestveno yavlenie*. Sofia: BKP, 1966, 95–100.
41 Veselin Hadzhinikolov, "Traditsiite na Aprilskoto vŭstanie i Bŭlgarskata komunisticheska partiya." In *Aprilskoto vŭstanie*, 221–242.

The Bulgarian Revival as a National Myth

The Revival as an epoch of national formation and liberation struggles functions for the Bulgarians as a founding myth, a myth about the birth of the nation and its entering into the modern world. This has far-reaching implications for historical scholarship. To begin with, the Revival is presented in a bright, cheerful, and optimistic tonality. It is conceived of in organic metaphors (taken from its own self-representation) as a "rebirth," a kind of childhood and youth of the Bulgarian people, an epoch of accelerated maturing and the accumulation of experience. In contrast to the preceding existence that passed in a "slumber," the Revival is an "awakening," followed by a quickening of the pace of development, a dynamic epoch of upsurge and advance in all spheres of life. It is flanked by the darkness of the "yoke" from one side, in "downwards" direction. On the other side—in "upwards" direction—is the loss of innocence after independence, that is, the entry into an age of crude political strife and the crass pragmatism of "primitive accumulation" as well as the dissipation of national energies in unsuccessful unification wars and national catastrophes. The darkness before and after is condensed, so that the Revival may shine in radiant light. The halo enveloping it is reflected in numerous sublime statements in fiction but also in professional historical scholarship.[1]

As a "birth" (or at least a "rebirth") of the Bulgarians, the epoch plays a major role in the building of Bulgarian self-identity and the anchoring of the collective "we." The identity engendered here presents the highest and most idealized portrait of the nation. It is composed of virtues and deeds of valor—charity, pure idealism, self-abnegation, heroism and self-sacrifice—all performed for the people and the motherland. The best of the nation is personified in its most worthy "sons" (more rarely "daughters") that build up the "pantheon" of national heroes. The Bulgarian nation of any time may thus look at itself in the mirror of its highest and rarest, not in its mass (average) or lower element. It can feel proud of this image of itself and use it as a source of national dignity. In fact, the embedding of the positive national identity in the Revival obstructs a more critical look at the epoch thus sanctified. The attitude toward it remains sentimental and largely "romanticized," which is true also of most professional scholarship, even if it pretends to have overcome the earlier "romanticism."

The men of the Revival, and the revolutionaries in particular, are instituted as national heroes, who had dedicated their life to the struggle against foreign domination and for national independence. In this way they bring nation and state together, legitimating the nation-state. At the same time they are model personalities, an outgrowth (emanation) of the people, the highest embodiment of the nation. Monuments and mausoleums have been erected in their honor (and in honor of the Russian soldiers who fell in the fight for Bulgarian liberation). Dedicated to these heroes are annual commemorations (on the dates of their birth or death), the celebration of anniversaries, official state holidays, etc. The solemn rhetoric and ritual, as well as plastic representations in paintings and monuments, serve to convert abstract national ideas into tangible experience and thus reproduce the national consciousness among the present-day generations.[2]

The Revival has a double temporality. As a historical epoch, it is localized in the past as a period of the linear historical time-events. But it also exists in parallel transcendence of the present, of any present. The co-present status of this epoch derives from its sanctification and its being chosen as a seat for national heroes and national virtues. It is as if the heroes look down from "above" and watch their co-nationals (and what they are doing with the deed they began) with care and concern; the transcendence of the Revival opens up to the stream of profane everyday life during moments of national self-celebration. Unlike epochs that the Bulgarians want to see harmlessly isolated from the present and forgotten (e.g., the first centuries of the Ottoman "yoke"), the Revival is often evoked as a source of confidence, strength, purity, and edifying examples.[3]

The epochs that followed the Revival did not live up to its promise. The potential was scattered in pursuit of chimerical national goals, and economic development was disappointing. At least this is the prevailing mood among Bulgarian historians and the broader public (hardly changed by the Communist reference to the "bright future"). Hence the idealization of the Revival as some "lost paradise" (before the Fall) containing a host of opportunities and possible developments. The "irrepressible nostalgia" for this "most Bulgarian time" may be interpreted somewhat poetically as a yearning for the primordial completeness of Being, when aesthetics and pragmatics, Art and Life, Word and Deed were one—as in the feat of Botev.[4] Historians, intellectuals, and "time diagnosticians" have aspired to see the Revival continued, emulated, somehow repeated, so that the degraded present will be regenerated and renewed through the purifying and empowering contact with its spirit. The Revival is elaborated into a repository of all sorts of self-grown "authentic" ethnic and cultural contents—values, traditions, people's virtues, etc. The revivalist "spirit" of pure patriotism, devotion to the cause, and self-sacrifice for the people and the motherland, etc. is evoked to breath faith and reassurance in adverse times. Politicians and public figures of all colors and persuasions have referred to the national Revival, and so have intellectuals with various purposes—affirmative (to call forth pride), critical (a negative comparison with present-day realities, to decry the sullying of the ideals), or moralizing (calls for disinterested idealism, for devotion to public service, etc.). The very term is generalized into the attribute "revivalist," used with a certain loftiness of style in historical fiction and political journalism, for example in phrases such as "revivalist patriots," "revivalist spirit," "revivalist fullness of life," etc.[5]

In actual fact, the political mobilization of the Revival for nationalist objectives or to provide a rationale for authoritarian and totalitarian regimes has prevailed over its more sublime uses. Various political forces have made use of the Revival according to their convenience and selectively formulated its "legacy," which they claimed as they looked to it for "forerunners" (or "predecessors"), pretending to be their "heirs" and to follow their "bequests" or learn from their "lessons." By manipulations such as selection and condensing, and through outright falsification, the Revival was shaped into generalized visions or images. Such opposite poles as republicanism or monarchism, democracy or authoritarianism have all been derived from the epoch, which has been used both to justify an established order and to agitate for revolutionary change. All in all, it has been engaged in a kind of "politics of time"—in attempts to influence the present and the future of Bulgarian society.

The Revival is a part, and in fact the major part, of the Grand (i.e., "high" and official) historical narrative, whose protagonist is the Bulgarian people—a collective hero and martyr in the historical drama. The national epic has the formation of the nation and its struggles for freedom as its central meaning. The social aspect usually comes second. This decides the relevance of the events and actors—that is, what and who is worthy of entering the story, and what and who is not; what is a "historical" happening and what is of little import and can be omitted. The narrative of "great deeds" privileges certain themes and leaves others without attention. Such privileged themes are the spread of education and knowledge, the church struggles, and especially the armed revolts. The struggles, along with the heroism and martyrdom they involved, occupy the central place and they are all interpreted in a national sense. Under the magnifying glass of an interest like this, even the smallest local rising, undertaken for whatever reasons, becomes a fight for national liberation (or acquires such a meaning from the context). Such an extreme is the inclusion of the semi-brigand outlaws (*haiduti*) if not as outright national revolutionaries at least as their "spontaneous" forerunners in avenging the people's suffering.[6] At the same time, the narrative contains characteristic amnesia and *lacunae*, and peaceful times and aspects of life are barely touched upon. The reading public is expected to forget about the existence of the all-absorbing and not quite heroic everyday life, otherwise so familiar to it from experience.

Furthermore, the narrative is deeply partial toward "us" and biased against the "others" (Turks, Greeks) or "the other among us" (Bulgarians that assimilated as Greeks or converted to Islam, *chorbadzhii*). Sharp lines, black and white colors, emotionally condensed statements are used in drawing the picture. The usual device is to generalize about collective heroes or villains—nations, classes, political trends, etc., and to suppress contradictory facts as "anomalous"[7]—for example, worthy *chorbadzhii*, Turks who showed kindness to Bulgarians or Bulgarian brigands that robbed their own countrymen.[8] The front lines should be clearly delineated according to ethnic (or class) criteria. Anomalous and abnormal from this point of view are Muslim Bulgarians (*pomaks*), or Bulgarian collaborators with the Turks. Also anomalous is the "Time of troubles" (the second half of the eighteenth century), with the impossible sorting out of good and evil according to nationality, because the peaceful Turkish population suffered in the same way at the hands of robber bands (*kŭrdzhalii*, *daalii*) among whom there were Bulgarians (e.g., the famous or infamous brigand leader Indzhe).

The historical scholarship of the Revival has as its (tacit) objective to reproduce the national identity by establishing a continuity across time between "forefathers" and "descendants." Besides being the protagonist of the historical drama, "the people" is the addressee of the historical message, the reader of its own past exploits and suffering. In a characteristic doubling, the narrative of how the Bulgarian nation came to be born during the Revival becomes an instrument for the reproduction of national consciousness at any time through the national upbringing of the younger generations (in schools and elsewhere). It is to be noted that there are no clear-cut boundaries between supposedly "serious" professional history writing, popular historical expositions, and high-school textbooks in this respect.[9] What is supposedly dictated by the pedagogical needs of the school applies to most academic writing as well. And it is precisely university specialists who are the authors of lecture courses for wider audiences, and of textbooks. A "double game" is being played in the sense that ideas supposedly "overcome" in the specialized historical literature (e.g. the myth of the "dark ages," forced conversion to Islam *en masse*, the *chorbadzhii* as an internal enemy, etc.) are being reproduced time and again in history textbooks for high schools and even find their way into university courses,[10] passing from there into the "collective consciousness" as undoubted truths.

Not that it is impossible to offer an ideologically more neutral and scholarly, distanced treatment of the epoch of the Revival, the phenomenon of the nation (or class) included, and such examples have been provided. An analytical treatment that goes into subtle differentiation, attention to empirical detail, "exceptions" from biased expectations, and the relativizing practice of contextualization all have the effect of diluting the hard-line theses and blurring the clear-cut fronts; dramatism is downplayed if "prosaic" but curious everyday matters are included. But the narrative is then in discord with the attitudes and expectations of most historians and of the wider readership or audience formed in a national spirit; nor does it serve the national purpose with which national historiography is entrusted by the state in the first place. Rather than being epistemological, the problem is actually one of tasks and intentions. Acting in the same direction is the feeling of personal significance that many scholars acquire in servicing national needs and tending the fire around their subject.

In sum, it is the above-mentioned need to reproduce the national identity and legitimate Bulgarian statehood that stand substantially in the way and obstruct the "cooling down" of the subject matter and its shift toward the "purely academic." Bulgarian historical scholarship on the Revival will most probably remain, in the foreseeable future, divided between the academic and the patriotic, the scholarly and the romantic, and will, in fact, present a mixture of both.

Notes

1 Just some examples are Mishev, *Nachalo na bŭlgarskata*, 10; Arnaudov, "Dukh i nasoki," 191, 229; Mutafchiev, "Dukh i zaveti," 197–200; Bakalov, *Bŭlgarskoto natsionalno-revolyutsionno*, 158; Natan, *Ikonomicheska istoriya*, v; Konstantin Kosev, *Kratka
   istoriya*, 7, 11. There is full agreement between nationalist and leftist authors in this
   respect.
2 Anthony Smith, *National Identity*. London: Penguin Books, 1991, 77.
3 For example by Mutafchiev, "Dukh i zaveti," 197–200; Mishev, *Nachalo na bŭlgarskata*, 10; Arnaudov, "Dukh i nasoki," 191, 229; Konstantin Kosev, *Kratka istoriya*,
   11–12. Also in the right-wing discourse of the 1930s.
4 Peleva, *Ideologŭt na natsiyata*, 208–209.
5 Some value uses of the term are given in Konev, *Bŭlgarskoto vŭzrazhdane i prosveshtenieto*. Vol. 1, 48–52.
6 For example Bistra Tsvetkova, *Haidutstvoto v bŭlgarskite zemi prez XV–VIII vek*. Vol. 1,
   Sofia: Nauka i izkustvo, 1971, 7–12.
7 Various strategies for imposing conceptual order upon reality are described by Mary
   Douglas, *Purity and Danger. An Analysis of the Concepts of Pollution and Taboo*. London: Routledge, 1996, 2–3, 36–41.
8 Such "borderline" cases of "good Turks" and "bad Bulgarians" are mentioned in
   memoirs, e.g. Kostentsev, *Spomeni*, 95–96, 137–141.
9 The boundaries are entirely blurred by authors such as Nadezhda Dragova, who use
   both a more "scholarly" style and write popularizing historical fiction. See Dragova,
   Otets Paisii. Patriarkh na bŭlgarskoto vŭzrazhdane. Stara Zagora: Znanie, 1994; *Kniga
   za Paisii*. Sofia: Bŭlgarski pisatel, 1972; *Probuzdane*. Sofia: OF, 1963.
10 For a recent picture of the Ottoman domination in the spirit of the "dark ages," see
   Konstantin Kosev, *Kratka istoriya*, 23–26, 28, 30–32.

GLOSSARY

aba	= woolen cloth
aga	= Muslim landowner
ayans	= notables, landed aristocracy in the late Ottoman Empire
bakali	= shopkeepers
beglikchii	= collectors of the tax on sheep (*beglik*)
bey	= Muslim landowner
chetniks	= members of an armed band (*cheta*)
chiflik	= big land estate
chitalishte	= reading-room
chorbadzhiya (pl. *chorbadzhii*)	= traditional Bulgarian notables, mediators between the Turkish authorities and the population
dzhelepi	= traders in sheep
esnaf	= guild of craftsmen
Exarchate	= the autonomous Bulgarian Church
gaitan	= decorative braid
gospodarlŭk	= a type of land estate (and the arrangement for the running of it)
haiduti	= outlaws
has	= the estates of the sultan and other magnates
Hatt-i-Humayun	= reform act of 1856
Hatt-i-Sherif	= reform act of 1839
hŭshove	= outcasts and exiles
iltizam	= the leasing out of crown lands to tax farmers
ispolitsa	= a certain kind of sharecropping arrangement
Janissaries	= elite infantry corps in the Ottoman Empire
kesim	= a certain kind of sharecropping arrangement

kiradzhii	=	ambulant traders
komiti (*komitadzhi*)	=	members of a secret revolutionary organization ("secret committee")
kŭrdzhalii	=	brigands, robber gangs
millet system	=	representation and organization according to faith in the Ottoman Empire
mukataa	=	the leasing out of crown lands to tax farmers
mülk	=	unconditional land grant
narodniki	=	Russian populists
obshtina	=	local community and self-government, commune
pasha	=	high ranking Ottoman official
Phanariots	=	rich Greeks from the Phanar district in Istanbul
Pomaks	=	Muslim Bulgarians
pomeschiki	=	big landowners in Russia before the revolution
raeti	=	free peasant smallholders
reaya (or raya)	=	flock, rural and urban non-Muslim producers
sipahi	=	Ottoman feudal cavalryman, owner of (*timar*) fief
Tanzimat	=	the reform era (1839–1856) in the Ottoman Empire
timar	=	mostly military land fief
vakf	=	pious (Muslim) endowment, untaxable property belonging to Muslim religious institutions
vilayet	=	large administrative unit in the Ottoman Empire

A NOTE ON TRANSLITERATION

Bulgarian words have been transliterated according to a modified Library of Congress system.

ts	–	*Ts*onev as in *ts*ar
ŭ	–	Dimit*ŭ*r as in "m*o*ney"
yu	–	*Yu*ri as in "*u*nion"
ya	–	Ili*ya* as in "*ya*rd"
zh	–	*Zh*echev as in "vi*si*on"
dzh	–	Un*dzh*iev as in "*G*eorge"

However, I have retained the spelling of well-known geographical names (such as Sofia, pronounced Sofiya) and the accepted spellings of Serbo-Croat and Russian names and words (e.g., Dositej Obradović, Jovan Rajić, "Voprosy Istorii").

BIBLIOGRAPHY

Adanir, Fikret. "Tradition and Rural Change in Southeastern Europe during Ottoman Rule." In *The Origins of Backwardness in Eastern Europe*, edited by Daniel Chirot. Berkeley–Los Angeles–Oxford: University of California Press, 1989, 131–176.

Aleksiev, Nikola. "Obrazŭt na ottsa Paisiya" (Father Paisii's image). *Otets Paisii* 12, no. 10 (1939): 444–446.

Anderson, Benedict. *Imagined Communities*. Thetford, Norfolk, 1983.

Andonov, Ivan. *Iz spomenite mi ot tursko vreme* (My recollections from the times under the Turks). Plovdiv, 1927.

Angelov, Bozhan. *Bŭlgarska literatura. Chast 2. Istoricheski ocherk na novata bŭlgarska literatura ot Paisiya do dnes* (Bulgarian literature. Part 2. Historical review of the new Bulgarian literature from Paisii until the present). Sofia, 1923.

Aprilov, Vasil. Dopŭlnenie kŭm knigata "Dennitsa na novobŭlgarskoto obrazovanie" (Addition to the book "Dawn of the new Bulgarian education.") In Aprilov, *Sŭchineniya*. Sofia: Bŭlgarski pisatel, 1968, 148–189. (Originally in Russian: Dopolnenie k knige "Dennitsa novo-bolgarskago obrazovaniya.") In Aprilov, Sŭbrani Sŭchineniya. Sofia, 1940, 165–198.

Aprilskoto vŭstanie, 1876–1966 (The April uprising, 1876–1966), edited by Ivan Undzhiev et al. Sofia: BAN, 1966.

Aretov, Nikolai. *Bŭlgarskoto vŭzrazhdane i Evropa* (The Bulgarian Revival and Europe). Sofia: Kralitsa Mab, 1995.

Arkhiv na Vŭzrazhdaneto (Archive of the Revival), edited by Dimitŭr Strashimirov. Vol. 1, Sofia, 1908.

Arnaudov, Mikhail. *Bŭlgarsko vŭzrazhdane* (The Bulgarian Revival). Sofia: Bŭlgarska misŭl, 1941.

Arnaudov, Mikhail. *Paisii Hilendarski (1722–1798)*. Sofia: Hemus, 1942.

Arnaudov, Mikhail. "Dukh i nasoki na bŭlgarskoto vŭzrazhdane" (Spirit and trends of the Bulgarian Revival). In *Prez vekovete*, edited by Krŭstyu Mitev. Sofia: Bŭlgarska istoricheska biblioteka, 1938, 190–191.

Arnaudov, Mikhail. "Paisii Hilendarski." In Arnaudov, *Tvortsi na bŭlgarskoto vŭzrazhdane*. Vol. 1, Sofia: Nauka i izkustvo 1969, 7–61 (first edition in 1942).

Atanasov, Shteryu. *Koi sa bili kŭrdzhaliite i protiv kogo sa se borili te?* (Who were the Kŭrdzhalii and whom did they fight?). Sofia: Dŭrzhavno izdatelstvo, 1954.

Bakalov, Georgi. *Nashite revolyutsioneri. Rakovski, Levski, Botev* (Our revolutionaries. Rakovski. Levski. Botev). Sofia, 1924.

Bakalov, Georgi. *G. S. Rakovski*. Sofia, 1934.

Bakalov, Georgi. *Hristo Botev*. Sofia, 1934.

Bakalov, Georgi. *Bŭlgarskoto natsionalno-revolyutsionno dvizhenie. Ocherki* (The Bulgarian national-revolutionary movement. Sketches). Sofia, 1937.

Bakalov, Georgi. *Zavetite na bŭlgarskoto vŭzrazhdane.* (The legacy of the Bulgarian Revival). Sofia, 1937.

Bakalov, Georgi. *Aprilskoto vŭstanie i Benkovski* (The April uprising and Benkovski). Sofia, 1938.

Bakalov, Georgi. "Dvete linii v Bŭlgarskoto vŭzrazhdane" (The two lines in the Bulgarian Revival). In Bakalov, *Bŭlgarskoto natsionalno-revolyutsionno,* 3–7.

Bakalov, Georgi. "Otets Paisii. Deloto na Paisii" (Father Paisii. The Deed of Father Paisii). In Bakalov, *Izbrani istoricheski proizvedeniya.* Sofia: Nauka i izkustvo, 1960, 33–37.

Balabanov, Marko. *Filosofski i sotsiologicheski sŭchineniya* (Philosophical and sociological works). Sofia: Nauka i izkustvo, 1986.

Balabanov, Marko. "Bŭlgarskii napredŭk" (Bulgarian progress). *Chitalishte* 1, no. 11 (1870/71); no. 12 (1870/71). Reprinted in Balabanov, *Filosofski i sotsiologicheski,* 108–124.

Balabanov, Marko. "Nachaloto na narodnostta" (The beginnings of nationality). *Vek,* no. 45 (15 November 1875). Reprinted in Balabanov, *Filosofski i sotsiologicheski,* 135–140.

Balabanov, Marko. "Narodno bitie" (The people's way of life). *Vek,* no. 26 (6 July 1874). Reprinted in Balabanov, *Filosofski i sotsiologicheski,* 141–145

Balabanov, Marko. "Po narodnoto probuzhdane" (On the people's awakening). *Periodichesko spisanie na Bŭlgarskoto Knizhovno Druzhestvo.* 16 (1905): 577–598.

Balabanov, Marko. "Politikata na narodite v tursko" (The politics of the peoples under the Turks). In Balabanov, *Filosofski i sotsiologicheski,* 219–224.

Balabanov, Marko. "Sŭvremenniyat dukh na bŭlgarskiya narod" (The contemporary spirit of the Bulgarian people). *XIX vek,* no. 11 (13 March 1876). Reprinted in Balabanov, *Filosofski i sotsiologicheski,* 214–224.

Balan, Aleksandŭr. "Otkoga da zapochvame novata si knizhnina?" (From when should we date our new literature?). *Bŭlgarska misŭl* 8, no. 1 (1933).

Balan, Aleksandŭr. "Pochetŭk na stara i nova bŭlgarska knizhnina" (Beginnings of old and new Bulgarian literature). *Uchilishten pregled* 20, nos. 1–3 (1921): 1–18.

Bendix, Reinhard. "Tradition and Modernity Reconsidered." In *Comparative Studies in Society and History* 9, no. 3 (1967): 318–344.

Bitsilli, Petŭr. "Shto e natsiia?" (What is a nation?) *Rodina* 2, no. 1 (1939): 150–164.

Black, Cyril. *The Dynamics of Modernization. A Study in Comparative History.* New York–Evanston–London: Harper & Row, 1966.

Blagoev, Dimitŭr. "Hristo Botev kato poet i zhurnalist" (Hristo Botev as poet and journalist). In Blagoev, *Za Bŭlgarskoto vŭzrazhdane,* 129–145 (first published in 1897).

Blagoev, Dimitŭr. "Hristo Botev." In Blagoev, *Za Bŭlgarskoto vŭzrazhdane,* edited by D. Raikov. Sofia: Partizdat 1982, 86–103 (the work is dated 1887).

Blagoev, Dimitŭr. "Iz Vŭtreshen pregled" (Chronicle of domestic events). In Blagoev, *Za Bŭlgarskoto vŭzrazhdane,* 146–150 (first published in 1898).

Blagoev, Dimitŭr. "Prinos kŭm istoriyata na sotsializma v Bŭlgaria" (Contribution to the history of socialism in Bulgaria). In: Blagoev, *Izbrani istoricheski sŭchineniya v dva toma,* edited by Mariya Veleva. Vol. 1, Sofia: Nauka i izkustvo, 1985, 180–556. The work appeared in 1906.

Blŭskov, Iliya. *Spomeni* (Memoirs), edited by Docho Lekov. Sofia: Otechestven front, 1976 (the memoirs were written in 1907–1917).

Bobchev, Stefan. "Elensko prez vreme na turskoto vladichestvo" (Elensko in the times of Turkish Rule). In *Elenski sbornik.* Vol. 2. Sofia, 1938, 1–108.

Bochev, Stefan. "Kapitalizmŭt v Bŭlgariya" (Capitalism in Bulgaria). *Spisanie na bŭlgarskoto ikonomichesko druzhestvo* 30, no. 2 (1931): 65–78.

Boneva, Vera. *Istoricheski etyudi po Bŭlgarsko vŭzrazhdane.* (Historical studies on the Bulgarian Revival). Veliko Tŭrnovo,1997.

Boneva, Vera. "Ivan Kasabov kato teoretik na vŭzrozhdenskiya revolyutsionen liberalizŭm." (Ivan Kasabov as theoretician of revolutionary liberalism during the Revival). In Boneva, *Istoricheski etyudi,* 59–69.

Boyadzhiev, Hristo. "Sŭshtnost na natsionalnata bŭlgarska dŭrzhava i rolyata na uchitelya za izgrazhaneto i" (The essence of the Bulgarian nation-state and the role of the teachers in building it). *Uchilishten pregled* 41, no. 10 (1942): 1259–1273.

Bozveliev, K. *Spomeni* (Memoirs). Vol. 1, Kazanlŭk, 1942.

Bŭlgariya 1000 godini (927–1927) (Bulgaria's 1000 years, 927–1927). Sofia: Ministerstvo na narodnata prosveta, 1930.

Bŭlgarskata natsiya prez Vŭzrahzdaneto (The Bulgarian nation during the Revival), edited by Hristo Hristov. Vol. 1, Sofia: BAN, 1980; Vol. 2, Sofia: BAN, 1989.

Bŭlgarskata vŭzrozhdenska inteligentsiya. Entsiklopediya (The Bulgarian intelligentsia during the Revival. Encyclopedia), edited by Nikolai Genchev and Krassimira Daskalova. Sofia: Petŭr Beron, 1988.

Burmov, Aleksandŭr. *Izbrani proizvedeniya v tri toma* (Selected works in three volumes). Sofia: BAN, 1974–1976.

Burmov, Aleksandŭr. "Borba za ideino-revolyutsionna chistota v BRTsK v Bukuresht (1869–1871)" (The struggle for ideological revolutionary purity in BRTsK in Bucharest, 1869–1871). In Burmov, *Izbrani proizvedeniya.* Vol. 2, 201–218 (first published in 1966).

Burmov, Aleksandŭr. "BRTsK (1868–1877)." In Burmov, *Izbrani proizvedeniya,* 9–114 (first published in 1943).

Burmov, Aleksandŭr. "Bŭlgarskoto natsionalno-revolyutsionno dvizhenie i bŭlgarskata emigratsionna burzhoaziya prez 1867–1869 g" (The Bulgarian national-revolutionary movement and the Bulgarian émigré bourgeoisie in 1867–1869). In Burmov, *Izbrani proizvedeniya.* Vol. 2, 140–164 (first published in 1961).

Burmov, Aleksandŭr. "Marin Drinov kato istorik na Bŭlgariya" (Marin Drinov as a historian of Bulgaria). In *Izsledvaniya v chest na Marin Drinov.* Sofia: BAN, 1960, 105–118.

Burmov, Todor. *Bŭlgaro-grŭtskata tsŭrkovna raspra* (The Bulgarian–Greek church controversy). Sofia, 1885.

Buzhazhki, Evlogi. "Burzhoazno-fashistki falshifikatsii na bŭlgarskoto natsionalno-revolyutsionno dvizhenie" (Bourgeois-fascist falsifications of the Bulgarian national-revolutionary movement). *Istoricheski pregled* 8, no. 3 (1951/52).

Buzhahzki, Evlogi. "Politicheskata formula na burzhoaziyata za 'mnimo bŭlgarsko vŭstanie' prez 1876 g." (The political formula of the bourgeoisie for a "faked Bulgarian uprising" in 1876). *Vekove* 15, no. 3 (1986): 5–20.

Chakŭrov, St. "Novobŭlgarsko obrazovanie" (New Bulgarian education). *Uchilishten pregled,* 34, nos. 5–6 (1935): 545–578.

Chervenkov, Vŭlko. "Kŭm 80–godishninata ot gibelta na Levski" (Toward the eightieth anniversary of Levski's death). *Novo vreme* 29, no. 2 (1953): 32–37. The speech was first published in *Rabotnichesko delo,* no. 49 (18 February 1953).

"Chestvane na ottsa Paisiya (rech na Boris Yotsov)" (Celebration of Father Paisii–Speech by Boris Yotsov). *Uchilishten pregled* 42, no. 8 (1943): 998–1003.

Chilingirov, Stiliyan. *Bŭlgarskite chitalishta predi osvobozhdenieto. Prinos vŭrkhu istoriyata na bŭlgarskoto vŭzrazhdane* (The Bulgarian reading rooms before the liberation. Contribution to the history of the Bulgarian Revival). Sofia, 1930.

Clarke, James. "Father Paisii and Bulgarian History." In Clarke, *The Pen and the Sword,* edited by Dennis Hupchick. East European Monographs. Boulder, New York: Columbia University Press, 1988, 87–111.

Crampton, Richard. *A Concise History of Modern Bulgaria.* Cambridge University Press, 1977.

Crampton, Richard. *A Short History of Modern Bulgaria.* Cambridge University Press, 1987.

Damyanova, Tsveta. "Nyakoi aspekti na renesansoviya mirogled–skhodstva i razlichiya s Bŭlgarskoto vŭzrazhdane" (Some aspects of the Renaissance world-view–Similarities to and differences from the Bulgarian Revival). *Literaturna misŭl* 22, no. 5 (1978): 106–119.

Danova, Nadya. *Konstantin Georgi Fotinov v kulturnoto i ideino-politichesko razvitie na Balkanite prez XIX vek* (Konstantin Georgi Fotinov in the cultural and ideological-political development of the Balkans during the nineteenth century). Sofia: BAN, 1994.

Daskalov, Roumen. *Images of Europe: A Glance from the Periphery.* Working Paper, European University Institute, SPS, 94/8, 1994.

Daskalov, Roumen. "Natsiya, natsionalna ideya i nie" (Nation, national idea, and us). In Daskalov, *Mezhdu Iztoka i Zapada. Bŭlgarski kulturni dilemi.* Sofia: LIK, 1998, 187–225.

Daskalov, Roumen. "Transformations of the East European Intelligentsia: Reflections on the Bulgarian Case." *East European Politics and Societies* 10, no. 1 (1996): 46–84.

Daskalova, Krassimira. *Bŭlgarskiyat uchitel prez Vŭzrazhdaneto* (The Bulgarian teacher during the Revival). Sofia: Universitetsko izdatelstvo "Kliment Ohridski," 1997.

Daskalova, Krassimira. *Gramotnost, knizhnina, chitateli i chetene v Bŭlgariya na prekhoda kŭm modernoto vreme.* (Literacy, literature, readers and reading in Bulgaria in the transition to modernity). Sofia: LIK, 1999.

Davidova, Vera. *Istoriya na zdraveopazvaneto v Bŭlgariya. Ochertsi* (History of healthcare in Bulgaria). Sofia: Nauka i izkustvo, 1956 (translated from Russian).

"Den na narodnite buditeli (rech na Boris Yotsov)" (Day of the People's Awakeners–Speech by Boris Yotsov). *Uchilishten pregled* 41, no. 9 (1942):1119–1124.

"Den na narodnite buditeli (rech na Boris Yotsov)" (Day of the People's Awakeners–Speech by Boris Yotsov). *Uchilishten pregled* 42, nos. 9–10 (1943): 1168–1172.

"Den na narodnite buditeli (rechi na Boris Yotsov i na D. Dyulgerov)" (Day of the People's Awakeners–Speech by Boris Yotsov and D. Dyulgerov). *Uchilishten pregled* 40, nos. 9–10 (1941): 1230–1240.

"Den na Ottsa Paisiya" (Day of Father Paisii). *Uchilishten pregled* 40 (1941): 1008–1111.

Derzhavin, Nikolai. *Istoriya Bolgarii* (History of Bulgaria). Vol. 4, Moscow–Leningrad: Izdatel'stvo Akademii Nauk SSSR, 1948.

Derzhavin, Nikolai. "Paisii Hilendarskii i ego 'Istoriia Slavenobolgarskaia', 1762" (Paisii Hilendarski and his "Slavonic–Bulgarian history"). In Derzhavin, *Sbornik stat'ei i issledovanii v oblasti slavianskoi filologii.* Moscow: Izdatel'stvo Akademii Nauk SSSR, 1941, 63–124.

Dimitrov, Angel. *Uchilishteto, progresŭt i natsionalnata revolyutsiya. Bŭlgarskoto uchilishte prez vŭzrazhdaneto.* (Schools, progress and the national revolution. The Bulgarian schools during the Revival). Sofia: BAN, 1987.

Dimitrov, Angel. *Knizharyat, kogoto narichakha ministŭr. Biografichen ocherk za Hristo G. Danov* (The book trader who was called minister. A biography of Hristo G. Danov). Plovdiv: Hristo G. Danov, 1988.

Dimitrov, Ilcho. *Epokha 1885. Istoricheski ocherk za Sŭedinenieto na Severna i Yuzhna Bŭlgariya* (Epoch 1885. A historical study of the unification between northern and southern Bulgaria). Sofia: Taliya, 1995 (first edition in 1985 under the title: *Predi 100 godini. Sŭedinenieto*).

Dimitrov, Mikhail. *Hristo Botev. Idei. Lichnost. Tvorchestvo* (Hristo Botev. Ideas. Personality. Oeuvre). Sofia: Novo Uchilishte, 1919.

Dimitrov, Mikhail. *Lichnostta na Botev*. (The personality of Botev). Sofia, 1938.

Dimitrov, Strashimir and Krŭstyu Manchev. *Istoriya na balkanskite narodi, XV–XIX vek* (History of the Balkan peoples, fifteenth to nineteenth centuries). Sofia: Nauka i izkustvo, 1971.

Dimitrov, Strashimir. *Formirane na bŭlgarskata natsiya*. (Formation of the Bulgarian nation). Sofia: OF, 1980.

Dimitrov, Strashimir. "Chiflishkoto stopanstvo prez 50–te i 70–te godini na XIX vek" (The *chiflik* economy in the 50s and the 70s of the nineteenth century). *Istoricheski pregled*, 11, no. 2 (1955): 3–34.

Dimitrov, Strashimir. "Kŭm vŭprosa za otmenyavaneto na spakhiiskata sistema v bŭlgarskite zemi" (The problem of the dismantling of the *sipahi* system in the Bulgarian lands). *Istoricheski pregled* 12, no. 6 (1956): 27–58.

Dimitrov, Strashimir. "Predgovor" (Foreword). In Hristo Stambolski, *Avtobiografiya. Dnevnitsi. Spomeni*, 5–15.

Dimitrov, Strashimir. "Za agrarnite otnosheniya v Bŭlgariya prez XVIII vek" (On agrarian relations in Bulgaria during the eighteenth century). In *Paisii Hilendarski i negovata*, 129–165.

Dimov, Damyan. "Narodnost, narodnosten chovek i obrazovanie" (Nation, man of the people, and education). *Uchilishten pregled* 34, nos. 5–6 (1935): 521–544.

Dinekov, Petŭr. *Pŭrvi vŭzrozhdentsi* (First men of the Revival). Sofia: Hemus, 1942.

Dinekov, Petŭr. *Vŭzrozhdenski pisateli* (Writers of the Revival). Sofia: Nauka i izkustvo, 1964.

Dinekov, Petŭr. "Problemŭt za romantizma v bŭlgarskata literatura do Osvobozhdenieto" (The problem of Romanticism in Bulgarian literature until the liberation). In Dinekov, *Vŭzrozhdenski pisateli*. Sofia: Nauka i izkustvo, 1964, 49–79.

Douglas, Mary *Purity and Danger. An Analysis of the Concepts of Pollution and Taboo*. London: Routledge, 1996.

Dragova, Nadezhda. *Probuzdane* (Awakening). Sofia: OF, 1963.

Dragova, Nadezhda. *Kniga za Paisii* (A book about Paisii). Sofia: Bŭlgarski pisatel, 1972.

Dragova, Nadezhda. *Otets Paisii. Patriarkh na bŭlgarskoto vŭzrazhdane* (Father Paisii. Patriarch of the Bulgarian Revival). Stara Zagora: Znanie,1994.

Drinov, Marin. "Otets Paisii, negovoto vreme, negovata istoriya i uchenitsite mu" (Father Paisii, his times, his history, and his disciples). *Periodichesko spisanie na Bŭlgarskoto Knizhovno Druzhestvo* 1, no. 4 (1871): 3–26. Reprinted in Drinov, *Izbrani sŭchineniya*. Vol. 1. Sofia: Nauka i izkustvo, 1971, 163–185.

Drosneva, Elka. *Folklor, Bibliya, Istoriya. Kŭm 230–godishninata na "Istoriya Slavyanobulgarska."* (Folklore, the Bible, history. Toward the 230th anniversary of the *Slavonic–Bulgarian History*). Sofia: Universitetsko izdatelstvo "Kliment Ohridski," 1995.

Drumev, Vasil. "Materiali za istoriyata na dukhovnoto vŭzrazhdane na bŭlgarskiya narod" (Materials for the history of the spiritual revival of the Bulgarian people). *Periodichesko spisanie na Bŭlgarskoto Knizhovno Druzhestvo*, nos. 11–12 (1876): 3–7.

Drumev, Vasil. "Zhivotoopisanie" (Biography). *Periodichesko spisanie na Bŭlgarskoto knizhovno druzhestvo* 1, no. 3 (1971). Reprinted in Drumev, *Sŭchineniya*. Vol. 2, Sofia: Bŭlgarski pisatel, 1968, 201–293.

Drumev, Vasil. "Zhivotoopisanie. Stoiko Vladislavov–Sofronii." (Biography. Stoiko Vladislavov–Sofronii). *Periodichesko spisanie na Bŭlgarskoto Knizhovno Druzhestvo* 1, nos. 5–6 (1872): 3–4.

Elenkov, Ivan. "Denyat na narodnite buditeli. Za funkstiite na uchilishtnite praznitsi vŭv vremeto mezhdu dvete svetovni voini" (The Day of the People's Awakeners. On the functions of school holidays in the interwar period). In *Simpozion ili Antichnost i humanita-*

ristika. Izsledvaniya v chest na prof. Bogan Bogdanov, edited by Violeta Gerdzhikova et al. Sofia: SONM-2000, 269–281.

Filipov, Al. "Uchitel na natsionalno sŭznanie" (The teacher in the national consciousness). *Otets Paisii* 6, nos. 8–9 (1933): 14–15.

Fingov, Dimitŭr, arkhimandrit Sofronii, Asen Kisyov. "Spomeni" (Recollections). In *Sbornik Kaloferska druzhba*. Vol. 1, Sofia, 1908.

Firkatian, Mari. *The Forest Traveller. Georgi Stoikov Rakovski and Bulgarian Nationalism.* New York: Peter Lang, 1996.

Furet, François. *Interpreting the French Revolution.* Cambridge University Press, 1981 (Original: Penser la Revolution Française. Editions Gallimard, Paris, 1978).

Gabrovski, Nikola. *Nravstvenite zadachi na inteligentsiyata* (The moral tasks of the intelligentsia). Sofia, 1889.

Gachev, Georgi. *Uskorenoto razvitie na kulturata* (The accelerated evolution of culture). Sofia: Nauka i izkustvo, 1979.

Gandev, Hristo. *Ranno vŭzrahdane, 1700–1860* (The Early Revival, 1700–1860). Sofia, 1939.

Gandev, Hristo. *Faktori na bŭlgarskoto vŭzrazhdane, 1600–1830* (Factors of the Bulgarian Revival, 1600–1830). Sofia: Bŭlgarska kniga, 1943.

Gandev, Hristo. *Vasil Levski. Politicheski idei i revolyutsionna deinost* (Vasil Levski. Political ideas and revolutionary activity). Sofia, 1946.

Gandev, Hristo. *Kratka bŭlgarska istoriya. Populyaren ocherk* (A short history of Bulgaria. Popular outline). Sofia, 1947.

Gandev, Hristo. *Aprilskoto vŭstanie* (The April uprising). Sofia: Narodna mladezh, 1956.

Gandev, Hristo. *Aprilskoto vŭstanie, 1876.* (The April uprising, 1876). Sofia: Nauka i izkustvo, 1974.

Gandev, Hristo. *Problemi na bŭlgarskoto vŭzrazhdane* (Problems of the Bulgarian Revival). Sofia: Nauka i izkustvo, 1976.

Gandev, Hristo. *Ot narodnost kŭm natsiya* (From people to nation). Sofia: Nauka i izkustvo, 1988.

Gandev, Hristo. "Burzhoaznata natsiya i osobenostite v neinoto razvitie" (The bourgeois nation and the peculiarities in its development). In *Bŭlgarskata natsiya.* Vol. 1, 23–43.

Gandev, Hristo. "Kŭm ideiniya razbor na Paisievata istoriya" (An analysis of the ideas in Paisii's *History*). In Gandev, *Problemi na bŭlgarskoto*, 166–177 (first published in 1946).

Gandev, Hristo. "Kŭm istoriyata na promishleniya kapitalizŭm u nas prez Vŭzrazhdaneto" (A contribution to the history of industrial capitalism in our lands during the Revival). In Gandev, *Problemi na bŭlgarskoto*, 426–460 (first published in 1954).

Gandev, Hristo. "Kŭm vŭprosa za periodizatsiyata na bŭlgarskata istoriya" (On the problem of periodization of Bulgarian history). In Gandev, *Problemi na bŭlgarskoto*, 501–514 (first published in 1951).

Gandev, Hristo. "Natsionalnata ideya v bŭlgarskata istoriopis" (The national idea in Bulgarian historiography). In Gandev. *Problemi na bŭlgarskoto*, 720–743 (first published in 1940).

Gandev, Hristo. "Turski izvori za agrarnata istoriya na Bŭlgariya prez Vŭzrazhdaneto" (Turkish sources for the agrarian history of Bulgaria during the Revival). *Istoricheski pregled* 10, no. 2 (1954):120–127.

Gandev, Hristo. "Zarazhdane na kapitalisticheski otnosheniya v chiflishkoto stopanstvo na Severozapadna Bŭlgariya prez XVIII vek" (The emergence of capitalist relations in the *chiflik* economy of northwestern Bulgaria during the eighteenth century). In Gandev, *Problemi na bŭlgarskoto*, 271–394 (first published in 1962).

Gavrilova, Raina. *Vekŭt na bŭlgarskoto dukhovno vŭzrazhdane* (The age of the Bulgarian spiritual revival). Sofia: Slov–D, 1992.

Gavrilova, Raina. *Bulgarian Urban Culture in the Eighteenth and Nineteenth Centuries.* Selinsgrove: Susquehanna University Press; London: Associated University Press, 1999.

Gavrilova, Raina. *Koleloto na zhivota. Kŭm vsekidnevieto na bŭlgarskiya vŭzrozhdenski grad* (The wheel of life. Everyday life in the Bulgarian towns during the Revival). Sofia: Universitetsko izdatelstvo "Kliment Ohridski," 1999.

Gecheva, Krŭstina. *Bŭlgarskata kultura prez Vŭzrazdaneto. Bibliografiya. Bŭlgarska i chuzhda knizhnina, 1878–1983.* (Bulgarian culture during the Revival. A bibliography. Bulgarian and foreign literature, 1878–1983). Sofia: BAN, 1986.

Gellner, Ernest. *Nations and Nationalism.* Oxford: Blackwell, 1983, 47–48.

Gellner, Ernest. *Nationalism.* London: Weidenfeld & Nicolson, 1997, 41–43.

Genchev, Nikolai. *Levski, revolyutsiyata i bŭdeshtiya svyat* (Levski, the revolution, and the future world). Sofia: OF, 1973.

Genchev, Nikolai. *Frantsiya v bŭlgarskoto dukhovno vŭzrazhdane* (France in the Bulgarian intellectual revival). Sofia: Universitetsko izdatelstvo "Kliment Ohridski," 1979.

Genchev, Nikolai. *Vasil Levski.* Sofia: Voenno izdatelstvo, 1987.

Genchev, Nikolai. *Bŭlgarskata kultura XV–XIX vek* (Bulgarian culture from the fifteenth to the nineteenth century). Sofia: Universitetsko izdatelstvo "Kliment Ohridski," 1988.

Genchev, Nikolai. *Bŭlgarsko vŭzrazhdane* (The Bulgarian Revival). Sofia: Otechestven front, 1988 (third revised edition, first edition in 1978).

Genchev, Nikolai. *Bŭlgarskata vŭzrozhdenska inteligentsiya* (The Bulgarian intelligentsia of the Revival). Sofia: Universitetsko izdatelstvo "Kliment Ohridski," 1991.

Genchev, Nikolai. *Bŭlgaro–ruski kulturni obshtuvaniya prez Vŭzrazhdaneto* (Bulgarian–Russian cultural exchanges during the Revival). Sofia: LIK, 2002.

Genchev, Nikolai. "Dvizhenie na ideite i izsledvaniyata v bŭlgarskata istoriografiya" (Changing ideas and research in Bulgarian historiography). In *Universitetski izsledvaniya i prepodavaniya na bŭlgarskata istoriya u nas i v chuzhbina.* Vol. 1. Sofia, 1982, 31–55.

Genchev, Nikolai. "Pak po nyakoi vŭprosi ot istoriyata na bŭlgarskoto vŭzrazhdane" (On some problems of the history of the Bulgarian Revival). *Istoriya i obshtestvoznanie,* no. 4 (1985): 13–22.

Genchev, Nikolai. "Sotsialnata struktura na bŭlgarskoto obshtestvo prez Vŭzrazhdaneto" (Social structure of the Bulgarian society during the Revival). *Sotsiologicheski problemi,* no. 6 (1980): 3–13.

Genchev, Nikolai. "Za osnovnoto sŭdŭrzhanie na bŭlgarskiya vŭzrozhdenski protses" (On the basic content of the Bulgarian Revival processes). In *Kultura, tsŭrkva i revolyutsiya,* 40–46.

Genov, G. "Politicheskite lozungi na vŭzrazhdaneto" (The political slogans of the Revival). *Otets Paisii* 7, no. 10 (1934): 211–213.

Genov, Krŭstyu. *Romantizmŭt v bŭlgarskata literatura* (Romanticism in Bulgarian literature). Sofia: BAN,1968.

Georgiev, Emil. *Obshto i sravnitelno slavyansko literaturoznanie* (General and comparative Slavic literary studies). Sofia: Nauka i izkustvo, 1965.

Georgiev, Emil. *Bŭlgarskata literatura v obshtoslavyanskoto i obshtoevropeisko literaturno razvitie* (Bulgarian literature in the Slavic and European literary evolution). Sofia: Nauka i izkustvo, 1973.

Georgiev, Emil. "Bŭlgarskoto i obshtoevropeisko vŭzrazhdane" (The Bulgarian and European Renaissance). In Georgiev, *Bŭlgarskata literatura,* 149–176.

Georgiev, Emil. "Bŭlgarskoto literaturno i obshtoistorichesko razvitie i Prosveshtenieto"

(Bulgarian literary and historical development and the Enlightenment). In Georgiev, *Bŭlgarskata literatura*, 203–215.

Georgiev, Emil. "Paisii Hilendarski–mezhdu Renesansa i Prosveshtenieto" (Paisii Hilendar-ski–Between the Renaissance and the Enlightenment). In *Paisii Hilendarski i negovata epokha*, 253–283.

Georgiev, Emil. "Ranniyat Renesans i Predrenesansŭt v yuzhnoslavyanskata literaturna obshnost" (Early Renaissance and pre-Renaissance in the South Slav literary commu-nity). In Georgiev, *Obshto i sravnitelno*, 78–82.

Georgiev, Emil. "Renesansovo-prosveshtenskiyat period v yuzhnoslavyanskata literaturna obshtnost" (The Renaissance-Enlightenment period in the South Slav literary commu-nity). In Georgiev, *Obshto i sravnitelno*, 83–90.

Georgiev, Emil. "Romantizmŭt v yuzhnoslavyanskata literaturna obshnost" (Romanticism in the South Slav literary community). In Georgiev, *Obshto i sravnitelno*, 91–101.

Georgiev, Emil. "Tipologichen relef na romantizma v bŭlgarskata literatura" (Typological profile of Romanticism in Bulgarian literature). In Georgiev, *Bŭlgarskata literatura*, 231–261.

Georgieva, Tsvetana. "Za genezisa na burzhoaznite elementi v sotsialnata struktura na bŭlgarite" (Origins of the bourgeois element in the social structure of the Bulgarians). *Istoricheski pregled* 33, no. 2 (1977): 87–90.

Georgov, Ivan. "Materiali po nasheto vŭzrazhdane" (Materials on our Revival). *Sbornik narodni umotvoreniya, nauka i knizhnina* 24 (1908): 1–47.

Gergova, Ani. *Knizhninata i bŭlgarite prez Vŭzrazhdaneto. Izvestiya na nauchno-izsledova-telskiya institut po kulturata.* (Literature and the Bulgarians during the Revival. Publica-tions of the Cultural Research Institute). Vol. 2, Sofia, 1984.

Gergova, Ani. *Knizhninata i bŭlgarite XIX–nachaloto na XX vek* (Literature and the Bulgari-ans in the nineteenth and the beginning of the twentieth centuries). Sofia: BAN, 1991.

Grozdanova, Elena. *Bŭlgarskata selska obshtina prez XV–XVIII vek* (The Bulgarian peasant commune from the fifteenth to the eighteenth centuries). Sofia, 1979.

Gruev, Ioakim. *Moite spomeni* (My memoirs). Plovdiv, 1906.

Gŭlŭbov, Konstantin. "Psikhlogiya na bŭlgarina" (Psychology of the Bulgarian). *Bŭlgarska misŭl* 9, no. 2 (1934): 109–119.

Hadzhiiski, Ivan. *Sŭchineniya v dva toma* (Works in two volumes). Sofia: Bŭlgarski pisatel, 1974.

Hadzhiiski, Ivan. "Aprilskoto vŭstanie i Benkovski" (The April uprising and Benkovski). In Hadzhiiski, *Sŭchineniya v dva toma*. Vol. 1, 344–366 (first published in 1943).

Hadzhiiski, Ivan. "Istoricheskite koreni na nashite demokraticheski traditsii" (The histori-cal roots of our democratic traditions). In Hadzhiiski. *Sŭchineniya v dva toma*. Vol. 1, 85–99 (first published in 1937).

Hadzhiiski, Ivan. "Psikhologiya na Aprilskoto vŭstanie" (Psychology of the April uprising). In Hadzhiiski. *Sŭchineniya v dva toma*. Vol. 1, 299–343 (first published in 1940).

Hadzhinikolov, Veselin. "Iz zhivota na Instituta za bŭlgarska istoriya" (The activities of the Institute for Bulgarian History). *Izvestiya na Instituta za bŭlgarska istoriya* 1–2 (1951): 351–386.

Hadzhinikolov, Veselin. "Nachalni godini na Instituta po istoriya." *Istoricheski pregled* 53, no. 4 (1997): 130–154.

Hadzhinikolov, Veselin. "Traditsiite na Aprilskoto vŭstanie i Bŭlgarskata komunisticheska partiya" (The traditions of the April uprising and the Bulgarian Communist Party). In *Aprilskoto vŭstanie*, 221–242.

Harrison, David. *The Sociology of Modernization and Development.* London: Unwin Hyman, 1988.

Hassinger, Erich. *Das Werden des neuzeitlichen Europa. 1300–1600.* Braunschweig, 1959.

Hinkov, Hristo. "Vŭzrazhdaneto i stopanska Bŭlgariya" (The Revival and the Bulgarian economy). *Otets Paisii* 11, no. 6 (1938): 201–207.

Hristov, Hristo. *Paisii Hilendarski.* Sofia: Nauka i izkustvo, 1972.

Hristov, Hristo. *Bŭlgarskite obshtini prez vŭzrazhdaneto* (The Bulgarian communes during the Revival). Sofia: BAN, 1973.

Hristov, Hristo. *Agrarniyat vŭpros v bŭlgarskata natsionalna revolyutsiya* (The agrarian question in the Bulgarian national revolution). Sofia: Nauka i izkustvo, 1976.

Hristov, Hristo. "Harakter i znachenie na Osvoboditelnata voina" (The character and impact of the liberation war). In *Osvobozhdenieto na Bŭlgariya, 1878–1968*, 15–26.

Hristov, Hristo. "Kŭm vŭprosa za klasite i klasovite otnosheniya v bŭlgarskoto obshtestvo prez Vŭzrazhdaneto (proizkhod, sotsialna prinadlezhnost i rolya na chorbadzhiite)" (The problem of classes and class relations in Bulgarian society during the Revival [Origins, social status, and the role of the *chorbadzhii*]). *Izvestiya na Instituta po istoriya* 21 (1970): 51–85.

Hristov, Hristo. "Kŭm vŭprosa za zarazhdaneto na kapitalizma i obrazuvaneto na bŭlgarskata natsiya prez Vŭzrazhdaneto" (The problem of the emergence of capitalism and the formation of the Bulgarian nation during the Revival). In *Bŭlgarskata natsiya.* Vol. 2, 9–36.

Hristov, Hristo. "Nyakoi problemi na prekhoda ot feodalizma kŭm kapitalizma v istoriyata na Bŭlgariya" (Some problems of the transition from feudalism to capitalism in the history of the Bulgarians). *Istoricheski pregled* 17, no. 3 (1961): 83–107.

Hristov, Hristo. "Paisii Hilendarski i Bŭlgarskoto vŭzrazhdane" (Paisii Hilendarski and the Bulgarian Revival). In *Paisii Hilendarski i negovata epokha*, 33–69.

Hristov, Hristo. "Za rolyata na bŭlgarskata burzhoaziya v natsionalnata revolyutsiya" (On the role of the Bulgarian bourgeoisie in the national revolution). *Istoricheski pregled* 33, no. 3 (1977): 91–97.

Hvostova, K. "Sotsiologicheskie modeli 'Zapadn'ye i vostochn'ye tip'y obshtestvenn'yh otnoshenii'" (Sociological models "Western and Eastern types of social relations"). In *Obshtee i osobennoe*, 202–212.

Igov, Svetlozar. *Kratka istoriya na bŭlgarskata literatura* (Short history of Bulgarian literature). Sofia: Prosveta, 1996.

Ilchev, Ivan. *Reklamata prez Vŭzrazhdaneto.* (Advertising during the Revival). Sofia: Marin Drinov, 1995.

Inalcik, Halil. *The Ottoman Empire. The Classical Age 1300–1600.* London: Weidenfeld & Nicolson, 1973.

Inalcik, Halil. *The Ottoman Empire: Conquest, Organization, Economy. Collected Studies.* London: Variorum Reprints, 1978.

Inalcik, Halil. "Application of the Tanzimat and its Social Effects." In Inalcik, *The Ottoman Empire: Conquest*, chapter 16, 1–33.

Inalcik, Halil. "L'Empire ottoman." In *Actes du premier Congrès International des Etudes Balkaniques et sud–est Européennes.* Vol. 3 (Histoire). Sofia, 1969, 75–103.

Istoriya na Bŭlgariya v dva toma (History of Bulgaria in two volumes), edited by D. Kosev, D. Dimitrov et al. Vol. 1, Sofia: Nauka i izkustvo, 1954.

Istoriya na Bŭlgariya v tri toma (History of Bulgaria in three volumes). Vol. 1, Sofia, 1961.

Istoriya na Bŭlgariya v 14 toma (History of Bulgaria in 14 volumes). Vol. 5, Sofia: BAN, 1985; Vol. 6, Sofia: BAN, 1987.

Istoriya za 11 klas (History for eleventh grade). Sofia: Anubis, 1996.

Ivanov, Yurdan. *Bŭlgarite v Makedoniya* (The Bulgarians in Macedonia). Sofia, 1915.

Ivanov, Yurdan. "Dokumenti po nasheto vŭzrazhdane" (Documents for our Revival). *Sbornik narodni umotvoreniya, nauka i knizhnina* 21 (1905): 1–111.

Iz arkhivata na Naiden Gerov (The Archive of Naiden Gerov), edited by T. Panchev. Sofia: BAN. Vol. 1, 1911; Vol. 2, 1914.

Janos, Andrew. "Modernization and Decay in Historical Perspective. The Case of Romania." In *Social Change in Romania, 1860–1940*, edited by Kenneth Jovith. Berkeley: University of California, 1978, 72–116;

Janos, Andrew. *The Politics of Backwardness in Hungary, 1825–1945*. Princeton, N. J.: Princeton University Press, 1982.

Janos, Andrew. "The Politics of Backwardness in Continental Europe, 1780–1945." *World Politics* 41, no. 3 (1989): 323–359.

Jireček, Konstantin. *Istoriya na bŭlgarite* (History of the Bulgarians). Sofia: Nauka i izkustvo, 1978 (first Bulgarian edition in 1886).

Karanov, Efrem. *Spomeni* (Memoirs). Sofia: Otechestven front, 1979 (the memoirs were written in 1920).

Karayovov, Todor. "Prosvetiteli i revolyutsioneri" (Enlighteners and revolutionaries). *Prosveta* 4, no. 4 (1938): 400–412.

Kasabov, Ivan. *Moite spomeni ot Vŭzrazhdaneto na Bŭlgariya s revolyutsionni idei* (My recollections of the Revival of Bulgaria with revolutionary ideas). Sofia, 1905.

Kazandzhiev, Spiridon. "Natsionalno sŭznanie" (National consciousness). *Otets Paisii* 8, no. 2 (1935).

Kiossev, Aleksandŭr. "Spisŭtsi na otsŭstvashtoto" (Lists of absences). In *Bŭlgarskiyat kanon? Krizata na literaturnoto nasledstvo*, edited by Aleksandŭr Kiossev. Sofia: Aleksandŭr Panov, 1998, 5–49.

Kisimov, Panteli. *Istoricheski raboti. Moite spomeni.* (Historical works. My memoirs). Vols. 1–4, Plovdiv, 1897.

Kitromilides, Paschalis. "The Enlightenment East and West: A Comparative Perspective on the Ideological Origins of the Balkan Political Traditions." In Kitromilides, *Enlightenment, Nationalism, Orthodoxy. Studies in the Culture and Political Thought of Southeastern Europe.* Variorum, 1994, 51–70.

Klincharov, Ivan. *Hristo Botev. Zhivot i dela.* (Hristo Botev. Life and deeds). Sofia, 1926.

Kniga za bŭlgarskite hadzhii (Book about the Bulgarian pilgrims), edited by Nadya Danova and Svetla Gyurova. Sofia: Bŭlgarski pisatel, 1985.

Kolarov, Vasil. "Vŭrkhu Aprilskoto vŭstanie" (On the April uprising). In Kolarov, *Izbrani proizvedeniya*. Vol. 3, Sofia: BKP, 1955, 180–190 (first published in 1945).

Konev, Iliya. *Bŭlgarskoto vŭzrazhdane i prosveshtenieto* (The Bulgarian Revival and the Enlightenment). Vol. 1, Sofia: BAN, 1983; Vol. 2, Sofia: Universitetsko izdatelstvo "Kliment Ohridski," 1991.

Konobeev, Vasilii. *Bŭlgarskoto natsionalno-osvoboditelno dvizhenie. Ideologiya, programa, razvitie.* (The Bulgarian national-liberation movement. Ideology, program, evolution). Sofia: Nauka i izkustvo, 1972.

Konobeev, Vasilii. "Genezisŭt na kapitalizma v Bŭlgariya" (The genesis of capitalism in Bulgaria). In Konobeev, *Bŭlgarskoto natsionalno-osvoboditelno*, 7–58.

Konobeev, Vasili. "Za agrarnata programa na bŭlgarskite revolyutsioneri prez 60-te i 70-te godini na XIX vek" (On the agrarian program of the Bulgarian revolutionaries in the 1860s and 1870s). In Konobeev, *Bŭlgarskoto natsionalno-osvoboditelno*, 368–437.

Konobeev, Vasilii. "Za klasovoto sŭdŭrzhanie na ideologiyata i programata na Paisii Hilendarski" (On the class content of the ideology and the program of Paisii Hilendarski). In Konobeev, *Bŭlgarskoto natsionalno-osvoboditelno*, 59–79.

Konstantinov, Georgi. *Vŭzrazhdaneto i Makedoniya* (The Revival and Macedonia). Sofia, 1943.

Konstantinov, Georgi. "Otets Paisii. Po sluchai 175 godini ot napisvaneto na negovata is-toriya" (Father Paisii. On the occasion of 175 years since the writing of his history). *Otets Paisii* 10, no. 7 (1937): 259–270.

Konstantinov, Georgi. "Zaveti na nashite vŭzrozhdentsi" (The legacy of our men of the Revival). *Otets Paisii* 7, no. 10 (1934): 209–210.

Koselleck, Reinhart. "Das Achtzehnte Jahrhundert als Beginn der Neuzeit." In *Epochen-schwelle und Epochenbewusstsein*, edited by Reinart Herzog and Reinhart Koselleck. Munich: Wilhelm Fink Verlag, 1987, 269–282.

Koselleck, Reinhart. "Moderne Sozialgeschichte und historische Zeiten." In *Theorie der modernen Geschichtsschreibung*, edited by Pietro Rossi. Frankfurt/Main, 1987, 173–190.

Koselleck, Reinhart. "'Neuzeit': Remarks on the Semantics of the Modern Concepts of Movement." In Koselleck, *Future's Past. On the Semantics of Historical Time*. Cambridge, Mass. and London: The MIT Press, 1985, 231–266.

Kosev, Dimitŭr. *Lektsii po nova bŭlgarska istoriya* (Lectures on the new Bulgarian history). Sofia: Nauka i izkustvo, 1952.

Kosev, Dimitŭr. "Aprilskoto vŭstanie–vrŭkhna tochka na bŭlgarskata natsionalno-demokra-ticheska revolyutsiya" (The April uprising–Apex of the Bulgarian national-democratic revolution). In *Aprilskoto vŭstanie*, 7–17.

Kosev, Dimitŭr. "Devetdeset godini ot Osvobozhdenieto na Bŭlgariya" (Ninety years from the liberation of Bulgaria). In *Osvobozhdenieto na Bŭlgariya, 1878–1968*. Sofia: BAN, 1970, 7–13.

Kosev, Dimitŭr. "Harakter i znachenie na rusko-turskata voina prez 1877–1878 g." (Character and impact of the Russo-Turkish war in 1877–1878). In *Osvobozhdenieto na Bŭlgariya ot tursko igo, 1878–1958*. Sofia: BKP, 1958, 3–12.

Kosev, Dimitŭr. "Idealistichesko i materialistichesko razbirane na bŭlgarskoto vŭzrazh-dane" (The idealistic and the materialist view of the Bulgarian Revival). *Istoricheski pre-gled* 4, no. 3 (1947/8): 317–332.

Kosev, Dimitŭr. "Klasovite otnosheniya v Bŭlgariya prez Vŭzrazhdaneto" (Class relations in Bulgaria during the Revival). *Istoricheski pregled* 7, nos. 4–5 (1951); 443–463.

Kosev, Dimitŭr. "Kŭm izyasnyavane na nyakoi problemi ot istoriyata na Bŭlgariya prez XVIII i nachaloto na XIX vek" (Toward the clarification of some problems of the history of Bulgaria in the eighteenth and the beginning of the nineteenth century). *Istoricheski pregled* 12, no. 3 (1956): 26–62.

Kosev, Dimitŭr. "Kŭm vŭprosa za periodizatsiyata na Novata bŭlgarska istoriya" (On the problem of periodization of the new Bulgarian history). *Istoricheski pregled* 6, no. 3 (1950): 360–366.

Kosev, Dimitŭr. "Misli po diskusiyata za rolyata na bŭlgarskata burzhoaziya v natsionalno-osvoboditelnoto dvizhenie" (Thoughts on the discussion of the role of the Bulgarian bourgeoisie in the national-liberation movement). *Istoricheski pregled* 33, no. 1 (1977): 103–105.

Kosev, Dimitŭr. "Za ideologiyata na Paisii Hilendarski" (On the Ideology of Paisii Hilendar-ski). In *Paisii Hilendarski i negovata epokha*, 7–30.

Kosev, Konstantin. *Za kapitalisticheskoto razvitie na bŭlgarskite zemi prez 60–te i 70–te godini na XIX vek* (The capitalist development of the Bulgarian lands in the 1860s and 1870s). Sofia: BAN, 1968.

Kosev, Konstantin. *Bismarck, Iztochniyat vŭpros i bŭlgarskoto osvobozhdenie, 1856–1878* (Bismarck, the Eastern question, and the Bulgarian liberation, 1856–1878). Sofia: Nauka i izkustvo, 1978.

Kosev, Konstantin. *Aprilskoto vŭstanie–prelyudiya na Osvobozhdenieto* (The April uprising–Prelude to the liberation). Sofia: Hristo Botev, 1996.

Kosev, Konstantin. *Kratka istoriya na Bŭlgarskoto vŭzrazhdane* (A short history of the Bulgarian Revival). Sofia: Marin Drinov, 2001.

Kosev, Konstantin. "Kŭm vŭprosa za deistvieto i vzaimodeistvieto na vŭtreshnite i vŭnshnite faktori v bŭlgarskoto natsionalno-osvoboditelno dvizhenie prez vŭzrazhdane-to" (On the problem of the action and interaction of internal and external factors in the Bulgarian national-liberation movement during the Revival). In *V chest na akademik Hristo Hristov*. Sofia: BAN, 1976, 35–48.

Kosev, Konstantin and Nikolai Zhechev. *Aprilskoto vŭstanie, 1876* (The April uprising, 1876). Sofia: Nauka i izkustvo, 1966.

Kostentsev, Arseni. *Spomeni* (Memoirs). Sofia: Otechestven front, 1984 (first edition in 1917).

Krŭstnikov, Nikola. *Opit za psikhologicheski analiz na nashiya obshtestven zhivot* (An attempt at a psychological analysis of our public sphere). Sofia, 1922.

Kultura, tsŭrkva i revolyutsiya prez Vŭzrazhdaneto (Culture, church, and revolution during the Revival), edited by Krumka Sharova. Sliven, 1995.

"Kŭm chitatelite" (To the Readers). *Periodichesko spisanie na Bŭlgarskoto Knizhovno Druzhetvo* 1, no. 1 (1870): 1–7.

Kurtev, Nedyalko. "Formirane na bŭlgarskata burzhoazna natsiya" (The formation of the Bulgarian bourgeois nation). *Godishnik na Sofiiskiya universitet. Ideologichni katedri.* Vol. 57, Sofia, 1964.

Kuyumdzhieva, Miglena. *Intelektualniyat elit prez Vŭzrazhdaneto* (Intellectual elites during the Revival). Sofia: Universitetsko izdatelstvo "Kliment Ohridski," 1997.

Lambrev, K. "Bŭlgarskoto vŭzrazhdane i dneshnite uchilishtni ideali" (The Bulgarian Revival and the ideals of our schools today). *Uchilishten pregled* 38, no. 1 (1939): 3–18.

Lampe, John. "Imperial Borderlands or Capitalist Periphery? Redefining Balkan Backwardness." In *The Origins of Backwardness in Eastern Europe*, edited by Daniel Chirot. Berkeley–Los Angeles–Oxford: University of California Press, 1989, 177–209.

Lampe, John and Marvin Jackson. *Balkan Economic History, 1550–1950. From Imperial Borderlands to Developing Nations.* Bloomington: Indiana University Press, 1982.

Lazarkov, Nikola. *Spomeni. Iz robskoto minalo na Dupnitsa* (Memoirs. The past under the yoke in Dupnitsa). Dupnitsa, 1924.

Lekov, Docho. *Literatura, obshtestvo, kultura. Literaturno-sotsiologicheski i literaturno-istoricheski problemi na bŭlgarskoto vŭzrazhdane* (Literature, society, culture. Literary-sociological and literary-historical problems of the Bulgarian Revival). Sofia: Narodna prosveta, 1982.

Lekov, Docho. *Bŭlgarska vŭzrozhdenska literatura* (Bulgarian literature of the Revival). Vol. 1, Sofia: Universitetsko izdatelstvo "Kliment Ohridski," 1993.

Lenin, Vladimir. "Agrarnaia programma sotsial-demokratii v pervoi russkoi revoliutsii 1905–1907 godov" (The agrarian program of the social democrats in the first Russian revolution, 1905–1907). In Lenin, *Polnoe sobranie sochinenii*. Moscow: Gosudarstvennoe izdatel'stvo politicheskoi literatury, 1961, vol. 16, 193–413.

Lenin, Vladimir. "Agrarny vopros v Rossii k kontsu XIX veka" (The agrarian question in Russia at the end of the nineteenth century). In Lenin, *Polnoe sobranie suchinenii*. Vol. 17, 57–137.

Lerner, Daniel et al. "Modernization." In *International Encyclopedia of the Social Sciences*. Vols. 9–10. New York and London: The Macmillan Company and the Free Press, 1972, 386–408.

Levintov, N. G. "Agrarnye otnosheniya v Bolgarii nakanune osvobozhdeniia i agrarny perevorot 1877–1879 godov" (Agrarian relations in Bulgaria on the eve of the liberation and the agrarian overturn in 1877–1879). In *Osvobozdenie Bolgarii ot turetskogo igo. Sbornik stat'ei*. Moscow, 1953.

Lewis, Bernard. *The Emergence of Modern Turkey.* London–New York–Toronto: Oxford University Press, 1965, 438–442.

MacDermott, Mercia. *The Apostle of Freedom. A Portrait of Vasil Levsky.* Sofia Press, 1979.

Madzhrakova-Chavdarova, Ognyana. "Predpostavki i nachalo na legalnata politicheska borba na bŭlgarskiya narod prez Vŭzrazhdaneto" (The prerequisites and beginning of the legal political struggle of the Bulgarian people during the Revival). *Istoricheski pregled* 48, no. 7 (1992): 3–29.

Madzrakova-Chavdarova, Ognyana. "Bŭlgarskoto narodno predstavitelstvo–idei i opiti za sŭzdavaneto mu (40–te–60–te godini na XIX vek)" (Representation of the Bulgarian people–Ideas and attempts at its formation in the 1840s to 1860s). *Istoricheski pregled* 49, no. 2 (1993): 3–35.

Makdŭf, *Chii e Botev? Nravstveniyat lik na taya zloveshta lichnost.* (Whose is Botev? The moral outlook of this sinister personality). Sofia: Armeiskiya voenno-izdatelski fond, 1929.

Manchev, Vasil. *Spomeni. Dopiski. Pisma* (Memoirs. Articles. Letters). Sofia: Otechestven front, 1982 (the memoirs were written in 1904).

Manov, Vasil. *Uchilishteto i novata dŭrzhava* (The school and the new state). Sofia, 1935.

Markova, Zina. *Bŭlgarskoto tsŭrkovno-natsionalno dvizhenie do Krimskata voina* (The Bulgarian church-national movement until the Crimean War). Sofia: BAN, 1976.

Markova, Zina. *Bŭlgarskata Ekzarkhiya, 1870–1879.* (The Bulgarian Exarchate, 1870–1879). Sofia: BAN, 1989, 5–30, 315–323.

Marx, Karl. *Capital. A Critique of Political Economy.* London: Penguin Books, 1981, Vol. 3.

Meininger, Thomas. *The Formation of a Nationalist Bulgarian Intelligentsia, 1835–1878.* New York and London: Garland Publishing, 1987.

Mendels, Franklin. "Proto-industrialization: The First Phase of the Industrialization Process." *Journal of Economic History* 32, no. 1 (1972): 241–261.

Migev, Vladimir. *Utvurzhdavane na monarkho-fashistkata diktatura v Bŭlgariya, 1934–1936* (The consolidation of the monarchical-fascist dictatorship in Bulgaria, 1934–1936). Sofia: BAN, 1977.

Mikhailovski, Stoyan. "Kak zapadat i se provalyat dŭrzhavite" (How states decline and fail). In Mikhailovski, *Neizdadeni sŭchineniya.* Vol. 1 Sofia, 1940.

Mikhalchev, Dimitŭr. "Mozhe li dneshna Bŭlgariya da se vŭrne kŭm dukha na nasheto vŭzrazhdane?" (Can today's Bulgaria return to the spirit of our Revival?). *Filosofski pregled* 11, no. 3 (1939): 330.

Milev, Nikola. "Faktorite na bŭlgarskoto vŭzrazhdane" (Factors of the Bulgarian Revival). In *Sbornik v chest na prof. Ivan Shishmanov.* Sofia, 1920, 129–157.

Milkova, Fani. *Pozemlenata sobstvenost v bŭlgarskite zemi prez XIX vek* (Land ownership in the Bulgarian lands during the nineteenth century). Sofia: Nauka i izkustvo, 1969.

Miller, Ilya. "Formirovanie natsii. Mesto problemy v sovokupnosti protsessov perekhoda ot feodalizma k kapitalizmu v stranakh tsentral'noi i iugovostochnoi Evropy" (Formation of the nations. The location of the problem in the overall process of transition from feudalism to capitalism in the states of Central and Southeast Europe). *Sovetskoe slavyanovedenie,* no. 6 (1975): 93–98.

Mishaikov, Dimitŭr. "Belezhki vŭrkhu domashnata shaechna industriya v Bŭlgariya" (Notes on the domestic woolen cloth industry in Bulgaria). *Spisanie na Bŭlgarskoto ikonomichesko druzhestvo* 7, no. 8 (1903): 527–553.

Mishev, Dimitŭr. *Bŭlgariya v minaloto* (Bulgaria in the past). Sofia, 1916, 284–285.

Mishev, Dimitŭr. "Nachalo na bŭlgarskata probuda" (The beginnings of Bulgarian awakening). *Tsŭrkoven arkhiv.* Vols. 1–2, Sofia, 1925.

Mitev, Plamen. *Sŭzdavane i deinost na Bŭlgarskiya revolyutsionen komitet—1875* (The creation and activities of the Bulgarian revolutionary committee of 1875). Sofia: LIK, 1998, 16–21.

Mitev, Plamen. *Bŭlgarsko vŭzrazhdane. Lektsionen kurs.* (The Bulgarian Revival. Lectures). Sofia: Polis, 1999.

Mitev, Plamen. "Razmisli vŭrkhu Rusko-turskata osvoboditelna voina (1877–1878)" (Reflections on the Russo-Turkish liberation war, 1877–1878). *Istoriya* 3, no. 2 (1994): 52–59.

Mitev, Yono. "Dvizheshti sili na bŭlgarskata natsionalna revolyutsiya s ogled uchastieto na burzhoaziyata v neya" (Driving forces of the Bulgarian national revolution with regard to the participation of the bourgeoisie). *Istoricheski pregled* 33, no. 1 (1977): 105–116.

Mitev, Yono. "Obrazuvaneto na bŭlgarskata natsiya" (The formation of the Bulgarian nation). *Istoricheski pregled* 4, no. 3 (1947/8): 291–316.

Mitropolit Simeon Varnensko Preslavski, Stoyan Chomakov, "Spomeni" (Recollections). In *Yubileen sbornik Koprivshtitsa,* edited by Archimandrite Evtimi. Sofia, 1926, 15–24.

Mizov, Nikolai. *Praznitsite kato obshtestveno yavlenie* (Holidays as public events). Sofia: BKP, 1966.

Mutafchiev, Petŭr. "Deloto i primerŭt na Paisiya" (The deed and example of Paisii). *Otets Paisii* 8, no. 7 (1935): 333–337.

Mutafchiev, Petŭr. "Dneshna Bŭlgariya i dukhŭt na nasheto Vŭzrazhdane" (Today's Bulgaria and the spirit of our Revival). *Prosveta* 5, no. 10 (1940): 1169–1181.

Mutafchiev, Petŭr. "Dukh i zaveti na Vŭzrazhdaneto" (The spirit and legacy of the Revival). *Otets Paisii* 7, no. 10 (1934): 197–200.

Mutafchiev, Petŭr. "Kŭm novo vŭzrazdane" (Toward a new revival). *Otets Paisii* 8, no. 1 (1935): 3–9.

Mutafchieva, Vera. *Agrarnite otnosheniya v Osmanskata imperiya prez XV–XVI vek.* (Agrarian relations in the Ottoman Empire during the fifteenth and sixteenth centuries). Sofia: BAN, 1962.

Mutafchieva, Vera. *Kŭrdzhaliisko vreme* (The times of the Kŭrdzhalii). Sofia: Nauka i izkustvo, 1987.

Mutafchieva, Vera. *Osmanska sotsialno-ikonomicheska istoriya* (Ottoman social-economic history). Sofia: BAN, 1993.

Mutafchieva, Vera. "Kategoriite feodalno zavisimo naselenie v nashite zemi pod turska vlast prez XV–XVI vek" (Categories of feudal dependent population in our lands under Turkish rule in the fifteenth and sixteenth centuries). In *Izvestiya na instituta po istoriya.* Vol. 9, 1960, 57–90.

Mutafchieva, Vera. "Otkupuvaneto na dŭrzhavnite prikhodi v osmanskata imperiya prez XV–XVII v. i razvitieto na parichni otnosheniya" (The leasing of state revenues in the Ottoman Empire from the fifteenth to the seventeenth centuries and the development of money relations). *Istoricheski pregled* 16, no. 1 (1960): 40–74.

Mutafchieva, Vera. "Po nyakoi sporni vŭprosi iz osmanskata sotsialno-ikonomicheska istoriya" (On some controversial issues of Ottoman social-economic history). In Mutafchieva, *Osmanska sotsialno-ikonomicheska,* 435–448.

Mutafchieva, Vera. "Za roliata na vakŭfa v gradskata ikonomika na Balkanite pod turska vlast, XV–XVII v" (On the role of the *vakf* in the urban economy of the Balkans under Turkish rule, fifteenth to seventeenth centuries). *Izvestiya na Instituta po istoriya* 10 (1962): 121–145.

Narodna otbrana, no. 1724 (9 October 1934); no. 1725 (16 November 1934); no. 1758 (3 July 1935); no. 1762 (31 July 1935); no. 1765 (21 August 1935); no. 1766 (28 August 1935); no. 1775 (30 October 1935).

Nashata borba. Kratŭk razbor na programata na Sŭyuza na Bŭlgarskite Natsionalni Legioni

(Our struggle. A short analysis of the program of the union of the Bulgarian national legions). Varna, 1938.

Natan, Zhak. *Ikonomicheska istoriya na Bŭlgariya* (Economic history of Bulgaria). Sofia, 1938.

Natan, Zhak. *Bŭlgarskoto vŭzrazhdane* (The Bulgarian Revival). Sofia: Bŭlgarski pisatel, 1949 (fourth, revised edition. First edition in 1939).

Natan, Zhak. "Kŭm vŭprosa za pŭrvonachlnoto natrupvane na kapitala v Bŭlgariya" (On the initial accumulation of capital in Bulgaria). *Isvestiya na ikonomicheskiya institut* 1–2 (1954): 13–46.

Natan, Zhak. "Otnovo po vŭprosa za klasite i klasovite otnosheniya v Bŭlgariya prez Vŭzrazhdaneto" (Once again on the issue of classes and class relations in Bulgaria during the Revival). *Istoricheski pregled* 7, nos. 4–5 (1951): 467–469.

Natan, Zhak. "Po vŭprosa za periodizatsiyata na nashata istoriya" (On the periodization of our history). *Istoricheski pregled* 6, no. 2 (1950): 210–216.

Nichev, Boyan. *Uvod v yuzno-slavianskiya realizŭm* (Introduction to South Slav Realism). Sofia: BAN, 1971.

Nikov, Petŭr. *Vŭzrazhdane na bŭlgarskiya narod. Tsŭrkovno-natsionalni borbi i postizheniya.* (The Revival of the Bulgarian people. Church-national struggles and achievements). Sofia: Nauka i izkustvo, 1971 (first edition in 1929).

Nikov, Petŭr. "Vŭzrazhdane chrez tsŭrkva" (Revival through the church). In *Bŭlgariya 1000 godini*, 321–381.

Novaia istoriia. Chast 1. Ot frantsuzkoi burzhoaznoi revoliutsii do franko–prusskoi voiny i parizhkoi kommuny (1789–1870) (Modern history. Part I. From the French bourgeois revolution to the Franco–Prussian war and the Paris Commune, 1789–1870), edited by E. V. Tarle, A. V. Efimov, and F. A. Heifets. Moscow: Gosudarstvennoe sotsial'no-ekonomicheskoe izdatel'stvo, 1939.

Novaia istoriia. Vol. 1, 1640–1789 (Modern history. Vol. 1, 1640–1789), edited by V. V. Birukovich, B. F. Porshnev, and S. D. Skazkin. Moscow: Gosudarsvennoe izdatel'stvo politicheskoi literatury, 1951.

Novichev, A. D. *Istoriia Turtsii. T. 2, Novoe vremia. Chast 1 (1793–1834)* (History of Turkey. Vol. 2, the modern epoch. Part 1, 1793–1834). Izdatel'stvo Leningradskogo universiteta, 1968.

Obshtee i osobennoe v istoricheskom razvitii stran Vostoka: Materialy diskusii obshtestvennyh formatsiiakh na Vostoke (Common features and peculiarities in the historical development of the Eastern states: Materials of the discussion of the social formations in the East), edited by G. Kim. Moscow: Nauka, 1966.

Robin Okey, *Eastern Europe, 1740–1985. Feudalism to Communism.* Minneapolis: University of Minnesota Press, 1985.

Ormandzhiev, Ivan. *Otets Paisii i epokhata na Vŭzrazhdaneto* (Father Paisii and the epoch of the Revival). Sofia: Kazanlŭshka dolina, 1938, 19–23.

Ormandzhiev, Ivan. *Nova i nai-nova istoriya na bŭlgarskiya narod* (Modern and contemporary history of the Bulgarian people). Sofia: Zaveti, 1945.

Pachkova, Petya. *Ideinoto razvitie na pobornitsite sled Osvobozhdenieto* (The ideological evolution of the national activists after the liberation). Sofia: Nauka i izkustvo, 1988.

Paisii Hilendarski i negovata epokha, 1762–1962 (Paisii Hilendarski and his epoch, 1762–1962), edited by D. Kosev et al. Sofia: BAN: 1962.

Palairet, Michael. *The Balkan Economies c. 1800–1914. Evolution without Development.* Cambridge University Press, 1997.

Panov, Todor. *Psikhologiya na bŭlgarskiya narod* (The psychology of the Bulgarian People). Sofia, 1914.

Paskaleva, Virdzhiniya. *Bǔlgarkata prez Vǔzrazhdaneto* (Bulgarian women during the Revival). Sofia: BKP, 1964.

Paskaleva, Virdzhiniya. "Predpostavki i nachenki na rannoto Bǔlgarsko vǔzrazhdane" (The prerequisites and beginnings of the early Bulgarian Revival). *Istoricheski pregled* 34, no. 2 (1978): 83–98.

Paskaleva, Virdzhiniya. "Razvitie na gradskoto stopanstvo i genezisǔt na bǔlgarskata burzhoaziya prez XVIII vek" (The development of the urban economy and the genesis of the Bulgarian bourgeoisie in the eighteenth century). In *Paisii Hilendarski i negovata epokha*, 71–126.

Paskaleva, Virdzhiniya. "Za samoupravlenieto na bǔlgarite prez Vǔzrazhdaneto" (On the self-government of the Bulgarians during the Revival). *Izvestiya na Instituta po istoriya*. Vols. 14–15 (1964): 69–84.

Pavlov, Todor. *Izbrani proizvedeniya* (Selected works). Vol. 3, Sofia: BAN, 1960.

Pavlov, Todor. "Bezsmǔrtnoto delo na Paisii Hilendarski" (The immortal deed of Paisii Hilendarski). In Pavlov, *Izbrani proizvedeniya*. Vol. 3, 7–14 (first published in 1952).

Pavlov, Todor. "Hristo Botev. Bezsmǔrten sin, uchitel i vozhd na naroda" (Hristo Botev. Immortal Son, teacher and leader of the people). In Pavlov, *Izbrani proizvedeniya*. Vol. 3, 60–74.

Pavlov, Todor. "Hristo Botev i nasheto vreme" (Hristo Botev and our times). In Pavlov, *Izbrani proizvedeniya*. Vol. 3, 41–51 (dated 1945).

Pavlov, Todor. "Kǔm vǔprosa za nashata nauchna istoriya i po-spetsialno za istoriyata na Aprilskoto vustanie" (On the issue of our scientific history and on the history of the April uprising in particular). In Pavlov, *Izbrani proizvedeniya*. Vol. 3, 263–291.

Pavlov, Todor. "Natsiya i kultura" (Nation and culture). In Pavlov, *Natsiya i kultura*. Sofia: Izdatelstvo Gologanov, 1940, 106–133.

Pavlov, Todor. "Po vǔprosa za ideologiyata na Lyuben Karavelov" (On the ideology of Lyuben Karavelov). In Pavlov, *Izbrani proizvedeniya*. Vol. 3, 81–90.

Pavlov, Todor. "Za marksicheska istoriya na Bǔlgariya" (Toward a Marxist history of Bulgaria). In Pavlov, *Izbrani proizvedeniya*. Vol. 3, 335–379.

Pavlov, Todor. "Za sǔdǔrzhanieto i formata na istoricheskiya protses" (On the content and form of the historical process). In Pavlov, *Izbrani proizvedeniya*, Vol. 3, 397–431.

Peleva, Inna. "Epopeya na zabravenite—istoriya, mit, ideologiya" (Epic of the forgotten—History, myth, ideology). In Peleva, *Ideologǔt na natsiyata. Dumi za Vazov*. Plovdiv: Plovdivsko universitetsko izdatelstvo, 1994, 5–88.

Peleva, Inna. "Natsionalno vreme, kontinentalno vreme—figuri na neprevodimostta" (National time, continental time—Tropes of untranslatability). *Literaturen vestnik*, no. 31 (11 October 2000); no. 32 (18 October 2000).

Peleva, Inna. "'Pod igoto' i bǔlgarskoto znanie za 1876" ("Under the yoke" and the knowledge of the Bulgarians about 1876). In Peleva, *Ideologǔt na natsiyata*, 89–199.

Penev, Boyan. *Paisii Hilendarski*. Sofia, 1918 (first published in 1910).

Penev, Boyan. *Nachalo na bǔlgarskoto vǔzrazhdane* (The beginning of the Bulgarian Revival). Sofia: T. Chipev, 1929 (first edition in 1918).

Penev, Boyan. *Istoriya na novata bǔlgarska literatura* (History of the new Bulgarian literature), edited by Boris Yotsov. Vol. 1, Sofia, 1930; vol. 2, Sofia, 1933; vol. 3, Sofia, 1933; vol. 4, part 1, Sofia, 1936.

Penev, Boyan. "Hristo Botev." In *Hristo Botev. Po sluchai petdeset-godishninata ot smǔrtta mu* (Hristo Botev. On the fiftieth anniversary of his death). Sofia, 1926, 81–115.

Peshev, Petǔr. *Istoricheskite sǔbitiya i deyateli ot navecherieto na Osvobozhdenieto ni do dnes.* (Historical events and activists from the eve of the liberation until the present). Sofia: BAN, 1993 (first edition in 1925).

Petkanova-Toteva, Donka. "Pazvitie na prosvetnite idei v Bŭlgariya prez XVIII vek" (The development of ideas on education in Bulgaria during the eighteenth century). In Petkanova-Toteva, *Hilyadoletna literatura*. Sofia: Nauka i izkustvo, 1974, 211–238.

Pletnyov, Georgi. *Chorbadzhiite i bŭlgarskata natsionalna revolyutsiya* (The *chorbadzhii* in the Bulgarian national revolution). Veliko Tŭrnovo: Vital, 1993.

Pletnyov, Georgi. *Midhat pasha i upravlenieto na Dunavskiya vilayet* (Midhat pasha and the governing of Dunavski Vilayet). Veliko Tŭrnovo: Vital, 1994.

Pletnyov, Georgi. "Borba za obshtinskata vlast prez vŭzrazhdaneto" (Struggles for the communal government during the Revival). *Trudove na Velikotŭrnovskiya universitet "Kiril i Metodii."* Vol. 8, no. 2 (Istoricheski fakultet), 1970/71, Sofia, 1973, 163–191.

Pletnyov, Georgi. "Chorbadzhiite ot Tŭrnovsko v natsionalnoosvoboditelnoto dvizhenie" (The *chorbadzhii* from the Tŭrnovo region in the national-liberation movement). *Istoricheski pregled* 33, no. 3 (1977): 105–109.

Pletnyov, Georgi. "Proizkhod i sotsialna prinadlezhnost na chorbadzhiite ot Tŭrnovsko" (The origins and social status of the *chorbadzhii* in the Tŭrnovo region). *Trudove na Velikotŭrnovskiya universitet "Kiril i Metodii."* Vol. 9, no. 2 (Istoricheski fakultet) 1971/2, Sofia, 1973, 69–104.

Pletnyov, Georgi. "Rolyata i myastoto na chorbadzhiite ot Tŭrnovsko v prosvetnoto dvizhenie prez Vŭzrazhdaneto" (The role and place of the *chorbadzhii* from the Tŭrnovo region in the education movement during the Revival). *Trudove na Velikotŭrnovskiya universitet "Kiril i Metodii."* Vol. 10, no. 2 (Istoricheski fakultet) 1972/3, Sofia, 1973, 53–83.

Pletnyov, Georgi. "Sotsialnata prinadlezhnost na kotlenskite chorbadzhii prez Vŭzrazhdaneto" (The social status of the *chorbadzhii* from Kotel during the Revival). *Istoricheski pregled* 31, no. 2 (1975): 69–74.

Pollard, Sidney. *Peaceful Conquest. The Industrialization of Europe 1760–1970*. Oxford University Press, 1981.

Popov, Stefan. *Bŭlgarskata ideya* (The Bulgarian idea). Munich, 1981.

Pravdolyubov, I. *Hristo Botev ne e marksist* (Hristo Botev is not Marxist). Sofia, 1933.

"Predgovor na 'Mati Bolgariya'" (Introduction to "Mother Bulgaria"). *Periodichesko spisanie na Bŭlgarskoto Knizhovno Druzhestvo*, nos. 9–10 (1874): 1–13.

Radev, Simeon. *Stroitelite na sŭvremenna Bŭlgariya* (The builders of contemporary Bulgaria). Vol. 1. Sofia, 1910.

Radkova, Rumyana. *Bŭlgarskata inteligentsiya prez Vŭzrazhdaneto* (The Bulgarian intelligentsia during the Revival). Sofia: Nauka i izkustvo, 1986.

Radkova, Rumyana. *Inteligentsiyata i nravstvenostta prez Vŭzrazhdaneto* (The intelligentsia and morality during the Revival). Sofia: Marin Drinov, 1995.

Radkova, Rumyana. "Natsionalno samosŭznanie na bŭlgarite prez XVIII i nachaloto na XIX vek" (The national self-consciousness of the Bulgarians during the eighteenth and at the beginning of the nineteenth centuries). In *Bŭlgarskata natsiya*, 178–238.

Radkova, Rumyana. "Za vrŭzkite mezhdu inteligentsiyata i burzhoaziyata v bŭlgarskoto osvoboditelno dvizhenie" (On the connections between the intelligentsia and the bourgeoisie in the Bulgarian liberation movement). *Istoricheski pregled* 33, no. 2 (1977): 90–93.

Rakovski, Georgi. "Bŭlgarskii naroden vŭpros pred otomanskata porta" (The Bulgarian national question before the Ottoman Porte). *Dunavski lebed* 1, no. 9 (18 November 1860).

Rakovski, Georgi. "Bŭlgarskii za nezavisimo im sveshtenstvo dnes vŭzbuden vŭpros i nikhna narodna cherkva v Tsarigrad" (Today's Bulgarian question about an independent clergy and a Bulgarian people's church in Constantinople). *Dunavski lebed* 1, no. 2 (22 September 1860); no. 3 (29 September 1860).

Rakovski, Georgi. "Istinskoto rodoliubie" (True patriotism). *Dunavska zora* 2, no. 49 (8 December 1869).

Rakovski, Georgi. "Posledni izvestiya vŭrkhu nash vŭpros" (Last news on our question). *Dunavski lebed* 1, no. 19 (31 January 1861).

Rakovski, Georgi. "Velikata ideya na bŭlgarite" (The great idea of the Bulgarians). *Dunavska zora* 2, no. 51 (24 December 1869).

Rakovski, Krŭstyu. "Stranitsa iz bŭlgarskoto vŭzrzhdane" (A page from the Bulgarian Revival). In *Misŭl. Literaturen sbornik* 1 (1910): 142–173.

Robinson, Andrei. *Istoriografiia Slavianskogo Vozrozhdeniia i Paisii Hilendarski* (The historiography of the Slavic revival and Paisii Hilendarski). Moscow: Izdatel'stvo Aka-demii nauk SSSR, 1963.

Sakazov, Ivan. *Bulgarische Wirtschaftsgeschichte.* Berlin and Lepzig: Walter de Gruyter, 1929.

Sakŭzov, Ivan. "Razvitie na gradskiya zhivot i zanayatite v Bŭlgariya prez XVIII–XIX vek" (The development of urban life and of the crafts in Bulgaria during the eighteenth and nineteenth centuries). In *Bŭlgariya 1000 godini*, 685–703.

Sbornik ot otbrani okrŭzhni ot osvobozhdenieto do kraya na 1942 g. (Collection of selected instructions from the liberation to the end of 1942), edited by Nikola Balabanov and Andrei Manev. Vols. 1–2, Sofia, 1943.

Seliminski, Ivan. *Izbrani sŭchineniya* (Selected works). Sofia: Nauka i izkustvo, 1979.

Semov, Marko. *Bŭlgarinut–poznat i nepoznat* (The Bulgarian–Familiar and unfamiliar). Sofia: Voenno izdatelstvo.

Semov, Marko. *Dushevnost i otselyavane. Razmisli za haraktera na nashiya narod* (Psychology and survival. Reflections on the character of our people). Plovdiv: Hristo Danov, 1982.

Senghaas, Dieter (ed.). *Peripherer Kapitalismus. Analysen über Abhängigkeit und Unterentwicklung.* Frankfurt/Main, 1974.

Sharova, Krumka. *Lyuben Karavelov v bŭlgarskoto osvoboditelno dvizhenie, 1860–1867* (Lyuben Karavelov in the Bulgarian liberation movement, 1860–1867). Sofia: Nauka i izkustvo, 1970, 7–23.

Sharova, Krumka. "Bŭlgarskoto natsionalnorevolyutsionno dvizhenie i edrata burzhoaziya" (The Bulgarian national-revolutionary movement and the big bourgeoisie). *Istoricheski pregled* 33, no. 2 (1977): 71–80.

Sharova, Krumka. "Bŭlgarskiyat revolyutsionen komitet–1875" (The Bulgarian revolutionary committee of 1875). In *Bŭlgarsko vŭzrazhdane. Idei. Lichnosti. Sŭbitiya.* Sofia: Obshtobŭlgarski komitet "Vasil Levski" i Universitetsko izdatelstvo "Kliment Ohridski," 1995, 42–128.

Sharova, Krumka. "Krizisni yavleniya v BRTsK prez lyatoto i esenta na 1872 g" (Crisis signs in BRTsK in the summer and autumn of 1872). *Istoricheski pregled* 47, no. 3 (1991): 3–24.

Sharova, Krumka. "Mithad pasha i bŭlgarskoto revolyutsionno dvizhenie prez 1972 g." (Midhat pasha and the Bulgarian revolutionary movement in 1972). *Istoricheski pregled* 47, no. 6 (1991): 3–16.

Sharova, Krumka. "Nauchni rezultati ot diskusiyata za rolyata na burzhoaziyata v bŭlgarskoto osvoboditelno dvizhenie i predstoyashti izsledovatelski zadachi" (Scientific results from the discussion on the role of the bourgeoisie in the Bulgarian liberation movement and future research tasks). *Istoricheski pregled* 34, no. 1 (1978): 93–102.

Sharova, Krumka. "Problemi na Bŭlgarskoto vŭzrazhdane" (Issues of the Bulgarian Revival). In *Problemi na Bŭlgarskoto vŭzrazhdane*, edited by Krumka Sharova. Sofia: BAN, 1981, 5–44.

Sharova, Krumka. "Vzaimodeistvie na dvizheniyata za natsionalna kultura, tsŭrkva i politichesko osvobozhdenie prez Vŭzrazhdaneto" (Interaction between the movements for national culture, church, and political liberation during the Revival). In *Kultura, tsŭrkva i revolyutsiya*, 11–39.

Sheitanov, Naiden. "Dukhŭt na otritsanie u bŭlgarina" (The spirit of negation of the Bulgarian). *Filosofski pregled* 5, no. 2 (1933): 128–141.

Sheitanov, Naiden. "Predosvoboditelno ili tsyalostno vŭzrazhdane" (Pre-liberation or complete revival). *Filosofski pregled* 9, no. 2 (1937): 183–191.

Shishmanov, Ivan. *Izbrani sŭchineniya* (Selected works). Vol. 1 (Bŭlgarsko vŭzrazhdane). Sofia: BAN, 1965.

Shishmanov, Ivan. "Koga se nacheva novobŭlgarskata literatura" (When does the new Bulgarian literature start?). *Rodna rech* 1, no. 3 (1928).

Shishmanov, Ivan. "Paisii i negovata epokha. Misli vŭrkhu genezisa na bŭlgarskoto vŭzrazhdane" (Paisii and his epoch. Thoughts on the genesis of the Bulgarian Revival). *Spisanie na BAN* 8 (1914),:1–18. Reprinted in Shishmanov, *Izbrani sŭchineniya*. Vol. 1, 81–92.

Shishmanov, Ivan. "Paisii i Rousseau. Aperçu." (Paisii and Rousseau. Aperçu). *Dennitsa* 1, nos. 7–8 (1890): 353–354.

Shishmanov, Ivan. "Uvod v istoriyata na bŭlgarskoto vŭzrazhdane" (Introduction to the history of the Bulgarian Revival). In Shishmanov, *Izbrani sŭchineniya*. Vol. 1, 31–73. (First published in 1930.)

Shishmanov, Ivan. "Zapadnoevropeiskoto i bŭlgarskoto vŭzrazhdane" (The West European and the Bulgarian Renaissance). In Shishmanov, *Izbrani sŭchineniya*. Vol. 1, 74–80. (First appeared in 1928.)

Skalweit, Stephan. *Der Beginn der Neuzeit. Epochengrenze und Epochenbegriff*. Darmstadt, 1982.

Smith, Anthony. *National Identity*. London: Penguin Books, 1991.

Snegarov, Ivan. *Natsionalno i obshtestveno znachenie na bŭlgarskite tsŭrkovni borbi* (The national and public impact of the Bulgarian church struggles). Sofia: Kuzman Katsarov, 1920.

Snegarov, Ivan. *Istoriya na Ohridskata arkhiepiskopiya-patriarshiya, 1394–1767*. (History of the Archbishopry-Patriarchy of Ohrid, 1394–1767). Sofia, 1932.

Snegarov, Ivan. *Solun v bŭlgarskata dukhovna kultura*. (Thessaloniki in Bulgarian spiritual culture). Sofia, 1937.

Snegarov, Ivan. *Skopskata eparkhiya*. (The Eparchy of Skopje). Sofia, 1939.

Sprostranov, E. "Po vŭzrazhdaneto na grad Ohrid" (On the Revival of the town Ohrid). *Sbornik narodni umotvoreniya, nauka i knizhnina*. 13 (1896): 621–681.

Stalin, Joseph. *Marksizm i natsional'no-kolonial'nyi vopros* (Marxism and the national-colonial question). Partizdat, 1936. (English translation: "Marxism and the national question." In Stalin, *Marxism and the National Question. A Collection of Articles and Speeches*. San Francisco: Proletarian Publishers, 1975, 15–99).

Stalin, Kirov, Zhdanov, *Zamechaniia o konspekte uchebnika novoi istorii, "K izucheniiu istorii"* (Notes on the conspectus of the textbook of modern history, "Toward the study of history"). Moscow: Partizdat, 1937.

Stambolski, Hristo. *Avtobiografiya. Dnevnitsi. Spomeni* (Autobiography. Diaries. Memoirs), edited by Strashimir Dimitrov. Sofia: Bŭlgarski pisatel, 1972. (First edition in 1927–1931).

Stanev, Nikola. *Borba na bŭlgarite za dukhovna svoboda* (The struggle of the Bulgarians for spiritual freedom). Sofia, 1920.

Stefanova, Milena. *Kniga za bŭlgarskite chorbadzhii* (A book about the Bulgarian *chorbadzhii*). Sofia: Izdatelstvo na Sofiiskiya universitet "Kliment Ohridski," 1998.

Stokes, Gale. "Dependency and the Rise of Nationalism in Southeast Europe." In Stokes, *Three Eras of Political Change in Eastern Europe.* Oxford University Press, 1997, 23–35.

Stokes, Gale. "Introduction: In Defense of Balkan Nationalism." In *Nationalism in the Balkans. An Annotated Bibliography*, edited by Gale Stokes. New York and London: Garland Publishers, 1984.

Stoyanov, Hristo. *Vŭzpitanieto v svetlinata na natsionalniya ideal* (Upbringing in the light of the national ideal). Sofia, 1935.

Stoyanov, Ivan. *Istoriya na Bŭlgarskoto vŭzrazhdane* (History of the Bulgarian Revival). Tŭrnovo: Sv. Evtimii Patriarkh Tŭrnovski, 1999.

Stoyanov, Zakhari. Biografii. Chetite v Bŭlgariya (Biographies. The *cheti* in Bulgaria). In *Sŭchineniya*. Vol. 2, Sofia: Bŭlgarski pisatel, 1983. (The biography of Vasil Levski appeared in 1883, that of Lyuben Karavelov in 1885, and that of Hristo Botev in 1888).

Stoyanov, Zakhari. Publitsistika (Political journalism). In *Sŭchineniya*. Vol. 3, Sofia: Bŭlgarski pisatel, 1983.

Stoyanov, Zakhari. Zapiski po bŭlgarskite vŭstaniya (Notes on the Bulgarian uprisings). In *Sŭchineniya*. Vol. 1, Sofia: Bŭlgarski pisatel, 1983. (First edition 1884–1892).

Strashimirov, Anton. *Kniga za bŭlgarite* (A book about the Bulgarians). Sofia, 1918.

Strashimirov, Dimitŭr. *Istoriya na Aprilskoto vŭstanie* (The history of the April uprising). Vols. 1–3, Plovdiv, 1907.

Strashimirov, Dimitŭr. *V. Levski. Zhivot, dela, izvori* (V. Levski. Life, deeds, sources). Vol. 1, Sofia, 1929.

Strashimirov, Dimitŭr. "Komitetskoto desetiletie (epokha na komitetite), 1866–1876" (The decade of the committees. An epoch of the committees, 1866–1876). In *Bŭlgariya 1000 godini*, 781–888.

Strashimirova, Svetla. *Bŭlgarinŭt pred praga na novoto vreme. Orientiri na vŭzrozhdenskiya svetogled* (The Bulgarians on the threshold of modernity. Orientation signs in the worldview of the Revival). Sofia: Universitetsko izdatelstvo "Kliment Ohridski," 1992.

Studia culturologica. Vol. 1, spring 1992.

Sudŭt nad istoritsite. Bŭlgarskata istoricheska nauka. Dokumenti i diskusii, 1944–1950 (The trial of the historians. Bulgarian historical scholarship. Documents and discussions, 1944–1950), edited by Vera Mutafchieva, Vesela Chichovska et al. Vol. 1, Sofia: Marin Drinov, 1995.

Sugar, Peter. "The Enlightenment in the Balkans. Some Basic Considerations." *East European Quarterly* 9, no. 4 (1985): 499–507.

Tabakov, Simeon, *Opit za istoriya na grad Sliven* (An essay on the history of the town of Sliven). Vol. 2, Sofia, 1924.

Tishkov, Petŭr. *Istoriya na nasheto zanayatchiistvo do Osvobozhdenieto ni* (A history of our crafts until the liberation). Sofia, 1922.

Todev, Iliya. *Novi ochertsi po bŭlgarska istoriya. Vŭzrazhdane* (New essays in Bulgarian history. Revival). Sofia: Vek 22, 1995.

Todev, Iliya. *Kŭm drugo minalo ili prenebregvani aspekti na bŭlgarskoto natsionalno vŭzrazhdane* (Toward a different past, or ignored aspects of the Bulgarian national Revival). Sofia: Vigal, 1999, 45–46, 63.

Todev, Iliya. "April 1876 ili Bŭlgarskoto razpyatie" (April 1876 or the Bulgarian crucifixion). In Todev, *Novi ochertsi*, 105–113.

Todev, Iliya. "Dr. Stoyan Chomakov ili ot osvoboditelen kŭm imperski natsionalizŭm" (Dr. Stoyan Chomakov—from liberation to imperial nationalism). In Todev, *Kŭm drugo minalo*, 149–164.

Todev, Iliya. "Dualizmŭt kato durzhavnostroitelna initsiativa v Bŭlgarskoto vŭzrazhdane.

Begŭl pogled ot 1992 g." (Dualism as a state-building initiative in the Bulgarian Revival. An overview from 1992). In Todev, *Novi ochertsi*, 123–136.

Todev, Iliya. "Kŭm problema za genezisa i rolyata na natsionalnata ideya v bŭlgarskoto vŭzrazhdane" (On the genesis and the role of the national idea in the Bulgarian Revival). In Todev, *Kŭm drugo minalo*, 13–22.

Todev, Iliya. "Paisii–avtor na bŭlgarskata natsionalna ideya" (Paisii–Author of the Bulgarian national idea). In Todev, *Kŭm drugo minalo*, 23–34.

Todev, Iliya. "Partiite v bŭlgarskoto natsionalno dvizhenie i osvobozhdenieto" (The parties in the Bulgarian national movement and the liberation). In Todev, *Novi ochertsi*, 66–82.

Todev, Iliya. "Problemŭt za smisŭla na Aprilskoto vŭstanie v bŭlgarskata marksicheska istoriografiya" (The issue of the meaning of the April uprising in Bulgarian Marxist historiography). In Todev, *Novi ochertsi*, 83–104.

Todorov, Goran. "Istoricheskite vŭzgledi na Paisii" (The views of Paisii on history). *Izvestiya na instituta po istoriya*. Vol. 20 (1968).

Todorov, Goran. "Sotsialno-politicheskata obuslovenost na Aprilskoto vŭstanie. Otzvukŭt na Aprilskoto vŭstanie v Rusiya" (Social-political conditions of the April uprising. The reverberation of the April uprising in Russia). In *Aprilskoto vŭstanie, 1876–1966*, 117–130.

Todorov, Nikolai. *Balkanskiyat grad XV–XIX vek* Sofia: Nauka i izkustvo 1972. (Translated into English as *The Balkan City, 1400–1900*. Seattle and London: University of Washington Press, 1983.)

Todorov, Nikolai. "Po nyakoi vŭprosi za ikonomicheskoto razvitie i za zarazhdaneto na kapitalizma v bŭlgarskite zemi pod tursko vladichestvo" (On some issues of the economic development and the emergence of capitalism in the Bulgarian lands under Turkish rule). *Istoricheski pregled* 17, no. 6 (1961): 87–105.

Todorova, Maria. "The Course and Discourses of Bulgarian Nationalism." In *Eastern European Nationalism in the Twentieth Century*, edited by Peter Sugar. The American University Press, 1995, 55–102.

Topalov, Kiril. *Vŭzrozhdentsi* (Men of the Revival). Sofia: Universitetsko izdatelstvo "Kliment Ohridski," 1999.

Topalov, Kiril and Nikolai Chernokozhev. *Bŭlgarskata literatura prez Vŭzrazhdaneto* (Bulgarian literature during the Revival). Sofia: Prosveta, 1998.

Topencharov, Vladimir. *Portretŭt na Paisii.* (Paisii's portrait). Sofia: Narodna Mladezh, 1959.

Topuzanov, Simeon. *Ideologiya, stroezh i zadachi na Bŭlgarskiya rabotnicheski sŭyuz* (Ideology, construction, and objectives of the Bulgarian Workers' Union). Sofia, 1937.

Traikov, Veselin. *Ideologicheski techeniya i programi v natsionalno-osvoboditelnite dvizheniya na Balkanite do 1878 godina* (Ideological trends and programs in the national-liberation movements in the Balkans until 1878). Sofia: Nauka i izkustvo, 1978.

Traikov, Veselin. "Dva aspekta za rolyata na burzhoaziyata v bŭlgarskoto natsionalnoosvoboditelno dvizhenie" (Two aspects of the role of the bourgeoisie in the Bulgarian national-liberation movement). *Istoricheski pregled* 33, no. 2 (1977): 82–90.

Tsanev, Dimitŭr. *Bŭlgarskata istoricheska knizhnina prez Vŭzrazhdaneto. XVIII–pŭrvata polovina na XIX vek* (Bulgarian historical writing during the Revival, eighteenth to mid-nineteenth centuries). Sofia: Nauka i izkustvo, 1989.

Tsanev, Dimitŭr. "Proyavi na natsionalno chuvstvo i sŭznanie v bŭlgarskata vŭzrozhdenska istoricheska knizhnina prez pŭrvata polovina na XIX vek" (Manifestation of national feeling and consciousness in Bulgarian historical writing during the first half of the nineteenth century). In *Bŭlgarskata natsiia*. Vol. 1, 239–263.

Tsonev, Benyu. "Novobŭlgarska pismenost predi Paisiya" (The New Bulgarian writing before Paisii). *Bŭlgarski pregled* 1, no. 8 (1894): 80–98.

Tsonev, Benyu. "Ot koya knizhovna shkola e izlyazŭl Paisii Hilendarski" (From which literary school did Paisii Hilendarski come?). *Slavyanski glas* 10, nos. 5–6 (1912): 165–174.

Tsonev, Stefan. "Kŭm vŭprosa za razlozhenieto na esnafskite organizatsii u nas prez perioda na Vŭzrazhdaneto" (On the issue of the decline of the craft guilds in our lands during the Revival). *Trudove na Visshiya institut za narodno stopanstvo v grad Varna* 1 (1956): 3–80.

Tsvetkov, A. "Nashite narodni buditeli" (Our people's awakeners). *Otets Paisii* 10, no. 9 (1937): 330–335.

Tsvetkova, Bistra. *Haidutstvoto v bŭlgarskite zemi prez XV–VIII vek* (The *haiduti* in the Bulgarian lands, fifteenth to eighteenth centuries). Vol. 1, Sofia: Nauka i izkustvo, 1971.

Tsvetkova, Bistra. "Prinos kŭm izuchavaneto na turskiya feodalizŭm v bŭlgarsite zemi prez XV–XVI vek" (A contribution to the study of Turkish feudalism in the Bulgarian lands in the fifteenth and sixteenth centuries). *Isvestiya na Instituta za bŭlgarska istoriya* 5 (1954): 71–153.

Tsvetkova, Bistra. "Promeni v osmanskiya feodalizŭm na balkanskite zemi prez XVI–XVIII v." (Changes in Ottoman feudalism in the Balkan lands, sixteenth to eighteenth centuries). *Istoricheski pregled* 27, no. 4 (1971): 55–73.

Tŭpkova-Zaimova, Vasilka. "Nachaloto" (The beginning). *Istoricheski pregled* 54, nos. 1–2 (1998): 51–62.

Undzhiev, Ivan and Tzveta Undzhieva. *Hristo Botev. Zhivot i delo* (Hristo Botev. Life and deeds). Sofia: Nauka i izkustvo, 1975.

Vankov, Nikola. *Istoriya na uchebnoto delo otkrai vreme do osvobozhdenieto* (A history of education from earlier times to the liberation). Lovech, 1903.

Vasilev, Vasil. "Akademik Dimitŭr Kosev kakŭvto go vidyakh i zapomnikh" (Academician Dimitŭr Kosev as I saw and remember him). *Istoricheski pregled* no.1 (1997): 105–129.

Vazov, Ivan. *Under the Yoke* (translated by M. Aleksieva and T. Atanasov). Sofia: 1955.

Velchev, Velcho. *Paisii Hilendarski. Epokha, lichnost, delo* (Paisii Hilendarski. Epoch, personality, deed). Sofia: Narodna prosveta, 1981.

Venelin, Yuri. *O zarodyshe novvo bolgarskoi literatury* (On the origins of the new Bulgarian literature). Moscow: Tipografiya N. Stepanova, 1838. (*Zaradi Vozrozhdenie novoi bolgarskoi slovesnosti ili nauki*, translated into Bulgarian by Mikhail Kefalov, Bucharest, 1842; Ruse, 1896.)

Venelin, Yuri. *Drevnie i nyneshnia bolgare* (Ancient and present-day Bulgarians). Moscow: Universitetska tipografiya, 1856. (First edition in 1829.)

Veselinov, Kosta. *Bortsi za natsionalna svoboda* (Combatants for national freedom). Sofia, 1940.

Vladikin, Lyubomir. *Istoriya na Tŭrnovskata konstitutsiya* (History of the Tŭrnovo constitution). Sofia: Hristo Danov, 1936.

Vladikin, Lyubomir. "Natsionalizmŭt kato kulturno-politicheski faktor" (Nationalism as a cultural-political factor). *Prosveta* 2, no. 3 (1936): 289–304.

Vlaikov, Marin. *Vŭzpitanieto v novata dŭrzhava* (Upbringing in the new state). Sofia, 1935.

Vlaikov, Todor. "Ako to ne beshe stanalo" (Had it not happened). *Prosveta* 1, no. 5 (1936): 528–532.

Vlaikov, Todor. "Nashata inteligentsiya" (Our intelligentsia). *Demokraticheski pregled* 18, no. 5 (1926): 289–309.

Vlaikov, Todor. "Sluchaini belezhki. Po vŭprosa za inteligentsiyata ni" (Casual notes. On the issue of our intelligentsia). *Demokraticheski pregled* 8, no. 1 (1910): 99–106.

Volkov, Evgeni. *Hristo Botev*. Sofia, 1929.

Vŭzrazdane (Revival), edited by Svetoslav Milarov, Todor Peev and Ivan Drasov. 1, Braila, 1876.

Yanev, Petko. *Traditsionni i novi praznitsi* (Traditional and new holidays). Sofia: OF, 1970.

Yanev, Yanko. "Dukhŭt na natsiyata" (The spirit of the nation). *Otets Paisii* 6, no. 1 (1933): 8–10.

Yaneva, Svetla. "Pŭtishta na industrializatsiyata: protoindustriite v Evropa i v bŭlgarskite zemi (XVIII–XIX v.)" (Roads of industrialization: Proto-industrialization in Europe and in the Bulgarian lands, eighteenth and nineteenth centuries). *Istoricheski pregled* 56, nos. 5–6 (2000): 99–118.

Yotsov, Boris. "Bŭlgarskata istoriya, neinata razrabotka do Osvobozhdenieto i znachenieto i za probudata na bŭlgarskiya narod" (Bulgarian history, its elaboration until the liberation, and its role in the awakening of the Bulgarian people). *Otets Paisii* 6, nos. 8–9 (1933): 6–11.

Yotsov, Boris. "Naroden buditel" (People's awakener). *Otets Paisii* 3, nos. 19–20 (1930): 287–295.

Yotsov, Boris. "Paisii Hilendarski." *Uchilishten pregled* 41, no. 7 (1942): 838–841.

Yotsov, Boris. "Pŭt na bŭlgarskoto vŭzrazhdane" (The path of the Bulgarian Revival). *Rodna rech* 8, no. 5 (1935): 197–204.

Yotsov, Boris. "Vasilii Aprilov." *Prosveta* 1, no. 2 (1935): 129–139.

Zaimov, Stoyan. *Minaloto. Ocherki i spomeni iz deyatelnostta na bŭlgarskite taini revolyutsionni komiteti ot 1869–1877 g.* (The past. Essays and memories about the activities of the Bulgarian secret revolutionary committees, 1869–1877). Sofia: BZNS, 1986. (First edition in 1884–1888).

Zarev, Pantalei. *Bŭlgarskoto vŭzrazhdane* (The Bulgarian Revival). Sofia: Nauka i izkustvo, 1950.

Zhechev, Toncho. *Bŭlgarskiyat Velikden ili strastite bŭlgarski* (The Bulgarian Easter or the Bulgarian passions). Sofia: Marin Drinov, 1995. (First edition in 1875.)

Zhechev, Toncho. "Ivan Hadzhiiski i nie" (Ivan Hadzhiiski and we). In Zhechev, *Istoriya i literatura*. Sofia: Bŭlgarski pisatel, 1982, 468–483. (First published in 1966.)

Zlatarski, Nikola. *Nova politicheska i sotsialna istoriya na Bŭlgariya i Balkanskiya poluostrov* (New political and social history of Bulgaria and the Balkan peninsula). Sofia, 1921.

Zlatarski, Vasil. "Deinostta na d-r Konstantin Jireček v Bŭlgariya" (The activities of Dr. Konstantin Jireček in Bulgaria). *Periodichesko spisanie* 66, nos. 1–2 (1905).

INDEX

Abdül-Mecid 2, 100
agrarian thesis (reform, revolution) 77, 79, 82, 83–85, 113, 206, 208, 216
anarchism 185, 186, 187, 188, 229
Andonov, Ivan 228, 241
April uprising (1876) 4, 6, 81, 88, 113, 119, 121, 123, 125, 132, 133, 140, 143, 162, 163, 166, 169, 170, 174, 187, 189, 190, 197–210, 211, 213, 220, 227, 237, 241, 244, 245
Aprilov, Vasil 2, 12, 26, 162
Asiatic mode of production 67, 73
Awakeners 2, 25, 27, 151, 176, 177, 232

Bacho Kiro 245
Bakunin 184, 185
Balabanov, Marko 2
Balkan wars (1912–13) 162, 163, 199, 228
Batak 201
beglikchii 57, 109, 111
Belinski 187
Benevolent Society (*Dobrodetelna Druzhina*) 140, 142, 171
Benkovski, Georgi 201, 245
Berlin Congress (1879) and peace treaty 162, 163, 197, 198, 219, 227
Beron, Petŭr 38, 42
Bismarck 175
Board of Trustees in Odessa (*Odesko nastoyatelstvo*) 171
Bogoridi, Stefan 168, 172
Botev's Day (June 2) 244
Botev, Hristo 4, 25, 61, 101, 121, 138, 140, 141, 142, 143, 156, 171, 176, 177, 178, 179, 182, 183, 184–187, 188, 189, 212, 214, 216, 220, 239, 240, 241, 242, 244, 245, 251
bourgeois (democratic) revolution 44, 58, 60, 62, 63, 64, 65, 71, 77, 79–84, 116, 125, 126, 168, 206, 208, 212–216
Bulgarian Revolutionary Central Committee 6, 165, 180, 188
Bulgarian Revolutionary Committee (of 1875) 188, 189

capitalism (and transition) 11, 29, 47, 58, 60, 62–68, 71–73, 77, 79, 80, 81, 83, 87, 90, 208, 213, 214, 218, 241
Chernishevski, Nikolai 180, 184, 185, 187
cheti, chetnik 192, 122, 140, 171, 178, 187, 189

chiflik 59, 67, 69, 70, 71, 77, 78, 84, 85, 114, 115, 130, 208, 212, 216
Chistemenski, Kocho 245
Chomakov, Stoyan 171, 172
chorbadzhi 61, 67, 110, 111, 112–119, 123, 124, 126–129, 131, 135–138, 139, 140, 141, 168, 176, 177, 203, 205, 212, 227, 229, 234, 235, 238, 240, 241, 242, 245, 252, 253
communards 184, 214
commune, communal council (*obshtina*) 21, 22, 110, 126, 136, 236
Conservatives 110, 227
Crimean war (1853–56) 6, 25, 72, 101, 102, 103, 115, 119, 126, 127, 128, 139, 168, 172, 206

damaskini 30, 33, 39, 43, 100, 101
Day of People's Awakeners (November 1) 231, 244
Dobrolyubov, Nikolai 184, 187
Drinov, Marin 2, 26, 100, 151
Drumev, Vasil 25
dualism, dualists 114, 139, 165, 172, 173, 177
dzhelepi 109, 111

Eastern Question 47, 174, 216
Eastern Rumelia 197, 227, 239
Edirne peace treaty (1829) 57, 102, 103
educationism, educationists 118, 122, 164, 165, 170, 171, 177, 179, 188, 189
Enlightenment 11, 25, 27, 28, 29, 30, 32–38, 40, 42, 43, 44, 103, 106, 151, 160
esnaf 68, 110, 111, 117, 135, 136, 231, 235
Europeanization 46, 47, 90
evolutionism, evolutionists 6, 112, 128, 138, 145, 151, 162–169, 172–175, 190, 199, 227, 239
Exarchate 1, 6, 22, 30, 101, 102, 104, 112, 138, 169, 197, 235

Father Paisii's Day (September 27) 153, 231, 232, 244
feudalism 11, 58, 60, 62, 63, 64, 70, 72, 73–79, 80, 81, 84, 87, 90, 113, 116, 208, 212, 218
French revolution 13, 62, 82, 126, 139–141

Gabrovo 68, 162
Greek Patriarchy 6, 40, 99, 126, 134, 135, 144, 155, 158, 161, 218
Gyurgevo Committee 189, 220

haiduti 102, 109, 178, 184, 243, 252
Hatt-i-Humayun 173
Hatt-i-Sherif 96, 173
Herzen, Alexander 180, 184, 187
Hetairia Philike 13
hŭshove 113, 138, 140, 227

Ilinden Uprising 228
Ikonomov, Todor 168
Indzhe 252
Istanbul (Constantinople) 68, 122, 197, 205